"What an astonishing thing a book is. It's a flat object made from a tree with flexible parts on which are imprinted lots of funny, dark squiggles. But one glance at it and you're inside the mind of another person, maybe somebody dead for thousands of years. Across the millennia, an author is speaking clearly and silently inside your head, directly to you. Writing is perhaps the greatest of human inventions, binding together people who never knew each other, citizens of distant epochs. Books break the shackles of time. A book is proof that humans are capable of working magic."
– Carl Sagan, in *Cosmos*

"Thought has the power to bring into being
the visible from the invisible."
– Ann Wigmore

# Play and Practice and Progress into Being You

"I've missed more than 9,000 shots in my career. I've lost almost 300 games. 26 times, I've been trusted to take the game winning shot and missed. I've failed over and over and over again in my life. And that is why I succeed."
– Michael Jordan

"Any who may wish to profit himself alone from the knowledge given him, rather than serve others through the knowledge he has gained from learning, is betraying knowledge and rendering it worthless."
– Haile Selassie

"I have found that if you love life, life will love you back."
– Lalit Arora

"If you are always trying to be normal, you will never know how amazing you can be."
– Maya Angelou

"By choosing your thoughts, and by selecting which emotional currents you will release and which you will reinforce, you determine the quality of your light. You determine the effects you will have upon others, and the nature of the experience of your life."
– Gary Zukav

"Emancipate yourselves from mental slavery. None but ourselves can free our minds."
– Bob Marley

"If you limit your choices only to what seems possible or reasonable,
you disconnect yourself from what you truly want,
and all that is left is compromise."
– Robert Fritz

# DREAM YOUR WORLD

## FATHOM A NEW LIFE
## IN WHICH YOU THRIVE

### DANIEL JOHN CAREY
Author of *Dream Another Dream*

Dream Your World: Fathom a New Life in which You Thrive

**Disclaimer:**

This book is sold for information purposes only. How you interpret and utilize the information in this book is your decision. Neither the author nor the publisher and/or distributor will be held accountable for the use or misuse of the information contained in this book. This book is not intended as medical advice because the author and publisher of this work are not recommending the use of chemical drugs or surgery to alleviate health challenges. It also does not stand as legal advice, or suggest that you break any laws. Because of the way people interpret what they read, and take actions based on their own intellect and life situations, which are not in the author's, publisher's, and/or distributor's control, there is always some risk involved; therefore, the author, publisher, and/or distributor of this book are not responsible for any adverse effects or consequences from the use of any suggestions, foods, substances, products, procedures, or lifestyles described hereafter.

**ISBN:** 978-1-884702-23-5
**Library of Congress Control Number:** 2023932388
**Dewey CIP:** 158.1.    **OCLC:** 24218880
**First Edition:** 2023
**Published by**: Oakonic, POB 1272, Santa Monica, CA 90406-1272, USA

# FOR THE LOVE OF BOOKS

"We read to know we are not alone."
– C. S. Lewis

"The failure to read good books both enfeebles the vision and strengthens our most fatal tendency – the belief that the here and now is all there is."
– Allan Bloom

"I suggest that the only books that influence us are those for which we are ready, and which have gone a little farther down our particular path than we have yet got ourselves."
– E. M. Forster

"When I look back, I am so impressed again with the life-giving power of literature. If I were a young person today, trying to gain a sense of myself in the world, I would do that again by reading, just as I did when I was young."
– Maya Angelou

"Books are the carriers of civilization. Without books, history is silent, literature dumb, science crippled, thought and speculation at a standstill."
– Barbara Tuchman

"From your parents you learn love and laughter, and how to put one foot before the other. But when books are opened, you discover that you have wings."
– Helen Hayes

"Reading is the sole means by which we slip, involuntarily, often helplessly, into another's skin, another's voice, another's soul."
– Joyce Carol Oates

"Books are a sort of cultural D.N.A., the code for who, as a society, we are and what we know."
– Susan Orlean

"There is no passion to be found playing small – in settling for a life that is less than the one you are capable of living."
– Nelson Mandela

# Prelude to You

"A teacher affects eternity; he can never tell where his influence stops."
– Henry Brooks Adams

A book can be like a teacher whose impact on a life path might never be realized.

As with *Dream Another Dream*, this book doesn't consist of only my thoughts, but includes the theories, philosophies, beliefs, opinions, considerations, and conclusions of many people from throughout history.

Maybe some parts of this book will be for you, and others not so much. Consider it to be an invitation to align with the better aspects of who you are, and to dive into living your life in health out loud as your solution.

Perhaps you have lived a lowly life, an unsatisfying life, a troubled life, or, for one or many reasons, a life simply not in alignment with your dreams, the potential of your better qualities, and the brilliance of your higher capacities.

As with my other book *Dream Another Dream*, I hope this book is helpful for those who are not only wishing for a better life, but are ready to break through being their enigma, and will work for a life in which they will thrive.

To benefit from reading a book of this sort, a reader can write their thoughts in a journal kept while reading. Their notes can be their own book about life concepts, theories, philosophies, beliefs, goals, and preferences.

"What is in my heart must come out, so I write it down."
– Ludwig Van Beethoven

As you read, do write your higher quality thoughts in a notebook. Write freely while focused on the positive. Otherwise, forget your edit button. Allow mistakes as you write random ideas, observations, and the workings of your mind onto the paper. Through and while reading and writing, explore what your better life can be. Write helpful, motivational thoughts of determination about creating a better quality life for yourself, including for your people, community, society, and Earth.

Believe in your higher potential.

"The start to a better world is the belief that it is possible."
– Lilly Tomlin

Stop spiraling into intrusive thoughts, and hanging onto structures of thinking and communication no longer serving you.

Break free of the thinking patterns developed to deal with a life you don't want to live.

Don't get caught in negativity that distracts and halts you.

Stop creating catastrophe in hypothetical thoughts that have nothing to do with your reality, but exist only as mental simulation, and as ruinous fantasy.

Seek what helps you to navigate into your better world.

Combine daily exercise, excellent and clean plant-based nutrition, and intentional living with integrity in alignment with your better qualities to grasp hold of who you are.

"There will always be obstacles and challenges that stand in your way. Building mental strength will help you develop resilience to those potential hazards so you can continue on your journey to success."
– Amy Morin

Dive into the process of making your more helpful thoughts align with your actions, communication, and choices. Use this process as the mechanism to arrive in the life you want to experience.

"It has been a long journey, but if you dream and have the ambition, and want to work hard, then you can achieve."
– Mo Farah

From here, your journey begins.

# Table of Contents

"Every morning you have two choices:
Continue to sleep with your dreams,
or wake up and chase them."
— Carmelo Anthony

# Inception

"You can change your fate. You can sit back, or you can go after your life and all that you want it to be."
— Hilary Swank

Someone asked me why I wrote two books with a similar theme. It is because I have much more to say than what could fit into one book. Even though there is some repeated information, each book contains information different from the other, and any repeated information goes along with the message.

At first, I didn't know what I was going to write, what I was going to conclude, what I was going to include, what I was going to advise. I wrote, anyway.

"If we are to wait for the moment when everything is absolutely ready, we shall never begin."
— Ivan Turgenev

What started out as writing some notes of theory and philosophy on life to leave for a child of mine eventually turned into books covering a wide range of topics, mixed with wisdom from all sorts of people from throughout history.

The books have sort of an editorial bricolage type of construction, which is a writing style I also used in my book about screenwriting. I wanted the books to contain the opinions and views of many people, and not only my own. I wanted them to be helpful for a range of people, and to encourage solutions.

1

I grew up in a poverty-stricken household of many misfortunes, with abuse, neglect, and assault common to me. My parents were not what people describe as "emotionally available." I had several older brothers, but they were also troubled in many ways, as well as unavailable. There were no grandparents, aunts, or uncles, and nobody to bounce ideas off of, to guide me, to help me explore life concepts, or to protect me. There was no Internet in those days, and electronic media was limited. I turned to books, newspapers, and magazines to learn about life.

"It was books that taught me that the things that tormented me most were the very things that connected me with all the people who were alive, or who had ever lived."
— James Baldwin

As a child, until I was thirteen, I could not retain what I had read. While my grades then briefly improved, some horrible events and a contentious, abusive, thoroughly troubled household kept me down. I continued to get lousy grades throughout school. I didn't relate to school, or the teachers, or most of the students. Family life was terrible, saturated with problems, uncertainty, abuse, and brutality. Sleep deprivation, stress, and random injuries were common.

Even under those conditions, I still thought I would write books. Specifically, books I hoped people would connect with, and would find helpful – for many generations. I wanted to speak to people in the present as much as in the future. Books do that.

"A true piece of writing is a dangerous thing; it can change your life."
— Tobias Wolff

I thought I would write a book I wish I would have had when I was young, to help people through life. It was my goal. What I had written was too long for one book. It is two.

"If you only read the books that everyone else is reading, you can only think what everyone else is thinking."
— Haruki Murakami

I wanted to write books unlike anything I or anyone had ever read. I wanted them to be unique, and contemplative, to stir thought, trigger questions, and help people factor answers, reimagine their existence, and inspire and motivate them to be their own solution.

"My task, which I am trying to achieve is, by the power of the written word, to make you hear, to make you feel – it is, before all,

to make you see."
   — Joseph Conrad

"If I can stop one heart from breaking, I shall not live in vain. If I can ease one life from aching, or cool one pain, I shall not live in vain."
   — Emily Dickenson

After writing for many years, I worked on the manuscripts of the two dream books during the pandemic. It was a surreal to spend so much time alone. I thought I should do something worthwhile, rather than obsess about news, and get caught up in the scandals, gossip, and other drama of whatever the media was focusing on as determined by algorithms. There wasn't much of anywhere to go, other than jogging and biking. For a time, even the parks, hiking trails, and beaches were closed. There was no place to gather with people. It was time to be safe as the virus the issue was being sorted out. It seemed to be a good time to get stuff done. For me, it was time to write.

"Alone. For the first time I understood the terrible significance of that word. Alone without witness, without anyone to speak to, without refuge."
   — Simone de Beauvoir

I don't know what I would have done during the pandemic shutdown, if I hadn't been able to write. Being alone so much was surreal — especially for someone used to being around numerous people. I was a ringleader of sorts. I had spent years running a screenwriting workshop consisting of hundreds of writers, in addition to working on TV and film productions, and having several other layers of social life going on.

Starting in March 2020, I took what I had written over many years, and overhauled, polished, and added to it. I wrote in silence, I wrote to music. I wrote in parks. I wrote on the beach. I wrote on the side of hiking trails. I wrote when camping.

I wrote, and spoke little. That included time I spent during the pandemic while recovering from vocal cord surgery that left me mute for months.

"I turned silences and nights into words. What was unutterable, I wrote down. I made the whirling world stand still."
   — Arthur Rimbaud

With these books, I feel I found something I could do to help be part of the solution. I hope they are worthwhile, and appreciated.

"The only way to do great work is to love what you do. If you haven't found it yet, keep looking. Don't settle. As with all matters of the heart, you'll know when you find it."
— Steve Jobs

When *Dream Another Dream* was published, friends asked me where this person came from who wrote the book. Some didn't know I was a person who would write such a thing. Others did.

"There may be a great fire in our soul, but no one ever comes to warm himself by it, all that passers-by can see is a little smoke coming out of the chimney, and they walk on."
— Vincent van Gogh

While parts of this book are a bit the same as *Dream Another Dream*, most if it is not. Even the similar parts have a slightly different angle to them, with information not contained in *Dream Another Dream*. It's all meant to incite helpful thought, action, and communication.

I simply wanted to do something beneficial for many people. I hope I succeeded with books presenting the right sort of challenges and helpful confrontations, ones that infuse beneficial thoughts, actions, and communication resulting in more satisfying, healthful, and helpful lives.

"It's impeccable how brutal the truth can be at times. But sometimes the truth arrives on you, and you can't get it off. That's when you realize that sometimes it isn't even an answer — it's a question."
— Markus Zusak

I aimed to present advice on what to do with and how to engage with life, each other, and our relationship with wildlife and Earth.

"He that to what he sees, adds observation, and to what he reads, reflection, is in the right road to knowledge."
— Caleb Colton

Let us get on with it. Let go of the past. Open your mind and imagination. Listen. Consider. Dive into being your solution.

"I know but one freedom and that is the freedom of the mind."
— Antoine de Saint-Exupery

"Your soul already knows the answer. You just have to be quiet enough to hear it, and brave enough to listen."
— Stacie Martin

# Dive into Your Imagination

"Tell me, what is it you plan to do with your one wild and precious life?"
– Mary Oliver

Are you continually allowing situations, events, and people to distract, muffle, and control you because you are not taking control of your life?

Or, are you accessing and using your intellect, instinct, intuition, discernment, talents, skills, abilities, anticipation, yearning, imagination, and beneficial qualities to form your life into what you want it to be?

Your future does not have to be some random spec that falls out of the cosmos. You also do not have to perpetually settle for a low-quality life.

"It is never too late to be what we might have been."
– George Eliot

If you are not experiencing the life you want, there is one person to whom you can turn to change your life. That person is you.

"Man is so made that when anything fires his soul, impossibilities vanish."
– Jean de La Fontaine

Your life is not going to stay the way it is. Instead, it is going to change in some way regardless of what you do.

5

"Success isn't a result of spontaneous combustion. You must set yourself on fire."
– Arnold H. Glasgow

If your life is going to reflect what you wish it to be, it is up to you to transform your wishes into reality.

"Thought is cause: experience is effect. If you don't like the effects in your life, you have to change the nature of your thinking."
– Marianne Williamson

If you are reading this type of book, it is likely that you are not satisfied with the condition of your life.

"May you overcome every darkness you face in your life with the light of your soul."
– Prem Tihan

Maybe you are at some level of dissatisfaction with how you have spent your life, and have decided that you do not want to waste one more moment replicating the results you have been experiencing.

Maybe you have reached what you feel to be the end of your rope and have made the decision that you do not want to go through another year, month, week, or day without experiencing life improvement.

"The truth is that our finest moments are most likely to occur when we are feeling deeply uncomfortable, unhappy, or unfulfilled. For it is only in such moments, propelled by our discomfort, that we are likely to step out of our ruts and start searching for different ways and truer answers."
– M. Scott Peck

Your life does not have to be guided by the formula of the myth in which your strongest life-altering revelation arrives at your darkest moment. A great change in your life also does not have to be spurred by a cataclysmic event. You also do not have to depend on others or on events for inspiration.

The personal revelations and inspirations triggering improvement can arrive when you open your thoughts to their possibility.

"Every exit is an entry somewhere else."
– Tom Stoppard

Maybe you are at the point of feeling as if your life has been shattered, and you are chaos. Instead of thinking of your life as shattering, consider that it may finally be recomposing into a more beautiful mosaic. You may be going through a major life cleanse as you are shedding what truly is not you while taking on a new understanding and form.

"Storms purify the atmosphere."
– Henry Ward Beecher

You might be going through a life storm, even deluged by a typhoon of issues and feeling as if you are in the center of a tornado. Storms are ways Nature rearranges and clarifies, renewing energy, opening new pathways, and infusing patterns of growth.

"Sometimes a breakdown can be the beginning of a kind of breakthrough, a way of living in advance through a trauma that prepares you for a future of radical transformation."
– Cherrie Moraga

"I began to understand that suffering and disappointments and melancholy are there not to vex us or cheapen us or deprive us of our dignity, but to mature and transfigure us."
– Hermann Hesse

What you may be going through is a level of what some call a shamanic conversion – or enlightenment – as you discover what it is you are truly about.

"Suffering has been stronger than all other teaching, and has taught me to understand what your heart used to be. I have been bent and broken, but – I hope – into better shape."
– Charles Dickens

It is difficult to know, but be assured that everyone experiences struggle. Pain and other matters are not always evident. Everyone has their issues, drama, stress, fear, loss, defeat, sadness, grief, loneliness, infirmity, rejection, and concern impacting their resonance, outlook, expectations, anticipation, hope, yearning, relationships, and the way they view, relate to, interact with, and participate in life.

"It's a delicate walk to balance hope with chaos."
– Stacie Martin

We are not only the product of self. We are the product of generations, history, experience, sensory engagement, nurturing (or the lack thereof), of Nature, atmosphere, and terrain, and of what we ate, considered, thought, saw, heard, and faced, and of what we have had – and of what we have not had. We are the product of us and all.

For you, there is the situation of acknowledging your problems, and dealing with them through wiser, educated choices. Hopefully in ways that will benefit you, those you love, and others in your community.

My other book *Dream Another Dream* goes into some of the situations I had to deal with, including growing up in an abusive, neglectful, financially stressed, brutal household of many troubles and tragedies, and ruled over by generations of alcoholism, infighting, sickly behavior, and toxic relations. I shared the information in the book with the hope of helping someone else in their self-realization and advancement into a more healthful life path.

**"Because we become what we live, the work that we do, and what and who we value while doing it, have a major impact on our character and who we become."**
– Kathleen Lynch

We are not one thing, we are layers upon layers of things, and have layers of mental and physical things going on. Luckily, we can be proactive in guiding some of it. We can focus every day on what is beneficial using our better qualities. Through knowing ourselves, we can know others, and, while wiser, have compassion for them.

**"I just want to feel as much as I can, it's what soul is all about."**
– Janis Joplin

During the pandemic, when much of what was everyday life had shut down, people were forced into a situation in which their sensory experiences were limited. No longer were they going to events, public venues, school, work, gyms, or places where they experienced what had been their normal stimuli. It was a trial for many people, not knowing how to function without their normal everyday experiences.

Not everyone processed the pandemic situation in the same way.

For other people, especially those who are highly sensitive, not being around crowds, not being around highly stimulating situations, and being in calmer situations, the pandemic worked better for them. Having fewer people and sounds around, and experiencing life on a more intimate level, including reading books, listening to music, having one-on-one conversations, exercising alone, being more in control of what they view, and working on their own projects would be more of their sort of thing. They are more agreeable with less hustle and bustle going on, feel more comfortable with time for introspection, and appreciate a lower spectrum of intensity so they don't get overwhelmed in situations. They might be so highly sensitive to quickly being overwhelmed and having a loss of control that it causes them to react harshly, or to implode and withdrawal. That is why the calmness of the pandemic shutdown might have worked better for them. It doesn't necessarily mean the person is introverted, which is a different thing. Humans are complex, layered beings. It also doesn't mean they have a personality disorder, or obsessive compulsive disorder (OCD), or have attention deficit hyperactivity disorder (ADHD), sensory processing disorder (SPD), generalized anxiety disorder (GAD), autism spectrum disorder (ASD), sensory processing disorder (SPD), or emotional dysregulation, which are a number of different things that shouldn't be expected to express in the same ways. Then, there are the issues relating to dominance, power, control, and even Puer Aetemrnus and Puella Aeterna issues (wanting to be eternally young), and c-PTSD (complex post-traumatic stress disorder) and it's intrusion into emotions, and inability to cope with or manage those out in society, so they find it easier to not be around people as they will then experience less anxiety and frustration. Then, there are depression, anxiety, sadness, grief, and other mental health states and stages, which can be different than – and tangled in with – neuro issues – and some are more common to experience with certain conditions. For some with one or more of those issues, the aloneness of the pandemic shutdown magnified their situations, sometimes to the point of tragedy. There are so many complexities to this. It is far too much to be explained here. It could include brain function, serotonin levels, dopamine issues, neurodivergence, nutrition and fitness issues, education level, family and childhood history, young adult history, relationship history, trauma, undiagnosed chronic or degenerative or genetic disorders, and other matters. (Google any of the above, and: "HSP = highly sensitive person.")

As always, if you feel life issues to be overwhelming, do explore ways of seeking help that can set you on a better life path. This could include visiting with a psychologist, joining a 12-step group to find what has helped others, reading books about your issues, cleaning up your diet, getting daily exercise, following a regular sleep pattern, using your talents, and other ways of helping yourself.

Maybe what had been normal for people before the pandemic wasn't so healthy, anyway. Some clearly had been caught up in the habituation of entitlement of having access to what they wanted whenever they wanted – at their whim. Then, when the pandemic shutdown happened, some felt as if they were being denied their life – when all that was being asked of them was that they participate in helping stop the spread of the virus. Their refusal and protest against helping only quickened and worsened the spread and suffering.

Some people were caught in situations where they were stuck in unhealthy households. The quarantine magnified and intensified their problems.

Sometimes a great change in life can be beneficial, in unexpected ways – including having to refactor who we are, and reconfigure how to participate in life, and who we spend our time with. Perhaps what a person dreads going through will spin them into a much healthier way of existing.

"What we consider to be normal in this society is actually neither natural or healthy, and in fact is a cause of much human pathology – mental and physical. And actually people's pathologies – what we call abnormalities – whether it's mental or physical illnesses – are actually normal responses to what is an abnormal culture."
– Gabor Maté

Nobody is going to get by without experiencing some hardships, but we can be here for each other, reduce the suffering, and lead each other out of the dark times.

Know that when you are experiencing dark times, others also are. Step back, reconsider, regroup, and place yourself in the forward row of the most helpful interpretation and function you can engage in.

"Knowing your own darkness is the best method for dealing with the darknesses of other people. It would help you to have a personal insight into the secrets of the human soul. Otherwise everything remains a clever intellectual trick, consisting of empty words and leading to empty talk."
– Carl Gustav Jung

"Are you unhappy because you have lost those things in which you took pleasure? But you can also take comfort in the likelihood that what is now making you miserable will also pass away."
– Boethius

"Sometimes our fate resembles a fruit tree in winter. Who would think that those branches would turn green again and blossom, but we hope it, we know it."
– Johann Wolfgang von Goethe

Know that part of who you are consists of your intuition, of your yearning, of what you feel satisfied by, and what you desire. These can be what initiate the thoughts driving your emotion, how you express yourself and communicate, how it is you go about seeking what you wish for, and how you participate in life.

"There is a life-affirming spark within you which constantly nudges you towards saying yes to life."
– Linda MacDonald

Maybe what you feel is that you are at the end, but that ending may be your beginning, and a time to find the path into your next life adventure. Use your power to take control of where you go.

"The world is round and the place which may seem like the end may also be the beginning."
– Ivy Baker Priest

"You aren't a machine with broken parts. You are an animal whose needs are not being met. You need to have a community. You need to have meaningful values, not the junk values you've been pumped full of all your life, telling you happiness comes through money and buying objects. You need to have meaningful work. You need the natural world. You need to feel you are respected. You need to secure your future. You need connections to all these things. You need to release any shame you might feel for having been mistreated."
– Johann Hari

What you are doing, or can be doing, is learning, practicing skills, and building yourself into what you will next become. If you are a student of life who pays attention, you will hear the message, see the opportunities, and work to build the new set of skills and dexterity you can use to advance into experiencing your better possibilities.

"For last year's words belong to last year's language. And next year's words await another voice. What we call the beginning is often the end. And to make an end is to make a beginning."
– T. S. Eliot

Like others, I have experienced a variety of life problems. I have attempted. I have failed. I have chosen to continue on, including seeking what will help me, even when anything of benefit seemed absent, or unobtainable. I realized that a person must work to self-motivate, and to continually take actions in the direction of what they wish to be and see.

"The most powerful weapon on earth is the human soul on fire."
– Ferdinand Foch

I have sought wisdom through books. I have made attempts at changing and improving my life. I have made some better choices, and some that were not so beneficial. I have met contention and my own varieties of issues.

One thing I've learned is: You have to keep pushing along, and to not allow yourself to be stopped by what you first perceive as a roadblock. You have to protect and honor your life.

We are animals. We observe and contemplate. We factor and calculate solutions. We make attempts. Those who are wise will continue to use their discernment, and work to be their solution.

Just as others have done throughout history, you could be the person who creates or discovers something beneficial to many other people, even millions.

"Your spark can become a flame and change everything."
– Edgar Daniel Nixon

I have read many books on the topic of life change. I found some to be helpful, and some that were not so much.

In particular, I think a book most helpful in manifesting a truly healthful life would be one helpful in determining the difference between the authentic beneficial traits of a person and the personality someone has tried to become so they are more likely to fit into what they have perceived to be acceptable society.

"Most people are convinced that as long as they are not overtly forced to do something by an outside power, their decisions are theirs, and that if they want something, it is they who want it. But this is one of the great illusions we have about ourselves. A great number of our decisions are not really our own but are suggested to us from the outside; we have succeeded in persuading ourselves that it is we who have made the decision, whereas we have actually conformed with expectations of others, driven by the fear of isolation and by more direct threats to our life, freedom, and comfort."
– Erich Fromm

Considering that many of us do conform to what we think is the most acceptable way of being, maybe it is the conformity that is holding us back, and which may have placed limits on the expression of our vision and on we do with our intellect, skills, and talents. The conformity may also have played a part in the feelings of awkwardness and inadequacy that crushes potential. In a good way, this may lead to the introspection that can bring about healthful life changes by doing away with the false self, and by allowing people to identify and cherish their true beneficial qualities.

"I have always believed, and I still believe, that whatever good or bad fortune may come our way we can always give it meaning and transform it into something of value."
– Hermann Hesse

Perhaps you feel as if your life has been injured, and that what you desire and need is to undergo healing. Understand that you hold the power and ability to heal your wounds to a level at which you can then move forward doing what you are capable of. You can use your desire, yearning, and energy as motivation to take the actions that make the changes resulting in better choices that can be solutions uniquely styled for you.

Maybe you are tilting on the edge of the life you have been leading, have realized how it is not what you desire, and you want to change course. Through changing your focus, better quality nutrition and exercise, and wiser time management you can follow a different path bringing you into a more desirable situation.

Maybe you are seeking options that can lead to a more satisfying life. The options you need may be right inside you, and these include thinking differently, which leads to taking actions, communicating, and otherwise expressing yourself in ways that give you different experiences from those you've been experiencing.

"Every human being is a problem in search of a solution."
– Ashley Montagu

If you want to change your life – no matter what step of life you are in – it is good to remember that people can rise out of their former ways of living and take charge of becoming more of what it is they hope to be. They can become more of an expression of their true selves. They can do away with the things holding them back. They can adapt to a more proactive state of mind that will propel their actions toward creating a better level of health and satisfaction. They can change the way they perceive things, and they can do so in more beneficial ways – including for others.

"The world is but a canvas to the imagination."
– Henry David Thoreau

"Only those who will risk going too far can possibly find out how far one can go."
– T.S. Eliot

13

This book often mentions thoughts. This is because if you want beneficial changes in your life, you need to equally change the way you conduct your thoughts. Changing your patterns of thinking in sync with taking action, and communicating is the key to life change and transformation. Part of that includes what you ingest nutritionally through food, and mentally through literature and other devices of learning – including learning from other people, and from your own practices, trials, attempts, errors, and drive to do better.

"Change your thoughts, and you change your world."
– Norman Vincent Peale

What you see around you partially consists of your thoughts made visible through the manipulation of your actions and communication.

What you think, as in how you perceive things, is what – more than anything else – may determine your future. Your actions and communication are the results of your thoughts.

What you have accomplished, or failed to accomplish, has often been the result of your thinking.

If you want a future that is very different from your past, observe, factor, conclude, and turn your thoughts into action and communication to guide things to happen in your favor.

"Life is not a 'brief candle.' It is a splendid torch that I want to make burn as brightly as possible before handing on to future generations."
– George Bernard Shaw

While future generations were in my thoughts as I worked on this book, I also thought that it might be a book for anyone of any age who desires a more satisfying life.

Rather than writing an instruction manual, I aimed for something that was exploratory in nature, as what works for one person might not be what works for another.

"If you have knowledge, let others light their candles in it."
– Margaret Fuller

My approach to the topic of changing thought to formulate life change was to write a book – or books – I could give to my children in the hope of helping to guide their lives. I also aimed to write for people who have been through any number of situations. I'm especially interested in motivating people who feel they have been trampled down, or otherwise have troubled backgrounds, including people who have been abused, neglected, homeless, addicted to substances, or imprisoned. My aim also is to motivate people to live in ways that are more environmentally sustainable, protective of wildlife, cause less harm to non-human animals, and universally healthful.

Writing the two dream books has provided me with the opportunity to use many of the quotations I've been collecting throughout my life. I use quotations from such a variety of people because I don't want the book to consist only of my thoughts. I want it to include the thoughts of many, and to inspire readers to have their own so they infuse their dreams into their lives with parallel actions creating the improvements they wish to be and see.

"The best of a book is not the thought which it contains, but the thought which it suggests; just as the charm of music dwells not in the tones but in the echoes of our hearts."
– Oliver Wendell Holmes

Many books about motivation are so scrubbed and polished they seem more like corporate handbooks. Creating that type of book like was absolutely not my goal.

I wanted to write a book to enliven people and to motivate them away from being anywhere within that description F. Scott Fitzgerald used in *The Great Gatsby*: "He's so dumb he doesn't know he's alive."

While writing this book, I aimed to get away from the sort of self-help mysticism some success and positive-thinking gurus seem to dwell in, and that I find hard to relate to. Instead, I aimed to write plainly, and with wording that I hope to be accessible, without grand dressing.

"A good coach will make his players see what they can be, rather than what they are."
– Ara Parsegian

When I've looked at other motivational books, I have found that I can't relate to many of them. The authors seem to project spiffy images of people living lives of opulence while focusing on extreme materialistic abundance. That is not me. It also is hardly what most people can relate to. It is also the type of lifestyle that is not sustainable, nor does it appeal to those of us who like to live simply, and who like to keep our hands in the soil.

"When we stop working with our hands, we cease to understand how the world really works."
– Clive Thompson

I'm more of the hands-on person, like to dig my own garden, bury my own kitchen scraps to grow more food, and am not interested in a lifestyle surrounded by technological and glamorous spectacles. Nor am I interested in pretending to have the perfect life, posing as some sort of ideal, nor in setting myself as an example of a flawless specimen. Like you and everyone else, I am flawed.

Because of numerous circumstances, many people don't have the type of situation giving them access to the so-called perfect life idealized in some of the most popular success books, or in the imagery produced by corporate advertising. Even when they do have a situation allowing them to replicate advertising imagery, they may harbor no desire to live that type of high-maintenance life.

What many people desire isn't about luxury and posh living. Instead, they simply want to experience happiness, health, and satisfaction while maintaining loving relationships. As I see it, none of the things people truly want have anything to do with the materials that make up the corporate imagery in advertising, which is of huge financial wealth.

"Always having what we want may not be the best good fortune. Health seems sweetest after sickness, food in hunger, goodness in the wake of evil, and at the end of daylong labor, sleep."
– Heraclitus

Many people do not care to make their lives into the images seen in commercials, but would like to own a life more in tune with true happiness – and in which their loves can thrive.

No matter what life presents to them, in managing their lives, many people unfortunately choose what they may consider the easiest route – which may turn out to be the most difficult.

It is likely that if people really did put themselves to work making their lives into what their higher potential can present when it is truly used, they would find that the more healthful life in which they do wisely use their resources, intellect, skills, and talents would be much less troublesome.

"Let him who would move the world first move himself."
– Socrates

I hope this book helps people live more sustainably, and to be a part of the solution. That is, rather than participating in what many people consider success: a money-hoarding, mansion-dwelling, and unsustainable lifestyle of high maintenance and luxurious excess.

"Try not to become a man of success. Rather, become a man of value."
– Albert Einstein

As you read through the book, realize the repetition is intentional. It wrote it that way because people often need to hear the same message repeatedly, before they grasp a concept. This can be especially true if they are going to take the concept to heart and apply its principles to life.

Repetition of the knitting needle creates the sweater. Repetition of a bricklayer's hands creates a structure. Repetition of a swimmer's movements creates fitness. And repetition of messages creates a learned mind.

"Self-education is, I firmly believe, the only kind of education there is."
– Isaac Asimov

I don't think a book like this could ever be finished. This is especially so because this book covers such a broad range of issues that are not the same for each person. The subject of personal fulfillment is also a rich one that cannot be explored within one book.

"Discovery consists of seeing what everyone else has seen and thinking what no one else has thought."
– Albert Szent-Gyorgyi

"The whole idea is to earn the flavor. No one gives it to you."
– Jamie Oliver

"To read without reflecting is like eating without digesting."
– Edmund Burke

Readers of books about personal growth can more effectively apply what they learn by making notes as they read, exploring their thoughts and options, then acting upon what they discover and factor.

With this book, the process may be brought about more effectively if you:

A) Use a notebook to take notes and record thoughts relating to the parts of the book that most strongly speak to you.

B) Write a game plan that applies your goals to your thought patterns. Then…

C) Act upon the information. And…

D) Keep a journal detailing the changes and successes you have made happen in your life.

17

E) Review and adjust your goals every morning so you begin each day focused on what you wish to attain.

Do all of these things with the goal of improving every level of your situation.

"The thirst after happiness is never extinguished in the heart of man."
– Jean Jacques Rousseau

While there are millions of people ready to sell something they claim will improve life, there also seems to be an endless parade of people ready to purchase the products – which often do not hold any of the promises contained in the marketing claims.

I have no products to sell, nor is this book about marketing things based on claims they will improve your life. The initial tools you need to improve your life can't be purchased. They are what you already have. It is the desire and drive to become more healthful and satisfied with your life. A key to all of this is to: Value your self.

"If I am not for myself, who is for me? And if I am only for myself, what am I? And if not now, when?"
– Hillel

This book is about restructuring your being through excellent nutrition, exercise, positive-thinking, visualization, and goal setting in tune with continual actions, helpful communication, and intentional living. It is about uplifting your thoughts and accelerating your actions to propel your life toward health and fulfillment in the best way you can while using what is available to you.

"I'm worth it. And the next time you hesitate before going after something you want, the next time you blush and brush off a compliment, the next time you doubt your place in the world, and the workplace, in your home, or in your own skin, say these words to yourself: I'm worth it."
– Viola Davis

The nutritional aspects of the book are based on returning to what Nature provides. Since their beginnings, humans survived on a natural diet. It is only in the last century that humans have consumed unnatural substances containing synthetic chemicals proven to contribute to learning disabilities, developmental disorders, anxiety, depression, birth defects, cancers, kidney and cardiovascular disease, and other degenerative diseases, and in damage to the environment, the death of wildlife, and a poisoned Earth.

"We are living in a world today where lemonade is made from artificial flavors, and furniture polish is made from real lemons."
– Alfred E. Newman

Inadequate nutrition and the consumption of junk food contribute to everything from skin problems to obesity, from heart disease to visual impairment, from depression to blood disorders, and from the inability to concentrate and focus to a weakened immune system.

Eating whole foods, such as unprocessed fruits and vegetables, provides the body with important nutrients, including vitamins, minerals, essential fatty acids, amino acids, enzymes, and health-inducing phytochemicals, such as isoflavonoids and lignans.

A plant-based diet rich in fresh fruits and vegetables is also rich in biophotons (or bions), an often overlooked nutrient of light energy produced, emitted, and absorbed by the cells of plants and animals. Biophotons are in our DNA, and in the nucleus of all our cells from head to toe. Biophoton meridian fields run through our cells and body structures. Biophoton light energy fields are one way our cells communicate. The presence of biophotons and photoreceptor proteins within our tissues allows for our cells to not only communicate, but to vibrate with energy, and otherwise function.

A diet with an abundance of uncooked plant matter is rich in antioxidants, enzymes, EFAs, anti-inflammatories, biophotons, and other micro- and macro-nutrients, and helps the body to generate, regenerate, and function at a higher level.

As explained later, those who are truly interested in experiencing vibrant health should banish fried and sautéed foods; synthetic food additives; MSG (monosodium glutamate); hydrogenated oils; processed sugars, including corn, rice, and agave syrups; processed salts; bleached grains; and other low-quality substances from their diet. They would benefit by following a fresh-foods diet consisting of a rotation of raw fruits, vegetables, nuts, seaweeds, and germinated or sprouted seeds and legumes. A key is also: Daily exercise. (See my book *Plant-Based Regenerative Nutrition*.)

When you consider that your body is constantly replacing its cells, your blood cells only live a little more than a week before they are replaced with new cells, and your muscle cells live about three months before they are replaced, perhaps you can begin to understand how nutrition plays a major role in creating, recreating, and maintaining your life.

While your body cells today may have been constructed of the substances of the low-quality foods you have consumed, understand that you can transform your body structure in a matter of months by consuming a diet consisting of high-quality, plant-based nutrition – and especially a diet largely consisting of fresh, fruits and vegetables. Plant substances provide enzymes, high-quality essential fatty acids, bioavailable amino acids, fiber, and a full spectrum of vitamins, minerals, and trace nutrients, and, as mentioned, antioxidants, anti-inflammatories, and biophotons.

"To keep the body in good health is a duty, otherwise we shall not be able to keep our mind strong and clear."
– Buddha

I include a plant-based diet as the basis for the best nutrition because it is a major key in experiencing the highest levels of vibrant health.

As Dr. Edward Howell explained in the 1940s, edible raw plant matter provides the nutrients we need, including *life force energy*.

The natural state of the body is to be healthful and free from toxins and disease.

The keys to health are a proactive thought patterns triggering parallel actions and communication, a daily exercise regimen, a plant-based diet, a regular sleep pattern, and a healthful atmosphere. It also is of great help to well-being to be in uplifting, loving relationships.

"If you want to meet someone who can fix any situation you don't like, who can bring you happiness in spite of what other people say or believe, look in a mirror and say this magic word: Hello."
– Richard Bach

You can begin to improve your life at any moment. It is largely your decision to take the initiative, and the necessary actions.

If you are to experience satisfaction, it is more likely to happen if you formulate thoughts that result in you taking the actions and communicating in ways that create it. Know that it is within your power and ability to do so.

"The value of achievement lies in the achieving."
– Albert Einstein

From your mind to your voice and body, it is likely that you can communicate and work to make all parts of your being function in ways that are more beneficial to you. At the same time, you can begin to bring things into your life that will build it into what you want it to be. You can also begin to turn away those things in your life that do not harmonize with the way you hope for your life to be.

"Most powerful is he who has himself in his own power."
– Lucius Annaeus Seneca

There is no better time to begin improving your life than the present.

Now is the time to take control of your existence so you can begin leading a more healthful and helpful life in which to thrive.

"A moments insight is sometimes worth a life's experience."
– Oliver Wendell Holmes

You can decide at this very moment that you will work each day to change your life for the better.

You can decide right now that you will no longer settle for the qualities and standards you have been experiencing.

You can decide as you read this that you will work each day to achieve your goals.

"The greatest revolution of our generation is the discovery that human beings, by changing the inner attitudes of their minds, can change the outer aspects of their lives."
– William James

The ancient peoples of the world, the cave dwellers on every continent, the originators of religious teachings and philosophies, the creators of mythological stories handed down for generations, everyone from the Aztecs and Buddhists to the Egyptians, Eskimos, Hebrews, Hindus, Hopi, Mayans, Polynesians, Sumerians, and every other group of people have shared the message that a person's happiness in life greatly relies not on government or industry, but on the choices of the individual to use his or her power – in action and communication.

Throughout this book I use quotations from a wide variety of people. I did not pay attention to their religion, race, nationality, gender, sexuality, political leanings, or even to their history of purity or corruption. I simply sought to use quotations that spoke what I felt was truth, and I did so with one goal: to motivate you, the reader.

"What we call our destiny is truly our character and that character can be altered. The knowledge that we are responsible for our actions and attitudes does not need to be discouraging, because it also means that we are free to change this destiny. One is not in bondage to the past, which has shaped our feelings to race, inheritance, background. All this can be altered if we have the courage to examine how it formed us. We can alter the chemistry

provided we have the courage to dissect the elements."
— Anais Nin

As human beings, health and happiness is what we desire.

You can choose to keep following a pattern of dissatisfaction, or you can get busy with your beneficial qualities creating a new pattern.

"I don't think people realize how much strength it takes to pull your own self out of a dark place mentally. If you did that today, or any day, I am proud of you."
— Morgan Freeman

This book is the invitation to aim for and go toward that which makes you a more healthful and satisfied expression of your self. It invites you to do so while also encouraging you to be part of the solution to society's and Nature's ills.

"We learn wisdom from failure much more than from success. We often discover what will do by finding out what will not do; and probably he who never made a mistake never made a discovery."
— Samuel Smiles

Get busy doing what you want to do, be, and see.

"Skill to do comes of doing."
— Ralph Waldo Emerson

One hundred percent of the rest of your life starts right now. Be active and engaged with and in it. Make it be part of the solution for a more sustainable future in which Nature and wildlife can thrive.

Avoid being a participant in what Carl Sagan called "the celebration of ignorance." This can be viewed as the dumbing down of a humanity focused on nonsense, being involved with nonstop shopping, trying to be validated by owning stuff, consuming toxic foods, and participating in what drives humans, wildlife, and the land, water, and air into steeper decline. It is what is leading to ocean acidification, climate change, degraded soil, desertification, dying plant life, crop failures, plunging wild animal populations, and an Earth saturated with pollution.

Research permaculture, organic food gardening, and wild food foraging. Learn what can be done to improve the conditions of your local wildlife habitat.

Learn the varieties of reasons why industrial hemp is considered to be the most valuable and useable crop – and how hemp can be used in ways that replace products made of trees, cotton, and petroleum (including petroleum plastics and fuels).

# Ending or Beginning Results

If you are not doing what you want to do, consider that you may be doing what you don't want to do.

**"Action may not always bring happiness, but there is no happiness without action."**
– Benjamin Disraeli

Many people say they don't have time in their days to accomplish the things they want to. Maybe they aren't managing their time and other resources as wisely as they could.

**"We have more possibilities available in each moment than we realize."**
– Thich Nhat Hanh

Everyone on this planet has the same number of hours in a day, week, month, and year. Some accomplish great things, while others spend hours watching TV, playing video games, obsessively following celebrity culture, and/or otherwise engaging in wasteful and slothful activities.

What you do with your life is up to you. You can either let the whimsy of whatever happens create your life, or you can become proactive in creating a more desirable life.

**"What you are is a question only you can answer."**
– Lois McMaster Bujold

Decide right now to spend your time more wisely.

23

Stop drifting in the ocean of dissatisfaction. Instead, discover or revive and nurture your higher ambitions. Live with aim. Develop and follow a plan to get you to a desirable destination.

"All serious daring starts from within."
– Harriet Beecher Stowe

Unless you are in a war zone, in prison, or in some other trying situation, there likely are things you can manage better, including what you eat, your attitude, how you communicate, and what you engage in. You can immediately begin to select the higher-quality foods available to you. You can decide to think in a way more conducive to a healthful life. You can communicate more healthfully. You can decide from now on to set goals and be involved in activities more likely than less likely to bring you what you want. As you do this your body and life will begin to function at a level equal to your nutrition, thoughts, communication, and actions.

Whether you like it or not, there are outside influences impacting your life. It is likely that you can have some power over how they do so.

Consider that you may be treating your life the way society collectively reacts to its own problems, and this usually means lazily, without the most helpful solutions, and while doing things that will lead to similar unsatisfactory conditions, while only applying bandages to wounds that are untreated and continue to fester.

Your surroundings are impacting you. You absorb the energy surrounding you. The people and things in your atmosphere affect you. These can have a positive impact, or they can have a negative impact. You also can learn to have more control over these things – or, at least, how you deal with them.

Each person is a power source, generating energy that is manifested in their thoughts, actions, communication, relationships, and results.

By plugging into your potential, using your talents and skills, guiding your thought processes, and actively choosing what to do with your energy and time, communication and actions, you can fuel a life you want to lead. Or, like many people, you can do none of it, or do it sloppily, and end up in a life you may not care to have.

"Some men see things as they are and say, 'Why?' I dream of things that never were, and say, 'Why not?'"
– George Bernard Shaw

Many people live life reacting to things that have already happened with energy already spent to form those things.

Much of the activity you see, including on the daily news, may consist of people reacting to things that have happened, getting dulled by and lost in results, and doing what amounts to taping bandages on societal wounds that continue to hemorrhage because the underlying thought processes, actions, and issues causing the problems have not been changed in a way that would bring more satisfying results.

Are you caught in what seems to be a revolution of dullness, and perhaps as being an active co-perpetrator of humanity's downfall?

Your life does not have to resemble the dysfunction and corruption you witness. Instead, you can decide to live life working for a better future by making wiser choices in all areas of your life.

"A life of reaction is a life of slavery, intellectually, and spiritually. One must fight for a life of action, not reaction."
– Rita Mae Brown

Many people trip and stumble over their constant concern and worry about finances. But finances are the end result of thoughts and actions. Many people also fumble over issues that are the result of unwise decisions that continue to be acted on and replicated through actions and communication – even though the very same people hate the results of those decisions.

Reacting to secondary causative factors is how many people lead their lives. They don't take action to rule their lives. Instead, they allow themselves to be ruled and formed by what has been expressed – or is being expressed – by others.

Focusing on end results prevents you from creating solutions and taking actions leading to better results and greater satisfaction.

"There is nothing as easy as denouncing. It don't take much to see that something is wrong, but it takes some eyesight to see what will put it right again."
– Will Rogers

No longer allow yourself to get tangled in end results. They are unraveling before you and the energy that led to their manifestation has already been spent. Instead, use the energy you have now to be involved in thoughts, actions, and communication more likely than less likely to end up with the beneficial results you want.

"The sole purpose of human existence is to kindle a light in the darkness of mere being."
– Carl Gustav Jung

Thoughts drive your actions and communication, and your engagement with potential and opportunities. The real power is not of wealth, but it is the power of thought. The power of your thought is guided by your belief in what you are capable of doing mixed with the level at which you have tapped into the power of your essence, which is the dwelling of your intellect, talents, instinct, intuition, abilities, yearning, elegance, and other graces fueling your potential. The real power is in how enlightened you are combined with how you choose that enlightenment to guide your being.

"You must live in the present, launch yourself on every wave, find your eternity in each moment."
– Henry David Thoreau

Behavior is triggered by what you anticipate. Your anticipatory behavior is something that defines you and formulates your existence.

Anticipation is a constant, is intertwined with your thoughts, and guides every action you take and every communication you make.

"I always entertain great hopes."
– Robert Frost

"To the question whether I am a pessimist or an optimist, I answer that my knowledge is pessimistic, but my willing and hoping are optimistic."
– Albert Schweitzer

"Hope is a waking dream."
– Aristotle

Your behavior reveals what you hope for, or your lack thereof. It reveals intention and attention. It displays how deeply you are tuned into your better qualities. It shows what you are conscious of, what you desire, your motives, and your passions.

"Every decision you make – every decision – is not a decision about what to do. It's a decision about who you are. When you see this, when you understand it, everything changes. You begin to see life in a new way. All events, occurrences, and situations turn into opportunities to do what you came here to do."
– Neale Donald Walsch

Through your actions and communication you reveal what you think of your self, and whether you believe in your beneficial attributes enough to use them to transform your self and turn your wishes into reality. Your actions and communication not only reveal who you are, they also help to determine what you become.

"What disappoints me the most is somebody who can do something well and does not do it."
– Sean Penn

What I am talking about is not about limiting yourself. It is about opening yourself to what could be yours: health, satisfaction, happiness, and loving relationships. It is about discovering higher quality nutrition, new energy, new thought processes, better quality communication, and a level of vibrant health you have not experienced. It is about accessing your beneficial yearning, and utilizing your intellect, talents, skills, and potential for your good.

"By sowing frugality we reap liberty, a golden harvest."
– Agesilaus

When I am speaking of improving your life, I'm not talking about increasing your material possessions, which are a façade. I am not about hoarding wealth and trying to impress people with money and expensive stuff, which is silly, wasteful, and unsustainable nonsense. If anything, I'm talking about having fewer things than what commercialized and corporate greed-driven culture grooms us to believe in as a validation of a successful, satisfying life.

"We can only be said to be alive in those moments when our hearts are conscious of our treasures."
– Thornton Wilder

I am advising that you get involved in having a bigger, more satisfactory, and more sustainable life saturated with health and the true expression of the good things about you. You do it through work. The work you have to perform to access the life you wish for.

"Everything can be taken from a man but one thing: the last of the human freedoms – to choose one's attitude in any given set of circumstances, to choose one's own way."
– Victor Frankl

I'm advising that you get and stay involved in making your better life happen through the wise use of your intellect, yearning, talents, skills, time, energy, and passions, which are your tools and treasures.

"How can you follow the course of your life if you do not let it flow?"
– Lao Tzu

27

Set a course for your life that will reveal all you wish your life to be.

"An intense anticipation itself transforms possibility into reality; our desires being often but precursors of the things which we are capable of performing."
– Samuel Smiles

There is anticipation that hinders, and anticipation that helps. There is also anticipation that is the stem of and triggers anxiety, dismissal, disbelief, narcissistic behavior, and denial, lies, deception, and greed, which all can damage.

Let your anticipation be of a healthful sort, and not of what others will think of you, and what you will do if they don't react as your anticipation had assigned. Use anticipation to help build a healthful life in which you thrive.

"Conscience in most men is but the anticipation of the opinions of others."
– Jeremy Taylor

"If I had to live my life in anticipation of what others thought of me, little would get done."
– Henry Rollins

We can't expect to control what others think or will think. Instead, we can have some control over what we think, do, and say. Work on the practice of doing what is helpful and healthful.

"Not being in the present moment is no less foolish than looking forward to the past."
– Mokokoma Mokhonoana

Tune yourself to continually anticipate good things happening in your life. Plan on them happening. Visualize them happening. Stay in the present and work to strive through work to cause them happen.

"Life can seem like a gloomy wait in the thick of black shadows. And still there are those who smile at the darkness, anticipating the beauty of an eventual sunrise."
– Richelle Goodrich

Work daily to manufacture results that are your solutions.

"A major component of health and wellness, gratitude helps us to appreciate the blessings we already have, and sparks the anticipatory pleasure of blessings to come."
– Laurie Buchanan

# Consider Your Possible

"Granted that I must die, how shall I live?"
– Michael Novak

"The most important thing in life is to stop saying 'I wish' and start saying 'I will.' Consider nothing impossible, then treat possibilities as probabilities."
– David Copperfield

On some level, and probably in a much more dominant way than you might have considered, you are in charge of how happy and healthful you can be. Part of it depends on your focus, your anticipation, your nutrition, and how you perceive things.

If you do not like the health you are experiencing, you can change it. If you do not like the thoughts and visions out of alignment with who you truly are, and what you hope to happen using your better qualities, change them. If you do not like the type of life you are leading, you can lead it onto a more satisfying path.

"Each of us has much more hidden inside us than we have had a chance to explore. Unless we create an environment that enables us to discover the limits of our potential, we will never know what we have inside of us."
– Muhammad Yunus

Changing your life takes work. That is, work in a good way – because it fuels growth toward the expression of potential. It means working to access your inner wealth of character resources to create a better outside. It means exploring your options and acting on your better ones. It means working to create an environment in alignment with how you wish your life to be. It means considering, planning, working toward, and expressing your possible.

"My grandfather once told me there are two kinds of people: those who do the work, and those who take the credit. He told me to try to be in the first group; there is much less competition."
– Indira Gandhi

"If you don't make the time to work on creating the life you want, you're eventually going to be forced to spend a lot of time dealing with a life you don't want."
– Kevin Ngo

Some people say it is too difficult to work on changing their life. Instead of working toward creating a more satisfying life, they conform to the mundane and less vibrant. Little do they seem to realize that their choice also takes time, energy, resources, and effort. They are still maintaining a life, but a life that won't give them as much satisfaction as the life they desire.

You can either work toward improving, or give into whatever happens. Consider that it might be easier and more enjoyable to work toward improving your life and experiencing that journey.

"Hope is passion for what is possible"
– Soren Kierkegaard

"The very least you can do in your life is to figure out what you hope for. And the most you can do is live inside that hope. Not admire it from a distance but live right in it, under its roof."
– Barbara Kingsolver

Whether a person succeeds or continues to succeed, experiences health or sickness, enjoys life or grovels in despair often depends on what happens within. And it depends on if there is hope for a better life, and if the person engages in actions to manifest the vision of the hope into existence.

"Hope is beautiful, and so are those who have it."
– Cathy Rowland

If you are living a life undesirable to you, it is time to explore solutions and work toward the life you want. It is time to make plans in alignment with what you hope for, to turn those hopes into possibilities, and to convert those possibilities into your reality. As you do this with your thoughts, actions, and communication, you will be engaging the most helpful parts of your self.

In his book *Curious? Discover the Missing Ingredient to a Fulfilling Life*, psychologist and George Mason University professor Todd Kashdan writes that scientists have found that anticipating satisfactory things to happen in your life activates the nucleus accumbens in the ventral striatum region of the brain, which is known as the pleasure center. The simple contemplative and curiosity thought processes of considering the possible increases both the dopamine neurotransmitter activity between the nerve cells and the opiate neurotransmitter presence within the brain, preparing the body to experience what we are expecting to happen. It is then, when we feel the motivation to make our expectations form into our reality that we are daring enough to take action. As we continue to visualize and then attain our goals through intentional actions, the hippocampus region of the brain – which is involved with thoughts of curiosity and imagination, and with memory – will get accustomed to the patterns of visualizing and accomplishing. The process will help form into patterns of behavior that become habits.

"The moment of enlightenment is when a person's dreams of possibilities become images of probabilities."
– Vic Braden

It appears that working with the thought processes that create the body chemicals in relation to those thoughts, and to do so in an uplifting, anticipatory manner that will stimulate actions, and then specifically and intentionally taking those actions in alignment with the set goals will be what gives you the most fulfilling feeling of satisfaction. Actively and knowingly participating in this process by setting goals and achieving them will instill a habit of the process involving many areas of your brain, which always is involved in wiring and rewiring itself in tune with your thoughts, actions, communication, habits, and experiences.

As Norman Doidge explains in his book, *The Brain That Changes Itself: Stories and Personal Triumph from The Frontiers of Brain Science*, what we think and what we do plays a large role in the formation of the network of nerves in our brain. These processes, and how being actively aware of and engaged in using them can play a large role in changing your life, are also explained in the book, *Buddha's Brain: The Practical Neuroscience of Happiness, Love, and Wisdom*, by Rick Hanson and Richard Mendius, and in books by

31

Daniel Goleman, such as *Social Intelligence: The New Science of Human Relationships*.

Either you are visualizing the life you want, and working toward manifesting the vision, or you are not. Either you are creating the life you want, and forming and engaging with the habits that create the neuropathways in tune with the activities of the life you want, or you are not.

Take time to consider the things you can succeed in. Work to experience satisfaction in those areas.

Become devoted to making your life function as your solution, and hopefully in ways that help your community and benefits your society, including the regional environment you and the people around you depend on. Make it your reality and common way of functioning.

"People think I'm disciplined. It is not discipline. It is devotion. There is a great difference."
– Luciano Pavarotti

Successful people know what it is they want. They know where they want to land. They know what they want to get. And they continually study, factor, focus, and work to get it.

Successful people seek information to help them. They research. They plan and prepare. They practice what they need to do to get the things they want. They work to transform themselves into their vision of how they see themselves living. They remain actively engaged in working to manifest their goals. In doing so, their brains are in the habit of functioning at the level of their success.

You can do the same. And you can begin doing it now with everything you think, plan, practice, say, and do.

"The happiness of your life depends on the quality of your thoughts."
– Marcus Aurelius

Many people are fully engaged in low-grade lifestyles in which they never connect with their beneficial qualities. You don't have to be one of them.

Why not work to improve your life? Otherwise, what are you doing, other than agreeing to be stuck and unsatisfied?

Be proactive in sculpting your life. To do it, be involved with working with your beneficial qualities, clarifying what you choose to do in life, and intentionally apply those thoughts to your actions and communication.

Again, you are more likely to be what you desire to be if you continually engage in the thoughts, actions, and communication in tune with what you want to be.

"In psychotherapy, enthusiasm is the secret of success."
– Carl Gustav Jung

Anyone can take the life lessons presented to them, and use them to improve their life. They can go about it in ways to create smaller improvements that build upon one another like brickwork to construct a more healthful and satisfying life.

"We know what we are, but know not what we may be."
– William Shakespeare

"Do not follow where the path may lead. Go instead where there is no path and create a trail."
– Ralph Waldo Emerson

"We do not need magic to change the world. We carry all the power we need inside ourselves already: We have the power to imagine better."
– J. K. Rowling

Stop listening to commercialism that broadcasts falsities, and formulates the agreement that you will be happy only when your life resembles the corporate images seen in advertising.

"Most people are other people. Their thoughts are someone else's opinions, their lives a mimicry, their passions a quotation."
– Oscar Wilde

Make your life become the genuine situation you want to experience. Understand that nobody can do it for you. You have to do it for yourself. Visualize it. Plan it. Nurture it. Do it. Become it. Live it. Love it.

Focus on what you want to accomplish.

"It was best when I forgot about everything and just thought about the music."
– Linda Ronstadt

Be your original you.

"The work will teach you how to do it."
– Estonian proverb

# The Condition

"We fear our highest possibility – as well as our lowest one. We are generally afraid to become that which we can glimpse in our most perfect moments."
– Abraham Maslow

"The first step to getting the things you want out of life is this: Decide what you want."
– Ben Stein

If you are waiting around for your life to begin, for things around you to change, for your days to be more to your liking, and to be in company you would better enjoy, it is likely that you will be stuck in the waiting zone. What you see around you is your life. If you don't like it, stop waiting for it to change. Make it change.

"I am a part of all that I have met."
– Alfred Tennyson

"If you gaze for long into the abyss, the abyss also gazes into you."
– Friedrich Wilhelm Nietzsche

The way your life has turned out up to this point is not something that simply happened. Consider the chance your life largely has been formulated by the things you have done, said, worn, accumulated, sought, and eaten, and the people with whom you have associated, the places you have gone, and especially the things you have thought.

"If you wish to make an apple pie truly from scratch, you must first invent the universe."
— Carl Sagan

"You can count how many seeds are in the apple, but not how many apples are in the seed."
— Ken Kersey

The power to formulate the thoughts that trigger positive life change is free, and continually at play. It is up to each person to discover, access, and use the power, to manage how it is used, and to apply it to life.

"There's a lot happening in many of us. I think you have to celebrate every part. It's what you are. You have to try to find all of those secret names."
— Cassandra Wilson

It is you who can transform your life. It is done by clarifying your interaction of thoughts, intention, action, and communication.

Make the plans, think the thoughts, take the actions, speak the words, and live with intention to get your life to work for you in the way you desire.

"The whole problem is to establish communication with one's self."
— E. B. White

Through being conscious of and following high-quality nutrition, engaging in daily exercise, and combining those in alignment with your goals through daily intentional living, you can activate a proactive energy within you to experience a more satisfying expression of your being. To get those things into position as strongly present in your life, turn your goals into actions and helpful communication – and make it your life practice.

Don't wait around for better circumstances to occur. Mentally and physically prepare for, and be engaged with creating your better circumstances to help own the satisfaction you desire to experience.

"Don't compromise yourself. You are all you've got."
— Janis Joplin

"The potential of the average person is like a huge ocean unsailed, a new continent unexplored, a world of possibilities waiting to be released and channeled toward some great good."
— Brian Tracy

Look at your life as though it is a garden. Eliminate the clutter and overgrowth choking the beauty and damaging the harvest of good things you want from life. Continually plant the seed thoughts and nurture them through action, communication, and your power of creation to get the harvest you desire.

"When you examine the lives of the most influential people who have ever walked among us, you discover one thread that winds through them all. They have been aligned first with their spiritual nature and only then with their physical selves."
– Albert Einstein

"The best people possess a feeling for beauty, the courage to take risks, the discipline to tell the truth, the capacity for sacrifice. Ironically, their virtues make them vulnerable; they are often wounded, sometimes destroyed."
– Ernest Hemingway

Changing your life from what it is to what it can be, especially if the change is radical, may require strengths you never have accessed, and perhaps powers you never knew you possess.

Improving your life takes a continual expression of bravery, courage, planning, focus, practice, and intentional thoughts and actions in alignment with goals. You have to teach yourself, and use what you learn to make it all work.

"I now see my life, not as the slow shaping of achievement to fit my preconceived purposes, but as the gradual discovery of a purpose which I did not know."
– Joanna Field

Many people spend years creating and maintaining an unhealthful lifestyle. They feed themselves with unhealthful foods while entertaining low-quality thoughts resulting in passive, mundane, or self-loathing actions as they utilize little of their faculties to get through their days. They do so in a pattern building the life and health they do not desire. By default, the unsatisfying life and low-quality health they end up with are quite literally what they worked for. They were the most active participant in creating their situation.

"We either make ourselves happy or miserable. The amount of work is the same."
– Carlos Castaneda

If people have become lazy in their lives, the thoughts and activities they will need to engage in to break away from their old patterns of behavior while putting their intellect to work and improving their nutrition by following healthful diet may feel incredibly vitalizing and amazingly liberating.

"If you want to build a ship, don't herd people together to collect wood and don't assign them tasks and work, but rather teach them to long for the endless immensity of the sea."
– Antoine de Saint-Exupery

Perhaps one of the main motivators in changing your life will come from the realization that you can make your life happen the way you want it to happen.

You do not have to collapse under whatever weight you perceive is being forced onto you; instead, you can rise, use your power, and build the life you want.

You don't have to conform to conditions others have created, but can form your own conditions.

Educate yourself, align your situation, create a game plan, and otherwise do what you need to do to capture the vision of what you want your life to be. Then work every day toward creating the vision as reality.

"The higher education so much needed today is not given in the school, is not to be bought in the market place, but it has to be wrought out in each one of us for himself; it is the silent influence of character on character."
– William Osler

We all began our lives with nothing. Some of us have been provided with material possessions, and some of us have been lucky to have been nurtured by parents – or other figures – who somehow helped to bring out our best characteristics.

Some people are born with the euphemistic golden spoon in their mouth, and go on to live a life where they seem to be handed everything. Others are born into the most unfortunate conditions, and go on to a life of discouragement, regret, and misfortune. Sometimes it works the opposite way in which those handed everything end up in tragedy, and those born into tragedy go on to live a life of vibrant health and satisfaction.

"Failure is the condiment that gives success its flavor."
– Truman Capote

In a way, it seems those who appear to have been handed everything are the unfortunate ones. They might never experience the exhilarating satisfaction of succeeding from the depths of miserable circumstances children born into poverty, abuse, and neglect may experience.

However, even though it may not appear so, those who seem to have been handed everything are also continually faced with challenges that easily could result in a reversal of fortune.

No matter what our background, we can penetrate through challenges to improve and maintain our situation.

Perhaps it is best to not think of challenges as a wall. Instead, think of challenges as opportunities.

"People who have attained things worth having in this world have worked while others have idled, have persevered while others gave up in despair, and have practiced early in life the valuable habits of self-denial, industry, and singleness of purpose. As a result, they enjoy in later life the success often erroneously attributed to good luck."
– Grenville Kleiser

"Let me tell you the secret that has led me to my goal: my strength lies solely in my tenacity."
– Louis Pasteur

No matter what conditions you were born into, please recognize your talents and strengths, and use your intellect to create a life geared more to being part of the sustainable solution.

"I wasn't exactly brought up in one of those Norman Rockwell paintings you used to see on the cover of the *Saturday Evening Post*."
– Reggie Jackson

No matter what your background has been, you have to take what you have and make the best of your life. Otherwise you stagnate and devalue your life – and the lives around you – through not trying, not exercising your talents, not utilizing your skills, not using your intellect, and not contributing to the solutions the world needs.

"If you don't take chances, you can't do anything in life."
– Michael Spinks

Whether people are rich or poor, old or young, living in the north or south, east or west, they are depending on the same things for their survival. Those include: environment, wildlife, air, water, soil, food, thought, movement, community, and love. The quality of each one of these plays a part in the level of life they get to experience.

"Winners have simply formed the habit of doing things losers don't like to do."
— Albert Gray

Work the things into your life you need for accomplishing the life you want to have. Be your answer.

Be part of the solution the world so badly needs.

"There is no chance, no destiny, no fate, that can hinder or control the firm resolve of a determined soul."
— Ella Wheeler Wilcox

"With our minds we can make anything happen. I believe in immersion – it's one thing to know the principals, and it's another thing to live it day-to-day so it becomes a pattern"
— Anthony Robbins

"No matter who you are, we are creatures of habit. The better your habits are, the better they will be in pressure situations."
— Wayne Gretzky

# Your Filter

"A human being is a part of the whole, called by us, 'Universe,' a part limited in time and space. He experiences himself, his thoughts and feelings as something separated from the rest – a kind of optical delusion of his consciousness.

This delusion is a kind of prison for us, restricting us to our personal desires and to affection for a few persons nearest to us. Our task must be to free ourselves from this prison by widening our circle of compassion to embrace all living creatures and the whole of nature in its beauty.

Nobody is able to achieve this completely, but the striving for such achievement is in itself a part of the liberation and a foundation for inner security."
– Albert Einstein

People build their mental landscape out of what they think, study, feel, hear, see, smell, taste, do, communicate, and the ways in which others treat them. They apply it to the things they think, study, see, hear, smell, feel, taste, and do, including how they treat others. This landscape, which is your filter, can be limited by the life experiences that formulated it, including the limits you and others have placed on your life, and what you do with it.

The early humans also applied their mental landscape to everything, including the planets and stars they saw in the vastness of the sky. They looked at the various terrestrial groupings and named them after familiar shapes, such as creatures of the land, air, and sea.

Your mind filter began to form at the earliest stages of your life, and continues to form throughout your life.

Consider what your mind filter consists of, how it was formulated, how you apply it, and how you allow it to alter and guide you.

"Human beings are perceivers, but the world they perceive is an illusion created by the description that was told to them from the moment they were born."
– Carlos Castenada

Fetal programming is what happens to you before birth, including hearing sounds while in the womb. Fetal programming can play a role in what you feel, respond to, and desire after birth.

Parents often talk to their babies as the babies sleep. This plays into the subconscious mind of the child. Often this talk involves suggesting how successful the child will be, and how much the child is loved. These early interactions, even if only amounting to a simple comprehension of sound patterns and tones, are what helps to formulate the child's filter.

The uterus and placenta are not impervious barriers. Fetuses are sensitive not only to sounds, but to the foods their mothers eat, smells their mothers smell, the emotions their mothers experience, and the molecules created by those emotions.

While science has concentrated on fetal exposure to industrial pollutants, bacteria, fungi, and parasites, and on the genetic expression factors of what forms and affects fetuses and newborns, it is increasingly recognizing that everything a fetus and a newborn is exposed to can impact a child. This includes the mother's health, diet, substance use, mental state, living arrangement, relationships, workplace, and lifestyle issues. It also includes the conditions of other parent or supervising figures who nurture – or neglect – the infant and child.

Because fetal conditioning has an influence on gene expression, it may help determine what sort of health the child experiences throughout life, and also may have an impact on the next generations. This is called *epigenetics*.

Certain drugs that have had damaging effects on fetuses can also cause the next generation to have birth defects, or health issues. There are all sorts of ways in which this plays out. Some examples are that children born to parents who are obese are more likely to have children who experience weight and blood sugar issues, and people who have diabetes are more likely to have children who become diabetic.

A number of things impacting a fetus can play a part in future generations. Some of this has to do with learning, conditioning, economics, stress, and environment, and also with what the mother chooses to keep as a part of her life, including thoughts, activities, relationships, dietary patterns, alcohol use, and pharmaceutical and "recreational" drugs.

This does not mean an expectant mother should go into a cocoon away from every single thing with the potential of bringing about an emotion, or that she should hide from sounds, smells, and people.

It is important for expectant mothers to remain physically and socially active – and intellectually engaged – while following a regular sleeping pattern and a healthful diet. The variety of chemical changes occurring in sync with the expectant mother's emotions in a healthful environment are helpful to the formation of a healthy baby.

As an adult, your filter partially consists of both sense-perceived memories that have tuned you, as well as the chemicals surrounding you, the foods you have been exposed to, the sounds you have heard, the smells you have smelled, the sights you have seen, the textures you have felt, the words that have been spoken to and by you, and the emotions and health of the people who birthed and raised you.

In addition to foods, smells, and emotions, certain words, sounds, colors, textures, flavors, shapes, temperatures, and even shades of light can bring about memories that affect your cell structures, tissue function, and hormonal production.

As your experiences in life create a filter in your mind through which you judge all that is presented to you, your filter will help determine what things, colors, shapes, textures, foods and flavors, smells, sounds, and people you like to have in your life.

"Habits of thinking need not be forever. One of the most significant findings in psychology in the last twenty years is that individuals can choose the way they think."
– Martin Seligman

Your filter is not permanently fixed in its present state. It continues to change throughout your life. Luckily, you have some control over your filter, and over how you reconfigure your logic in that you can decide and reformulate how you factor and react to things. That is, other than perhaps not in your sexuality and gender, and some other matters, as those tend to remain the same, and trying to change those could be damaging, reductive, and unhealthful.

People hold prejudices, and desires developed in their minds, based on their experiences. They may not like to be around people who resemble, or who sound or act similar to certain unhelpful, damaging, or undesirable people from their past. This all might be subconscious to them. These are examples of how their filter was shaped by their experiences.

All of this does not mean you need to remain completely susceptible to your past, or that you should be freakishly fanatical about understanding and deciphering the impact of every thing about what you have seen, heard, smelled, tasted, touched, or experienced.

I'm not suggesting to obsess about your epigenetics.

I am mentioning how your past shaped you because it is part of understanding who you are, and what you respond to, and this can give you ideas about what you can do to transform into the healthier expression of yourself.

While considering these angles about your filter, it may be interesting to observe how people live their lives and to listen to what concerns them, what interests them, what they hope for, what displeases them, and what they cherish.

**"If you want something you've never had, you have to do something you've never done."**
– Kimnesha Benns

Many people are so caught up in the mess that has become their life they lose sight of what it was they wanted out of life in the first place. They become so burned out they do things to escape into a life that is not their own. They eat foods they know are not good for them, spend time doing things they know are not best for them, watch loads of television, shop for stuff they don't need with money they don't have, don't get enough exercise or movement, and end up being surrounded by people who zap their energy, take up their time, negate their good qualities, badly influence them, and blur their focus. They don't get the things done they know they need to do, if they are to lead a healthful life. Altogether, they don't advance toward where they want to be. Their filter is broken, clogged, neglected, frazzled, and in need of repair, restructuring, and nurturing.

Your filter can be as rigid or as malleable as you allow it to be. This has to do with having a closed or open mind, and how you allow yourself to perceive what life presents to you – and what you present to life.

43

"The future is not some place we are going to, but one we are creating. The paths to it are not found, but made – and the activity of making them changes both the maker and the destination."
– John Schaar

Your perceptions play a part in how you deal with your past and present, and what you agree to do based on your calculations of these in the present. Perceptions play so much a part of you they might be considered to be one of the senses, or attached to them. They are at least sense perceptions.

Perceptions are continually in play as you survey what is presented to you and then compare, contrast, and factor them to derive a conclusion of how the things act or react, consider what they can do, and if you can use them in ways to satisfy you, benefit you, or help you to attain a goal. The calculation process of your perception may have as much to do with your past as it does your present.

"Look at the past as a bullet. Once it's fired it's finished."
– Catherine Bauby

Your past isn't as spent as the above quotation may lead you to believe. But you can reinterpret, reconfigure, and realign the filter created by your past so it works better for you in the present and future.

We are somewhere between the extremes of complete amnesia and a condition called hyperthymestic syndrome, in which a person remembers impeccably accurate details of their life, including dates, times, and sequences. Most of us are some blend of the two conditions, wherein we don't remember much of anything about certain things, but remember great details about others.

Whatever you remember, or don't, you can reshape how you react to memories, and use them to bring forth good for your present and future.

"Make not your thoughts your prisons."
– William Shakespeare

If you had a sad or unsatisfactory past, and want a happy future, choose not to dwell in the past. Decide that you will not be a walking wound. Look and live forward, not backward. Be continually involved with creating a better future.

"People who look ahead are very rare. Most people look to the past. We walk backwards, we back our way through life. We move

44

forward but always while looking backwards. People who envision their future and move toward it, peering ahead are incredibly rare."
– Henri Langlois

"Even a happy life cannot be without a measure of darkness, and the word 'happy' would lose its meaning if it were not balanced by sadness. It is far better to take things as they come along with patience and equanimity."
– Carl Gustav Jung

You can play a large role in how limiting or broadening your ability to experience life will be. It can be largely up to you if you are being held back from or moving toward the life you want. It is largely up to you if you are healing your life, or are enabling an unhealthful lifestyle to dominate you. It is up to you if you are going to be welcoming to the things, people, thoughts, nutrients, activities, and love beneficial to you. In the long run, it is most likely to be largely up to you if your joy is being limited, diminished, or broadened.

"You are so young; you stand before beginnings. I would like to beg of you, dear friend, as well as I can, to have patience with everything that remains unsolved in your heart. Try to love the questions themselves, like locked rooms and like books written in a foreign language. Do not now look for the answers. They cannot now be given to you because you could not live them. It is a question of experiencing everything. At present you need to live the questions. Perhaps you will gradually, without even noticing it, find yourself experiencing the answer, some distant day. Perhaps you are indeed carrying within yourself the potential to visualize, to design, and to create for yourself an utterly satisfying, joyful, and pure lifestyle. Discipline yourself to attain it, but accept that which comes to you with deep trust, and as long as it comes from your own will, from your own inner need, accept it, and do not hate anything."
– Rainer Maria Rilke

It is up to you to take risks, to learn, to make mistakes, to experience sorrow and pain, to gain wisdom, to construct and reweave your filter, to dare to love, and to manage your yearning, needs, perceptions, and calculations to help you factor and formulate the conditions you need to take the actions and make the communication to experience your desired life.

"If we but try to live uprightly, then we shall be all right, even though we shall inevitably experience true sorrow and genuine

disappointments, and also probably make real mistakes, and do wrong things, but it's certainly true that it is better to be fervent in spirit, even if one accordingly makes more mistakes, than narrow-minded and overly cautious."
— Vincent van Gogh

"You have powers you never dreamed of. You can do things you never thought you could do. There are no limitations in what you can do — except the limitations of your own mind."
— Darwin P. Kingsley

I don't think it is any coincidence that the word life is so similar to the word love. If you want to experience the best life possible for you, lift yourself through love, which is the power capable of creating miracles in and around you.

"Where there is great love there are always miracles."
— Willa Cather

Let love be the filter through which you see the world.

# What Is Your Truth?

"All truth is an achievement. If you would have truth at its full value, go win it."
— Munger

People can choose to believe whatever they want. But belief does not always jive with reality. You can believe the sky is made up of psychedelic orange gas with green polka-dotted blue cows floating in it, but your belief does not mean it is true. You can believe a certain terrible person is beneficial to you, when they might be working against your best interests, limiting your ability to live healthfully, diminishing your potential, and damaging you.

The longer you live, the more likely you will realize that not everything you consider to be true actually is. It is also likely that you will recognize this condition as being common among humanity.

"There is great hunger and thirst in all of us for the truth whether we are aware of it or not. There is no-one unfeeling or unseeing. To think ourselves unique is the height of ignorance."
— Agnes Martin

"Truths are universally and not individually rooted; a truth cannot be created, but only perceived."
— Paramhansa Yogananda

It is a common thing to have to adjust your views to what is better and more accurate information, otherwise, you are a stuck in antiquated concepts and ignorance. It is something scientists have to continually deal with, as they discover more accurate information about things they study, even to the point of obliterating former beliefs once considered as solid.

We are continually observing, calculating, and reevaluating our conclusions and often factoring other conclusions, which are essentially agreements with ourselves based on what we believe to be true, and perhaps what we wish to be true.

"My greatest challenge has been to change the mindset of people. Mindsets play strange tricks on us. We see things the way our minds have instructed our eyes to see."
– Muhammad Yunus

"All truths are easy to understand, once they are discovered; the point is to discover them."
– Galileo Galilei

As humans have progressed in their understanding of things, they have disposed of inaccurate past beliefs. Where once they believed exposing wounds to air was what caused infection, they now understand that tiny things called "germs" grow and multiply in moist, warm wounds, and this germ colony and how the immune system responds to it is what has been named *infection*.

There is a long list of falsehoods humans have believed, and they have based much of their life choices on these falsehoods.

"The real does not die. The unreal never lived."
– Nisargatta Maharay

For many years, people believed Earth was the center of the universe. In the 1600s Galileo Galilei argued with Catholic Church leaders over their insistence Galilei was wrong in his belief that Earth revolved around Sun. His 1632 work, *A Dialogue Concerning the Two Great Systems of the World*, included his theory. Galilei had to go to Rome to plead with Catholic leaders not to ban his teachings. He was tried on suspicion of heresy and ordered to recant his theory, was put under house arrest, and the publication of any more of his ideas was banned.

Galileo Galilei's concepts furthered the theory of Nicholas Copernicus, who lived from 1473 to 1543, and who also concluded Earth revolves around Sun. Copernicus was hardly the first to believe in that reality. Ancient drawings found on various parts of Earth reveal that many people who lived long before Galilei and Copernicus had realized Earth revolves around Sun.

Remarkably, it wasn't until 1992 that the Catholic Church officially conceded that Earth revolves around Sun.

Even though many people before Galilei had realized that Earth revolves around Sun, Galilei's predicament stands as an example of how people – including many so-called authority figures – refuse the truth, and choose to continue living in and promoting ignorance.

"The mind can assert anything and pretend it has proved it. My beliefs I test on my body, on my intuitional consciousness, and when I get a response there, then I accept."
– D. H. Lawrence

No matter what people believe or do not believe, there are basic fundamental truths unaltered by belief. False beliefs do not change the truth.

There are many things people believe, but which are not reality. Even after they learn that something isn't how they thought it had been, they may continue to try to hold onto their disproved beliefs, and drift into denial. Many people refuse to change behavior associated with former false beliefs, and it lands them in unfortunate situations.

"God is near me (or rather in me), and yet I may be far from God because I may be far from my own true self."
– C. E. Rolt

False beliefs are limiting in that they can block you from accomplishing what you are capable of becoming, and reduce you to less than what you are capable of being.

You may believe in something about yourself falsely, and the agreement to believe it limits you.

"The difference between what we do and what we are capable of doing would suffice to solve most of the world's problems."
– Mahatma Gandhi

You may think you cannot accomplish something you are perfectly capable of accomplishing.

The simple process of thinking you are only capable of a certain level of something will likely limit you to that level – or to far less.

Wake up from the nightmare of living far below your capabilities.

"We need limitations and temptations to open our inner selves, dispel our ignorance, tear off disguises, throw down old idols, and destroy false standards. Only by such rude awakenings can we be led to dwell in a place where we are less cramped, less hindered by the

49

ever insistent External. Only then do we discover a new capacity and appreciation of goodness and beauty and truth."
– Helen Keller

False beliefs in health are limiting. Believing in something that doesn't work for the body, even though it may provide some very little good, limits your ability to experience better health. Doing something you believe is good for the body, even though it is damaging, reduces your potential.

"This above all: To thine own self be true, for it must follow as dost the night the day, that canst not then be false to any man."
– William Shakespeare

Your truth already exists within you. You simply need to exercise the tool to bring out your truth. The tool you need to make it happen is something you already have. It is what some people call intellect, intelligence, spirit, or soul.

Maybe the unwise words of others have brought you down.

Work to do away with the false beliefs you carry about yourself, and don't be overwhelmed with considering what others think of you.

Your frustration with others not believing in your capabilities may be because you falsely believe you are not capable. Consider that others may be reflecting back to you what you project about your belief in yourself. Realize they may also be displaying their own fears, self-doubt, and lack of self-esteem: a lack of belief in their own intellect, talents, sills, craft, abilities, potential, instinct, and love.

"Fears are educated into us, and can, if we wish, be educated out."
– Karl A. Menninger

Many people live their lives by fear. They are fearful about not succeeding, are not going to be able to pay their bills, are not going to experience or hold onto love, and are going to lose any security they may be experiencing. Their fears may become their driving force, and bring them into the energy of desperation, which can fuel irrational thought patterns that lead to damaging actions and communication, which creates unfortunate consequences.

"I saw a study that the more television people watched, the more afraid of their neighbors they became. The researchers called it 'the dangerous world syndrome.' The mathematical correspondence was compelling. The more television people watched, the more crime they thought there was in their neighborhood, and the more

exaggerated their belief about how many murders and burglaries were taking place."
— John Robbins

When we live while ruled by fear, we are more likely to live dishonestly, to rob others of their energy and resources, to eat unhealthful foods, to entertain low-quality thoughts, to be slothful, to engage in risky behavior, and to partake of damaging substances.

When we allow ourselves to live by fear, we doubt others because we doubt ourselves. We feel the fear, and it drags us down.

"We tell lies when we are afraid — afraid of what we don't know, afraid of what others will think, afraid of what will be found out about us. But every time we tell a lie, the thing that we fear grows stronger."
— Tad Williams

When we doubt ourselves, we are more likely to lie to others, and to ourselves. When we fear, we are more likely to lie. When we lack confidence, we are more likely to lie. When we aren't truthful to ourselves, we are likely to be untruthful to others. We feel the lie. It drags us down, and we know it will torment us to maintain it.

"As we are liberated from our own fear, our presence automatically liberates others."
— Nelson Mandela

Confidence and intentional positive living is the opposite of fear. It challenges and disperses fear. And it has to do with people knowing they are capable of improving and carrying on with their life in a way that utilizes their intellect, yearning, talents, skills, craft, abilities, potential, instinct, intuition, honesty, and love.

"Perhaps the most important thing we can undertake toward the reduction of fear is to make it easier for people to accept themselves, to like themselves."
— Bonaro W. Overstreet

When we live confidently, we have hope and faith in ourselves and in others. In this way, being confident is charitable as it spreads confidence into those around us.

When we live confidently in tune with our natural attributes, we take care of ourselves, we have heart, and we are less likely to allow ourselves to drag our chins on the floor.

When we live confidently, the positive energy of doing so can spread into our community.

"As we let our light shine, we unconsciously give other people permission to do the same."
– Marianne Williamson

If you want to be aligned with a manner more conducive to improvement, you might wish to especially work to do away with the energy of fear and doubt. They are not what you want to be your truth, reality, or ruling force. They are of the dreadful victim mentality consisting of energy opposing faith and hope.

"Everything that happens in all material, living, mental, or even spiritual processes involves the transformation of energy. Every thought, every sensation, every emotion is produced by energy exchanges."
– J. G. Bennett

"Each of us makes his own weather, determines the color of the skies in the emotional universe which he inhabits."
– Fulton J. Sheen

"Life is the sum of what you focus on."
– Winifred Gallagher

Isn't it interesting that many so-called elected officials continually focus their attention and words on fear, doubt, crime, and punishment? This is where many public servants fail the people. It also displays their concept of the world. Rather than recognizing problems and creating solutions toward better results, they are focusing on the unsatisfactory end results of energy already spent, and fueling more of the same, thus perpetuating what they claim to be working to get rid of.

People who continually talk about fear and terror might be all about fear and terror. It is what is in their mind, and is their energy.

Some so-called leaders may consider the spreading of fear – and getting people to act in relation to fear – to be beneficial to industry, nation-building, and the careers of those same corrupt politicians who work to keep the poor people down – which serves the rich. Greed.

"It is not whether your words or actions are tough or gentle; it is the spirit behind your actions and words that announces your inner state."
– Chin-Ning Chu

Refuse to dwell in fear and doubt. Allowing fear and doubt to rule your thoughts, emotions, and motions distracts and weakens you, and stifles your ability to succeed.

"People deal too much with the negative, with what is wrong. Why not try and see positive things, to just touch those things and make them bloom?"
— Thich Nhat Hanh

Build your inner state to consist of what you want by visualizing what you want, setting goals, and acting on those goals through actions and communication to bring about what you want.

Dwell in, live for, and rule your life by creating the life you want.

"If we were logical, the future would be bleak indeed. But we are more than logical. We are human beings, and we have faith, and we have hope, and we can work."
— Jacques Cousteau

Your belief helps formulate your reality. Belief rules your reasoning, which is continually adjusted as you are exposed to and factor different experiences, which helps you determine what you believe to be true or untrue, what to accept, what to reject, what you like and don't like, and what you anticipate. It all plays into the actions you take, words you speak, relations you make, and life you live.

Continually adjusting to simple truths, living your truth, aligning your goals to it, and working to achieve those goals leads to improvement in life.

"Truth is a demure lady, much too ladylike to knock you on the head and drag you to her cave. She is there, but the people must want her and seek her out."
— William F. Buckley, Jr.

"Integrity is telling myself the truth."
— Spencer Johnson

"Our own life is the instrument with which we experiment with truth."
— Thich Nhat Hanh

"If you cannot find the truth right where you are, where else do you expect to find it?"
— Dogen Zenji

# Break Free of Fallacies

"What gets us into trouble is not what we don't know. It's what
we know for sure that just ain't so."
– Mark Twain

An example of what people are capable of doing based on false
information occurred on October 20, 1938. It was the day Orson
Welles broadcast a reading of H.G. Welles's *The War of the Worlds*
on Mercury Theatre Radio. Many thousands of people who heard the
broadcast believed Martians were attacking Earth. People became
engulfed in fear. Massive panic took place in and around New York
City. People frantically ran from their homes, abandoned their
workplaces, and clogged the streets to escape the Martians. Their
decisions were based on imagination.

Consider the possibility that you are currently making decisions
in your daily life based on fallacy.

"The eye sees only what the mind is prepared to comprehend."
– Henri L. Bergson

Consider the possibility that all you believe about the past, from
what you think you know about world history, to what you think to be
the truth about the people around you, and even about yourself, may
largely consist of created perceptions not based on reality.

What you consider to be true may be a figment of somebody's
imagination. Even the most intricate details of what you consider to
be reality may be falsehoods. This includes everything from the so-

54

called old wives' tales to what you have read in books and heard in the media, at school, or otherwise from the mouths of others.

"In every age it has been the tyrant, the oppressor, and the exploiter who has wrapped himself in the cloak of patriotism, or religion, or both to deceive and overawe the people."
– Eugene Victor Debs

Many people have realized that what they learned about history from textbooks when they were schoolchildren was largely fictionalized, romanticized, and revisionist history filled with lies. Often, this is done for political reasons, such as to build blind national patriotism. For instance, here in the United States, many students were taught Christopher Columbus both "discovered" America and was the first to find that Earth is round. Columbus has also been portrayed as a heroic figure who brought civility to the heathens.

In truth, Columbus didn't "discover America" in 1492. Many people from other continents, including Africa and Asia, had already been to what became known as the American continents. The indigenous peoples have been shown to be of Asian ancestry.

The Americas were named by German cartographer Martin Waldseemuller in about 1507. Waldseemuller may have used the name of the Welsh merchant, Richard Amerike, who sponsored John Cabot's 1497 boat adventures to what is now known as Newfoundland. Waldseemuller also may have used the feminized name of Italian explorer Amerigo Vespucci, who traveled with a group exploring the coasts in 1499; or the name of the gold-rich Amerrique district of Nicaragua – which may have been visited by both Vespucci and Columbus. Before Columbus made his famous boat ride, millions of people had already been living on what became known as the American continents.

Columbus landed on an occupied island that is now part of the Bahamas, thus the teaching of his landing on a continent is also flawed. Columbus and his group also went on to other islands, including what are now Cuba, Haiti, Jamaica, and Puerto Rico.

In reality, for thousands of years before Columbus there were people who knew the world is round. Evidence of this can be found in ancient drawings from every continent, and in navigational maps and on cave walls.

Columbus was also not a heroic figure worthy of praise or honor. He and his group of thugs were homicidal rapists who robbed, enslaved, and tortured the indigenous people of the islands where Columbus' fleet of ships had landed. Who else would be more suitable to expand an imperialistic empire than a group of cold-hearted thugs?

In truth, the island people were better off without Columbus. The islanders had their own culture, which was much more peaceful and civil than the practices Columbus and his group introduced – which involved cutting off the hands of those who were believed to be lazy, or who were otherwise viewed as uncommitted to following the dictates of Columbus' group.

The "Columbus Day" holiday of October 10th has been an insult to indigenous cultures, and is based on lies. Columbus was not a figure to be admired; he was someone who should be abhorred and exemplified as a genocidal maniac rapist who enslaved people. It's appropriate for October 10th to be renamed Indigenous Peoples Day.

Just as there are mistruths being taught to schoolchildren in the belief they will be more dedicated citizens to the reigning government if they believe a certain whitewashed and fictionalized history, there are authority figures today working to groom their country's citizens to believe in lies to advance the careers of politicians, promote the monsters of the military, and lavish wealth on corporate giants.

"War itself is, of course, a form of madness. It's hardly a civilized pursuit. It's amazing how we spend so much time inventing devices to kill each other, and so little time working on how to achieve peace."
– Walter Cronkite

Throughout history there have been those who have fashioned themselves as heroic figures. Their self-promotion has been accomplished through the sacrifice of many lives. Their activities involve sending forth their troops to rob, plunder, kill, and overtake.

Consider that there are people today who are in positions of so-called power and who are doing great damage to Earth, to the environment, to wildlife, and to your ability to live healthfully with the people you love. Perhaps some of these corrupted political and corporate leaders are those you have perceived as good and righteous.

"Re-examine all you have been told at school or church or in any book, dismiss whatever insults your own soul, and your very flesh shall be a great poem."
– Walt Whitman

The way you perceive other cultures, your government, global corporations and their leaders, your local community, and your life may be a part of the mistruths spread by others with unwise agendas not about improving your condition, but keeping you in a place to benefit the wealthy. Perhaps you are living beneath their design and agenda of benefitting from you as you purchase their products, and replicate the imagery they produce of what your life should resemble.

Maybe you are oppressed, and have not realized it simply because you are set on replicating what you have been convinced is important.

"If you live in an oppressive society, you've got to be resilient. You can't let each little thing crush you. You have to take every encounter and make yourself larger – rather than allow yourself to be diminished by it."
– James Earl Jones

Maybe you are caught within an illusion, a bubble, an imaginary life not your own, but that is the creation of others who benefit from the lifestyle you have chosen to agree to be living. You do so by spending your time working for the same corporations deceiving you as you spend money on products they manufacture, as you have agreed to place yourself in debt – which also benefits the corporations. Maybe your life is so ruled by the scenario that you are no longer much of your own person, but more of a replicant of commercialized imagery, and a participant in the illusion.

"You cannot fix an illusion. You can only wake up from one."
– Michael Beckwith

What if everything you have believed in and learned up to this point has been based on false information fashioned by the dreams or clever minds of others?

"The courage to penetrate and power to see clearly the meaning of things hidden beyond the situation prevailing around us, and to act up to the discovered meaning, is what is known as revolutionary insight. Revolution can take place only where there is this power of penetrating insight."
– Vinoba Bhave

Learn about permaculture. That includes growing food, wild edible harvesting, and planting and nurturing wild fruiting trees and bushes. It's about reconnecting to the land and replanting paradise.

Learn about how there are many toxic products that can be replaced with natural materials that can be composted – including materials made from industrial hemp. (Research industrial hemp.)

Learn about protecting the wildlife and its terrain that has been so damaged by corporate greed. Be part of that solution.

# Bring Forth Good

"Goodness is the only investment that never fails."
— Henry David Thoreau

"The single largest pool of untapped resource in this world is human good intentions that never translate into action."
— Cindy Gallop

"There is a spark of good in everybody, no matter how deeply it may be buried, it is there. It's waiting to govern your life gloriously."
— Mildred "Peace Pilgrim" Norman

Improving your life is about tuning in to your potential and bringing forth good things. It is about preparing for and creating your life, about taking care of your body through excellent nutrition and exercise, about awakening to and working with your intellect, and about using your talents and abilities to experience satisfaction.

"There is a you, lying dormant. A potential within you to be realized. It does not matter whether you have an intelligence quotient of 60 or 160, there is more of you than what you are presently aware of. Perhaps the only peace and joy in life lies in the pursuit of and development of this potential."
— Leo Buscaglia

Reiterating what is suggested earlier, as you read this book, make notes in alignment with preparing yourself for a better life. Exercise your body and mind daily to build your mental and physical fitness level. Nurture your mind with that which uplifts you. Nourish your body with a plant-based diet free of junk food, and that advances you toward experiencing vibrant health.

A better future as an expression of your better qualities is within your grasp. Know you can create it through intentional beneficial thoughts, planning, actions, and communication.

"Success is simple. First, you decide what you want specifically; and second, you decide you're willing to pay the price to make it happen, and then pay that price."
– Bunker Hunt

Your life is like a sculpture. You are either chiseling away at your life in a very specific manner to create something beautiful, or you are allowing life to batter away at you to become like a decomposing ship stranded on a rocky shore. It is your decision which of these scenarios your life resembles.

"If ya keep on doing what you've always done, you'll keep on getting what you've always got."
– Momma Turtle

Whether on a profound or subtle level, there is some area in each person's life that could be improved. Many of the answers of how to go about making the changes toward improving an individual's life lie within the person. Other answers may have to be found by study, by contemplation, and by utilizing outside sources. It all has to do with thinking the thoughts that fuel the actions and interactions.

You might be struggling in life because you don't know what the answers could be. There are ways. Find and be answers.

"Reconsider all your limitations as if they were self-imposed, Many of them are."
– Chris Waugh

There is a way to open doors of opportunity that you may have considered to be closed to you.

Many of the doors you wish to be open may already be, and they only may be closed to you because of your perception.

"Reflect upon your present blessings, of which every man has plenty; not on your past misfortunes, of which all men have some."
– Charles Dickens

Many opportunities to improve your life have escaped you simply because you did not notice them, did not recognize them, believed you were not capable of attaining the benefits of them, gave into defeat, or because you may have been preoccupied with focusing on what you don't want and don't like while you have loitered in places you would rather not be, and with people doing the same.

Focus on what you want, and on what you like, in sync with better health. Be involved in doing what you can do in relation to what you see yourself doing. Plan it. Focus. Take the actions to propel yourself into your better life.

"You are precisely as big as what you love and precisely as small as what you allow to annoy you."
– Robert Anton Wilson

"The only limit to our realization of tomorrow will be our doubts of today."
– Franklin Roosevelt

Be brave and wise enough to face up to the tasks you need to accomplish to improve your life, and to engage your mind in figuring out a helpful way of dealing with any issues holding you back. Figure out the solutions, and work them into being.

Many people become so stuck in knowing their life is a mess that the fact of knowing it becomes their focus. It is as if they are in shock as they stare at the accident. Having their vision stuck in the disaster leads to doubt they can get out of the mess. Their doubts become their ruling factor as their vision becomes stalled at the site of the accident. Some have focused on the accident for so long that they got towed away to a junkyard, which is what their life resembles.

"If one desires a change, one must be that change before that change can take place."
– Gita Bellin

Stop believing in your doubts, and focusing on what you perceive to be your misfortunes. Instead, believe in your future, and your potential, your better qualities, and what you can make of them.

Maybe you did make unfortunate choices, and caused the accident your life resembles. You can choose to stay there, or you can cause solutions through wise actions and helpful communication that will place you in a more satisfactory life. It's your choice.

"When I dare to be powerful – to use my strength in the service of my vision, then it becomes less and less important whether I am afraid."
– Audrey Lorde

Listening to encouragement, and being encouraged is good. Refusing to listen to discouragement helps people to be invincible in their pursuits, but people who are undergoing intentional life change would likely benefit from remembering this: There is a difference between being reasonably optimistic about changing your life and being so extreme that your choices create problems and harm.

"The differences between optimists and extreme optimists are remarkable, and suggest that over-optimism, like overconfidence, may in fact lead to behaviors that are unwise."
– Manju Puri

While going about changing your life, it is important to remember that there are wiser choices and choices that aren't so wise. This is why you might consider reading a variety of books on self-improvement and about your interests; to do your homework, to be open to revising and redefining your plans; and to seek out professional help to make wiser choices in the clarity of health.

There are numerous ways people may go about determining what they desire to change in their life. Through self-review and goal-setting you can help identify what may work best for you.

"Possessions, outward success, publicity, luxury – to me these have always been contemptible. I assume that a simple and unassuming manner of life is best for everyone, best for both the body and the mind."
– Albert Einstein

When people talk about improvement they might think of the word *success*. Often their definition of success involves money and material possessions.

When I talk about success, I am not speaking of mansions, expensive things; the trendiest labeled products; piles of money; the latest technogadgets; closets filled with expensive clothes; and material nonsense. It is best to live simply, and to do less damage to Earth, the environment, and wildlife.

Rather than belongings and luxury, when I mention success I mean satisfaction and comfort with self, including health; fulfilling, nurturing, and loving relationships; and responsible use of talents, skills, and intellect in alignment with work.

"It is health that is the real wealth and not pieces of gold and silver."
– Mahatma Gandhi

Consider what minimal belongings you would require to fulfill your needs. Make a list of these things you could configure into a workable plan you could use if you needed or wanted to get rid of things.

"Remember this, that very little is needed to make a happy life."
– Marcus Aurelius

Make a list of actions you need to take to bring you closer to a satisfying lifestyle. Then, take daily actions to implement the plan.

"If you don't risk anything – you're risking even more."
– Erica Jong

What you need to do may involve new ways of dealing with belongings, education, professions, people, food, exercise, and community, or all of these.

"The best way to predict the future is to create it."
– Peter F. Drucker

"Taking in the good is not about putting a happy shiny face on everything, nor is it about turning away from the hard things in life. It's about nourishing inner well-being, contentment, and peace – refuges to which you can always return."
– Rick Hanson

"What we do flows from who we are."
– Paul Vitale

You may have made mistakes, as everyone has. You may have given up, which sometimes happens. You may have fumbled and fallen. Be like the athlete who rises, heals, and works harder.

It is time to rise, regroup, and take the actions and communicate the messages to redeem you. Use your power and make better choices. Carry on toward creating the life you want to own.

"Concerning all acts of initiative and creation, there is one elementary truth, the ignorance of which kills countless ideas and splendid plans: That the moment one definitely commits oneself, the Providence moves too. Whatever you can do or dream you can do, begin it. Boldness has genius, power, and magic in it. Begin it now."
– Johann Wolfgang von Goethe

Always remember, everyone has difficulties you are not aware of. Pain, physical and mental health issues, life drama and trauma, stress, fear, loss, rejection, sadness, grief, and sadness are common. Be kind – including toward yourself.

# Courage

"Whatever you do, you need courage. Whatever course you decide upon, there is always someone to tell you that you are wrong. There are always difficulties arising that tempt you to believe your critics are right.

To map out a course of action and follow it to an end requires some of the same courage that a soldier needs. Peace has its victories, but it takes brave men and women to win them."
— Ralph Waldo Emerson

"Life expands or contracts in direct proportion to one's courage."
— Anais Nin

Those interested in self-improvement are more likely to experience it if they are constantly involved in some sort of thought pattern fueling the work needed for creating the improvement. The process of continually engaging in the process will create patterns of thought-driven behavior resulting in more of the same.

"I'm not afraid of storms, for I'm learning to sail my ship."
— Louisa May Alcott

There is bravery, courage, integrity, and dignity in working to establish improvements in your life. Exercising these in ways that bring satisfaction will strengthen the resolve to create and experience more of it. Key factors are to do it with a set plan of clear goals, and to do it consistently, responsibly, and wisely.

"The most glorious moments in your life are not the so-called days of success, but rather those days when out of dejection and despair you feel rise in you a challenge to life, and the promise of future accomplishments."
– Gustave Flaubert

Many people are afraid to face their problems. This is so even when their troubles overwhelm their life. This includes people who dig themselves into denial. They might so regret the reality of issues facing them that they bury themselves in escapism – which can lead a variety of other problems creating health issues, defeat, and ruin.

"To live a spiritual life we must first find the courage to enter into the desert of loneliness and to change it by gentle and persistent efforts into a garden of solitude."
– Henri J. M. Nouwen

Ignoring problems does not make them go away. Instead, it may make them much worse. Like an infection, problems untreated can spread into other areas of people's lives, and into the lives of those who they live and associate with.

"Every time I close the door on reality, it comes in through the window."
– Ashleigh Brilliant

"You cannot find peace by avoiding life."
– Virginia Woolf

People often spend loads of time doing things to delay having to face an issue. In the modern-day, procrastination often involves staring at TV, spending hours and more hours playing video games, getting entangled in the worldwide Web, obsessing about celebrity culture, and shopping to replicate advertising imagery that corporate marketing departments define as what happiness consists of.

Escapism can also involve substance abuse, consuming unhealthful foods, sleeping too much, wasting time doing meaningless things, crass and degrading "entertainment," engaging in anonymous and risky sex, and/or spending time with people who are also not dealing with their issues and who enable problems to fester and slothfulness to perpetuate.

What some people are best at is achieving defeat, sadness, deflated hope, laziness, atrophy, regret, and ruin.

"Procrastination is the thief of time."
– Edward Young

"Nothing is so fatiguing as the eternal hanging on of an uncompleted task."
– William James

"Procrastination is the passive assassin of opportunity."
– Roy Williams

"A lot of disappointed people have been left standing on the street corner waiting for the bus marked perfection."
– Donald Kennedy

The sooner you face up to, work to, and take care of your problems while continually working to achieve daily goals, the better your situation will be.

Consider your hands, your feet, your lips, and your eyes. All probably are similar to others of anyone who accomplished great things. Some were smaller, some were larger, some may have lost parts along their way. Some may have even been born without certain parts. But successful made do with what they had. Some started out with few – and others with fancy – things.

Be one of the wise ones. Like those who seemed to be – or were considered to be – disadvantaged, take what you have, and create and achieve with it what you can.

Some people with physical ailments certainly are disabled. Some use it as an excuse for just about everything. Some with more debilitating ailments succeed far beyond even those who could be considered the most physically ideal.

Use the mechanism of your mind to formulate the combination to release you from any mental locks, cages, and chains binding you down.

Do not allow your problems to overwhelm your life. Refuse to let past or present events own your soul.

Do not let the past rob you of your future. Continually and intentionally live your days as if they are golden, and not stolen.

"I always wanted to be somebody, but I should have been more specific."
– Lily Tomlin

Stop looking away from those parts of your life needing attention. Instead, courageously turn and face them. Make the situation change in your favor according to what is healthful.

"One of the great lessons I've learned in athletics is that you've got to discipline your life. No matter how good you may be, you've got to be willing to cut out of your life those things that keep you from going to the top."
– Bob Richards

Do not give in to people who doubt you are capable of succeeding. Never allow yourself to think you are not capable or worthy of experiencing a life worthy of your better qualities.

It is likely that four of the most helpful things you can do for yourself are to:

A) Stop feeling as if you need to explain yourself.

B) Stop allowing yourself to react to other people's drama.

C) Refrain from slandering or negating other people.

D) Be aware of the picture you paint of others when you speak of them, as your words help paint the community you live in.

I mention slandering other people in that list because how you treat other people is reflective of the beliefs you hold within and in how you treat yourself.

No matter what other people do, be ambitious and involved with creating the life you want. Do this even if you were raised by people who had neither ambition nor manners. Be your better self.

"Do the things that interest you and do them with all your heart. Don't be concerned about whether people are watching you or criticizing you. The chances are that they aren't paying any attention to you. It's your attention to yourself."
– Eleanore Roosevelt

Completely overhaul the way you communicate with the people who are overly critical of you and/or who strongly doubt that you are going to succeed in improving your life. This may mean communicating with them far less, in limited ways, or not at all.

"As I grow older, I pay less attention to what men say. I just watch what they do."
– Andrew Carnegie

People may doubt your words, but they can't doubt your actions.

What you do, say, and accomplish might be things nobody has ever done or said, but what needs to be done and to be said.

What you do and say, and accomplish, might inspire others. The group of you might break into your own constellation of enlightened humanity who other people will look up to, even to revolutionize life to be healthier for all.

"Never doubt that a small group of thoughtful, committed citizens can change the world. Indeed, it is the only thing that ever has."
– Margaret Mead

Value your talents and intellect enough not to feel devalued using your better qualities. No matter what you do, some people will trash and devalue your intellect, belittle your character, undermine your goals, or otherwise drag you down. They only reveal themselves.
Believe in your self, no matter what.

"Use what talents you possess; the woods would be very silent if no birds sang there except those that sang best."
– Henry Van Dyke

Do not spend your time or energy explaining your dreams and goals to the doubters, to the haters, to the underminers, to those who belittle, or to the wasters of time. Instead, spend your time and energy planning for and working to improve and create the life you yearn for. Do it through focus, intention, action, and communication.
Some people are so concerned about their reputation that they never build much of one. Or, their reputation is of someone who lives woefully, who does little, who uses few of their capabilities, and who is more about worry and fear. They lack confidence.
Grab onto courage and build your confidence.
Bravely take charge of your days by setting a plan to succeed, and then spend your days working toward it.
Be determined to rid yourself of that which clutters your path, stalls you, robs you of time, and holds you back.
Do not look back toward what you consider to be your errors and failures. Instead, look forward to that which you can attain through planning and continued perseverance to improve through action.

"Courage is not the absence of fear, but rather the judgment that something else is more important than fear."
– Ambrose Redmoon

As you go forward into a healthful life and learn of the benefits of it, you will gain confidence and tune to your power. You will surpass the limits under which you once lived. You will understand that you are capable of attaining an improved life. This will strengthen, edify, and motivate you.

"We must all suffer one of two things: the pain of discipline or the pain of regret or disappointment."
— E. James Rohn

"Believe in yourself and there will come a day when others will have no choice but to believe with you."
— Cynthia Kersey

"Obstacles don't have to stop you. If you run into a wall, don't turn around and give up. Figure out how to climb it, go through it, or work around it."
— Michael Jordan

Stop allowing anything that challenges you to be a distraction pushing aside your focus, or to dismiss your drive to succeed.

Work to be invincible in practicing your intention to succeed at your goals through everyday actions.

Be relentless in pursuing the life you want to own.

Command your thoughts, do your homework, engage in your talents, build your skills, and force your life to happen in your favor.

"Nurture your mind with great thoughts, for you will never go any higher than your thoughts."
— Benjamin Disraeli

Give energy to thoughts fueling to work toward your goals. Let the vision of accomplishment drive parallel actions.

Like an athlete who constantly works toward victory, you can surpass your records in ways you never considered. Believe in, work toward experiencing, and own this satisfaction.

Allow yourself to be propelled toward a better life by visualizing your life the way you want it to be, and then making it happen through intentional living.

"Nothing is, unless our thinking makes it so."
— William Shakespeare

Be courageous about and focus on your goals the way runners and bikers focus on the finish line, the way swimmers focus on form and speed, the way mountain climbers focus on the top, and the way ball players focus on upping the score. Work on creating your goals into reality the way classical musicians organize musical notes to make beautiful sound: That is, through thoughts and actions called *practice*.

Within the bravery of courage in action is the beauty of elegance in practice.

"Dreams are renewable. No matter what our age or condition, there are still untapped possibilities within us and new beauty waiting to be born."
    – Dale E. Turner

"You may be whatever you resolve to be. Determine to be something in the world, and you will be something. 'I cannot,' never accomplished anything; 'I will try,' has wrought wonders."
    – J. Hawes

"Fortune sides with him who dares."
    – Publius Vergillus "Virgil" Maro

"Chained by their attitudes, they are a slave, they have forfeited their freedom. Only a person who risks is free."
    – Unknown

"That is will never come again is what makes life so sweet."
    – Emily Dickinson

"Let me not pray to be sheltered from dangers, but to be fearless in facing them. Let me not beg for the stilling of my pain, but for the heart to conquer it."
    – Rabindranath Tagore

"Courage is never to let your actions be influenced by your fears."
    – Arthur Koestler

"You miss 100 percent of the shots you never take."
    – Wayne Gretzky

"Man cannot discover new oceans, unless he has the courage to lose sight of the shore."
    – Andre Gide

"Each person has inside a basic decency and goodness. If he listens to it and acts on it, he is giving a great deal of what it is the world needs most. It is not complicated, but it takes courage. It takes courage for a person to listen to his own good."
    – Pablo Casals

"Life shrinks and expands in proportion to one's courage."
    – Anais Nin

"The fact is, that to do anything in the world worth doing, we must not stand back shivering and thinking of the cold and danger, but jump in and scramble through as well as we can."
    – Robert Cushing

Be courageous for yourself, even when nobody is looking.

"With courage you will dare to take risks, have the strength to be compassionate, and the wisdom to be humble. Courage is the foundation of integrity."
– Keshavan Nair

Have the integrity to continue on doing your best while experiencing trials.

Through the complicated times, maintain the stamina in your drive to create the life you yearn for.

"Everyday courage has few witnesses. But yours is no less noble because no drum beats for you and no crowds shout your name."
– Robert Louis Stevenson

"It is courage the world needs, not infallibility. Courage is always the surest wisdom."
– Wilfred T. Grenfell

# Plan Your Life

"Twenty years from now you will be more disappointed by the things you didn't do than by the ones you did do. So throw off the bowlines. Sail away from the safe harbor. Catch the trade winds in your sails. Explore. Dream. Discover."
— Mark Twain

Maybe your life is so out of order that it pains and sickens you.

"The more severe the pain or illness, the more severe will be the necessary changes. These may involve breaking bad habits, or acquiring some new and better ones."
— Peter McWilliams

"People who say that life is not worthwhile are really saying that they themselves have no personal goals which are worthwhile. Get yourself a goal worth working for. Better still, get yourself a project. Always have something ahead of you to look forward to, to work for and hope for."
— Maxwell Maltz

"When plans are laid in advance, it is surprising how often the circumstances fit in with them."
— William Osler

"If we do not know what port we're steering for, no wind is favorable."
— Lucius Annaeus Seneca

71

Many people reach a breaking point where they declare, "I can't live my life like this." But their intention to carry out the declaration has no definition, because they don't formulate a plan and act on it. By not having a plan, and being dedicated to it through action, they are committed to nothing. Rather than a declaration that they are going to change, through inaction their words are simply commentary.

"The man without a purpose is like a ship without a rudder – a waif, a nothing, a no man. Have a purpose in life, and having it, throw such strength of mind and muscle into your work as God has given you."
– Thomas Carlyle

If you are going through life without an idea of how you want it to be, you are spending your days aimlessly.

If you have an idea of what you want your life to be, but aren't spending your days both planning and working for it, you are only fantasizing.

If you have the idea of how you want your life to be, and are actively spending your days not only planning it, but also working toward it, that is more likely than less likely to build the sort of life you hope to own.

"Vision isn't enough unless combined with venture. It's not enough to stare up the steps unless we also step up the stairs."
– Vance Havner

"Reach high, for stars lie hidden in your soul. Dream deep, for every dream precedes the goal."
– Pamela Vaull Starr

The mind works in accordance with the influences suggested to it. To get your mind to work in your favor, define your intentions.

"People who do not see their choices do not believe they have choices. They tend to respond automatically, blindly influenced by their circumstances and conditioning. Mindfulness, by helping us notice our impulses before we act, gives us the opportunity to decide whether to act, and how to act."
– Gil Fronsdal

As an example of what people become based on their thoughts, consider those who have accomplished amazing things. The reason they are likely to have experienced such success is that they set goals for themselves, and combined their intention with their intellect, yearning, talents, abilities, skills, intuition, and instinct to accomplish those goals through everyday actions.

"You have got to know what it is you want, or someone is going to sell you a bill of goods somewhere along the line that can do irreparable damage to your self-esteem, your sense of worth, and your stewardship of the talents that God gave you."
– Richard Nelson Bolles

Many sports events have been won through the power of suggestion from coaches, cheering fans, friends, family, and cheerleaders. The players also did it because they had a vision and plan to win, they trained and practiced to win, and they acted out those plans and visions, turning them into the win.

"How do you go from where you are to where you want to be? I think you have to have an enthusiasm for life. You have to have a dream, a goal, and you have to be willing to work for it."
– Jim Valvano

"Our goals can only be reached through a vehicle of a plan, in which we must fervently believe, and upon which we must vigorously act. There is no other route to success."
– Stephen A. Brennan

Sports teams work with game plans. Architects work with plans called blueprints. Corporations function under corporate plans. Farmers run their farms by following plans of what to plant and where and when to plant it. People who knit blankets do so with plans. Take these examples of having and working with plans to obtain goals.

Make a game plan for your life to improve. Write it on paper, read and adjust it every morning, and spend your days acting on it.

"The greater our awareness of intentions, the greater our freedom to choose."
– Gil Fronsdal

Keeping a list of goals and priorities and reading it every morning is one of the most powerful tools you can use to help you focus on what you want to accomplish, and on carrying through with your goals.

"The term 'power' comes from the Latin posse: to do, to be able, to change, to influence or effect. To have power is to possess the capacity to control or direct change. All forms of leadership must

73

make use of power. The central issue of power in leadership is not: Will it be used? But rather: Will it be used wisely and well?"
  – Al Gini

There is power in suggestion – in suggesting things to others, and in suggesting things to yourself. Repeated suggestion is particularly effective.

Reading your goals every morning to focus your mind is using the power of suggestion.

Tell yourself you are worthy.

Tell yourself you are worth it.

Act on the suggestions as your list of goals. Every day.

By doing so you build skill, strength, experience, and wisdom.

"Don't let the fear of the time it will take to accomplish something stand in the way of your doing it. The time will pass anyway; we might just as well put that passing time to the best possible use."
  – Earl Nightingale

"Don't be fooled by the calendar. There are only as many days in the year as you make use of. One man gets only a week's value out of a year while another man gets a full year's value out of a week.
  – Charles Richards

Many people use suggestive or self-affirming notes to motivate them toward succeeding at goals. These notes might be generic and as simple as, "Believe in yourself." The notes may be task-specific, such as, "I will spend less money, and save more," or, "I will finish [name of project]." Some people get tattoos of affirmations, or images reminding them of what they care to remain focused on.

Daily affirmations may also include chanting, repeating motivational thoughts, writing uplifting and encouraging thoughts, listening to motivational material while exercising, and by literally defining your path by mapping it, and verbally proclaiming intentions – or whatever it is that will keep you focused on and engaged with succeeding at accomplishing your goals through daily actions.

Reading and writing affirmations at the start of every day helps to set energy patterns in your thoughts that travel throughout your brain and body tissues – which work in unison – as one through action and communication. It builds who you are, and what you will be.

"What I do today is important because I am exchanging a day of my life for it."
  – Hugh Mulligan

If you don't have a plan you are continually working with, you are simply bumping into life, people, experiences, and things as if you are in an amusement park bumper car with a broken steering wheel.

"One person with a belief is equal to a force of 99 who have only interests."
– John Stuart Mill

Keeping a "journaling" notebook of your thoughts regarding your concepts, intentions, observations, progress, nutrition, experiences, and dreams can help guide you along in your process of self-improvement. Slowly allow it to be a workbook that will assist you in leading a more healthful and intentionally satisfying life.

Write down the thoughts that motivate and inspire you to work for and to be a healthy version of yourself using your better qualities.

Write down what you desire to overcome, and provide some detail on how you plan to overcome it.

"Time is an equal opportunity employer. Each human being has exactly the same number of hours and minutes every day. Rich people can't buy more hours. Scientists can't invent new minutes. And you can't save time to spend it on another day. Even so, time is amazingly fair and forgiving. No matter how much time you've wasted in the past, you still have an entire tomorrow."
– Denis Waitely

"Learning to understand our dreams is a matter of learning how to understand our heart's language."
– Anne Faraday

"I am a writer who came from a sheltered life. A sheltered life can be a daring life as well. For all serious daring starts from within."
– Eudora Welty

In your notebook, detail the things you want from life; the things you dream about; and the thoughts you have regarding these issues. But don't get so obsessive about journaling that it takes away time and energy that would be more helpful to spend on accomplishing your goals. To make your life change you must be actively engaged in actions to make it change, and not simply in dreaming of, or fantasizing of, or writing about it.

The journal you keep of your goals, priorities, wants, dreams, and thoughts will be a "before and after" snapshot of your thought processes. Your better quality actions and communication will create the "after" picture.

"Think clearly and deeply, go into the structure of your desires and their ramifications. They are a most important part of your mental and emotional makeup, and powerfully affect your actions."
– Nisargadatta Maharaj

### Journaling exercises that will help you discover your passions and achieve goals.

This is to explore thoughts, define character, awaken creativity, trigger self-invention, and begin the consideration of your possible.

"Remember, you cannot abandon what you do not know. To go beyond yourself, you must know yourself."
– Nisargadatta Maharaj

1. Make a list of a few things you were good at when you were a child. Or a short list of what you wished to be good at.

2. Make a list of several things you thought were interesting and caught your attention when you were a child. Specifically, these should relate to what you would like your healthful life to include.

3. Make a list of some things you did that gave you satisfaction when you were a child. Specifically, these should be accomplishments, such as in music, art, sports, craft, or skills. Focus on what you had to work to achieve. Not on what you ate or wore, or where you went.

4. Make a list of some of the memorable compliments you have received about your character, talents, and/or skills. Or, what you wish you could have heard about yourself. Be your own coach.

5. Make a list of some of your favorite things, such as colors, sports, activities, hobbies, books, music, movies, flowers, plants, and wildlife. If it is of art, maybe you will draw some of these in your journal. Do so without being critical of your artistic skills.

6. Make a list of some of the things currently in your life that you do not want in your life. Keep it simple.

7. Make a list of some of the realistic and healthful things you do not have in your life, and want to have present in your life.

8. Go to a library and look for nonfiction books that interest you.
Keep in mind that you are looking for books to teach you things that will improve your life, not books that are meant for entertainment and/or for leisure. For instance, look for books that will improve your

skills, craft, and intellect, and/or that will help you to be more accomplished in your talents, skills, craft, and profession.

9. Make a list of some of the things you are capable of doing in relation to skills and talents.

10. Make a list of some things you would like to do during your life.

"The secret of getting ahead is getting started. The secret of getting started is breaking your complex overwhelming tasks into small manageable tasks, and then starting on the first one."
– Mark Twain

"Unless commitment is made, there are only promises and hopes; but no plans."
– Peter F. Drucker

"We are what we repeatedly do; therefore, excellence is not an act, but a habit."
– Henry David Thoreau

Working at improving your life every day is the key.

When things seem to be getting complicated, hold onto your integrity, and keep the basics of your goals in mind.

If you find that you are growing doubtful, go back to your goals and work it out. Focus on things that are the basics of your life, talents, intellect, abilities, skills, and needs.

"If you don't set a baseline standard for what you'll accept in life, you'll find it's easy to slip into behaviors and attitudes or a quality of life that's far below what you deserve."
– Anthony Robbins

Each item on your list of goals is like a rudder in your life. They will be similar to the small rudders of a large ship that guide it across vast oceans. A slight change in the angle of your intentions can guide you to a whole other destination.

Have faith in yourself, in the small things you do that bring about larger things. Doing so will build strength in your belonging.

Turn improving your life into being your ruling habit.

"You don't get to choose how you're going to die, or when. You can only decide how you're going to live. Now."
– Joan Baez

"Not choice, but habit rules the unreflecting herd."
– William Wordsworth

"Our challenge is to see beyond the world and invoke new beginnings."
– Marianne Williamson

"The final destination of a journey is not, after all, the last item on the agenda, but rather some understanding, however simple or provisional, of what one has seen."
– Pico Iyer

"It is good to have an end to journey toward; but it is the journey that matters, in the end."
– Ursula K. Le Guin

"I would rather be ashes than dust! I would rather that my spark should burn out in a brilliant blaze than it should be stifled by dry rot. I would rather be a superb meteor, every atom of me in magnificent glow, than a sleepy and permanent planet. The proper function of man is to live, not exist. I shall not waste my days in trying to prolong them, I shall use my time."
– Jack London

# Reengineer Your Self

"Through fear of knowing who we really are we sidestep our own destiny, which leaves us hungry in a famine of our own making. We end up living numb, passionless lives, disconnected from our soul's true purpose. But when you have the courage to shape your life from the essence of who you are, you ignite, becoming truly alive."
– Dawna Markova

If you are tired of leading an unsatisfying life, change it. Move the obstacles from your way, or go around them. Don't focus on what is stopping you. Do not dwell on what you perceive to be the unfortunate or unfair things that may have happened to you, and refuse to allow them to shade your world or halt your progress. Refuse to be held bound by things, events, situations, and/or people you perceive as working against you. Do not make any time for self-pity in your days. Do not allow your talents to be caged in by the bars of regret. Remove the walls and chains holding you from what you want. Awaken your life from any slumber.

"The best way to make your dreams come true is to wake up."
– Muhammad Ali

Look for the good in things, and build upon the good. Start with whatever good you have and use it to bring yourself closer to the person you want to be. Work at this every day from the moment of awakening. Do so in a calm, determined manner that will propel you toward being the person you wish to become.

"Realize that if you have time to whine and complain about something, you have time to do something about it."
– Unknown

"When you complain, all you do is broadcast, 'There's a victim in the neighborhood.'"
– Maya Angelou

"Don't be disquieted in time of adversity. Be firm with dignity and self-reliant with vigor."
– Chiang Kai-Shek

Refuse to be overthrown by problems.

Continually engage in the efforts to unlock your potential, to more forward within the potential, and engage in using it every day. You will build strength and dexterity that way.

Perhaps what is stopping you from experiencing more satisfaction in life is that you have not exercised your intellect, used your yearning, engaged in your talents and skills, connected with your other beneficial qualities, and become the stronger, more confident, resilient, and healthful person you are capable of being.

Maybe moving forward into the life you want to own is not about things becoming easier, but about you becoming stronger. Do that.

The message transcending generations is that you are to decide which of your yearnings become reality.

"Strong lives are motivated by dynamic purposes."
– Kenneth Hildebrand

Just as your grandest successes may be self-created, so too may be much of what you consider to be your greatest failures. It is likely that it is largely up to you to decide which one of these possibilities are realized.

"We carry within us the wonders we seek without us."
– Thomas Browne

"Deep within man dwell those slumbering powers; powers that would astonish him, that he never dreamed of possessing; forces that would revolutionize his life if aroused and put into action."
– Orison Swett Marden

Don't think of creating your life as a way of finding it. Creating your life is not about finding it, it's about opening it. What you become is nurtured from within you. It is there. It is real. And you can use it any way and at any time you wish.

"You must be lamps unto yourselves."
– Buddha

"If you have built castles in the air, your work need not be lost. Now put foundations under them."
– Osa Johnson

Take actions in tune with the power of believing in yourself and your helpful, beneficial qualities that can work miracles in your life.

Surround yourself in all ways with what motivates you, and brings out your best qualities as you work for what you want.

Make the positive, uplifting, nurturing, loving, and kind substances of your life the most vibrant and present in a way that they will continually capture and hold your attention. The strongest vibrations will always win, just as when listening to two voices at the same time, it is the loudest that will get your attention.

"A man's life is what his thoughts make it."
– Marcus Aurelius

Thoughts are seeds of the mind. Thoughts that are nurtured are more likely to grow into actions, words, and results.

Make your most helpful thoughts grow into reality through actions as you would grow seeds into an orchard to produce fruit.

"To see things in the seed, that is genius."
– Lao Tzu

Being proactive in changing your life is about propagating your most helpful thoughts, making positive decisions, and taking actions in alignment with these that lead to satisfaction.

Uplifting thoughts lead to uplifting words, actions, communication, and events. When uplifting thoughts lead to uplifting words, they can uplift you and those around you. When uplifting thoughts are combined with nutritious, vibrant foods, exercise, and daily, intentional, goal-oriented actions, transformative experiences can result.

Get outside in Nature to help yourself experience life. You can't live without Nature. It is a part of you, and you are a part of it. It impacts your thoughts, energy, and health. The energy of being out in Nature can help you factor what matters.

Because you are a manifestation of what your thoughts consist of, you are a being reflective of what enlightens you. Because of this, your words and actions are continually revealing the level of your enlightenment.

The positive life change you are undergoing likely is equal to your level of how your actions and communication are in tune with your self-realization combined with your determination expressed in your actions.

Respect and believe in your higher potential, and in that of others. It instills motivational power and energy to overcome, to carry on, to persevere, and to improve.

You won't always make the best choices, but you can always learn from mistakes, and use the gained knowledge as wisdom.

"While one person hesitates because he feels inferior, the other is busy making mistakes and becoming superior."
– Henry Link

Don't let your bad choices defeat you. Learn from them, grow from them, use them as your teachers, and as something that makes you stronger and more determined with the wisdom you need to move forward making smarter choices.

"You can't wait for inspiration. You have to go after it with a club."
– Jack London

Connect with and refuse to relinquish your power. Make persistent actions toward achieving your goals your common to the point of being both habits and your normal way of conducting the energy ruling your life.

"Energy and persistence alter all things."
– Benjamin Franklin

The more persistent you are in accomplishing your goals, and the more sustained your focus, the more you will see and realize it is possible to do what you want to do.

If you do anything habitually, make it the constant wise use of your time, resources, yearning, talent, abilities, skills, craft, intellect, intuition, energy, and love.

"Without heroes, we are all plain people and don't know how far we can go."
– Bernard Malamud

By doing all of these things while trusting in your heart, you will see that you are capable and worthy of changing your life.

While you once may have given up on attaining your goals, as you instead give up on that defeat, but go about accomplishing your plan with a renewed and continually intentional focus mixed with action, and better quality communication, you will be your own witness to the truths contained within you.

"The simple act of caring is heroic."
– Edward Albert

Care about yourself so much and so consistently that you become your own hero.

"Heroes take journeys, confront dragons, and discover the treasure of their true selves."
– Carol Pearson

"His high endeavors are an inward light, that makes the path before him always bright."
– William Wordsworth

"Every aspect of our lives is, in a sense, a vote for the kind of world we want to live in."
– Frances Moore Lappe

"When you are inspired by some great purpose, some extraordinary project, all your thoughts break their bonds: Your mind transcends limitations, your consciousness expands in every direction, and you find yourself in a new, great, and wonderful world. Dormant forces, faculties and talents become alive, and you discover yourself to be a greater person by far than you ever dreamed yourself to be."
– Patanjali

"Go confidently in the direction of your dreams. Live the life you've always imagined."
– Henry David Thoreau

# Intentional Living

"Regret for the things we did can be tempered by time; it is regret for the things we did not do that is inconsolable."
– Sidney J. Harris

The way you perceive things has to do with your life experiences, including with whom you have spent time, how you have been treated, what you have been taught and told, where you have gone, what you have done, seen, felt, smelled, heard, and tasted, what you have read, and the pattern of thinking with which you have allowed yourself to align.

How you do go about changing your life to have experiences different from your past is to choose to do so, to focus on doing so, and to continually take actions to make it so.

"First say to yourself what you would be; and then do what you have to do."
– Epictetus

Some people get caught in a cantankerous way of thinking as they continually consider the problems, irritants, and drama – or what they perceive as these. It is likely that their attitude helps to attract or create more of the same. Other people seem to glide along while continually focusing on the positive, acknowledging what makes them glad, and on creating the life they wish to have. Perhaps the greatest difference between these two types of people is they consider and treat their issues differently, with a different way of calculating what could be perceived as problems, and a different way of finding and working – or not working – on solutions.

"Three rules of work: Out of clutter find simplicity; From discord find harmony; In the middle of difficulty lies opportunity."
– Albert Einstein

Perhaps one way of looking at the issues facing you is to do what many positive-thought coaches suggest, which is to not think of them as problems. Instead, think of them as teachers, as lessons to learn, and as opportunities to achieve. They may be challenges, but that is not necessarily a bad thing.

The difference between a problem and an opportunity may be a matter of perception, and what you choose to do about the situation.

"I discovered I always have choices, and sometimes it's only a choice of attitude."
– Judith M. Knowlton

"Could we change our attitude, we should not only see life differently, but life itself would come to be different. Life would undergo a change of appearance because we ourselves had undergone a change of attitude."
– Katherine Mansfield

Some say you only experience what will bring you the lessons you need. While that concept is debatable – and likely unrealistic – perhaps it can be helpful to form an attitude of conducting yourself in such a way that allows you to learn from your experiences.

Use challenges the way a martial arts fighter uses the energy of the opponent. Use challenges as power to make better decisions.

With your gained knowledge that is wisdom gathered through living, avoid repeating unwise choices.

"I really do think that any deep crisis is an opportunity to make your life extraordinary in some way."
– Martha Beck

Through the power of thought it is likely that you can transform many of your otherwise unfortunate experiences into being motivational and beneficial life lessons for making wise choices.

"Reality is like a bud that keeps opening. The petals keep revealing themselves. It's not as if that bud becomes something that it wasn't before. It just keeps showing its potential."
– Adyashanti

"The good life is a process, not a state of being. It is a direction, not a destination."
– Carl Rogers

The line of progress toward the life people want is largely determined by their thoughts and life lessons mixed with actions and communication. Progression is up to them to create. What they experience often has to do with their yearning, perception, intentions, drive, focus, and determination, and their connection with their intellect, talents, and better potential.

"Choose your intention carefully, and then practice holding your consciousness to it, so it becomes the guiding light in your life."
– John Roger

The more you sustain your focus and determined participation in your goals through dedication, intention, and work, the more likely your life will become what you hope for.

"I never suspected that I would have to learn how to live – that there were specific disciplines and ways of seeing the world I had to master before I could awaken to a simple, happy, uncomplicated life."
– Dan Millman

Mastering your life includes not only thought and action, but also diet, exercise, and environment.

The issue of nutrition and how important your food choices are in the function of your body, mind, and brain are covered later in the book.

Diet is linked with environmental issues. Your food choices are the principal way in which you interact with Earth. Your role in creating a healthful planet is in alignment with how healthy you choose to be through a natural, vibrant diet.

"You are a product of your environment. So choose the environment that will best develop you toward your objective. Analyze your life in terms of its environment. Are the things around you helping you toward success – or are they holding you back?"
– W. Clement Stone

Arrange your life in every way possible that will allow your better intentions to be fulfilled using your higher qualities.

"Ya gotta be ready for the fastball."
– Ted Williams

"Somebody should tell us, right at the start of our lives, that we

are dying. Then we might live life to the limit, every minute of every day."
— Michael Landon

"Do not wait for extraordinary circumstances to do good action; try to use ordinary situations."
— Jean Paul Richter

"The purpose of life is a life of purpose."
— Robert Byrne

Intentional living is defining your path, acting on it, and following it every day.

"A man cannot be comfortable without his own approval."
— Mark Twain

If you want your life to be reflective of the good things inside you, work to reveal those.

If you want your life to be less cluttered, unclutter it.

If you want good in your life, bring good into it and create the good in your community.

If you want love, kindness, and gratitude in your life, you will be more likely to experience these if you are a projector of love, kindness, and gratitude.

"Kind words do not cost much. They never blister the tongue or lips. They make other people good-natured. They also produce their own image on men's souls, and a beautiful image it is."
— Blaise Pascal

If you want good people in your life who will uplift you, you are more likely to have them present if you uplift those around you.

If you want to stop living in denial and get your life in order, face and figure out your situation, factor solutions, set the goals, and work to create a better reality.

Nurture health and fitness through nutrition and daily exercise.

Cut out health-degrading foods. Choose a diet rich in the vibrant nutrients in raw fruits and vegetables. This will help you to experience a more vibrant life.

If you are tired of seeing through tired eyes, and living in a stale life, refactor how you factor things. Revitalize your life through more motivating conclusions, helpful actions, and better communication.

"If we wait for the moment when everything, absolutely everything is ready, we shall never begin."
— Ivan Turgenev

If you want to reveal your true talents and intellect, then live your truth, stimulate your intellect, and make your talents fully functional through practice.

If you want satisfaction to dominate your life, then decide what would satisfy you and work every day to bring it about.

"The best way out is always through."
– Robert Frost

If you want to get through the unfavorable issues veiling you from living a favorable life, then persist in working through them.

"For the things we have to learn before we can do them, we learn by doing them."
– Aristotle

If you want to have the mental power to change your life, then exercise your power to bring about a strong determination in the same way you exercise your body to make it stronger.

Daily physical exercise will help you to learn and understand the concept of powering and changing your life through thoughts that bring transformative intentional actions.

"If you have a great ambition, take as big a step as possible in the direction of fulfilling it. The step may only be a tiny one, but trust that it may be the largest one possible for now."
– Mildred McAfee

Envision your life the way you want it to be. Study, practice, and learn through challenges and errors, so you know what you need to bring about that life. Live more intentionally. Spend your time accomplishing goals. Dominate your thoughts with what it is you need to focus on, do, and communicate. Through doing these things, you will be intentionally creating the life you wish to own.

"Emotions reflect intentions. Therefore, awareness of emotions leads to awareness of intentions."
– Gary Zukav

"The great and glorious masterpiece of humanity is to know how to live with a purpose."
– Michel Eyquem de Montaigne

"Action is the foundational key to all success."
– Pablo Picasso

# Expecting and Experiencing

"Most of us serve our ideals by fits and starts. The person who makes a success of living is the one who sees his goal steadily and aims for it unswervingly. That is dedication."
– Cecil B. De Mille

Many people get caught up in expecting life to happen in a certain way in tune with conditions they wish to experience. Unfortunately, through the way they negligently engage in life, what they may be doing is experiencing the opposite of what they would like. They can be caught up in not living anything resembling their ideal life because they are stalled in a pattern of what they have been experiencing while thinking the same thoughts that brought about the life they don't want. They may be living in a way that simply happened without much use of their intellect, talents, or skills. They may be living in a way that is more in tune with how they believe others are expecting them to live, which could be the direct opposite of what would be most satisfying and healthful.

"What we achieve inwardly will change outer reality."
– Otto Rank

I am one who wanted a radically different life than the one I had experienced as a child. To get a different life, I had to think, act, and communicate differently than I had been.

After experiencing a rough childhood filled with strife, ruled by poverty, abuse, neglect, and brutality in a dark and unbearable household of woe, with troubled parents and generations of alcoholism, dysfunction, and mental health issues, I moved away.

When I was nineteen, I was saturated with post-childhood issues. I was a mess living in ruin and with no idea of how to change it. Most of the people around me were also far from living up to their higher potential. Many were damaged, damaging, and slathered with failure, and lost in their post-childhood baggage causing more damage.

I didn't want to continue on the trajectory I was experiencing. It seemed to only be heading toward a life of poverty. It seemed set by the circumstances of my childhood, of my parents, of my ancestors. I didn't have to live within the confines of generations of ruin. I badly desired something much more healthful for myself. To do it, I needed to change my thought patterns. Otherwise I would have continued in the same lowly life pattern that had been set before me – or worse.

"Prosperity is a way of living and thinking, and not just money or things. Poverty is a way of living and thinking, and not just a lack of money or things."
– Eric Butterworth

Do you want to succeed? Then stop conforming to what you think others may or may not think you should be. Stop trying to fulfill the expectations of others that batter you down. Work daily to experience what you wish and expect your life to be.

Stop paying attention to whatever holds you back from having the life you want to experience – especially people who don't believe in you, or those who want you to continue to wade in the same shallow life they are choosing to remain in.

Stop entertaining thoughts that bring about the same actions that create the same experiences you don't like to have.

"No one knows your capability as well as you do. No one knows how big you can dream, and no one knows how far you can go. You, like water, can seek and reach your own level."
– Lynne Cox

Some people say they don't succeed because they have no support system of people who believe in them.

To allow people to believe in you, you have to believe in yourself. Your support system is within the constructs of your mind.

To allow people to view you as capable of accomplishing something, you first have to accomplish it.

Even if people don't recognize your accomplishments, succeed anyway.

"Let me listen to me, and not to them."
– Gertrude Stein

"If other people do not understand our behavior – so what?
Their request that we must only do what they understand is an
attempt to dictate to us. If this is being 'asocial' or 'irrational' in their
eyes, so be it. Mostly, they resent our freedoms, and our courage to
be ourselves. We owe nobody an explanation or an accounting, as
long as our acts do not hurt or infringe on them. How many lives
have been ruined by this need to 'explain,' which usually implies that
the explanation be 'understood,' i.e. approved. Let your deeds be
judged, and from your deeds, your real intentions, but know that a
free person owes an explanation only to himself – to his reasons and
his conscience – and to the few who may have a justified claim for
explanation."
– Erich Fromm

You don't need permission, acknowledgement, approval, or
recognition to lead a brilliant, healthful life in which you thrive.

"Poor is the man whose pleasures depend on the permission of
another."
– Madonna Ciccone

Don't get caught up in being a praise junkie who seeks
permission and approval to express brilliance.
Accomplish your goals without expecting praise from anyone.
The achievement is the reward, not the acknowledgment.

"Stop looking outside yourself for your substantiation. Learn to
love who you are."
– Alan Arkin

Live with integrity and intention. Use your strengths to advance.
Align and work with your skills, passions, perception, intuition,
yearning, and power to achieve your higher goals.

"Why are women immobile? Because so many feel they're
waiting for someone to say, 'You're good, you're pretty, I give you
permission.'"
– Eve Ensler

Seeking the approval and validation of others is really a desire to
get yourself to approve of you – to validate yourself.
You validate yourself using your better qualities to accomplish
your goals and live more of your higher potential.

"We shall all someday look back on our lives and see that, in spite of our company, we were alone the whole way. This is what makes your self-respect so important, and I don't see how you can respect yourself if you must look in the hearts and minds of others for your happiness."
– Hunter Thompson

"I think you have to take charge of your own life, and understand that you're either going to live somebody else's dream, or live your own dream."
– Wilma Mankiller

Use your time and resources wisely, and don't waste them on nonsense. Use your energy on doing, not on observing. Use your time on accomplishing, not on being distracted.

"When you take charge of your life, there is no longer need to ask permission of other people or society at large. When you ask permission, you give someone veto power over your life."
– Albert F. Geoffrey

Have you never experienced success? Consider that experiencing success depends more on what you think and do than on anything or anyone else.

Perhaps you have utilized your innate abilities most effectively to keep you in the poverty victim mentality, and in being a pushover.

"We can usually tell the quality of our subconscious mind by looking at the quality of the life we are living. If we are not pleased with our life, we must look at the content of our mind to discover how we have been programming our existence to meet our belief structure."
– Dudley Evenson

It is up to you to change the state of your mind, the patterns of your thoughts, the quality of your health, the level of your fitness, the standards of your behavior, the helpfulness of your communication, and the trajectory of your life.

Stop fantasizing about the life you want to lead.

Start living the life you want. If even in small activities and successes every day that build into larger activities and successes.

By continually and intentionally being involved in some level of doing what you want to do, and not just thinking about it, and especially not simply by talking about it, but through intentional daily actions, you will build your confidence through accomplishments.

You will build patterns of thoughts that turn into patterns of behavior, and patterns of accomplishments.

"Great things are not done by impulse, but by a series of small things brought together."
– Vincent Van Gogh

Just as a riverbed is created by water constantly flowing over it, you can embellish your mind with thoughts that improve your life by constantly thinking about and taking action to improve your life.

Your body can get accustomed to performing certain tasks as you keep doing them, and get stronger at them. This includes the practice of eating a healthful diet; forming a routine of daily exercise; thinking and planning with the intention of improving your life; focusing on the things you need; and by continually doing the things that need to be done to create your healthful life.

"The thing always happens that you really believe in; and the belief in a thing makes it happen."
– Frank Lloyd Wright

The practice of improving your life is just that, a practice, which results in achievement.

As you bring your mind, body, and life to be more in tune with what is most pleasing to you, the more you will recognize your potential, and the more you will build the skills and strength to achieve what you want. This can be accomplished just as the musician must continually practice to be able to play music the way they want it to sound. Thought, action, and practice build skill.

"Yesterday is a canceled check; tomorrow is a promissory note; today is the only cash you have – so spend it wisely."
– Kay Lyons

Many people allow themselves to be easily and repeatedly distracted from accomplishing their daily goals. This interruption can be so common in their life that it has become their practice to fail at meeting their most basic daily goals by using the excuse that other matters needed their attention.

Some people may say that things keep happening that are less than ideal than what they expected. If you relate to this scenario, realize that some of the less than ideal situations may be of your making, and many occur because you allow them to.

As you are presented with situations that may be less than ideal, look toward ways of remaining calm and dealing with them in a way that will bring about benefits. Also, realize that you may benefit more by staying focused on and remaining active in attaining your daily goals than by taking care of whatever matter it is that may be tempting to sway or distract you from what is more important.

Just as an artist must focus and work on a painting until it reflects the image they are trying to create, so must you use your intellect, talents, time, and energy to create the life you wish for.

"I am more and more convinced that our happiness or our unhappiness depends far more on the way we meet the events of life than on the nature of those events themselves."
– Wilhelm von Humboldt

Perhaps you are in a terrible situation, as I was while growing up. Maybe you are surrounded by people behaving badly. Know that you can safely and wisely factor and work for a way out.

"In a toxic family system, the healthiest person causes friction. They create resistance in the familiar dynamics, and other members become uncomfortable and triggered."
– Nicole LePera

"The scapegoat doesn't get picked randomly or by accident. Usually they are either sensitive, unhappy, vulnerable, ill, and/or the outspoken child or whistle blower
In other words, the scapegoat is the child who refuses to look content – or stay silent – in the unbearable atmosphere created in the family home."
– Glynis Sherwood, Healing from Complex Trauma & PTSD/CPTSD

Please, do not give up hope of living in a more healthy, safe situation. Do cautiously seek out the help you need.

"If you assume that there is no hope, you guarantee that there will be no hope. If you assume that there is an instinct for freedom, that there are opportunities to change things, then there is a possibility that you can contribute to making a better world."
– Noam Chomsky

"If you lose hope, somehow you lose the vitality that keeps life moving, you lose that courage to be, that quality that helps you go on in spite of it all. And so today I still have a dream."
– Martin Luther King, Jr.

Dream of a better way of living, and do so while working to make it happen so that it is your experience. Make it so.

# Self-hate, Deceit, and Sabotage

Perhaps you have been living under the shadow of not feeling worthy of having your dreams come true. Now is the time to start feeling worthy.

**"The worst tyrants are those which establish themselves in our own breasts."**
– William Ellery Channing

If you never have experienced success, consider that you might benefit from exploring the possibility that you are in a habit of having self-deceptive thoughts.

Self-deceptive thoughts revolve around believing you are not capable. Part of it might be about you remembering negative and discouraging words others have said to or about you.

**"Fundamentally the marksman aims at himself."**
– Eugene Herrigel

Self-deceptive thoughts may be about you thinking and believing the discouraging and degrading words of others are about you.

Something to be considered when people say lousy things about you is that they are revealing more about their own condition while aiming their comments toward you. You just happened to be the target at which they toss their damaging words of self-hate.

People often accuse others of what the accuser truly is. This sort of behavior sometimes plays out in the media, such as the famous

95

minister who always preached against homosexuality and drug use, but who was found to be leading a closeted life that involved hiring male prostitutes, taking drugs, and pressuring his subordinates into sexual situations. He was filled with self-deception and self-hate, and projected it onto others. It is likely that he had been around people who taught him to hate himself, pressing him into pretending to be what he wasn't – rather than living as a healthful version of himself.

Self-deceptive thoughts often reflect your ideas of how – and belief that – others are being judgmental of you.

"When a person drowns himself in negative-thinking he is committing an unspeakable crime against himself."
– Maxwell Maltz

Self-deceptive thoughts can be agreements you have made with yourself to allow the negative comments of others to impact you, thus enabling others to define you.

"Anger and hardness is a shield, it masks other things."
– Mickey Rourke

Self-deceptive thoughts are partially of your own making, and can also be created by damaging, negative, neglectful, or otherwise unhealthful relationships. They consist of unfairly judging and unwisely limiting yourself. They are about you agreeing to whatever it was that could be viewed as negative about you, and allowing the energy of that to alter your thoughts, decisions, actions, words, fitness, food choices, relationships, and life.

Self-deceptive thoughts fuel self-sabotage, doubt, low self-esteem, limiting beliefs, fear, awkwardness, inadequacy, insecurities, procrastination, damaging emotions, worry, junk diets, laziness, neglect of talents and skills, and failure.

"Don't worry about the future. Or worry, but know that worrying is as effective as trying to solve an algebra equation by chewing bubble gum."
– Mary Schmich

"The most exhausting thing in life is being insecure."
– Anne Morrow Lindbergh

Self-deceptive thoughts perpetuate guilt, shame, insecurity, and the feelings, emotions, and activities associated with self-hate.

Self-hate spurs you to dwell in ignorance, regret, and defeat.

When dealing in self-hate you create and feed your fear, doubts, and worries, and/or agree to accept, magnify, and dwell in the fear, doubts, and worries others have projected onto you. In the energy of self-hate, you wallow in these creations and drop below your higher potential. While dwelling in self-hate, you go along with what works against you while permitting low-quality communication, damaging relationships, slothfulness, and neglect to continue.

"Our doubts are traitors, and make us lose the good we oft might win by fearing the attempt."
– William Shakespeare

If you are hosting self-deceptive thoughts, self-hate, self-sabotage, and low self-esteem, it is likely that you have been around damaging and damaged people who are unhealthful and who are hosting the very same issues. One thing these people are very good at is abundantly spreading their unhelpful energies and cynical attitudes. They are good at wasting their time, and the time of others who participate in their club of failure that is forever accepting new members. Refuse to be a member.

Continually receiving negative messages from damaging people lowers your self-esteem and creates a belief that you are incapable of attaining your goals. It may stop you from setting goals, and may instill a sense that you are and always will be unworthy and a failure, which is the energy of defeat and self-annihilation. Do not eat from that buffet. It will not nurture your intellect, talents, skills, or life.

"You must fight off a 'bad luck' way of thinking as if you were dealing with an invasion of hostile forces – for that is precisely what you are dealing with."
– Maxwell Maltz

Your thoughts help create your body chemistry. By thinking you are going to fail makes you more likely to fail, and creates a body chemistry of failure. On the other hand, thinking of yourself as succeeding is more likely to bring about that experience as the thoughts will trigger related actions and communication. In other words, thoughts are self-achieving and trigger the body to act in relation to the thoughts.

Through low-quality thoughts, foods, communication, and actions, you are creating and are in alignment with the energy of failure.

Halt your downward spiral. Turn your life around. Reclaim it.

By choosing to consume high-quality foods, getting daily morning exercise, and guiding your actions with work in alignment with goal-oriented thinking, you are more likely to create a body chemistry aligned with health and success.

"It is well known that panic, despair, depression, hate, rage, exasperation, frustration all produce negative biochemical changes in the body."
– Norman Cousins

Part of what might be inducing self-defeat is believing you are part of a stigmatized group. Maybe you are part of a stigmatized group. The stress and frustration of thinking people are going to label you and treat you badly, limit your participation in society, reject, and perhaps harm you can be disheartening and bring much sadness, anxiety, and unfortunate feelings, and lead to self-harm.

You might be self-stigmatizing. That is of you believing in the stereotypes other people apply, and this has brought you shame, or you fear it will bring you shame. Maybe stigmatization has brought you to retreat from participating in much of life.

Perhaps people have magnified your defeat, as they treated you badly because you are thought of as being part of – or you are a part of – a stigmatized group.

Being stigmatized can get so very complicated, unfortunate, and even tragic.

Stigmatization could be built around perceived age, or actual age, body shape, disabilities, health status, culture, religion, dietary choices, education, family associations, heritage, income, legal or criminal history, occupation, gender, orientation, and sexual experience.

Being stigmatized can cause rejection from families, schoolmates, coworkers, neighbors, and various clubs, groups, careers, businesses, social situations, and associations.

Even if you are suspected of being in a certain group, all sorts of levels of unfortunate behaviors could be applied to you, including disbelief, denial, ridicule, mockery, dismissal, prejudices, stereotype treatment, discrimination, and violence. Simply having the thought of being subjected to the horrible treatment can be damaging to you, and halt your life progression. Both perceived stigma and anticipated stigmatization can be damaging.

If you feel alone, or simply need someone to speak with, don't be afraid to contact a psychologist, seek out and attend a 12-step program and ask for help there. Research ways in which you can be a more healthy and satisfied version of yourself. If you have or have had a problem in life, there are likely others who are dealing with or have dealt with similar issue. There is help out there for you. Be good for yourself. Find and be your solution.

Take the steps, make the moves, research, educate yourself, read books, look up interviews and documentaries about the issue, and speak with helpful people. Do what it takes to get into a better frame of mind, and into a situation in which you thrive in health.

Just as building a structure, creating a better life for yourself takes work. Be the one who gets it done.

To fracture a pattern of self-defeat and to get into a more healthful energy pattern, continually work toward thinking in a way that is more in keeping with a successful frame of mind. Don't allow yourself – or others – to fill your mind with negativity, hate, anger, fear, or other dramatic emotions associated with stress, worry, deception, slander, illness, defeat, and the poverty victim mentality.

Refuse to allow yourself to fall into the trap of making excuses that perpetuate a life of inconsistent commitments, lazy attempts, being stuck, and failure.

"Excuses are the nails used to build a house of failure."
– Don Wilder

Often people who are timid, shy, and full of excuses have been subjected to forms of neglect and abuse that result in low self-esteem, feelings of inadequacy and unworthiness, or full-fledged self-hate. Through the actions and words of others they have learned to hate themselves and/or feel they are dismissible, unimportant, unworthy, insignificant, and neglectable. If this defines you, it is time to get past the walls constructed by the mistreatment – or perceived mistreatment – you have been subjected to. Do so without placing blame on others, and without dwelling on former relationships – which would keep you focused in the past. Instead, stay focused on making a better today and a more promising future, which you can intentionally create by staying in the present and focused on your intentions and goals. Do so while no longer allowing yourself to be guided by the negative words, attitudes, and actions of others.

Stop catering to the depths of a lack of belief in your intellect and talents.

Do not listen to discouragement. Instead, treat discouragement like water and you are the buoy. Water can't sink a buoy, unless there is a leak. Positive thoughts, words, and intentional, goal-oriented actions combined with a healthful diet and daily morning exercise are what keep you up.

Stop hosting self-deceptive and self-hating thoughts.

Instead of harboring negative thoughts, abhor them.

Stop slandering and undermining yourself.

Stop conforming to the limits you have placed on your life based on disbelief of your self.

Stop giving in to, rooting in to, and feeding off of any unhealthful energy, thoughts, words, and actions of others – including in the past and/or present. Be resilient to them.

If you have been victimized, do not revictimize yourself by relishing in the unfortunate, by continually thinking about how you were victimized, by forever talking about how you were victimized, or by not gathering yourself up and moving on to some better way outside the path of your victimization.

Many people get caught up in thoughts of who has betrayed them, and about how they have been betrayed. They constantly talk about how they were betrayed. By doing so, they dwell in the energy of the betrayal – instead of learning, regrouping, and moving on.

**"We are the hurdles we leap to be ourselves."**
– Michael McClure

Most people need not even bother examining the way others may have betrayed them, because, truth be told, they themselves, not others, are likely to have turned into their betrayers. They betray themselves by not living up to their intellect and talents; by wasting their time on frivolity; by practically discarding their talent and resources; by consuming garbage foods; by falling into laziness and not exercising; by diminishing themselves with their thoughts and conduct; and by staggering around in the low-quality situation they have settled into. Because of their actions, their life has aged into a fine patina of self-denial and wretched waste.

**"If we don't change the direction we're going, we're likely to end up where we're headed."**
– Chinese proverb

As mentioned earlier, just as people are more likely to fail because they don't think they can succeed, those who believe they can succeed are more likely to do so. Either of these scenarios is simply a matter of which frame of mind a person chooses to hold, and what thoughts they choose, actions they take, and communication they make to manifest it.

**"If you doubt you can accomplish something, then you can't accomplish it. You have to have confidence in your ability, and then**

be tough enough to follow through."
– Rosalynn Carter

You can either choose to believe you are going to fail, or you can choose to believe you are going to succeed. Of course outside issues influence your frame of mind and surroundings. But you can also play a large role in both choosing and creating your surroundings, as well as in choosing how your surroundings affect you.

"This above all, to refuse to be a victim. Unless I can do that I can do nothing."
– Margaret Atwood

Do not get caught up in the degradation of negativity, defeat, and self-deceit that all feed failure and ruin. Peel away the stifling feelings of anger, anxiety, hatred, loathing, jealousy, low self-esteem, fear, unworthiness, blame, and victimization.

Stop inflicting your life with limiting thoughts, absurdly critical comments, cynicism, slander, stagnant energy, junk foods, laziness, lack of exercise, and wasteful activities.

"When you show yourself to the world and display your talents, you naturally stir all kinds of resentment, envy, and other manifestations of insecurity. You cannot spend your life worrying about the petty feelings of others."
– Robert Greene

Stop talking yourself out of living your life.

"Suffering can be our greatest asset. If we have the capacity to learn from our suffering we have the capacity to improve our lives, improve our families, and improve our communities."
– Alexander McKinnon

Believe that you are unique, special, significant, worthy, able, loveable, and have talents, skills, craft, and power you can nurture. Realize this and start living your days knowing you are a beautiful being capable of amazing things.

"You can achieve anything you want in life – if you have the courage to dream it, the intelligence to make a realistic plan, and the will to see that plan through to the end."
– Sidney A. Friedman

Make and aim to accomplish realistic goals.

"One does not advance when one walks toward no goal, or –

which is the same thing – when his goal is infinity. To pursue a goal which is by definition unattainable is to condemn oneself to a state of perpetual unhappiness."
– Émile Durkheim

Avoid getting stuck in the rut of thinking who is against your abilities. Instead, work daily to accomplish realistic goals.

Some people are so caught up in negative-thinking that they think the people around them are working against them. Think about the outcome these people would have if the opposite were true: that the people around them are hoping the person becomes successful, healthy, and happy, and that loving relationships are strongly present in the person's life. Be that person.

"I am a kind of paranoiac in reverse. I suspect people of plotting to make me happy."
– J. D. Salinger

Avoid feeling as if things and people are working against you, that you will not experience joy, or that your life will never improve. Instead, focus on making a better life for yourself, and take daily actions to make it happen.

"If you seek love, appreciation, and affection, then learn to give love, appreciation, and affection."
– Deepak Chopra

Rather than believing others are thinking negatively about you, believe instead that they are working to do good to and wishing good for you. In doing so you will be doing the same for you.

Know this: There is absolutely not one truly healthy person who wants bad things for you. Instead, the enlightened people in life are wishing you health, satisfaction, kindness, and love. Be one of them – for you, and for others.

Stop worrying about what other people think of you. Live your life knowing that what matters more is what you will think about yourself. What matters is what you do with the attributes of your character and the resources you have.

Stop resigning yourself to self-hate, which is overwhelming your being with negativity.

No longer slander yourself – or other people.

Your happiness depends largely on you, and not on others.

You are capable of performing the tasks that need to be done to form your life into what you want it to be. You don't need an authority figure to give you permission to do so.

"Luck is what you have left over after you give 100 percent."
– Langston Coleman

We are all being given and are worthy of receiving blessings. Choose to accept them.

Look within. Your mind is a great resource. You are an owner of imagination and intellect, a person of dreams and talent, and are worthy of experiencing happiness, health, and love. With integrity, think, plan, speak, and act in ways revealing this honor.

"Only when we are no longer afraid do we begin to live in every experience, painful or joyous, to live in gratitude for every moment, to live abundantly."
– Dorothy Thompson

"The difference between great people and everyone else is that great people create their lives actively, while everyone else is created by their lives, passively waiting to see where life takes them next. The difference between the two is the difference between living fully and just existing."
– Michael E. Gerber

# The Competition Myth

"We are raised on comparison; our education is based on it; so is our culture. So we struggle to be someone other than who we are."
— Jiddu Krishnamurti

"The only competition worthy of a wise man is with himself."
— Washington Allston

"You start getting into trouble in life when you start comparing and contrasting your life to anyone else's. You don't win when you do that."
— Jeremy Pivin

Many people continually compare and judge themselves in relation to the next person. Often this is done believing in the concept that those who seem to own certain possessions, or who appear a certain way, have their lives together, and are happier.

"The world I am trying to understand is one in which men think they want one thing and then upon getting it, find out to their dismay that they don't want it nearly as much as they thought or don't want it at all — and that something else, of which they were hardly aware, is what they really want."
— Albert Hirschman

Some people seem to think that the more expensive things they accumulate and the more money they have, the better their life will be. Those of us who have been around wealthy people, as well as around those who have few possessions, know that money and material things do not hold a promise of creating happiness, health, or love. Some of the wealthiest people I have known have been the most unhappy and lonely. Some of the poorest people I have known seemed to be the most happy and content.

"Greed is a bottomless pit which exhausts the person in an endless effort to satisfy the need without ever reaching satisfaction."
– Erich Fromm

"No man is more cheated than the selfish man."
– Henry Ward Beecher

"I fear the popular notion of success stands in direct opposition in all points to the real and wholesome success. One adores public opinion, the other, private opinion; one, fame, the other, desert; one, feats, the other, humility; one, lucre, the other, love."
– Ralph Waldo Emerson

There are many examples of those who hoard wealth, and live selfishly. Some must be driven by unresolved issues relating to loneliness and a confused existence. They may be acting to fill a void that never seems to be filled no matter what they do, where they go, how many things they purchase, or how successful they seem to be with investments. When they experience empty feelings, they try to fill them by purchasing things – cars, homes, furniture, clothes, gadgets, and stuff. They may try surrounding themselves with pretty people, or people they consider to be hip, which is a sure way to fill a life with fair-weather friends who vanish as soon as strength of character is needed. They may do so with the false belief that they think they need – or that they can't live without – these things. They may be working to make their life resemble the so-called perfect lives they see in advertising and corporate media. In so doing they surround themselves with commercialized and mass-produced stuff. But it ends up being more accumulated stuff that gets added to the other stuff they own. Just as soon as they sell some of it, or throw it away, they are on to buying more stuff. They may travel, visit places, and see things. And in the quiet times they talk about how they are lonely, bored, not happy, and feel the need for something, but they don't know what it is.

"One of the main reasons wealth makes people unhappy is that it gives them too much control over what they experience. They try to

translate their own fantasies into reality, instead of tasting what
reality itself has to offer."
— Philip Slater

Some people bring that mindset into their relationships, which
they go through like they do clothing. Just as soon as they think
someone is the right fit, they start to look for the flaws while
exaggerating what they see as the reasons they shouldn't be with the
person. Their communication is a pose they can't hold onto, and it
quickly becomes tiresome and weak. Any problem they may have is
blamed on another person. Through all of this it is likely that they are
not accessing their intellect, talent, skills, truth, or love.

Even when people turn to self-help books they may be presented
with the message that success in life is rewarded with and validated
by owning stuff, by the presence of pretty people, and by vast
quantities of money. For instance, one author of positive-thinking
books mentions his resort-like mansion, as if that possession validates
him as a success. His focus on wealth can be viewed as a failure in
that he appears to be idealizing an environmentally unsustainable life,
and promotes the greed lifestyle as ideal. Instead of being part of the
solution, he is part of Earth's problem. I wonder if he feels as if his
housekeeper, lands keeper, and other servants are failures in life
because they don't own mansions. Maybe he pays well.

"No richness is innocent. Richness around the world is the
result of other people's poverty."
— Eduardo Galeano

It seems people who are successful at hoarding wealth do just
that, become very good at it, and display it in extravagance.

Where does it get them?

There are people who have several mansions or posh dwellings
on various parts of the planet, and they spend their time shuffling
between their homes. It is as if they are not content with anything, and
they try to create the perfect resort homes to escape to when they
want to escape from their other resort homes. When they get more
money they also get more stuff that accumulates to the point that they
either have to hire someone to help get rid of it for them, or they
spend more money to place it in storage units. I know of one person
who owns several homes, and I have heard this person complain of
being bored. Ruling over all of those possessions apparently has
brought no meaning, and may have created a bigger quagmire.

"Once you start to see through the myth of status, possessions, and unlimited consumption as a path to happiness, you'll find that you have all kinds of freedom and time. It's like a deal you can make with the universe: I'll give up greed for freedom. Then you can start putting your time to good use."
– David Edwards

"The poor man is not he who is without a cent, but he who is without a dream."
– Harry Kemp

"I have never been a millionaire. But I have enjoyed a crackling fire, a glorious sunset, a walk with a friend, and a hug from a child. There are plenty of life's tiny delights for all of us."
– Jack Anthony

I have been around some of the wealthy people. One thing that is noticeable is that they aren't a whole lot different from anyone else. They sleep, they eat, they have to take care of their basic needs, they tie their shoes, and, probably most of all, they want to be loved. They just happen to be surrounded by stuff that is more expensive than stuff that other people are surrounded by. And they play that game.

"Happiness resides not in possessions, and not in gold, happiness dwells in the soul."
– Democritus

"If there is to be any peace it will come through being, not having."
– Henry Miller

Among all the people I have been around, no matter if they are rich or poor, I have noticed that the people who have connected strongly with their talents are the happier ones, and more so if they have healthful relationships, eat healthfully, and exercise.

"Let your capital be simplicity and contentment."
– Henry David Thoreau

Avoid getting caught up in the symbols of wealth, symbols of success, and symbols of happiness. Just because the symbol exists does not mean that what it represents also exists. Many people do get caught up in believing that if they surround themselves with certain things representative of wealth, success, and happiness, they are then truly wealthy, successful, and happy. That is one sure way to get into financial debt, such as by using credit cards to purchase things to carry on the façade that is only held up by more ruinous debt.

Symbols don't always correlate with reality. This is especially true in a society reliant on loans and credit cards, and in which people have placed such financial burdens on themselves they are working simply to maintain a life filled with mythological symbolisms of satisfaction in the form of possessions. They are using credit cards and bank loans to mask their true situation, which is that of someone not able to afford what they have fooled themselves into purchasing, and lied to themselves about owning. What they may be most successful at is in creating a façade and in pretending that it is okay to have huge financial burdens to maintain an image of wealth and fake success. Not that they are able to enjoy their faux success so much, because they are too busy working to pay the bills and the lenders.

As I am writing this, the news is filled with stories of people who have overextended themselves, who are losing their homes and belongings, and who are having to face homelessness, unemployment, hunger, the struggle of untreated health conditions, and destitution.

"Why are you so enchanted with this world when a gold mine lies within you? Open your eyes and advance. Return to the root of the root of your own soul."
— Jalal ad-Din Rumi

The majority of the global population lives on what others would consider anything from poverty to extreme poverty. On the other end of the spectrum is the small minority of people who are paid many millions of dollars per year. This includes those company leaders who have been widely criticized for accepting pay and bonuses amounting to several hundred times more than what is earned by the lowest paid workers in the company.

The work of the poorest of the poor maintains the lifestyles of the wealthy. Hoarding wealth damages the poor, society, culture, and community.

"We need 'wake up economics,' where people value each other rather than the accumulation of wealth, power, and prestige."
— Anna and Christine Rowinski

Fame or financial wealth does not equal happiness or health. If it did, the newspapers wouldn't be filled with stories of wealthy people experiencing torrential downpours of life problems, emotional breakdowns, and relationship meltdowns.

If you are constantly engaged in putting on the big façade of your life being royal when it is a big pit of debt, question why you are placing so much focus on appearance.

"If you win, but don't help somebody when you should have, what kind of win is that?"
— Bjoernar Hakensmoen

If you are a person with loads of money, and you feel yourself getting too proud, go spend time volunteering for homeless groups, for abused women's shelters, for organizations helping teenage runaways, and for charities working with those who are otherwise destitute. Help with inner-city reforestation and culinary gardening projects, with soup kitchens, with youth groups, and with animal shelters. Consider working with FoodNotBombs.net, which prepares and vegetarian meals and serves them to the homeless, poor, or anyone who is hungry. Pay for a student's tuition, books, food, clothing, and housing. Fund permaculture groups. Volunteer and/or donate money to groups working to protect the environment, such as The Natural Resources Defense Council, Earth Island Institute, EarthFirst, the Green World Campaign, Sea Shepherd, or an organization that restores forests or protects ocean life. In other words, be active in being a part of the solution to an ailing world.

"This we know: All things are connected. Whatever befalls the Earth befalls us. We did not weave the web of life; we are merely a strand in it. Whatever we do to the web, we do to ourselves."
— Chief Seathl

"Once the game is over, the king and the pawn go back into the same box."
— Italian proverb

"The essence of philosophy is that a man should so live that his happiness shall depend as little as possible on external things."
— Epictetus

Competition for possessions and wealth, and the hoarding of these to ensure happiness and security is a falsehood.

While money can bring certain privileges and freedoms, it does not guarantee happiness, health, friendship, or love.

Having money means only that you can buy stuff, and have access to things. For the wise, being wealthy means they can support organizations focused on improving the condition of wildlife, the environment, and Earth.

If you are one who has been caught up in hoarding money – or focusing on that as a goal – release the feeling that you need to judge yourself as successful or not successful based on money.

"Enjoy the journey, enjoy every moment, and quit worrying about winning and losing."
— Matt Biondi

"There are two ways to get enough: one is to continue to accumulate more and more. The other is to desire less."
— G. K. Chesterton

Free yourself of the false notion of competition. Realize there is none. You are only working to improve yourself – regardless of what others are doing, saying, accumulating, or experiencing.

"The trouble with the rat race is that even if you win you're still a rat."
— Lilly Tomlin

"I do not try to dance better than anyone else. I only try to dance better than myself."
— Mikhail Baryshnikov

Stop comparing yourself to other people. It is a waste of your talents, intellect, time, energy, and resources. The competition mindset will distract you from what you need to focus on, and will drag you down below any fault you could possibly find in others.

Comparing yourself to others is degrading to your spirit, and to others. It weakens you.

"Always dream and shoot higher than you know you can do. Don't bother just to be better than your contemporaries or predecessors. Try to be better than yourself."
— William Faulkner

"Each of us is meant to have a character all our own, to be what no other can exactly be, and do what no other can exactly do."
— William Ellery Channing

"Often people attempt to live their lives backwards: they try to have more things, or more money, in order to do more of what they want so they will be happier. The way it actually works is the reverse. You must first be who you really are, then do what you need to do, in order to have what you want."
— Margaret Young

By working to develop your intellect, talents, and abilities, as well as your confidence, health, and level of standards, without feeling as if you need to keep up with anyone else, or compare yourself to anyone, you will be living your life.

"We must break away from the widespread belief that bigger, faster, newer, and more is always better. We need to reconsider what constitutes 'wealth.'"
– Greg Seaman

Set the pace for improving your situation and you may be surprised how you can help inspire others to do the same.

Replace the false sense of competition with the real sense of inspiration, and then you will begin to feel a more healthful energy complementing your positive thoughts and actions.

"No matter how much money you have, you can lose it."
– Michael J. Fox

The world is filled with people living their lives by the standards of other peoples' principles. And the world is filled with people caught up in paying attention to the way other people live – including fictional characters that appear in movies and TV shows.

Just as you don't have any competitors, you also don't have any enemies. There may be people who you don't care to be around, those who you would be better off avoiding, and some who you would be better off avoiding at all cost, but you don't need to think of people as enemies or competitors.

"Your opponent, in the end, is never really the player on the other side of the net, or the swimmer in the next lane, or the team on the other side of the field, or even the bar you must high-jump. Your opponent is yourself, your negative internal voices, your level of determination."
– Grace Lichtenstein

When you relieve yourself of the feeling that you are not competing with others, you will begin to understand the concept that there is no competition. All you are doing is working to improve your life – regardless of what others are doing. Disconnecting from the competitive energy is liberating and empowering.

"A common conception of security is an achievement or possession on the physical plane. But an abiding sense of security can never come from possession or from achievement. Security comes only when we have established our constant oneness with our soul."
– Sri Chinmoy

"One characteristic of winners is they always look upon themselves as a do-it-yourself project."
– Denis Waitley

111

"Don't believe that winning is really everything. It's more important to stand for something. If you don't stand for something, what do you win?"
— Lane Kirkland

"One of the most expensive things you could ever do is pay attention to the wrong people."
— Ed Mylett

The person to pay attention to, to spend the time helping, to advance into their possible for a better future, is yourself. That is, so you can be the best version of yourself, and will be a benefit for you, for those you love, and for your community.

Seek and work to place yourself in a situation of health in which you can flourish so you can be the best you can be for you, for the people in your life, for the community, for society, for culture, and for helping to heal Earth and protect wildlife.

Don't judge yourself according to what pop society views as worthy or unworthy, or according to the endless game of gathering material possessions that can overwhelm, sink, and bury you.

"Seeking fame, money, or beauty is a bottomless pit. Pursuing growth, kindness, trust, and health is a path to flourishing."
— Adam M. Grant

"Success is the progressive realization of a worthy ideal."
— Earl Nightingale

Take the risk of being who you are, not who you think you should be based on comparing yourself to others, or conforming to trendy concepts.

"Maybe it won't work out. Maybe it won't be what you wanted. Or it may just be the adventure of a lifetime. Take some chances."
— J. Mike Fields

No longer compare yourself to others.

"Since you are like no other being ever created since the beginning of time, you are incomparable."
— Brenda Ueland

# Talent

"If you have a talent, use it in every which way possible. Don't hoard it. Don't dole it out like a miser. Spend it lavishly, like a millionaire intent on going broke."
— Brenda Francis

"Having talent is like having blue eyes. You don't admire a man for the color of his eyes. I admire a man for what he does with his talent."
— Anthony Quinn

Imagine if there were a Black child from an extremely poor family living in a society largely dismissive and inconsiderate of, and abusive to dark-skinned people. Imagine if this Black boy had a most unfortunate thing happen to him, such as losing his sight at an early age. Imagine that instead of working through that problem, and putting it in a place so he could at least function to the best of his abilities, he instead spent his life in the depths of self-pity. Imagine if he never discovered and developed his talents. Imagine that, if instead of trying to make his life work, he stayed in his parents' home, never went anywhere, and did nothing with his time because he was too busy dwelling in self-pity. Imagine if his parents then died while he was still a young boy and he ended up living on the streets doing nothing with his time, and only took the smallest bit of effort to get by in his blind and self-pitiful state. Furthering his difficulties, he allowed himself to be beaten down by the prejudices held by others

113

who didn't like dark-skinned people, and who didn't feel comfortable around blind people. Imagine if this boy grew into a man and never discovered what he could have become if he had discovered and used his talents.

"Things turn out best for the people who make the best of the way things turn out."
– Art Linkletter

Imagine a different set of life situations for the blind Black boy from the poor home. In this situation he had still lost not only his sight, but also his parents at a young age. He also lived in a time when laws and people worked strongly against Black Americans. But this time the boy did not dwell in self-pity. Imagine that he went on to develop his talents, and despite some other life difficulties – including some of his own making – he broke through the obstacles that seemed to chase him. Imagine that he used his intellect, talents, and abilities to become a talented, world-famous musician so inspirational and dramatic that his life was made into an award-winning film. Imagine if he happened to be named Ray Charles.

"Great talents, by the rust of disuse grow lethargic and shrink from what they were."
– Ovid

"What and how much had I lost by trying to do only what was expected of me, instead of what I myself had wished to do?"
– Ralph Ellison

Consider that you may have given up on some of the very best graces with which you have been blessed. Maybe you have buried what may be your most beneficial qualities beneath a pile of self-pity, repression, conformity, or denial. Perhaps your thinking has been altered to the point that there is a blackout of power in regions of your intellect in which your elegance dwells. You may have made the mistake of denying your abilities for so long that you forgot what they are. Maybe you are aware of this, and maybe you blame situations and other people. But who is it that really made the agreement to avoid nurturing your talent, craft, skill, and ability? Is it you who continues to do so?

"If you have made mistakes, even serious ones, there is always another chance for you. What we call failure is not the falling down, but the staying down."
– Mary Pickford

Understand that the life of Ray Charles turned out to be so incredible because he used the power of his mind to make it that way. When he fell down, he got back up. He worked his patterns of thought into patterns of sound called songs that continue to entertain and inspire the people all over the planet who listen to his music.

"I try to tell the young kids there are two cardinal rules: You should approach creativity with humility and have your success with grace. It's a gift from God. You don't deserve it. You are a vehicle of a higher power. Don't abuse it."
– Quincy Jones

The successes experienced by people who have physical limitations is inspirational. They reveal that determination and persistence can pay off, that a healthy attitude is empowering, and that working to attain goals is dignified.

"The only thing worse than being blind is having sight but no vision."
– Helen Keller

Helen Keller is often given as an example of someone who overcame seemingly impossible odds to live an amazing life. When she was nineteen months old Keller became ill with what was possibly meningitis or scarlet fever. The illness left her both blind and deaf. She became an angry, frustrated child.

Keller learned to communicate by feeling the hands of an incredible six-year-old girl named Martha Washington, who was the Keller family cook's daughter. It wasn't until Keller was nearly seven years old that she began to recognize the hand movements of her caretaker, Anne Sullivan, as being the alphabet she could use to spell words. By first learning to communicate by spelling with her hands, and feeling the hands of those spelling words to her, Keller went on to learn Braille in several languages.

By age 24 Keller had earned a Bachelor of Arts degree from Radcliff College. With companions, Keller traveled the world and became an author who spoke out against war, campaigned for women's rights, and engaged in other humanitarian causes.

"Just because a man lacks the use of his eyes doesn't mean he lacks vision."
– Stevie Wonder

There is a long list of physically challenged people who have made great successes of their lives. Interestingly, an even longer list

115

can be made of able-bodied people who have given into failure and defeat. There also are people who have accomplished things many thought would be impossible. This reveals that many people are only limited with what they can accomplish by the limits they place on themselves through their thoughts.

"Do not let what you cannot do interfere with what you can do."
– John Wooden

In the lives of people throughout history, and in present-day people who have become greatly successful, it is often easy to recognize a pattern of persistence in action, and a sustained focus on goals. They had faith that they could accomplish their goals, then they demonstrated this faith through actions utilizing their intellect. They didn't simply sit around talking and thinking about what they wanted to do, they went out and did it. Their concentration may have been broken on occasion, but they continued working on their goals and eventually experienced achievement.

I am often around creative people, including musicians, artists, actors, and especially, because I run a screenwriting workshop, writers. It is sad to see when they get discouraged, disappointed, and feel a lack of belief in their abilities and potential.

"The real tragedy of life is not in being limited to one talent, but in the failure to use that one talent."
– Edgar W. Work

Someone I know who is an amazing actor, with an incredible ability to do accents, and has what seems to be everything it would take to be getting work in TV and film, gave up on show biz, and he works a job that is far below his potential as he struggles in what is essentially poverty. I've encouraged him to at least stay involved in theatre after his day job, and continue to work with his talents. That hasn't happened, either.

There seems to be nothing anyone can do about it. He would have to be the one to think the thoughts to trigger the actions needed to get back into the game. He might feel as if nobody valid recognizes his talents, but if those talents go completely unused, how could anyone ever recognize what they don't see?

"We can't take any credit for our talents. It's how we use them that counts."
– Madeleine L'Engle

Use your talents. Build skills through repeatedly practicing your talents.

"You are the only person on Earth who can use your ability."
– Zig Ziglar

Some people only want to start at the stop, and are unwilling to put the work in to improve their skills, dexterity, and strengths. They might think it is too difficult. Is the life they chose to be living far below their potential any easier? Is it better for them? Are they happier and healthier that way?

To get what you hope to have, you, specifically you, with your mind, your actions, and your communications, that means specifically you need to take the steps to get there. Nobody can do it for you.

Develop your skills. Learn. Study. Do the mental and physical work. Every day.

You can work to attain the rightful things in life that you hope to attain. Put in the effort, daily, and, through work, continue aiming for the goals you'd like to reach.

"There is a vitality, a life force, an energy, a quickering that is translated through you into action, and because there is only one of you in all of time, this expression is unique. And if you block it, it will never exist through any other medium and it will be lost. The world will not have it. It is not your business to determine how good it is nor how valuable nor how it compares with other expressions. It is your business to keep it yours clearly and directly, to keep the channel open."
– Martha Graham

Go about your days knowing that you are a unique individual capable of using your talents, intellect, perception, yearning, instinct, knowledge, power, faith, and energy to do your best to create a life that is right for you.

"Tension is who you think you should be. Relaxation is who you are."
– Chinese proverb

Know that you do not have to compete with anyone. You are a unique person with no need of comparing yourself to anyone but yourself. You are capable of attaining that which is right for you, and for nobody else.

"Treat yourself like someone you love and respect."
– J. Mke Fields

"There is a fountain of youth: it is your mind, your talents, the creativity you bring to your life and the lives of people you love. When you learn to tap this source, you will truly have defeated age."
— Sophia Loren

"When I was 15, I spent a month working on an archeological dig. One of the archeologists asked those kinds of 'getting to know you' questions you ask young people: Do you play sports? What's your favorite subject? And I told him, 'No, I don't play any sports. I do theater, I'm in choir, I play the violin and piano, I used to take art classes.' And he went, 'That's amazing!' And I said, 'But I'm not good at any of them.' And he said something then that I will never forget and which absolutely blew my mind: 'I don't think being good at things is the point of doing them. I think you've got all these wonderful experiences with different skills, and that all teaches you things and makes you an interesting person, no matter how well you do them.' And that honestly changed my life. Because I went from failure, someone who hadn't been talented enough at anything to excel, to someone who did things because I enjoyed them. I had been raised in such an achievement-oriented environment, so inundated with the myth of talent, that I thought it was only worth doing things if you could 'win' at them."
— Kurt Vonnegut

# School Days

"A young child is, indeed, a true scientist, just one big question mark. What? Why? How? I never cease to marvel at the recurring miracle of growth, to be fascinated by the mystery and wonder of this brave enthusiasm."
– Victoria Wagner

"I have never let my schooling interfere with my education."
– Mark Twain

"The only thing that interferes with my learning is my education."
– Albert Einstein

When speaking with any group of people about their school days it becomes obvious that there is a wide variety of educational experiences. Some people had skilled and helpful teachers, and excelled in school. Some received better educations at public schools than other students received in what were considered to be the better, private schools.

Another thing that becomes obvious when speaking with people about their childhood education is that attitude and circumstances have much to do with what people learn, how they learn it, and what they do with it.

"Education is too important to be left solely to the educators."
– Francis Keppel

"A teacher affects eternity; he can never tell where his influence stops."
— Henry B. Adams

"We are always too busy for our children; we never give them the time or interest they deserve. We lavish gifts upon them; but the most precious gift — our personal association, which means so much to them — we give grudgingly."
— Mark Twain

Some people grew up in what appeared to be so-called ideal neighborhoods where everything appeared to be proper and in its place, but where certain children were not in good situations because of various issues within their community, within their families, or within their schools. Their situations may not have been conducive to a healthful place for them to study, to learn, or to live. Many opportunities that could have been present for them were shut off in ways that may have had to do with their parents' choices; their school administrator's or teacher's choices; or the children may simply have been caught up in wasting much of their time; or they were not in a household with attentive parents or parent figures who would have nurtured a better learning environment. They might have also had learning disabilities, and other issues that were not recognized, or were otherwise undermining for them.

"You may have tangible wealth untold, caskets of jewels, and coffers of gold. Richer than I you can never be — I had a mother who read to me."
— Strickland Gillilan

Other people may have grown up in households in the most undesirable neighborhoods, yet they were able to obtain an education far better than children living in the better neighborhoods with what appeared to be high-quality school systems.

The children who lived in the worst parts of town may have had attentive parents or parent figures; teachers who cared; nurturing mentors; special school programs; healthful food that provided for high brain function; and probably most important of all, an attitude and curious mind open to learning and study.

Even children who were in terrible neighborhoods and problematic households sometimes exceed far beyond what would be expected from a person in their situation.

"The mother's heart is the child's schoolroom."
— Henry Ward Beecher

Some parents only seek to have children who take after them, no matter how lowly or in which limited way those parents live. That alone can hold back many children, frustrating them in their forced disconnection to who they really are and what they can excel in, as their parents expect them to be replicants, which is an impossible situation. As if the children are expected and even required to become only what the parents want them to be, within a wall of required behaviors and choices, including clothing, relationships, profession, skills, beliefs, recreation, tastes, manners, music, and other matters. The situation might work out, with the children wanting to emulate their parents, and taking on the same interests, skills, talents, flavors, and life practices. Or, strife, frustration, and harmful rebellion could take over, fracturing the relationship, even to the point of abuse, assault, and ruinous relations, and greatly unwise choices.

"No man, for any considerable period, can wear one face to himself and another to the multitude without finally getting bewildered as to which may be the true."
– Nathaniel Hawthorne

Children are not robots that will function to set designs and thought patterns.

"Your children are not your children. They are the sons and daughters of life's longing for itself. They come through you, but not from you. And though they are with you, yet they belong not to you. You may give them your love, but not your thoughts – for they have their own thoughts. You may house their bodies, but not their souls, for their souls dwell in the house of tomorrow, which you cannot visit, not even in your dreams."
– Khalil Gibran

It is unfortunate that people anywhere would allow a child to be living in a situation where the child is endangered by, abused by, or otherwise treated terribly by adults. Children growing up in households where abuse and/or neglect are present typically are not able to learn on a level equal to their age – especially when the abuse situation is perpetual.

Stress, lack of sleep, and bad nutrition are three issues that directly impact the way the brain – and the person – grows and functions. Continual stress and poverty have been found to hinder brain cell growth, and to impact thought and memory processes.

Children in terrible situations, including those related to bad diet, abuse, financial insecurity, feelings of helplessness, constant drama,

121

chronic worry, and/or the continual presence of fear, can experience a sort of learning paralysis. Instead of being attentive, their minds may be so disturbed by their predicament that their attention level has broken, impeding their ability to learn and progress. They may be hyperactive, which might be related to the continual consumption of unhealthful food and lack of structure and meaning, or they may be so overwhelmed with their problems that they simply spend much of their time daydreaming, mentally escaping from their situations.

"It is easier to build strong children than to repair broken men."
– Frederick Douglass

If you grew up in a terrible situation and are troubled, do not give up on yourself, or sacrifice your future to the combination of low-quality diet, thought, communication, or behavior.

Know that you can use your body's amazing ability to heal and you can transform into a much more healthful being.

The depths of despair, anguish, sadness, and ruin you may have experienced are only examples of how far your life can advance in the other direction when you continually work to apply the healing and restorative processes to your life.

If you lacked the presence of responsible adults to nurture and foster your best qualities, know that you can become the responsible adult in your life who will bring out everything wonderful within you while maintaining a diet, exercise, study, and work schedule in which you can thrive. I implore you to rectify your situation.

Because the brain wires itself in accordance with our experiences, those who grow up under the constant threat of fear may have an abundance of neural growth in the amygdala region of the brain, which is the area dealing with anger and fear.

When those who have grown up in an extremely unhealthful household are exposed to healthful situations free of the presence of fear and danger, it can take time for them to begin functioning more healthfully. This is because the brain needs to learn how to deal with a new set of situations.

Low-quality nutrition and bad treatment are known to affect a person's voice quality, breathing, speech, eye movement, mannerisms, posture, sleep, and concentration. When low-quality nutrition is combined with stress and fear, which can trigger the brain to release the natural body chemicals, adrenaline and cortisol, which trigger defensive behavior. A child regularly experiencing those conditions is not in a state of mind conducive to concentration, learning, or healthful growth.

"Concentration is the secret of strength."
– Ralph Waldo Emerson

I was a below-average student, and barely passed every grade. I was called names, disregarded by teachers, even told by some that I was a waste. My parents rarely said much to me. When they did, it was almost always on the level of insults, belittlement, dismissal, discouragement, name-calling, mockery, and ridicule. Other family members mirrored that attitude toward me. While a child, I was never in a good situation. Fear, anxiety, avoidance, diversion, and keeping to myself was my common tone, and done with the goal of avoiding bad treatment. It often didn't work. As an unprotected, neglected, and abused child, all sorts of brutality and assaults happened. There were no grandparents, aunts, or uncles, and nobody to turn to for help. Alcoholism, depression, frustration, regret, poverty, tragedies, anger, and many unfortunate situations ruled the household. Because I didn't talk much, my communication skills were lacking, and I had an unusual accent. In high school, my classmates thought it was funny to give me the title of "most likely to fail." I graduated completely unprepared for life, and ignorant about just about anything that mattered to building a healthful existence. My view of life was a kaleidoscope of cluelessness, perplexity, inadequacy, and confusion.

It is unlikely anyone around me as a child would have thought I would write and co-write books that are in libraries around the world, or that I would work on screenplays made into movies and TV shows.

If you grew up in a terrible situation, it is likely that your brain didn't grow and function in healthful ways. Your concentration skills were not given an ability to blossom as you were busy dealing with defending yourself, strategizing your safety, and worrying about your situation. Sleep deprivation also could have been a factor in your ability to function healthfully. That was my childhood

If you grew up in an unfortunate situation, it is likely that you did not have access to foods providing the nutrients your brain needed for the most healthful growth. Unfortunately – and more commonly – even in households where money is abundant, children are often eating low-quality foods rich in processed sugars and salts, in bleached grains, in saturated fats, trans fats, fried fats, and in MSG (monosodium glutamate), inflammatories, synthetic chemical dyes, flavors, scents, and preservatives.

"Behaviors and thoughts that relate to hope, love, and happiness can change the brain – just as fear, stress, and anxiety can change it."
– Eric Kanel

123

Fortunately, the human brain can improve with a change in diet, exercise, activities, education, and surroundings. It can heal from damage and neglect. Keys include avoiding addictive substances, a diet rich in fruits and vegetables, and regular exercise, and study.

Through setting of goals, daily study, use of intellect, practicing of talents, regular exercise, healthful foods, and nurturing social interaction, the person's abilities in attention, memory, and sequencing can be improved, and they can reconfigure how to deal with life in a healthful environment in a way that advances their ability to prosper and experience higher satisfaction.

"Healing is not a matter of technique or mechanism; it is a work of spirit."
– Rachel Naomi Remen

All cells within the body continually work to eliminate waste products and toxins while taking in the better-quality nutrients they are exposed to while releasing lower-quality substances.

If you grew up eating the lowest-quality foods, your brain is badly in need of quality nutrients.

When you change your diet to one that is more healthful, and stick with it, you will begin to feel a clarity of thought you had not experienced. This is a sign your brain has begun to heal and function at a higher level. You will likely also notice a stronger drive to learn, to be more active, and to participate in activities where your talent and intellect can flourish, and where your better qualities become more present and alive.

"And the day came when the risk to remain tight in a bud was more painful than the risk it took to blossom."
– Anais Nin

The brain works and grows in tune with what it is you are doing, hearing, saying, seeing, feeling, experiencing, and eating. When you become involved in activities, your brain functions in tune with what you are doing. The more certain parts of the brain are used, the more neurons will wire into and function in those parts.

The better your level of nutrition with truly vibrant foods, the better the brain can repair, reconfigure, and function.

"We don't challenge kids in schools. We don't challenge them to think; we don't challenge them to create. We challenge them to get good enough grades to get into a good enough college."
– Bob Compton

Many of us were not intellectually challenged when we were young. What we were presented with may have bored us and set us in a pattern of being accustomed to mundanity. This may have been because it was not of our interest, or we existed in a situation preventing us from being open to our interests.

Peer pressure, low-quality nutrition, family drama, bad treatment, lack of nurturing, and many other aspects of our childhood may have interfered with our attention, perception, attitude, and ability to learn what would have been most beneficial for us.

"We worry about what a child will become tomorrow, yet we forget that he is someone today."
– Stacia Tauscher

"That is the difference between good teachers and great teachers: good teachers make the best of a pupil's means; great teachers foresee a pupil's ends."
– Maria Callas

Some of us may have had teachers who were not at a level most helpful to our capabilities and talents.

Some of us may have been in school situations with inadequate or absent resources, or where, for any number of reasons, certain concepts that would have provided intellectual stimulation and would have been most beneficial to our learning were not presented. We may have detected that what was being taught wasn't exactly the truth. This may ring true when common history books and their mythological and idealistically whitewashed hero aspects are taken into consideration.

In certain ways, while we were children, we may have functioned at a level that was above our age group while we were continually presented with information that was below our level of learning.

"It is a miracle that curiosity survives formal education."
– Albert Einstein

"If I ran a school, I'd give the average grade to the ones who gave me all the right answers, for being good parrots. I'd give the top grades to those who made a lot of mistakes and told me about them, and then told me what they learned from them."
– Richard Buckminster Fuller

"Knowledge has to be improved, challenged, and increased constantly, or it vanishes."
– Peter F. Drucker

Many school systems are not funded sufficiently to allow for students to be nurtured in ways beneficial for their talents, skills, intellect, yearning, and life.

Many people grew up being taught at only a certain level of education based on what a board of educators decided as being what the typical person needed to know to function in society.

Some school administrators may think there is no use trying to excel in educating certain children because the children are most likely to follow their parents' footsteps, living lives far below their potential. Some teachers may discourage students from learning.

Some of the educational neglect has to do with dominant religious pressure, religious scrupulosity, antiquated concepts, and toxic belief systems about what is proper and godly. Under those circumstances, children might be blocked from learning certain concepts, and banned from reading certain books.

Teachers are the product of their background and schooling – which may have been lacking. They are also products of what they were taught to believe about life, and their function within it. They might have grown up with limiting beliefs dominating their household, family, community, culture, and communication.

"We are each so much more than what some reduce to measuring."
– Karen Kaiser Clark

"Most of the people who make it through the education system and get into the elite universities are able to do it because they've been willing to obey a lot of stupid orders for years and years. That's the way I did it, for example. Some people go along with it because they figure, 'Okay, I'll do any stupid thing that asshole says, because I want to get ahead.' Others do it because they've internalized the values. But after a while, those two things tend to get sort of blurred. But you do it, or else you're out. You ask too many questions and you're going to get in trouble."
– Noam Chomsky

Some ways of teaching don't connect with students, don't speak to them, and have little or nothing to do with the reality in which the students are living. Some ways of teaching tell a child what to learn based on a certain ideal learning situation that often does not exist.

Some schools teach mostly trivial things, which is excellent for giving good grades to students who are good at memorizing. But it doesn't work for students who may have high intelligence and are capable of amazing things, are brilliant in their own ways, but who are not good at memorizing.

"The art of teaching is the art of assisting discovery."
– Mark Van Doren

Some teachers only pay attention to the students who are dressed and groomed in or structured in a certain way, while ignoring the students who are more unique, or who are from homes where resources are limited.

Some teachers may have been interested in teaching in ways that would have been greatly beneficial for the students, but the teachers were bogged down by a school system that worked against any sort of genuine education.

Some teachers may have been excellent, but the students were caught in the unfortunate bully mindset, that is of thinking it was cool to disregard their teachers – a trait they might have learned in a troubled household.

"The aim of public education is not to spread enlightenment at all: it is simply to reduce as many individuals as possible to the same safe level, to breed a standard citizenry, to put down dissent and originality."
– Henry Louis Mencken

Some students never saw what they wanted to be. They had nobody to relate to, had no good examples, had no role models, and may not have had anyone capable of nurturing them in accordance with their intellect. Because of these situations, they may not have succeeded, and may have become lost in living far from what they would naturally have exceeded in. By their teenage years they may have gotten into mind-altering substances that played with their imagination that was otherwise never used, or used very little, or was discouraged from being used. When they did express themselves, they may have been shamed as being eccentric, assuming, or outlandish. All of this may have brought them to live regretfully and to be filled with despisement, dismissiveness, frustration, and a jaded attitude.

"The important thing is this: to be ready at any moment to sacrifice what you are for what you could become."
– Charles Du Bos

People can decide at any moment to focus on being part of their problem, or choose to be part of their solution. They can use their energy and time to complain and point fingers to place blame and shame, and spend their time responding to end results. Or, they can choose to get busy with the work involved in making their dream of a new life formulate right where they are. It is up to them if they work to make life better for them, and for everyone around them.

"Education is not the filling of a pail, but the lighting of a fire."
– William Butler Yeats

At any time and in any part of the world there may be a child who is a potential prodigy. They may become one of those who revolutionizes their culture, or who formulate an entirely unexplored aspect of humanity, of sciences, of arts, of agriculture, or of something else not previously discovered, and who transform society.

The potential of becoming incredible is not limited to children. At any age people may awaken from slothful lives and excel at something transformative – not only their lives, but also the lives of others.

"If a man does not keep pace with his companions, perhaps it is because he hears a different drummer. Let him step to the music which he hears, however measured or far away."
– Henry David Thoreau

As the saying goes, you can't help someone who doesn't want to be helped.

No matter what our childhood situation was, our attitude may be the result of what level of education we received. Luckily for us, we can change our attitude.

The inner drive or yearning of a person may be the force that brings about a successful life. Clicking into that force is the person's choice. That plays into attitude.

A healthful attitude may always have been a part of a person's character. If it isn't, at any moment, they can decide to change it.

Part of transitioning into a more healthful person may have to do with learning new ways of communicating, of conducting ourselves, of spending our time, of supplying ourselves with higher-quality mind and body nutrition, of nurturing our talents, and of accessing our love.

Some people may have grown up in situations with everything good available to them, but they chose to be shut off from being healthful. Others may have grown up in troubling situations, but had an attitude somehow far more healthful than the people around them.

"Men take on the nature, the habits, and the power of thought of those with whom they associate."
– Napoleon Hill

"Nothing of me is original. I am the combined effort of everybody I've ever known."
– Chuck Palahniuk

Just as we may have adapted to the manners of the people we were around when we were young, we also may adapt to the spectrum of behaviors of the people who are presently around us.

As part of my healing, I've visited with psychologists. They've told me I'm "on the spectrum." That is, the autism spectrum. It should not be a surprise. I call it the "light spectrum," because I'm simply lit differently. That includes my nerve wiring, the electromagnetic fields within me, the biophotons among my cells, my molecules of emotion, and how I electromagnetically and chemically interact with the magnetic fields and chemistry of Nature.

In one way or another, we are all connected with the magnetic fields and chemistry of Nature – including through our food choices, the water and air we take in, the trillions of cells of our microbiome, the sun light, the solar electron neutrinos, the interplanetary energy fields, and the surface contacts.

Being different is normal. We can't realistically expect anyone to be just like us. We are all wired in our own way, functioning and carrying on in our way, having sensory experiences that impact us to our most base substances, and dealing with what life throws at us.

Some of us may have been in childhood situations where we were regularly exposed to lying, excuse-making, stealing, slander, dishonesty, deception, violence, the poverty mentality, substance abuse, bad nutrition, and every manner of ruinous and terrible behavior. The unfortunate choices and behaviors of the elders may have been adapted into our common way of thinking, and lowered us into accepting a low-level life. These are things from which we will need to educate ourselves away, and then retune our thoughts, expectations, communication, and actions.

"The impact of abuse, neglect, and assault on a child is profound, even as much as brain damage – which it is."
– Gabor Maté

You don't have to remain stuck in the wounds of trauma from what you experienced. You can learn and grow and participate in healthier life interaction, expression, and reception. Perhaps how you do this will help not only you, but the people you love, and others.

"Be an opener of doors for such as come after thee."
– Ralph Waldo Emerson

129

Don't wait around for your life to heal. Get busy doing it, every day.

You can choose to educate yourself in any area of knowledge you are lacking. In today's world many people have access to all sorts of resources to learn about whatever their interests may be. By using information provided by books, libraries, seminars, and the Internet, a person can receive an education that is likely far better than what was available to them when they were young.

The Internet has introduced a whole new opportunity for learning about everything from history to music, literature and art, from health, fitness, and nutrition, to economics, science, and social science, and from traditional topics to those that were not covered in school – and may have not even existed when we were young.

**"There are two kinds of light – the glow that illuminates, and the glare that obscures."**
– James Thurber

Unfortunately, many choose to use their time and resources to satisfy their most base desires, as they feed from the lowest aspects of life they could possibly open for themselves – including through the blaring grotesqueness found on the Internet.

Nowadays those people who feel they didn't receive the education they should have had can get busy educating themselves.

We are all educated, but in which way are we educated, and what can we do about it to educate ourselves in a more healthful way conducive to what we most need to be healthful?

**"I just wish people would realize that anything's possible, if you try; dreams are made, if people try."**
– Terry Fox

Many people have been stuck in the bottomless grease pit of not exceeding in life, of not using their intellect and talents, or of advancing their skills, of not taking advantage of their opportunities, and of not conducting their lives in ways beneficial to them and to those they love. Many people have given up on their dreams, have settled into a life free of goals, have become slothful in every way, and have otherwise made decisions not in tune with what their life could be if they would instead tune into and use their intellect and beneficial qualities.

**"Emancipate yourself from mental slavery. None but ourselves can free our minds"**
– Bob Marley

Stop thinking you are limited to the level of life you have been experiencing. If you don't like the level of life you are leading, please use your power, thoughts, actions, communication, exercise, nutrition, and whatever resources you have to bring yourself closer to both experiencing and expressing a more healthful level of life.

"You miss 100 percent of the shots you never take."
– Wayne Gretzky

You play a large role in creating your future. What will it be? That is the question. Your thoughts, words, actions, attitude, food choices, and how you spend your time and resources will create the answer.

"It's time to stop into your power – right now. Lose the baggage and deadweight, shake off the energy that doesn't belong, tune into your inner wisdom, take a deep breath. Remember yourself and what you're capable of, and what you are here to do. Visualize your next move, and get moving.."
– Nyle Beck

Fathom your possibilities, set the goals, take the actions, speak the words, and become aligned with what you wish to be within the network of your better qualities to advance into being part of a better human society for all of us.

You may be young. You may be old. Whatever stage of life you are in, these are your school days.

Be your teacher. Engage in life. Learn, live, labor, and love.

"A world full of happiness is not beyond human power to create; the obstacles imposed by inanimate nature are not insuperable. The real obstacles lie in the heart of man, and the cure for these is a firm hope, informed and fortified by thought."
– Bertrand Russell

Be acquainted with and a participant of your better self.

# You Are Not Here

"I think I think, therefore I think I am."
– Ambrose Bierce

"In each of you are one quadrillion cells, 90 percent of which are not human cells. Your body is a community, and without those other microorganisms you would perish in hours. Each human cell has 400 billion molecules conducting millions of processes between trillions of atoms. The total cellular activity in one human body is staggering: one septillion actions at any one moment, a one with twenty-four zeros after it. In a millisecond, our body has undergone ten times more processes than there are stars in the universe – exactly what Charles Darwin foretold when he said science would discover that each living creature was a 'little universe, formed of a host of self-propagating organisms, inconceivably minute, and as numerous as the stars of heaven.'"
– Paul Hawken

"The fundamental delusion of humanity is to suppose that I am here and you are out there."
– Yasutani Roshi

Did you know that you can't be found? I mean, as far as what actually makes you form and grow and think and act and reason, you can't be found. Science can detect substances that interact with each other, such as chemicals and matter that are pretty much somewhat mechanically predictable. Scientists can look into the cells of the body and see what common substances they are made of, and scientists can see how the substances are arranged in various geometric patterns, and how they react to and in combination with each other. Scientists can use lenses to peer into the genes that play a role in determining how certain structures form and function. And scientists have some understanding of the biochemical interactions of the proteins. But other than understanding the human mechanism in an electro/chemical context, scientists can't figure out exactly what is the us that controls us. Scientists can't even determine if what is us is even inside the structure that is us, or if we are outside of us.

"The nature of god is a circle of which the center is everywhere and the circumference is nowhere."
– Empedocles

"You live in illusion and the appearance of things. There is a reality, but you don't know this. When you understand this you will see that you are nothing. And being nothing, you are everything. That is all."
– Kalu Rinpoche

Another thing that is interesting about us is that nothing in our physical structures is touching. There is space between the molecules, protons, electrons, atoms, and the finer particles and substances. There is so much space between the things that comprise us that there are very small substances traveling through the spaces within us, and the substances do this without our even knowing.

"Everything you've learned in school as 'obvious' becomes less and less obvious as you begin to study the universe. For example, there are no solids in the universe. There's not even a suggestion of a solid. There are no absolute continuums. There are no surfaces. There are no straight lines."
– Richard Buckminster Fuller

Unknown numbers of solar electron neutrinos are flowing through our bodies during every split second of every minute of every hour of every day. There is so much space between all the substances we are made of that the neutrinos have no problem traveling through us. The neutrinos are produced by the fusion reaction occurring in the interior of Sun. As they travel away from Sun, the neutrinos travel through space and pass through ordinary matter, including people, plants, and Earth.

In addition to neutrinos, there are multiple types of other substances continuously making their way through us. Gasses consisting of millions of molecules are being absorbed by our lungs and skin during every second of every minute. Gasses consisting of millions of molecules are also being exhaled from our lungs, and are evaporating through our skin, and even through our eyes and fingernails. We also, through drinking, are taking in water, and eliminating it both through our eliminative organs and through our lungs and skin. So much water is continually flowing through us that if we don't replace it every day, our health degrades.

Similar to a lake, you are a body that is a continuum of a flow. A lake may sit, but it is not still. A lake appears to be complete in itself, but there is always something entering, and something exiting. Without the flow, it would not be a lake, but would cease to exist as a lake. So are you.

"Water which is too pure has no fish."
– Ts'ai Ken T'an

All of us consist of a number of life forms, including bacteria. If it weren't for bacteria living around and within us, we would not be alive. Just as we are dependent on bacteria within us, the foods we eat are dependent on bacteria and fungi in the soil.

When taken into consideration that our physical structure does not consist of only one organism, it is easy to understand that we are not a single life form, but many life forms. We depend on many other forms of life to survive, including the plants, the fungi, the soil organisms, and also the wildlife that helps nurture, fertilize, pollinate, and spread plant and other life.

"Every man is more than just himself; he also represents the unique, the very special and always significant and remarkable point at which the world's phenomena intersect, only once in this way, and never again."
– Hermann Hesse

There are spheres of energy surrounding the galaxy. There are also energy fields connecting the planets and moons. There are electrical currents traveling in and around the planets and their moons. There are energy streams between Earth and Sun.

Scientists have been able to measure changes in the current of electricity flowing through Earth where it flows through the magnetic field in mantle rock. The current is formed when the stream of electrically charged atomic particles in the solar wind emitted by Sun interact with the magnetosphere within Earth. All life on Earth is dependent on the communication of this electrical magnetic field just as much as we are dependent on water, air, soil, plants, insects, fish, and other animals, and bacteria, fungi, and all other life forms. That magnetic field is part of what we are interacting with at all times – along with all the substances that pass in and out of us.

"The invitation is about participation, not mere observation. We are not journeying in the universe but with the universe. We are not concerned about living in an evolving world but co-evolving with our world. We are parts of a whole, much greater than the sum of its parts, and yet within each part we are interconnected with the whole."
– Diarmuid O'Murchu

There is a flow of electricity passing through us, and a flow of energy being generated by us. We are generating electricity at all times within every one of our cells, and this electricity helps our body to function. Our actions, including our involuntary movements, generate electricity. Our thoughts affect the flow of electricity in our tissues and this thought-generated energy interacts with the energies of the substances around us.

Our thoughts are also producing molecules with electrical charges. These molecules of emotion are created throughout all our body tissues, and they travel out of us and into the atmosphere, saturating the substances and terrain around us.

"Once we recognize that all matter is actually energy, we can begin to form a new vision of ourselves and the world around us. We begin to realize that our surroundings are not what they seem."
– William Buhlman

Isn't it interesting that when you walk into an ancient building your body may be interacting with molecules once in the bodies of the people who lived in that building hundreds of years in the past? It is also interesting to consider that what we are thinking is creating substances that are saturating the structures around us, and that what we think and say sends forth patterns of energy that become part of the cosmic sound.

Unfortunately, what many people are thinking and saying involves low-quality thoughts and words, such as those revolving around messed up celebrity culture.

One wonders what people in the future will learn about us, and if they will develop tools capable of reading the thought molecules we left behind. They may think our generation once thought so much of a certain celebrity that we considered the person to be some sort of guru or idealized figure, when in reality the celebrity was truly a tragic disaster obsessed with creating and believing their own publicity.

"Keeping your body healthy is an expression of gratitude to the whole cosmos, the trees, the clouds, everything."
– Thich Nhat Hanh

Knowing that you are a form of energy, consider your power and what you are doing with your power. Recognize your consciousness and that you are a consciousness of ability, creativity, yearning, potential, impact, relationship, communication, and community.

"The more science I studied, the more I saw that physics becomes metaphysics and numbers become imaginary numbers. The farther you go into science, the mushier the ground gets. You start to say, 'Oh, there is an order and a spiritual aspect to science.'"
– Dan Brown

"Every human being has etched in his personality the indelible stamp of the Creator."
– Martin Luther King, Jr.

Know that you are a spirit. You hold within you energy that formed not only the structures of your being, but also the plants, animals, and other substances around you.

"No one can stand in these solitudes unmoved, and not feel that there is more in man than the mere breath of his body."
– Charles Darwin

You are a divine expression of love. You may scoff at that thought, but if you are not the expression of what was a loving relationship, you can decide to be an expression of your own love.

"Yes, I am me, but what animates me is what animates Uncle Bob, the cat, the tree, the rock, and all that is. We are packaged differently, but we share the same essence. There are many of us and we are not the same but we are all one."
– Cheri Huber

"When I look inside and see that I am nothing, that's wisdom. When I look outside and see that I am everything, that's love. Between these two my life turns."
– Sri Nisargadatta

Just as the genes within us are a combination of the genes from our Earth parents, the spirit that is truly us is the substance of spiritual genetics which originated from the masterful spirits of whatever

Divinity is – some kind of energy power. Although we may not always succeed in living up to such an honorable spiritual heritage, it is something we can strive for. (Okay, maybe you have, but I have not.)

"All of life is interrelated. We are all caught in an inescapable network of mutuality, tied to a single garment of destiny. Whatever affects one directly affects all indirectly."
– Martin Luther King, Jr.

"We see men haying in the meadow, their heads waving like the grass they cut. In the distance, the wind seemed to bend all alike."
– Henry David Thoreau

# Confidence and Belief

"Let no one be deluded that a knowledge of the path can substitute for putting one foot in front of the other."
– Mary Caroline Richards

Do you want satisfaction? If so, determine what will satisfy you, then work to design your life to bring it about.

Have confidence. Educate yourself on what you need to learn. Utilize the knowledge by doing the work to attain your goals.

Open your mind to possibilities, including that of confidently knowing you can have a life more in tune with your desires.

Write down the things about yourself that you have confidence in, or wish to have confidence in – including in your talents, skills, and abilities, which some people call, *your graces*. They are your better and refining qualities, and are what present your elegance.

"Imagination is the beginning of creation. You imagine what you desire, you will what you imagine, and at last you create what you will."
– George Bernard Shaw

Believe in the power of your self to confidently reformulate into what you want to be.

You have access to tools that can adjust and tune you to be more in alignment with your desired life. These tools are free to you. They are your powers of instinct, yearning, thought, creativity, talent, motivation, and determination. These can all fuel your work.

"Some of the world's greatest feats were accomplished by people not smart enough to know they were impossible."
– Doug Larson

Faith does not mean an organized religion, but of faith in things that are, that may be, and that can become. For you, it is confidence.

I don't follow or practice any one religion, and am not a member of any organized religion. I partially grew up Catholic, and was involved with other religions, but left that organized religious stuff behind, as it appears to be more about money and power than about anything else. Religions can be quite creepy, invasive, controlling, sexist, racist, homophobic, toxic, narcissistic, cultish, hazardous, ruinous, overtaking, and completely outside reality.

I looked around at varieties of religious belief systems. The posing, pretending, grandly washed and revised history, the toxic patriarchy, the strive for power, the random rules made up to control, the money grab, the brainwashing, and the belief in the absolute fiction of organized religion wasn't something I wanted to continue participating in. They are clubs that have nothing to do with eternity. Some say they at least provide a safe place for children. But... considering the number of child abuse and assault cases among various religions and their programs, they also aren't that.

I consider a lot of theories, find much of them to be interesting, and try to live by what I feel to be true. However, I'm also not one to sit around repeatedly reading scriptural writings, nor am I into regularly listening to preachers or ministers dictate their interpretation of theories they think they recognize in – or selectively and cleverly choose from – the various writings they decide to consider sacred, and present their views of it as absolute eternal truth. Often, I found them to be about hate, and relegating who they consider to be the lesser people – the so-called sinners – to be dismissed or banished to some sort of hell, outer darkness, or a permanent detachment from good. As if that validates the commitment to whatever rigidity the religion is advocating. No thank you to their moral doctrine.

Not that I am the perfect example of anything, but I have done enough reading of various religious texts to satisfy me, and would prefer to get out and live and be involved in life. I'm not about sitting in some building every week listening to repetitive religious blabber to participate in collective effervescence to tinge myself with religious scrupulosity. I found church to be not about being sanctified, saved, or helping people make it to some sort of imaginary heaven theme park. It's about wealth and control. Been there, done that.

"Some people regard themselves as perfect, but only because they demand little of themselves."
– Hermann Hesse

Many people get caught up in following various preachers, ministers, or other guru types. They spend money supporting, and spend time listening to someone preach, perhaps spend time hoping for enlightenment, to be validated, or to be rescued. From what?

Religions plant the fear, then pose as the solution to the fear.

What is enlightenment if you aren't getting out and using it? What is so important about being sure to spend hours every week listening to someone speak, and more hours working to make the money to donate to the church, and perhaps even more time volunteering to help run the organization? Is that enlightenment in action, or is enlightened action more defined by using your talents, skills, craft, intellect, and other beneficial qualities?

Why do people give up so much of their power by having someone tell them what to think and how to pray and what to hope for, especially when they end up not having much of a life because they are so involved in the so-called worship, rituals, and conforming to the belief system? Could it be that they don't have enough confidence in themselves, or that they have given up their power? Could it be that the religions are stagnating people to not question, to not be curious, and to perpetually be the same?

How deep into conformity are you supposed to go to remain a member of an institution focused on getting money from followers?

How shut off to other parts of life do you have to be, and what beneficial parts of you are you shutting down to conform to a belief system built on greed to gain status, power, and investment money?

What level of self-righteous piousness do you have to engage in, thinking you are living rightly while believing those outside of the organization are both lost and unfavored of some supreme being?

Conforming to a high-demand belief system is limiting, and can feed into mental health issues, making them worse. Pray, and pray more, and you will feel better, they might say. Remain active in the religion, so you remain pure and righteous, they advise.

Give money and you will be right with God, they claim. How much money are you supposed to give to be a good member?

Consider the lies of any wealthy church. For instance, Mormons:

"Tithing is an essential practice of Latter-day Saints, regardless of where they live, their social standing, or their material circumstances. By keeping this law, Church members receive

spiritual and temporal blessings in their lives and help further the Church's divine mission on earth."
– Presiding Bishop Gérald Caussé of the Mormon church, August 2022

"Pay your tithing and be blessed. Tithing is not a free will offering. It is a debt."
– Marion G. Romney, a leader in the Mormon church

The Mormon financial manipulation is spiritual blackmail. It is similar to other churches requiring their members to surrender ten percent of their money to the church – so the followers are "right with God." It's all nonsense. It is also deception, abuse, and grifting.

The Mormon church has hundreds of billions of dollars in investments. It very likely is worth more than a trillion dollars. Some consider a trillion dollars to be a conservative estimate, including because of the increase in global real estate values. The church investments include office buildings (including in Manhattan and other cities), schools, apartment buildings, retail and entertainment real estate, warehouses, a Hawaiian amusement park, radio and TV stations, newspapers, book publishing, farms, ranches, timberland, clothing manufacturing and sales, and stocks, bonds, and other investments. (Search: Mormon Billions. On YouTube see: The Mormon Church in Canada: Where did more than $1 billion go?)

Why is the Mormon church still requiring members to give ten percent of their income to the church? If the members don't pay the money, they are considered "not in good standing," and can't attend certain church gatherings, including inside the Mormon temples – including weddings. It's spiritual brutality, toxic patriarchy, deception, grifting, scamming, and lies.

The Mormon church is a cult started with lies. The *Book of Mormon* contains wording, storylines, characters, and styles from other books. It is creative writing by self-proclaimed prophet Joseph Smith, who married multiple wives, including sisters, and mothers and daughters. When he was 37, he pressured a 14-year-old girl to marry him. He also pressured orphaned girls to marry him, saying it is God's will. He sent men on missions, then married their wives. Men were sent to Europe to bring women back to join in plural marriages.

Mormon history is rich with spiritual brutality, sexism, racism, malignant narcissism, toxic patriarchy, homophobia, and child abuse. Many members feeling unable to keep up with the cult standards have committed suicide. (Google: Mormon suicides)

The cult-owned school, Brigham Young University, is named after the second leader of the church, who commonly expressed horrendously racist views, had multiple wives, and ordered the killing of people, including indigenous people in Utah.

The women of the Mormon cult have no authority, and are taught to "respect the priesthood," to obey, not to question church authority, to be innocent and pure until marriage, and then to be submissive to their husbands. The boys as young as 12 are "given the priesthood," and therefore have more authority and are more spiritually empowered than any woman. The women are treated as commodities.

The Mormon leadership is a fraternal brotherhood of misogynistic men protecting their position as leaders over women – who are suppressed as handmaids, and treated as baby-making machines.

It seems surreal that women would participate in such an organization. But from an early age, the church members are told that doubting the church leaders is being influenced by a dark power that is of the devil. They are not to read any literature, or view any material critical of (telling the truth about) the church. They are to only rely on church literature and leaders to learn about the church.

To learn more about the Mormon church, search: The C.E.S. Letter. On social media, see Mormon Stories Podcast. Google: "Top 40 most dishonest acts in Mormon church history."

Giving money to an organization doesn't do anything for your soul, or whatever you want to call it. It doesn't give you "temporal blessings," or "spiritual blessings." All it means is you gave money to an organization. Where is the money going? Just as the Mormon church does, other churches have stock investments, bond investments, money in various funds, and money in gold, in real estate, and in various businesses. Money also goes into the pockets of the "church leaders." When you donate money to a church your money isn't going to God, it is going into corporate investment holdings, and supporting greed, ego, and deceptive cult activity.

Be wise. Stop giving your money to religion. Stop allowing them to deceive, grift, scam, bully, brutalize, and rob you. You aren't going to guarantee your place in a cartoon heaven theme park by giving money to an organization. Break free of that nonsense.

It is easy to understand how people feel a community and fellowship in their religious gatherings. And it is understandable how they can feel uplifted by associating with people of like mind. I can understand going to church to engage in community when feeling down or lonely. What I don't get is the sitting around and listening for hours every single week. I also don't get into the man-made theatrics that have nothing to do with much of anything other than mythology, distortions, deception, and antiquated concepts.

The concept of donating so many resources to support a belief system that has nothing to do with eternity or salvation, and everything to do with making money and vainglory is not a reasonable or wise way to spend energy, time, money, or life.

"Most churches make people feel guilty about natural human inclinations, making them feel dependent on the church for forgiveness. Religion focuses on unresolved human problems of insecurity, shame, fear, and wish fulfillment, and offers hope for a better life in the next world. Science offers people the tools of reason and knowledge to help build self-reliance and free people from mythology and simple wish fulfillment."
  – Jacque Fresco

"Science is not only compatible with spirituality, it is a profound source of spirituality. When we recognize our place in an immensity of lightyears and in the passage of ages, when we grasp the intricacy, beauty, and subtlety of life, then that soaring feeling, that sense of elation and humility combined is surely spiritual."
  – Carl Sagan

"Science is a wondrously successful way of knowing the world, but it isn't the only way. Knowledge also derives from other sources, such as common-sense experience, imaginative literature, music, and artistic expression."
  – Francisco Ayala

It seems as if many people who are into church are waiting for something and trying to find something. Maybe they are the ones they are waiting for, they are the ones they seek, and they are the ones who can validate themselves, and they don't know it. Maybe what they need is what they already have, but they don't understand that it is already there. Maybe by getting active in creating the life they want by using their talents and intellect they would seek less, live more, be more satisfied, and understand that they can be their own guru to bring them joy, health, satisfaction, and love.

"I shall tell you a great secret, my friend. Do not wait for the last judgment. It takes place every day."
  – Albert Camus

Instead of using up hours every week, and a chunk of their income dedicated to a church, what if people spent their time developing their talents, becoming active in environmental causes, and helping organizations that restore and protect trees, forests, and wildlife? This would do more to help the sacredness of life than supporting a church which does nothing to protect Earth, but does everything to make sure the financial books of the church are in order, and that the church leaders have money in their pockets.

"It is difficult to free fools from the chains they revere."
– François-Marie "Voltaire" Arouet

I had a conversation with someone who spends large amounts of her time and income on her church. She said I wouldn't understand because I'm "not a spiritual person." She claims that churches stop people from being involved in bad things because the churches take the people out of their lives that would otherwise be ruinous. I think that is an interesting concept which is also wasteful, tragic, weak, and ruinous. Perhaps being so dedicated to conforming to some high-demand religion is about being willing to be robbed of a genuine life.

"Because we are imperfect souls, our knowledge is imperfect. The history of learning is an adventure in overcoming our errors. There is no sin in being wrong. The sin is in our unwillingness to examine our own beliefs, and in believing that our authorities cannot be wrong."
– Neil Postman

"The ultimate result of shielding men from the effects of folly is to fill the world with fools."
– Herbert Spencer

If there is some sort of judgment gate, there will likely be many people being asked why they didn't use their skills, resources, talents, and time to improve life, and to protect the wildlife and environment that supports all life. Their honest answer will be they were too busy sitting in church and making money to donate to church. Others will say they were too busy playing video games, watching TV, keeping up with celebrity culture, playing on the Internet, shopping, or working to pay off the debt they got into to purchase stuff to replicate the images seen in corporate advertising, or to buy status symbols they thought would validate them, give them a place of influence and power in society, and bring joy by feeding ego, fantasy, and vanity.

"The world is a dangerous place, not because of those who do evil, but because of those who look on and do nothing."
– Albert Einstein

I encourage people to get out and live. It is through doing and experiencing that you will relate with and know life. Sitting around believing in something is having faith without works. Sitting in front of screen technology for hours upon hours does nothing for you. Get up and go live your life, using your better qualities. Your actions are your intentions taking place, and are truly the practicing of your faith.

"What sort of God would it be who only pushed from without?"
– Johann Wolfgang von Goethe

Whether or not you believe in Buddhism, in Hinduism, in Jainism, in Christianity, in Catholicism, in Judaism, in Mormonism, in Scientology, in Islam, in Hopi wisdom, or in other popular or unpopular religious or spiritual beliefs, there is some variety of goodness. Rather than sit around building your life philosophy, get out and live it, construct it, and experience it by practice.

Inspire your self. Be confident about it. Tune into your power. Use your talents. Play your skills. Engage in your craft. Stimulate your intellect. Manifest your sacredness, commitment, inspiration, and divinity through good works.

Feed off the knowledge you get by living your life and building goodness in your life. Take good from wherever it may flow and use it in your life to fuel your confidence, and protect the sacredness of Earth by creating a more sustainable culture in which wildlife thrives.

"People are hungry for messages of hope and life."
– Morgan Brittany

The difference between those who achieve great things and those who don't is most often a very simple process. Those who do achieve great things don't sit around thinking about it without taking action. They both believe and have confidence they can accomplish the tasks, and consistently work with intention while staying focused on accomplishing their goals through actions.

"Acting on a good idea is better than just having a good idea."
– Robert Half

Many people believe they can accomplish something, but their belief is lost in fantasy – because they take no action to accomplish the imagery stuck in their mind because of inaction.

Belief combined with planning and intentional action and related communication results in accomplishment of goals.

"I have been impressed with the urgency of doing. Knowing is not enough; we must apply. Being willing is not enough; we must do."
– Leonardo da Vinci

145

There is a current of electricity in your body. The level of its vibrancy depends on what you think, what you do, what you are planning to do, how you spend your time, what you say, what you read, how you treat others, how you treat animals, the people with whom you spend time, the music you listen to, the environment in which you spend your time, and the quality of your nutrition. The current responds to the level of your determination, intention, action, communication, and confidence.

Whether you choose to be ruled by confidence or by doubt is a matter of which energy you choose to plug into. You can focus on good and invigorating energy that uplifts and builds confidence. Or, you can tune into that which is negative, overly critical, and unaccepting of the gifts that can be found throughout your days, and simply leave your life up to whimsy.

Consider that a person who is ill may get well with the assistance of various therapies, and that perhaps one of the most important of all matters in healing is the person's state of mind, attitude, and will. It may be most helpful for those people to have a confident belief that their health will improve. But it will be more helpful if they work to recover and rehabilitate themselves. Instead of allowing frustration to turn into stress, which can degrade health even more, they can spin that frustration into helpful actions.

How well people accomplish their desires may be determined by how much work they carry out in alignment with their want. Those who really want something, and work for it, are more likely to accomplish their desires.

"Hope is itself a species of happiness, and, perhaps, the chief happiness which this world affords."
– Samuel Johnson

Have confidence in both your self and in others. By showing your confidence in others you reveal confidence in your self. By believing in the power of others, you believe in the power of your self.

Go about your days using your beneficial qualities with confidence while knowing you are capable improving your situation to be healthy for you.

Embrace the concepts of positive-thinking, of building strength in a person, of the ability to master talents, and of fine tuning your being as an instrument filled with confidence. By doing those you are more likely to attain that which is good, positive, and satisfying in your life.

If you want your life to improve, be determined to improve it. Intentionally act to improve it. Have confidence that you can improve it. Use self-discipline combined with actions to make it improve.

"Some people regard discipline as a chore. For me, it is a kind of order that sets me free to fly."
– Julie Andrews

Be brave, caring, driven, kind, gallant, and active in changing your life. Intentionally create a confident, nurturing atmosphere of prosperity, clarity, and self-awareness where the strengths of your better qualities will prosper.

"The most important cage you can free yourself from is the one in which you care what others think of you."
– Stacie Martin

Don't get caught up in religious guilt, or scrupulosity, or thinking your every move is being supervised by some fictional being created by people with an agenda so they can gain wealth and power. Move away from antiquated and false beliefs, and stop allowing them to rule your days, relationships, and life. Stop fearing what doesn't exist.

"There is simply no polite way to tell people they've dedicated their lives to an illusion."
– Daniel Bennett

"Until I was twenty, I was sure there was a being who could see everything I did, and who didn't like most of it. He seemed to care about minute aspects of my life – like on what day of the week I ate a piece of meat. And yet, he let earthquakes and mudslides take out whole communities – apparently ignoring the saints among them who ate their meat on the assigned days.
Eventually, I realized that I didn't believe there was such a being. It didn't seem reasonable."
– Alan Alda

Refuse to accept doubt in your life. Defy fear with confidence.

Believe in your self. Believe in your power. Use your energy in beneficial ways. Have confidence in and build your confidence in your self. Work with your instincts, yearning, talents, and abilities.

Build your strengths to fine-tune your self as an instrument that can be conducted by the thoughts of your mind to bring your life into what it is capable of being.

What you do is the example of what you are.

147

# Words

"Kind words are a creative force, a power that concurs in the building up of all that is good, an energy that showers blessings upon the world."
– Lawrence G. Lovasik

Words are the expression of thoughts and they plant the seeds of other thoughts in the minds of the people who hear them.

Words are powerful. Just as others can say things to you that limit or motivate you, you can say words to yourself – and to others – which motivate, encourage, uplift, strengthen, and bring about improved relations and conditions.

Words play into the collaboration of the conscious mind with the subconscious mind.

Words can create energy signatures in the minds of people who hear them. They can bind people into believing things, even when the things are not true. For instance, many people have heard negative things about themselves and then alter their behavior according to those unfortunate words.

"Language exerts hidden power, like a moon on the tides."
– Rita Mae Brown

Have you heard or read words that make you feel a certain way, such as motivated and determined? Words are messages, and water responds to messages made of patterns of sounds, which consist of energy that can alter your energy and molecules.

148

We consist mostly of water. Water is impacted by sound patterns, which can be calming, stimulating, frantic, disturbing, invigorating, nurturing, or loving.

"Words and magic were in the beginning one and the same thing, and even today words retain much of their magical power."
– Sigmund Freud

Words placed in our memories can continue to bless or to curse us, make us feel good, or bad, happy, or sad, or other ways.

Just as poison makes people physically ill, which can impact the mind, so too might unkind, mean, grotesque words ail the mind, which can impact the body.

As foods can be healing, so too can be words.

As a person experiences life, neural pathways are developed in the brain and other tissues in relation to what the person has experienced. In this way, poisonous words can create memory patterns of negativity and form an imprint of judgment over which other thoughts travel, playing into the role we play in life.

"Before you speak, ask yourself: Is it kind? It is necessary? Is it true? Does it improve on the silence?"
– Shirdi Sai Baba

People often curse each other and use negative words toward one another. Many people have been told they are dumb, ugly, and otherwise flawed or broken. These are the types of words that destroy self-esteem.

Ugly words may echo in a person's memory and affect the way they think, act, and communicate. They focus on the words and form an opinion of themselves that binds them or limits them.

Remembering words spoken to us can bring about the same energy patterns that originally rippled through us when we first heard the words. In less than ideal circumstances, this may lead to limiting thoughts, self-hate, destruction of character, weariness, slothfulness, defeat, damaged relationships, and failure. This is an example of how words create energy signatures in the minds of people who hear them. Those signatures can be evident in the structures of the person, in their eyes, facial expression, stance, posture, body positioning, breathing patterns, and vocal tone.

"Conversation is a meeting of minds with different memories and habits. When minds meet, they don't just exchange facts: they transform them, reshape them, draw different implications from

them, engage in new trains of thought. Conversation doesn't just reshuffle the cards: it creates new cards."
– Theodore Zeldin

"Words are a lens to focus one's mind."
– Ayn Rand

I'm not the type of person who goes to fortunetellers. I was once at a house party that, for its apparent entertainment value, had a fortuneteller. While I sat and listened to the guests' fortunes being told, I played with the idea that perhaps fortunetellers don't so much as *fore*tell the future as *tell* it – explaining with such energy what may become that it paves the way for events to take place – beginning the energy wave with their thoughts and words in such a way that it plants the seeds of what may grow into an event through thought-directed actions and communication.

"For as he thinketh in his heart, so is he."
– King Solomon

Very often people experience something that a person once told them would happen. This may be the expression of some sort of belief in words once spoken and heard. If people are told they will one day accomplish or experience something, perhaps they might be more likely to play out the scenario of it happening in their thoughts. And as thoughts result in actions that bring about events, the whole process may be what is called a *self-fulfilled prophecy*.

"If you keep saying things are going to be bad, you have a good chance of being a prophet."
– Isaac Bashevis Singer

"Assume a virtue if you have it not."
– William Shakespeare

At any time, you can begin to instill uplifting thoughts into your mind, which will nurture positive actions and communication, and, perhaps, satisfactory life changes. You can do this with your thoughts, the words that you speak, the words that you read in the literature of your choosing, the goals you set and notes you write to yourself, and hopefully the nurturing and encouraging words of those around you.

"The best way to predict the future is to create it."
– Alan Kay

Perhaps all words could be considered to be some form of prayer, in that they reveal what we hope for, fear, love, dislike, yearn for, and anticipate. Maybe words are often more about our hearing them than about who else is hearing them. Know the power of words. Decide to think and speak combinations of words that create the energy of and prophecy a healthier way of life.

While it helps to have supportive loved ones, you can also encourage yourself to factor and live out more of the life you desire.

As an exercise, make a list of the good, kind, and encouraging things people have said about and toward you. Also make a short list of the things you would like people to say to you. Consider that it may be helpful for you to read these lists regularly to help set a pattern of positive-thinking. Know that you don't have to hear those words from others to validate you.

When you are feeling less valiant, ways of getting motivated include listening to music that inspires you, reading things that encourage you, watching films that uplift you, and listening to motivational videos and recordings that can be found online.

As a way to encourage yourself, simply grab a pen and paper and write a stream of positive words, statements, and intentions. Simply let intentionally positive thoughts flow freely onto the page.

Reading and writing positive statements can be an especially powerful exercise when you are experiencing times of doubt or worry. The reading and writing will help cancel negative thoughts you are experiencing, because the mind works in accordance with the influences suggested to it. Positive thoughts will flow into your actions because the body acts in accordance with thoughts.

Writing positive affirmations will help you declare your intentions and shift your gears to remain on a healthful path. Once you declare them, stay busy by infusing the positive thoughts into your actions. By doing so you will form your declaration into manifestation.

"Be observant to the words you use in writing, typing, or talking. Negative words sabotage that which you really want in your life. It's like getting halfway across the bridge to happiness and cutting the ropes with negative, critical words."
– Daniel Giovanni Morello

Continually arrange the words in your mind to create the terrain for healthful thought. Allow positive, encouraging, motivating, and loving words to become the constant flow of your mantra. Use this to collaborate your conscious mind to successfully cooperate with your subconscious mind in bringing about the change you wish to see in your life.

"One of the most powerful and transformational forces in the universe is our words. They are the creative energy of the world, and by our words we influence our world."
– Rick Roepke

Use the words you think and the words you speak to help accelerate your life toward happiness, vibrant health, and the fulfillment of your goals.

# Transforming

It is up to you to take hold of your transformative powers, and to continually engage in the initiative and process of stimulating and using your intellect, talents, and skills to benefit your existence.

It is up to you to grow into being the best version of yourself.

"Transforming yourself is a means of giving light to the whole world."
– Ramana Maharshi

To start from somewhere, you must first be someplace. We are all someplace, but some of us don't know where we are.

Many people don't know their state in life. They have little idea what happened in their past – because they weren't paying attention, were kept in the dark by people around them, or were so far in denial they skimmed right over it. They may have hidden behind lackluster activities, excuses, mundane normalcy, low quality behavior, and being lost in and used by the lives of others as an escape mechanism.

"When a man's self is hidden from everybody else, it seems also to become hidden even from himself, and it permits disease and death to gnaw into his substance without his clear knowledge."
– Sidney Jourard

"Normal is not something to aspire to, it's something to get away from."
– Jodie Foster

"I would much rather have regrets about not doing what people said, than regretting not doing what my heart led me to and wondering what life had been like if I'd just been myself."
— Brittany Renée

Some people are caught up in living undercover, which is a pattern of roleplaying to conform to what they think is the acceptable form of behavior in alignment with the people around them.

Living undercover can be damaging to a person, and cause their feelings, emotions, and existence to become rigid, stagnant, stale, and stuck. Even their facial and vocal expressions may be altered by an earnestness to fit a fake persona. It may be in tune with a controlled repression of their true personality, intellect, and soul.

"Most of the shadows of this life are caused by standing in one's own sunshine."
— Ralph Waldo Emerson

Some people get into the habit of functioning as if they are being held hostage by situations or people in their life – including things and people from their distant past. They may almost lean on their feelings about these situations and relationships to support their attitude, which is a choice more than it is a curse.

"There is no man, however wise, who has not at some period of his youth said things, or lived in a way the consciousness of which is so unpleasant to him in later life that he would gladly, if he could, expunge it from his memory."
— Marcel Proust

Some continually agonize over the past as if it is a wound being misted with alcohol. This is often done while placing blame and shame on others, and wallowing in regret and stagnation, as if in a form of shock. Meanwhile, they might not recognize their participation in creating the situation – or, at least, carrying it on.

The past can't change. You can.

"We are all exceptional cases. Each of us insists on being innocent at all cost, even if he has to accuse the whole human race and heaven itself. If you tell a criminal that his crime is not due to his nature or his character, but the unfortunate circumstances, he will be extravagantly grateful to you."
— Albert Camus

People also often don't know what is happening with their life, and don't know what resources they have available to organize into something they can use to build a more satisfying, healthful existence. Maybe part of it is that they blame others for their situation, and make it easier to think they can't do anything about it, as the damage is done, and they are stuck, even paralyzed from progression. It's the blame game taken to an extent of extinguishing self-responsibility. Or, at least, pretending to, as a way of escaping responsibility, and to avoid working to get into a better situation. Instead, they remain loathsome, unencouraged by themselves as a coping mechanism that is of self-defeat. Again, they blame everyone else, but refuse to recognize their own complicity in their situation they helped design.

Some go through life seeking to get things done for them. They may be manipulative in getting what they can from other people. They may depend on and expect others to take care of them, or they wait to be directed on what to do, and when and how to do it. They may look for what is free and easy, or for what they can attain with the least amount of work. By doing so they weaken themselves, drain those around them, and negate their community. They might not recognize that free and easy might be the most costly and taxing of what would be more healthful and helpful choices in actions and communication – the work needed to get into a better situation. What they might attain is laziness, failure, stagnation, and possibly ruin.

Some seem to be waiting around for someone else to provide the change they want to see in life.

Some think buying a weekly lottery ticket will improve their life.

Some seem to think it is up to their family to provide their change.

Some carry an illusion that the government is going to improve their situation. Unfortunately, the government is more focused on crime, punishment, and corporate welfare than it is on activities to improve the situation of humans. The government largely functions as a concierge service for corporations, caters to the demands of commerce and industry, and is more concerned about money and less concerned about people. The government is a business. Businesses don't have morals, they have managers, bookkeepers, lawyers, and other workers.

"Truthfulness has never been counted among the political virtues, and lies have always been regarded as justifiable tools in political dealings."
– Hannah Arendt

When the government does focus on an individual, it is most often not in the most helpful way.

The U.S. spends more on jails and prisons than it does on education. Throughout the decades, many state governments have cut funding for parks, for children's programs, and for schools, education services, and libraries. They have been doing so while increasing funding for prison construction, for prison guards, and for increasing the number of police officers and criminal prosecutors. Meanwhile, each person held in prison costs several times more than what is spent on school students.

As I'm writing this, California has about 130,000 prisoners. That is in 33 prisons designed to hold a total of 84,000 inmates. The state is usually number one in prison spending, and ranks low in education spending. In 2021, the University of California's Board of Regents voted to allow for the increase of tuition, every year, indefinitely.

Unfortunately, what has been taking place in California is reflective of what has been going on in many other states, and in some other countries – often in ways far worse than what is happening in California.

As I'm writing this, the U.S. is holding more than two million people in prisons, jails, and youth "correction facilities." More than twice that number of U.S. citizens are on probation or parole. According to the Bureau of Justice Statistics, the U.S. is spending more than $80 billion on incarcerating people.

The U.S. both holds more people in prison – and spends more money on prisons – than any country. The U.S. has built more prisons in the past six decades than in all the world's history.

Instead of an educated generation, the U.S. has produced a prison generation. It's ruinous for people, their families, and communities.

Part of the prison-building scenario is the result of cuts in education funding, cuts in arts funding, cuts in library funding, cuts in childcare funding, and a pathetic and expensive "healthcare system" that basically only works for those with money. The poor suffer, delay getting help, can't afford the care, and are overwhelmed by health problems, including unhoused people – many of whom are living on the streets specifically after losing everything because of health problems.

"If we don't stand up for children, then we don't stand for much."
– Marian Wright Edelman

With all the money spent on prisons in America, and all the cuts of funding in education, it seems there would be a realization that it is easier and far less expensive to educate a child and provide

156

opportunities for a quality childhood, excellent nutrition, and education than it is to try to fix someone who grew up disadvantaged, neglected, denied, and/or abused.

Unfortunately, enlightenment seems difficult to come by in the offices directing government spending.

As history shows, if the fossil fuels industries, automobile industries, livestock industries, farmed animal feed industries, and companies owned by billionaires want government welfare, they get it into the tens of billions of dollars.

"If it's possible to build prison camps powerful enough to destroy human personalities, perhaps it was also possible to create environments that can foster its rebirth."
— Bruno Bettelheim

"If the misery of the poor be caused not by the laws of Nature, but by our institutions, great is our sin."
— Charles Darwin

Just as your power is diminished by catering to the illusion that the government will improve your life, your power is also diminished by waiting for someone else to improve your life.

"You are responsible for the world that you live in. It is not the government's responsibility. It is not your school's, or your social club's, or your church's, or your neighbor's, or your fellow citizen's. It is yours, utterly and singularly yours."
— August Wilson

"Nobody made a greater mistake than the person who did nothing, because they thought that they could only do a little."
— Edmund Burke

"Nothing strengthens the judgment and quickens the conscience like individual responsibility."
— Elizabeth Stanton

Thinking someone else is responsible for your happiness weakens you, creates laziness, dulls the senses, atrophies the brain, is unrealistic, and may as well be considered foolish.

Relying on others to do for us what we can do for ourselves is unhealthful, limits our learning, and can create a dysfunctional environment for all involved.

You cannot ride on the coattails of anyone and realistically expect your life to be the best it can be.

"If I wanted to become a tramp, I would seek information and advice from the most successful tramp I could find. If I wanted to become a failure, I would seek advice from people who never succeeded. If I wanted to succeed in all things, I would look around me for those who are succeeding, and do as they have done."
– Joseph Marshall Wade

Many don't seem to realize their life is a classroom. They also don't seem to care if they get a good grade, nor are they paying attention to the teacher, doing their homework, or studying and incorporating life enhancement and advancement processes. They are quick to waste time on activities that do nothing for them, for their loved ones, for their community, or for society.

"The only reason some people get lost in thought is because it's unfamiliar territory."
– Unknown

"You have the power to choose your own happiness. People, situations, and events outside of yourself will affect you, but no one can give you happiness."
– Stephanie Dowrick

Your life is not about what it was. Your life is about what it currently is, and it is about what it can become. If you pay attention to it and use the lessons and opportunities presented to you, your life likely can become more satisfying than what it has been, and is.

Open your eyes to the possibilities within you. Change comes from within. It is up to you to bring out the substances of your self that will be most pleasing to you. Get busy. Renovate yourself.

Your life can become completely different from what it currently is. You can transform yourself through thoughts, diet, exercise, communication, emotions, activities, education, poise, daily choices, associations, and by adapting to the elegance of your intellect and the eloquence of your love. You can do this to such an extent that people who know you now may be unable to recognize you in one year.

"Let the beauty we love be what we do."
– Jalal ad-Din Rumi

Especially if you have been living a low-quality life, you can essentially intentionally mutate into a completely different and more healthful version of yourself. Through infusing your body with a nutritious, plant-based diet, while staying away from low-grade foods, and by maintaining a quality daily morning exercise regimen, you can transform your health.

Through working to improve the way you think through intellectual stimulation and self-education, and improving skills, you can transform your mind. By changing your actions, improving your communication, and practicing better manners, smarter time management, and wiser ways of doing things, your life will change.

Through improving the ways in which you spend time, energy, and resources, you can transform your existence.

These are the principles of transforming your life from the inside.

"To find yourself, think for yourself."
– Socrates

"Adventure is not outside, it is within."
– David Grayson

I reiterate, all transformation toward success and health begins with your thoughts. Your outward appearance and the things you do are reflective of what is going on inside you.

If you are going to appear healthier, you need to be more healthful on the inside.

If you want your structure to improve, you have to improve your diet, change what you feed your mind, and improve your exercise.

All this has to do with thought.

"When you are inspired by some great purpose, some extraordinary project, all your thoughts break their bonds; your mind transcends limitations, your consciousness expands in every direction, and you find yourself in a new, great and wonderful world. Dormant forces, faculties and talents become alive, and you discover yourself to be a greater person by far than you ever dreamed yourself to be."
– Patanjali

"Man stands in his own shadow and wonders why it's dark."
– Unknown

"Ideas won't work unless you do.
– Unknown

"We must not, in trying to think about how we can make a big difference, ignore the small daily differences we can make which, over time, add up to big differences that we often cannot foresee."
– Marian Wright Edelman

"Find someone to help you through life. Respect everyone. Know that life is not fair, and that you will fail, often. But if you take some risks, step up when the times are the toughest, face down the bullies, lift up the downtrodden, and never, ever give up, if you do these things, the next generation, and the generations that follow will live in a world far better than the one we have today."
– William H. McRaven

If you want to see change in yourself, do change yourself.

If you want the world to improve, do improve the way you behave in – and what you do for – the world.

If you want to change the way people treat you, do improve the way you treat people.

If you want to transform yourself, do begin the journey from within by transforming your thoughts.

"Strength does not grow from comfort zones. It grows from thorns, and high tides, and wild, wild winds that knock you off of your feet.."
– Ullie Kaye

Transforming your life to experience a satisfying journey is up to you, and nobody else. The journey starts in your mind. Get busy with it.

"Circumstances may cause interruptions and delays, but never lose sight of your goal. Prepare yourself in every way you can by increasing your knowledge and adding to your experience, so that you can make the most of opportunity when it occurs."
– Mario Andretti

"When you know who you are, you stop letting other people tell you who you are. Insults, projections, and false narratives no longer trigger your insecurities when you walk around with divine confidence."
– Stacie Martin

"The man who makes everything that leads to happiness depend upon himself, and not upon other men, has adopted the very best plan for living happily."
– Plato

160

# You Are Your Gatekeeper

Health is not something that will flow into us if we clog the gates with unhealthful foods, thoughts, relationships, and activities. It is something that will root and grow into our lives through healthful thoughts, actions, interactions, environment, and nutrition.

Health is transformative and a better quality of it is more likely be our experience if we continually nurture a desirable level of health – both from the inside out, and the outside in.

"Dark green, leafy vegetables are the world's healthiest foods. As whole foods go, they offer the most nutrition per calorie.'"
– Michael Greger

"It's no coincidence that four of the six letters in health are 'heal.'"
– Ed Northstrum

People can transform through many ways, including through quality, plant-based nutrition, and daily physical activity. It also includes building thought processes that will beneficially change the way they deal with their situations. It involves building healthful interior and exterior atmospheres providing the terrain where health, intellect, skill, and beneficial relationships can flourish.

"The quality of expectations determines the quality of our action."
– Andre Godin

161

When athletes succeed they know it is because of their own actions and choices. Nobody can exercise for them. Nobody can restrict everything athletes think, do, communicate, or eat. They have to be disciplined enough to maintain their dietary guidelines based on the nutrition they need to get their body to perform at the level of their goals. Similarly, we can succeed at life by training to succeed and working to attain the satisfaction we desire.

To achieve vibrant health and an active, satisfying life, engage your intellect, practice your skills and talents, study what benefits you, and train for life like an athlete trains for sport.

"By believing passionately in something that still does not exist, we create it. The nonexistent is whatever we have not sufficiently desired."
– Nikos Kazantzakis

Generally, once you are an adult, and no matter what your background, if you are physically able, you largely become responsible for the satisfaction you feel in life. If you do not work to attain success in health and in life, as the athlete trains to attain the win, you will not own the satisfaction you are capable of experiencing.

"There is absolutely nothing that separates the elite from the paupers except their expectations. If you wish to rise above the masses, then let the fire burn fiercely within you. Do this, and it shall be done!"
– J. Arthur Holcombe

Train yourself to continually attain your goals by conducting your daily activities in a way to bring you closer to what you want to be.

Like an athlete, if you drop the ball, pick it up and continue aiming for and progressing toward the goal.

Focus on your present, as that is the game you are in.

"A real decision is measured by the fact that you've taken a new action. If there's no action, you haven't truly decided."
– Anthony Robbins

When you consider someone who decided on and successfully accomplished an athletic goal, such as to run a marathon, you can see how they go through training that starts out slow and, over a matter of months or years, builds toward the goal of accomplishment. The training an athlete goes through is similar to experiencing success in any area of life.

"If you really want to get something done, start on it, keep at it, and it will eventually happen."
– Richard H. Goodwin

"Making the best of ourselves is the reason we were born, but it takes patience and perseverance."
– Sarah Ban Breathnach

The success of attaining a goal is bred by perseverance and dedication to experiencing accomplishment. Priorities must be drawn, goals must be set, actions must be taken, and communication must be made, including with self. All the reasons for doing everything throughout the days, weeks, months, and years it takes to accomplish the goal have to be done in association with the reason of wanting it badly enough.

"Failure is, in a sense, the highway to success, inasmuch as every discovery of what is false leads us to seek earnestly after what is true."
– John Keats

"Motivation is what gets you started. Habit is what keeps you going.
– Jim Ryun

It is often the little things you do that lead to accomplishment. Continually thinking of and doing things to attain a goal builds patterns of thoughts that play out in patterns of behavior, action, and communication. As these patterns continue to evolve they create your common way of existing.

"If you think that something small cannot make a difference, try going to sleep with a mosquito in the room."
– Unknown

"The greatest things ever done on Earth have been done little by little."
– William Jennings Bryan

The level of your body's performance is highly dependent on the level of life you are leading, which is dependent on the level of thoughts you are creating, and the level of foods you are consuming.

To accomplish a better, more healthful and satisfactory level of life, feed your body the highest-quality nutrients available to you.

To experience the best of health, strive for a diet largely consisting of live plant matter: fruits, berries, vegetables, sprouts, sea vegetables, soaked raw nuts, and germinated seeds. Even better, use them fresh or otherwise in their unheated state, and not fried, sautéed, microwaved, or tainted with processed sugars or salts, MSG, or synthetic preservatives, dyes, flavors, scents, or sweeteners. These foods from Nature will help you to experience vibrant health that will increase your energy and drive. High-quality nutrients from plant substances are fuel for regenerating your power and the accomplishment of goals. (See my book: *Plant-Based Regenerative Nutrition*.)

"I hope you get to dance more with joy, than you spin in drama. I hope you get to know your worth, more than you sell yourself short. I hope that you fall asleep more peacefully worn out, than you are exhausted. I hope you wake each day feeling more rested, than still tired. I hope that you find yourself where fulfillment is yours, a lot more than it is not. I hope that you have more days that add riches to your memory bank, than subtract from it."
– Stacie Martin

Make the changes you want by being a more present and effective gatekeeper of your life through the goals you set, the priorities you focus on, the foods you eat, the activities you engage in, the communication you make, the literature you read, the music you listen to, the thoughts you entertain, and the quality of your relationships.

For you, the people you love, and your community, be the one who engages your better qualities, and gets things done.

"Everything in this world is a manifestation of what you give the world. The laws of karma are in every scripture. They're in the Bible, and the Quran, the Torah, they're in the yoga sutras. Every prophet tells you the same thing. It is really what you give the world that you get back from the world. Not that you have to trade, but give the world the positivity you want back. And you have to have faith that is what is going on. That is what is going on."
– Russell Simmons

# Essence

"Look within. The secret is inside you."
– Hui Neng

You know there are permanent things about you that you cannot deny. They determine who you are, what you yearn for, need, want, desire, consider, look for, and help you to formulate your existence,

Some people call the permanence infinite intelligence. They compare it to wild animals who naturally do things in alignment with their species, such as wasps who build their nests out of specific materials, spiders who make webs of a certain pattern, creatures who migrate thousands of miles along the same routes, and all wild animals who seek out and eat exactly what nourishes them.

"If you do not express your own original ideas, if you do not listen to your own being, you will have betrayed yourself."
– Rollo May

Everyone has it in them to wish and hope, expect and anticipate, yearn, desire, and work for what they want to experience.

Your life will function better if you follow a diet containing what nourishes you to be at the best level of health. Combine that with exercise, learning, and aligning your thoughts, actions, and communication with your better qualities, and you will be more in alignment with who you are.

Just as there are things you desire and that make you more in alignment with health, there are things that do the opposite. These include unhealthful air, toxic surroundings, violated land, noise pollution, and the presence of negativity, harshness, and thought patterns of ugliness, belittlement, fear, pain, and doubt.

You don't want to be aligned with things that make you less attuned to what helps you. It is your natural instinct, and you don't like it to be frustrated. You don't want a disturbance that clogs your ability to be in tune with your healthier potential, and what you need for it. You want to avoid what limits your higher potential, and damages your expression and ability to live safely and healthfully.

**"Our own physical body possesses a wisdom which we who inhabit the body lack."**
– Henry Miller

You consist of a being who desires to be attuned with what is beneficial. This being is who you are. It is your intelligence, and can be utilized to resonate patterns of thought energy directing your actions and communication to formulate your life in the most beneficial way.

The true you that is your essence consists of infinite intelligence. It is what has brought the intricate structures of all living beings to form into what they are. It is what drives us to desire that which is beneficial, beautiful, nurturing, and loving.

It is likely that much of the infinite intelligence that would otherwise be available to many people mostly goes untapped and is muffled by leading a low-quality life while consuming low-quality foods, entertaining low-quality thoughts, participating in low-quality communication, engaging in low-quality activities, and anticipating less than ideal situations.

By living a low-quality life, you are not being the more healthful person you are capable of being. And you are not experiencing the joy, satisfaction, and love that would otherwise be available to you.

**"In the world to come they will not ask me, 'Why were you not Moses?' They will ask me, 'Why were you not Zusya?'"**
– Reb Zusya

When you follow a healthful, nutritious diet free of junk; maintain your physical structure through daily exercise; develop your talents through practice of art or craft; expand your knowledge through study and intellectual stimulation; focus your mind on an agenda of achievement; fuel your actions with positive-thinking; surround yourself with that which inspires you to become your higher potential; and improve your communication with other people through respect, kindness, patience, forgiveness, and love, you are tuning your frequency to be more in alignment with health, and less in alignment with troublesome thoughts and behaviors. By doing so you will be better able to recognize and utilize the potential and power that is the essence of who you are.

Living healthfully, including with a truly nutritious plant-based diet and daily exercise, awakens your cells, electrical fields, chemistry, mind, and your system to the thing that had been dormant and dulled because of unwise living, and an unhealthful diet, low-quality thinking, a troubling atmosphere, dysfunctional relationships, and ruinous and untrue concepts.

Through a plant-based diet free of junk, extracted sugars and oils, heat-generated chemicals, and processed and synthetic ingredients, your system communicates better with the frequency of Nature. As your system becomes more clean, this natural diet corresponds with and connects with the essence of what you naturally consist of – down to your genetic matter, molecular structures, and subatomic particles. You will be less likely to experience common chronic and degenerative conditions, and various other ailments. Together, this can guide you toward being more in alignment with true health, your beneficial qualities, a cleaner energy, and to be the beauty you are.

"There is an essence of the Divine in all living things. And each person is literally a microcosm of the universe."
– Gloria Steinem

Some religious teachers have an understanding of a power existing throughout us. They seem to have an idea of what acknowledging the power means, including aligning with it by way of beneficial thoughts, words, and actions. They teach that you can live your life better by paying attention to this power. Some have certain names for it. Some define it in a way that limits it to certain individuals or styles of living. Some say it is one thing, and others say it is another thing. But all seem to agree that it exists. Some call it a form of intelligence. Some call it an inner drive. Some call it spirit, or soul. Some call it Divinity. Some say it is the energy consisting of what connects all and is through all.

"Every time you don't follow your inner guidance, you feel a loss of energy, loss of power, a sense of spiritual deadness."
– Shakti Gawain

Whatever it is, and however you want to define it, use the power of your essence to help you.

"We don't realize that the gods are not out there somewhere. They live in us all. They are the energies of life itself.
– Joseph Campbell

Whatever the essence or infinite intelligence is, it has formed you, those around you, and the plants, animals, birds, fish, insects, and all living things. You know there are certain things you do that make you feel more comfortable and in alignment with this energy. Respect and reverence for your life, for the lives of others, and for the lives of animals, as well as living in a way more in tune with Nature will help you to tune into the high frequency wavelength of power that is infinite intelligence, and keep it working for you in your life.

"If the doors of perception were cleansed everything would appear to man as it is, infinite."
– William Blake

You are the manifestation of energy.
You are power and potential, and you can use your wisdom to create the life more in alignment with the one you wish to have.

"Flesh and bone cannot contain the electrical energy that physically operates our body. To me, that is a physical, tangible, real sign of a soul, or that there is something unique in all of us that does not die."
– Patrick Swayze

# Thinking

"Every action has an ancestor of a thought."
– Ralph Waldo Emerson

The slightest change in your thoughts can send you on a path you may have never considered.

Very often people change their lives on the precept of one thought that drives them to at least aim for experiencing a life likely to be more satisfying than the route they had been on.

"The most beautiful experience we can have is the mysterious – the fundamental emotion which stands at the cradle of true art and true science."
– Albert Einstein

Sometimes it is our curiosity that triggers us to recognize things that will greatly influence our lives. For instance, when Albert Einstein was five years old his father showed him a compass. The thought of the compass working off an invisible power made such an impression on Einstein that he attributed the thought to setting off his life's journey. Five years later, he was given a copy of Aaron Bernstein's multivolume *Popular Books on Natural Science*. The books fascinated young Einstein and further defined his path toward becoming one of the most recognized figures in history.

People say Einstein's brain was different from the brains of most people. But after he died, his brain was examined and found to have

169

no unusual features. His mind and his ability to utilize it is what made him distinctive.

Perhaps we may not be able to use our minds in the same manner as Einstein did with his, but most people do have opportunities to access their intellect at a much deeper level than they have been accessing it.

Consider that just as the level of your physical health has much to do with the quality of your foods and how physically active you are, the level of life you are experiencing is reflective of the amount of your talent and intellect you are using, the quality of your thoughts, and otherwise the way you use your mind to factor and formulate your actions, communications, surroundings, and world.

"The problems we have today will not be solved by thinking the way we thought when we created them."
– Albert Einstein

Thoughts fuel actions. Actions that improve your life are the results of thoughts.

The animation of your body is the emotion of your thought energy. If you want to improve your life, use your thoughts to fuel helpful actions and communication to get you more satisfying results.

"We are what we think. All that we are arises with our thoughts. With our thoughts we make our world."
– Buddha

All sizes of human accomplishments are the results of thoughts. At first you may think you want to go to a particular place or obtain or experience a particular thing. The more you think about these, and the more you reason about them, the more likely you are to act on those thoughts and to go where you want to go, and to get or do what you want to get or do.

Luckily for us, thoughts can be guided.

Every one of your thoughts sends out a vibration. That vibration starts within your mind, which exists throughout your body.

By thinking specific thoughts, you can bring about certain energies into your life.

Thoughts can be negative or positive in that they create energy charges that flow from within the body tissues and out into the surrounding atmosphere and substances.

By choosing your thoughts, you select what type of electrical frequency you are engaged in and sending into the community and world.

Thoughts affect the fluid and mechanical structures of the body. They do this by changing the chemistry and electrical charge within the body, even to the point of altering the hormones and expressions, including where the blood flows, and the pace and volume of the breath. In this way, thoughts are like food in that they affect body chemistry.

Just as an unhealthful diet results in an unhealthful, acidic, toxic body, thoughts create chemical reactions that affect body tissues. Negative, acidic thoughts create more acidity in the body tissues, and this is seen as stress that can damage organs, suppress the immune system, alter movement, and lead to injuries and disease. Examples are the types of thoughts that create stress, which can help trigger a number of physical reactions, including anger, and physical ailments, such as high blood pressure and cardiovascular disease – which can be a combination of stressful thoughts, unhealthful environment, dysfunctional relationships, low-quality food, and lack of exercise.

"I don't eat junk foods and I don't think junk thoughts."
– Mildred "Peace Pilgrim" Norman

In combination with daily exercise, a healthful diet and communication, uplifting thoughts can transform the chemistry of your body. Simply changing your thoughts can change your blood pressure, the production of natural body chemicals, the tissue tension, and the acidity level of your body.

"Stress is not what happens to us. It's our response to what happens. And response is something we can choose."
– Maureen Kiloran

Various types of thoughts are felt more strongly in certain parts of the body. Body chemicals formed in response to certain emotions are produced more prominently within specific body tissues. The emotion molecules travel through the body tissues, resulting in some sort of physical actions that then affect what is and who is around you, and then travel further into the surrounding pond of life. This is so just as a small leaf that falls onto calm water creates a trickle of waves that emanate out to the stretches of the pond.

"Thoughts, like fleas, jump from man to man. But they don't bite everybody."
– Stanislaw Lec

You can feel the thought energy of others. Just as you can feel how angry they are, you can feel how serene a person is. "I could feel

171

their vibes" might be dismissed as a New Age term, but it is true. A person's thoughts create an energy and molecular field that is absorbed into the surrounding people, other animals, plants, and objects.

Not only do thoughts matter, they create matter. Your body hosts and helps to create a variety of microbes making up your microbiome. Your body is also surrounded by an electrically-charged neurochemical biome created by your thoughts that produce molecules of emotion and electric energy patterns.

If you ever perceived that you could feel someone's thoughts, know that what you detected is real. It is communion impacting community, society, and culture.

"I know of no more encouraging fact than the unquestioned ability of man to elevate his life by conscious endeavor."
– Henry David Thoreau

"Throughout all history, the great wise men and teachers, philosophers, and prophets have disagreed with one another on many different things. It is only on this one point that they are in complete and unanimous agreement. We become what we think about."
– Earl Nightingale

If you want to transform your life, in addition to improving your diet, be particularly focused on your thoughts because – as the saying goes – your thoughts have your tomorrow inside.

Seeds produce after their own kind. A tomato seed sprouts into a tomato plant, not into an oak tree. Thoughts are the seeds of your words and actions that produce results. To experience results that are more satisfying than the ones you have been getting, plant better-quality thoughts in your mind.

If you are not planting thoughts in your mind that you can nurture to get the results you want by turning those thoughts into action, then your thoughts are random, like weeds.

"Whatever you persistently allow to occupy your thoughts will magnify in your life."
– Frederick Douglass

Thoughts help to guide what you become, and where you arrive.

Similar to seeds, thoughts can be fed, nurtured, and grown into their potential. If you want your life to be uplifted, plant the seeds that would produce the desired harvest by thinking helpful thoughts.

Your mind is always focused on something. Some of this you can control, and some is simply the way it is as part of who you are. You can choose to focus on things that are beneficial to creating the life you want.

You are going to think, so you may as well think in ways beneficial to you. You are going to exist, and you may as well work to exist in a way enjoyable for you.

"If we are to make reality endurable, we must all nourish a fantasy or two."
– Marcel Proust

If you focus on thoughts of accomplishing what you want, and take relatable actions, then you are more likely to attain your goals.

"You have it easily in your power to increase the sum total of this world's happiness now. How? By giving a few words of sincere appreciation to someone who is lonely or discouraged. Perhaps you will forget tomorrow the kind words you say today, but the recipient may cherish them over a lifetime."
– Dale Carnegie

A mind fed constructive, complimentary, loving, uplifting, motivational, and helpful thoughts is more likely to produce verbal and physical emotions corresponding with those positive thoughts.

Begin to think in a way that adjusts your energy to the frequency you yearn to enjoy.

Just as a music conductor determines the way an orchestra plays a symphony, people can conduct the symphony of thoughts playing out in their minds.

Thoughts are power tools. Successful people tune into a way of thinking that builds accomplishment. Similarly, a person who is a consistent failure is likely tuned into a way of thinking that fuels the experience. In this way thoughts create an energy web that can capture what is desired, or what isn't. Some people call this a karmic affect. This is because your thoughts create your actions, and you experience what your thoughts and actions create.

Many people only use a tiny bit of their thought power, while others learn to use it for what amounts to brilliance and magnificence.

"Every day, think as you wake up, today I am fortunate to be alive, I have a precious human life, I am not going to waste it. I am going to use all my energies to develop myself, to expand my heart out to others; to achieve enlightenment for the benefit of all beings. I

am going to have kind thoughts towards others, I am not going to get angry or think badly about others. I am going to benefit others as much as I can."
– Dalai Lama

Unfortunately, there are those who misuse their power, and who choose to live in ways inconsiderate of and damaging to wildlife, and destructive to Earth.

No matter what pattern of thinking you have allowed yourself to fall into, outside of sexuality, and some other matters, you can willfully change it.

Work to resist and break free of damaging thought patterns. Factor ways to elude destructive emotions, and maintain some sense of serenity. Consciously strengthen your abilities to think in a way more helpful to achieving health for you and those in your life. Reconfigure your relationship with life, and get out of self-destructive habits and tendencies. Retool your thoughts, actions, and communication to build a foundation for good things to happen.

"What we are today comes from our thoughts of yesterday, and our present thoughts build our life of tomorrow: Our life is the creation of our mind."
– Buddha

A natural law is that of cause and effect. It largely rules over the power of thought. It is evident in the lives of those who work to improve their condition. What you think about often comes about through your communication and action.

"A single gentle rain makes the grass many shades greener. So our prospects brighten on the influx of better thoughts."
– Henry David Thoreau

Stories originating from all parts of Earth carry a theme of people finding the answers to their questions right in front of them. For a time, they may have been blind to the messages surrounding them.

"We are all too much inclined to walk through life with our eyes shut. There are things all around us, and right at our very feet, that we have never seen; because we have never really looked."
– Alexander Graham Bell

Throughout history the story has been recorded on cave walls, in ancient scripts, in novels, plays, lyrics, poems, and films. It is the story that humans can overcome challenges. A common thread within these stories describes the change a person goes through within their mind enabling them to overcome obstacles and achieve success. The message is of how it is up to the individual to conquer their self-doubt and to prosper by using their intuition, instinct, perception, yearning, skills, talents, and intellect.

"Normally, we do not so much look at things as overlook them."
– Alan Watts

Understand that learning and doing keeps your brain growing and active. Teach yourself about the things you need to learn to take the actions that will have you living more of the type of life you want to have. Engage in thoughts and activities corresponding with what you ideally see yourself thinking and doing, and in healthful relationships.

"The mind is not a vessel to be filled, but a fire to be kindled."
– William Butler Yeats

When you begin to practice a task requiring a certain type of focus and movement, such as drawing, dancing, yoga, bike riding, or swimming, or other sport, and you practice this task over and over during a period of weeks, months, and years, your brain rewires itself in relation to the parts of the brain controlling the movements you are making. This is done in correspondence with your thoughts. This process reveals that what you think about and what you physically do alters not only your muscles, but also the nerve cells of your brain and throughout your body.

"A lot of what passes for depression these days is nothing more than a body saying that it needs work."
– Geoffrey Norman

Because your neurons grow in accordance with what you are thinking, saying, and doing, it is important to continually think, say, and do the things necessary to participate in the life you want, and to start doing it as soon as possible as your daily life practice.

Whatever it is you want to do, learn about it and do it. Read books about it. Think about doing it. Plan on doing it. Write goals tuned to the intention of telling yourself you are going to do and accomplish the goals. And, most important of all, do what you want to do both mentally and physically.

Be dedicated to improvement and the expression of your better qualities.

"It's the repetition of affirmations that leads to belief. And once that belief becomes a deep conviction, things begin to happen."
– Claude M. Bristol

Rather than thinking your good fortunes are up to uncontrollable luck, think of luck as a matter of bringing about thoughts that are then manifested by the expression of good will in action.

Use your actions to continually work for better fortunes to happen.

Cultivate your ideas into reality by using thoughts, communication, and action to bring substances and circumstances into your life that fulfill your needs and desires.

Let your thoughts liberate you from whatever it is in you that has prevented you from succeeding.

Think in a way that captures the good things about life, and also increases the possibility for good things to happen.

Focus on thoughts of health assisted by invigorating exercise and a vibrant diet rich in fresh, whole, unprocessed plant-based foods.

Focus on thoughts of accomplishment and satisfaction brought on by the actions of working on and completing projects.

Focus on thoughts of happiness resulting from intentional living that brings you to continually engage in goal-oriented actions you take to fulfill your wishes.

Focus on thoughts of loving, nurturing relationships cultivated by respect, appreciation, gratitude, and beneficial communication.

Start now through your thoughts and actions to create your future happiness, love, and existence.

# Focus

"Imagination is more important than knowledge. For knowledge is limited to all we now know and understand, while imagination embraces the entire world, and all there ever will be to know and understand."
– Albert Einstein

Nutrition, movement, thought, planning, communication, regular sleep, and intentional, goal-oriented actions are all important in improving well-being, and especially in balance to experience vibrant health.

"That which dominates our imaginations and our thoughts will determine our lives, and our character."
– Ralph Waldo Emerson

Positive-thinking is so important to health that it could be considered an essential nutrient. This is because the activities of the mind are intermixed with and affect the tissues and body chemistry.

Just as healthful foods, daily exercise, and a regular sleeping pattern balance body chemistry, healthful thoughts trigger the release of various hormones influencing the chemistry and function of all the tissues.

"The world is full of people looking for spectacular happiness while they snub contentment."
– Doug Larson

177

Wellness and spiritual teachers throughout history have stressed the importance of the thought processes in conditioning health. In particular, many have taught about the health benefits of meditation to focus and reduce stress, confusion, anger, frustration, and let go of the upset of control that you don't actually control.

Science has shown that meditation is healthful in that it reduces the production of cortisol, a natural hormone produced by the body when it is under stress and can degrade memory processes. Cortisol levels are also reduced by laughter, fun activities, and agreeable physical interaction – including massage, cuddling, and sex.

"In the attitude of silence the soul finds the path in a clearer light, and what is elusive and deceptive resolves itself into crystal clearness."
– Mahatma Gandhi

"As irrigators lead water where they want, as archers make their arrows straight, as carpenters carve wood, the wise shape their minds."
– Buddha

Through his study of Tibetan monks who practice meditation for decades, Richard Davidson of the University of Wisconsin-Madison found that meditation influences the neural growth patterns of the brain.

The temporal parietal junction region of the brain, which deals with processing empathetic feelings and expressions is one of the regions meditation has been found to alter neurons of. The insula region of the brain, which deals with emotional response, is also affected by meditation.

Meditation has also been found to build the cortex area of the brain, which is involved in higher functions, and typically thins as we age. Thus, meditation is an antiaging practice.

"Do you have patience to wait till your mud settles and the water is clear? Can you remain unmoving till the right action arises by itself?"
– Lao Tzu

When the word "meditation" is mentioned some people entertain images of people in trances. Some are uncomfortable with the concept of meditation because they think it suggests a religious, or cultish practice – which are both fallacies. Others may think of meditation as not in tune with what they consider to be mainstream. But maybe mainstream isn't as good as they may believe, and going outside of the mainstream could be greatly beneficial to them.

Some think of meditation as an Eastern form of spirituality. But some form of meditation has been a common practice among people the world over. Ancient societies on all continents had their own form of meditation – called by different names.

Still others may not like the concept of doing meditation because they simply may be uncomfortable with and unwilling to face up to their thoughts.

Some people have been in such unhealthful situations their entire life that engaging in something healthful is foreign to them. Maybe this is because it displaces the stress they are accustomed to feeling, and the dysfunction they normally exist in. Doing something truly healthful may make them uncomfortable, as if they are losing their footing and control because they are in an unfamiliar place – even if that unfamiliar place is better for them.

However, since meditation is simply deep thinking, it is doubtful that there is anyone who hasn't practiced it by default at some time when faced with a life-altering decision or situation. They didn't know they were meditating.

"Silence is the element in which great things fashion themselves together."
– Thomas Carlyle

"Let us be silent – so we may hear the whisper of the gods."
– Ralph Waldo Emerson

Many people became familiar with the Eastern spiritual practice form of meditation when it was reported that the Beatles music group were studying transcendental meditation under the guidance of its founder, Maharishi Mahesh Yogi. The Beatles first studied with him in Wales. They traveled to Rishikesh, India, to continue their studies – along with my late, great friend, musician Ricksharaj.

Maharishi was from India and held a degree in physics. After studying under various teachers, his spiritual regeneration movement began in 1957. With encouragement from his students, in 1958 he began traveling the world to spread the message that humanity can rid itself of discontent. Schools of Maharishi's teaching have been established in several countries. Some of the teachings include the study of the ancient Vedic text, the *Bhagavad Gita*, which Maharishi called "the scripture of yoga."

However, meditation isn't limited to followers of Maharishi.

"Meditation is the discovery that the point of life is always arrived at in the immediate moment."
– Alan Watts

Meditating puts a person in a quiet state, during which sensory input is reduced. This is similar to deep sleep, but with the consciousness remaining engaged. During this time, just as in sleep, the neurons of the brain can process new information and make the neural connections needed to remember and deal with recently learned thought and action processes.

Those who regularly practice meditation, such as Buddhist monks, have been found to have strong gamma wave brain energy patterns that are associated with alertness, learning, and memory.

"Meditation is not just the means to an end. It is both the means, and the end."
– Jiddu Krishnamurti

Going through your thoughts with which you are uncomfortable, reconsidering them, and arranging them in a helpful order is what can be done when meditating.

Meditation helps you let go of issues and grasp hold of concepts to help manage others.

Meditation can be beneficial in dealing with the trials of life, as well as learning how to associate with beneficial events and the constant present.

"It is as important to cultivate your silent power as it is your word power."
– William James

Using the mind to focus on self – or the essence of being – during meditation, allows people to look at the engine of their mind, and service it. It allows people to take an inventory of their life, to consider on what their energies have been focused, to let go of the thoughts and feelings that are not helpful and may need to be disposed of, and to assign focus to those things needing attention.

"Inspiration does not come like a bolt, nor is it kinetic, energetic striving, but it comes into us slowly, and quietly, and all the time, though we must regularly – and every day – give it a little chance to start flowing, prime it with a little solitude and idleness."
– Brenda Ueland

To focus, be where there is solitude, and calmness. If possible, get out into a forest, or other natural environment, to meditate.

"They go inside a building to talk to their God. We go into the natural world and listen – and our Creator speaks to us."
– Lakota Man

Meditation may be practiced in combination with yoga, calisthenics, with introspective journaling, with artistic activities, with gardening, and with priority and goal review.

"Meditation is the tongue of the soul and the language of our spirit."
– Jeremy Taylor

Meditation helps focus the mind and tune the energy into the actions that need to be accomplished that day.

Getting into a daily morning practice of meditation, yoga, calisthenics, and goal review is an excellent way to start the day. The practice will help create progressive thoughts that trigger related actions and communication.

"The struggle of the male to learn to listen to and respect his own intuitive, inner promptings is the greatest challenge of all. His conditioning has been so powerful that it has all but destroyed his ability to be self-aware."
– Herb Goldberg

Meditating, yoga, and journaling can be particularly helpful for someone during a day without food but only water, which is called "fasting." As you allow the body to take a rest from eating food while drinking only water, you allow it to focus its energies on elimination, detoxifying, and healing. Some people will go on a juice feast, which is when they spend a day or more avoiding solid food but will consume fresh vegetable and/or fresh fruit juices, and water.

Another alternative to a pure water or a juice fast is to consume nothing but highly nutritious green smoothies and water for a week. Green smoothies consist of water blended with a fruit and some green leaves (such as spinach, kale, Romaine lettuce, chard, collard, dandelion, parsley, cilantro, celery, chickweed, purslane, or other green vegetables). A green nutrient powder added to the smoothie can also be helpful. (See: InfinityGreens.com.) Green smoothies contain more antioxidants than pure vegetable or fruit juices because many antioxidants are contained in the cell walls of the plants. Wheatgrass juice and fresh aloe gel are also excellent additions to green smoothies. Avoid putting starchy vegetables in green smoothies because the starch mixed with the fruit can cause bloating and gas. It is good to consume a variety of green vegetables.

When fasting and meditation are done on a day of rest from work, the mind has a chance to clear and refocus.

Many people teach that fasting and meditation are helpful to practice at each change of season. Some people drink only water while abstaining from food for 24 hours on the day of the full moon.

Just as fasting allows the body to dispose of toxins and undigested foods, meditation can be used to clear toxic thoughts and to align with more helpful and healing thoughts in tune with the life the person desires.

"We are frightened by our own solitude. Yet only in solitude can we learn to know ourselves, learn to handle our own eternity of aloneness. And love from one being to another is when two solitudes come nearer, to recognize, and protect, and comfort each other."
– Han Suyin

Some people do a personal retreat, spending a day or two in meditation while fasting, doing yoga and calisthenics, journaling, and visualizing their life as they would like it to be. This retreat session can be an amazing experience. A personal retreat done regularly (such as once every season), can help a person transform. It is a way to become more focused on accomplishing intentions. The silence of a retreat helps you live your life out loud.

"I have learned to seek my happiness by limiting my desires, rather than in attempting to satisfy them."
– John Stuart Mill

A person going through a personal retreat can gain mental strength. The benefits can continue after the fast by following a healthful diet and living intentionally with thoughts, actions, and communication corresponding with goals.

"Life does not consist mainly, or even largely, of facts and happenings. It consists mainly of the storm of thought that is forever flowing through one's head."
– Mark Twain

To keep the mind healthful, think healthful thoughts; study literature relating to what you most desire to be doing; stay involved in healthful activities; work to maintain loving relationships; and give the brain the best nutrients through high-quality, unprocessed foods, and intellectual stimulation.

The better health you obtain, the more agile you will be in performing the tasks necessary to accomplish your intentions.

As you practice healthfulness, your brain gets accustomed to supporting the mind posture you work to hold. The body chemistry adjusts as the tissues produce molecules of emotion in tune with it. It is not random, but is a result of thoughts, actions, and communication creating synapses in the neurons.

Exercise is important because it helps the brain, heart, and body to function in sync. During exercise, the brain utilizes the nerve cells throughout the body. This increases the agility of the body, heart, and mind, and the communication between them.

A part of the brain shown to function better on a clean diet combined with intentional thoughts and actions is the pineal gland. It is located in the center of the brain. Some call it "the spiritual gland" and the brain's trigger. Some say it is the receiver of inspiration.

**"I am convinced that there are universal currents of Divine thought vibrating the ether everywhere, and that any who can feel these vibrations is inspired."**
– Richard Wagner

These concepts of taking care of the body to build a healthful mind are ancient, and part of building a healthful community.

What ancient people didn't have is the modern-day understanding of food chemistry. That is not to say they didn't know certain substances impact both physical function and thought. They did understand the medicinal qualities of plant substances, and used herbs, teas, extracts, and tinctures to assist health.

Ancient people used psychedelic plants and psilocybin to influence changes in health, and to explore awareness.

Psychedelics can help induce a sense of awe, and the positive emotions of amusement, gratitude, happiness, kindness, compassion, and love. This can help develop life philosophies, and theories.

Because psychedelics can usher in positive emotions, they are beneficial in relieving stress, and in improving immunity.

**"The new formula of physics describes humans as paradoxical beings who have two complementary aspects: They can show properties of Newtonian objects and also infinite fields of consciousness."**
– Stanislav Grog

Don't simply jump into taking psychedelics. Learn about what they are, and how they can be beneficial. Research them.

Be safe. If on medications, or you have a genetic propensity for, or history of psychosis, ask your doctor or therapist what they know of psychedelics. Nobody should be pressured into taking them. Also, nobody on them should drive, or be in an unsafe situation.

A guided psychedelic experience in a safe environment can be beneficial. It can help to explore what Carl Jung called "the shadow self." It might help a person to work through life trials, release tensions, aid in reasoning, open perceptions, introduce new concepts, improve creativity, and bring an awareness of their better aspects and potential. Dr. Gabor Maté finds them helpful in treating addiction, anxiety, depression, PTSD, and adults with childhood trauma.

Writing, making art, playing instruments, listening to music, gardening, being in Nature, reading, being with a pet or an agreeable loved one, and talk therapy can be helpful while on a psychedelic.

"Although many of us think of psychedelics as dangerous drugs, it's time for a rethink. They are non-toxic, non-addictive, have very few side effects, and could potentially offer relief for people suffering from a range of psychological difficulties."
– Rasalind Watts, of the Imperial College Psilocybin Trial

"I am certain that the LSD experience has helped me very much. I find myself with a heightened color perception, and an appreciation of beauty almost destroyed by my years of depression."
– Bill Wilson, founder of Alcoholics Anonymous

"As we experience a resurgence of interest in psychedelics, we can again fantasize about a different future."
– Erika Dyck, Chacruna Institute for Psychedelic Plant Medicines

"Psychedelics are illegal not because a loving government is concerned you may jump out of a third-story window. Psychedelics are illegal because they dissolve opinion structures and culturally laid down models of behavior and information processing. They open you up to the possibility that everything you know is wrong.
– Terence McKenna

"I don't think we have time to wait for the science to tell us these medicines are useful. The indigenous cultures already have."
– Gail Bradbrook

Consider the possibility you might be lacking in beneficial sensory experiences, even to the point of dormancy – including aspects of your better qualities. A book you might find helpful is Dacher Keltner's *Awe: The New Science of Everyday Wonder*.

# Visualization

"Never lose sight of the fact that all human felicity lies in man's imagination and that he cannot think to attain it unless he heeds all his caprices."
– Donatien Alphonse "Marquis de Sade" François

"All meaningful and lasting change starts first in your imagination and then works its way out."
– Albert Einstein

"Thought is action in rehearsal."
– Sigmund Freud

Much of your life is initially created in your mind. The visionary life within your thoughts manifests into reality through your actions and communication.

Your thoughts control what your body will be doing, the tasks you will be performing, the communication you will be engaging in, and what you do to shape, arrange, color, and tone your world. Because of this process, your life is more likely to resemble the ways in which you visualize your life. That is, if you take the actions and communicate in alignment with what you want to see, hear, and be.

"No matter how qualified or deserving you are, you will never reach a better life until you can imagine it for yourself and allow yourself to have it."
– Richard Bach

If you want your life to be a certain way, start thinking of it being that way. Work your thoughts into actions and communication to create that life. Pay attention to the things that will inspire or influence your mind to bring this about. Act to manifest it.

"Dream lofty dreams, and as you dream so shall you become. Your vision is the promise of what you shall one day be; your ideal is the prophecy of what you shall at last unveil."
– James Allen

It takes practice to get your mind to think about the things you want to happen. While in the past your life may have been slothful and unappealing, some or much of this likely had to do with the way you conducted your thoughts. To get out of that mindset, retrain your patterns of thought in a way that improves your time management, goal setting, communication, food choices, fitness, actions, surroundings, relationships, satisfaction, and the expression of your yearning, talents, skills, intellect, and better qualities.

"Vision is perhaps our greatest strength. It has kept us alive to the power and continuity of thought through the centuries, it makes us peer into the future and lends shape to the unknown."
– Li Ka Shing

Visualize yourself working hard, exercising, experiencing vibrant health, eating a healthful diet, enjoying nurturing and loving relationships, expressing kind and uplifting words and thoughts to those around you who reflect these back to you, utilizing your talents and better qualities in ways beneficial to your happiness and strengths, using your intellect to create peace, and being attuned to all that is good.

The key words in the previous paragraph are "working hard."

"The first step towards getting somewhere is to decide that you are not going to stay where you are."
– John Pierpont Morgan

Imagine your life free of the things that are unhealthful, unhelpful, unkind, damaging, wasteful, unsustainable, and that negate and suppress your better qualities.

Keep visualizing yourself consistently and persistently improving your life and the condition of Nature that supports you. Work for it.

"Your vision will become clear only when you look into your heart. Who looks outside, dreams. Who looks inside, awakens."
– Carl Gustav Jung

186

Make it a habit to visualize what you want to experience. Let it fuel actions and communication that bring about desired changes.

Permeate your thoughts with those in alignment with realizing your goals.

Bring a helpful emotional attitude into play to help you progress toward the better life you desire. In alignment with this, carry the posture of the healthful and thriving version of yourself that you yearn for and hope to be.

Mental imagery can help you improve. But a major key to obtaining the life you want is that you must engage in the physical processes of action and communication to attain the life you want, and not to be simply stuck in what can be the stagnation of fantasizing amid randomness and the agendas of others.

"In order to change an existing paradigm you do not struggle to try and change the problematic model. You create a new model and make the old one obsolete."
– Richard Buckminster Fuller

In one way or another, change will happen. It is likely that some of it will be less favorable. Use your intuition and intention to guide you through difficulties while focusing to somehow bring out positive from even the less desirable change.

"Go confidently in the direction of your dreams! Live the life you've imagined. As you simplify your life, the laws of the universe will be simpler."
– Henry David Thoreau

As I mention elsewhere, when you practice a task requiring a certain type of focus and movement, such as drawing, martial arts, dancing, yoga, biking, swimming, or other sport or skill, and you continue doing so over and over during a period of weeks, months, and years, your brain rewires itself in relation to the parts of the brain controlling the movements you make. This shows that what you think about and what you do alters not only your muscles, but also the form and function of the neurons, both inside your brain and throughout your tissues.

"If you are seeking creative ideas, go out walking. Angels whisper to a man when he goes for a walk."
– Raymond Inmon

"Paint the walls of your mind with many beautiful pictures."
– William Lyons Phelps

187

Choose to use the power of your motivational visualization to fuel, nurture, and formulate your work, days, surroundings, relations, and life.

Uplift your thoughts with inspirational literature, music, and other arts. Let the common theme of your thoughts be empowering motivation that guides your actions, communication, and how you choose to participate in life.

Continually engage in working to attain the goals you set in tune with your visualizations.

Become a participant in the change you wish to be and see.

"The soul is dyed the color of its thoughts. Think only on those things that are in line with your principles and can bear the full light of day. The content of your character is your choice. Day by day, what you think, and what you do is who you become. Your integrity is your destiny. It is the light that guides your way."
– Heraclitus

Spend time visualizing to clarify your intentions, and to be more present within them. Set the intentions on paper as a list of goals. Act on the intentions as your daily practice.

You will be reformulated through the combination of reading and adjusting your goals every morning, following an unprocessed plant-based diet, engaging in regular morning exercise, and putting your intentions into your actions and communication.

"Every single moment has a particular rhythm to it, and we have the capacity to expand or contract an individual moment as appropriate. One way to shift what's going on in our world is not to try to rush to do more, but to allow ourselves to go deeper into that moment of being present. Our ability to shift gears, to shift our rhythm to meet that moment and be present in it, is what allows us to experience the fullness of life."
– Stephan Rechtschaffen

Your transformation, integrity, drive, energy, work, creativity, confidence, improvement, intention, focus, strength, motivation, better qualities, how you tune into your intellect, and the practice of your skills, craft, and talent in tune with your goals can be contagious. You might be the light your loved ones, community, society, and culture needs.

Work on and heal your self. Focus there. Bring it forward into the manifestation of a better life.

# Visualizing into Your Future

"Most people are not really free. They are confined by the niche in the world that they carve out for themselves. They limit themselves to fewer possibilities by the narrowness of their vision."
– Vidiadhar Surajprasad Naipaul

"I shut my eyes in order to see."
– Paul Gaugin

Read this chapter. Then, close your eyes and participate in it.

"And, just as it only takes a moment to die, it only takes a moment to live. You just close your eyes and let every futile fear slip away. And then, in this new state, free from fear, you ask yourself Who am I? If I could live without doubt, what would I do? If I could be kind without the fear of being screwed over? If I could love without fear of being hurt? If I could taste the sweetness of today without thinking of how I will miss the taste of tomorrow? If I could not fear the passing of time and the people it will steal? Yes. What would I do? Who would I care for? What battle would I fight? Which paths would I step down? What joys would I allow myself? What internal mysteries would I solve? How, in short, would I live?"
– Matt Haig

As an exercise, close your eyes and visualize your life the way you want it to be. Keeping your eyes closed, hold that image of your desired life and explore what it looks like. Recognize what it is you see.

"What a man thinks of himself, that is what determines, or rather, indicates his fate."
– Henry David Thoreau

Visualize your life decluttered, organized, environmentally sustainable, fed with high-quality foods, intellectually stimulated, professionally successful, nurturing to your talents, skills, and craft, and infused with health and love.

What will you be doing in the satisfactory life? Which vibrant foods will you be eating? In which ways will you exercise and be active? What will you be working on? Where will you be? With whom will you be? What do the surroundings look like? What are you going to be doing to transform this image into reality?

Open your eyes.

Write down and/or draw what you saw in your visualization. Include details.

Make a list of goals you can read and adjust every morning to start your day with purpose and intention focused on creating a more healthful life.

Welcome to your future.

Create it.

"Every day is a journey, and the journey itself is home."
– Matsuo Basho

"Take the first step in faith. You don't have to see the whole staircase. Just take the first step."
– Marin Luther King, Jr.

# Be Your Life Architect

"Life is raw material. We are artisans. We can sculpt our existence into something beautiful, or debase it into ugliness. It's in our hands."
– Cathy Better

Just as a stone worker creates a structure out of a pile of rocks and some other materials, you can create a life for yourself out of whatever materials it now consists of.

Being a proactive architect of your life involves working with what you have as your recipe ingredients.

Whether or not you are actively engaging in it, you are helping to create your future – wanted, or otherwise. You may as well think the thoughts to fuel actions and words creating the life you will live in.

Just as the repetition of a wheel advances a vehicle to a new location, through your repetition of thoughts and actions combined with helpful communication, your life will get to a different place.

Constructing something is about working with patterns.

"Nature is an endless combination and repetition of a very few laws."
– Ralph Waldo Emerson

When considering a structure it is easy to recognize geometric patterns within its design. The structure was also constructed by a pattern of work that put the materials together. The materials were

191

also formed by a geometric pattern of growth and/or compaction of substances.

There are patterns in your body, in your fingers, eyes, and through all the structures of your being, including all of your cells, and within the substances making up the cells. These structures are formulated by an inner energy that has directed the formation of the structures in relation to a pattern. The things you eat contain patterns and were formulated by growth patterns that continually form within the laws of Nature. The pattern of digestion breaks down the substances you eat into materials that are of patterns, and these are used by the body in a pattern that creates the patterns of your tissues.

There are also patterns in thoughts.

"Thought is the sculptor who can create the person you want to be."
– Henry David Thoreau

There are patterns in music, which are created by patterns of thinking. Music is mathematical, and works like magic to create patterns in the minds of those who hear it. That process can alter the brain function, and the movement, communication, breathing, heart rate, and body chemistry of those who hear the music.

"Teaching music is not my main purpose. I want to make good citizens. If children hear fine music from the day of their birth and learn to play it, they develop sensitivity, discipline, and endurance. They get a beautiful heart."
– Shinichi Suzuki

After twenty years of research, in 1993 University of California Irvine physicist Gordon Shaw published a study in which he concluded that listening to classical music could temporarily increase a person's I.Q. Over the course of decades, Shaw studied the brain's ability to recognize symmetries and patterns in sounds. He found that people apply this process in solving math problems, in playing music, and in performing tasks, such as playing chess.

In his research, Shaw concluded that the brain's patterns resemble classical musical compositions. In reverse, he hypothesized that the brain could also be influenced by classical music.

In his research, Shaw worked with cellist and psychologist Frances Rauscher to put three year olds through a six-month test with half of them receiving voice lessons and the others receiving instruction in piano. After six months, those who had the piano lessons displayed improvement in spatial-temporal reasoning.

With another test, Shaw put college students through tests that showed their IQs improved by nine points after listening to classical music. The study involved having the students go through various stages of tests that included silence, relaxation tapes, and listening to Wolfgang Amadeus Mozart's Sonata for Two Pianos in D Major.

Shaw's research revealed an increase in the IQ of the college students who listened to the Mozart sonata. This discovery, now known as "the Mozart effect," brought Florida state-funded childcare centers to play music by Ludwig van Beethoven, and the state of Georgia to distribute classical music recordings to new mothers.

Using Shaw's research as a marketing tool, companies began selling classical music recordings specifically meant for parents to play to their babies and toddlers.

Shaw went on to write a book, *Keeping Mozart in Mind*, and developed a piano keyboard process specifically designed to improve math skills.

In subsequent studies, Shaw used magnetic resonance imaging to show that Mozart's music stimulated the brain's cortex more than music by Beethoven, which left Shaw puzzled.

"If I were not a physicist, I would probably be a musician. I often think in music. I live my daydreams in music. I see my life in terms of music."
– Albert Einstein

One of my favorite descriptions of how humans relate to the patterns of music is in the opening of Randall Grass' book, *Great Spirits: Portraits of Life-Changing World Music Artists*. In it, Grass writes, "Music has a way of ineffably penetrating our hearts and minds and souls. Perhaps, then, it should not be surprising that the most recent theory concocted to explain the universe is string theory, which posits that the smallest, irreducible element at the core of any piece of matter is a single, vibrating string. In other words, according to this theory, music is the essence of the universe: the cosmos is one massive symphony of vibrations and waves pulsating at myriad frequencies, tempos, and rhythms." Grass, who is a musician and master in world music, theorizes that, "The capacity of humans to relate to music may be simply an innate means for people to comprehend and connect with the cosmos at the most profound level."

"Rhythm and harmony are essential to the whole of life."
– Plato

"To understand is to perceive patterns."
– Isaiah Berlin

Just as the notes of music put in a certain pattern can be either chaotic or pleasant, so too are the patterns of your thoughts, which play out as chaotic or pleasant in your actions and words.

Thoughts help form the network of neurons within you, the actions your tissues make, and the arrangement of the things around you. As you do, hear, feel, say, and see things, the memories of those are stored as patterns in connections between neurons that are formed according to what you are involved in.

It is the repetition and patterns formed within the neurons of your brain and body combined with the way certain experiences, memories, behaviors, and chemistry turn on and off specific genes, and the patterns of those genes, that collectively create what you call "my life."

"Mathematics possesses not only truth, but also supreme beauty."
– Bertrand Russell

There are patterns in leaves, in seeds, in cells, and in all the structures of all living things. The surface structures of animals and plants have patterns. More patterns are in the structures of the tissues. Other patterns are in the microscopic structures of the cells, in the intercellular structures, in the nucleus, chromatin, DNA, molecules, and in the subatomic electrons and protons, and the intricacies of smallness. There are patterns in the trillions of activities taking place within cells during every split second. The patterns are partially created by electromagnetic energy, which is the power of Nature, which is in us, throughout us, and surrounds us.

There too are patterns in your essence. And there is power there. These powers are your talents, abilities, instinct, intellect, and yearning guided by the elegant power of your spirit. You can, with your power, use these to formulate your life and build it into its potential. You have the strength within you to help make this happen. You know it is there; it drives you to be attracted to and to be pleased by particular sounds, colors, shades, textures, smells, shapes, and feelings – which all consist of patterns. Left to randomness these attributes can be like the pieces of a puzzle in a pile. Organized and managed, they can create the gorgeous picture of what your life can become, if you would engage your powers to compose it.

Think and align with, and work to awaken the patterns of powerful energy resting within. Build patterns in everything you think and do in alignment with the results you desire.

"A successful man is one who can lay a firm foundation with the bricks that others throw at him."
– David Brinkley

Every building, machine, product, business, document, and work of literature, music, sculpture and other form of art and human creation is the product of an idea, which is a thought.

The first structure existing before something is built or created is the vibrational structure made of thoughts formulated inside the architect's mind. Similarly, your mind is the architect of your actions helping to create your future.

Just as an architect first thinks up plans, then illustrates them before bringing them into reality by creating a structure, you too can work your thoughts into reality by writing your goals, and then working to create them into reality. Writing your goals is one of the most basic steps toward manifesting them.

Consider that the cells of your body have a game plan, or a blueprint they follow. It is called the DNA and the pattern, chemistry, and energy within it determines the design and function of the cells.

Each person is like a vine constantly growing. The vine can be guided to grow in a certain way, or it can be left to form in whatever way it happens to grow.

Like a gardener coaxing a vine to grow along the pattern of a trellis, each person can guide the ways in which their life develops and what pattern it follows.

Actions result in learning, which is knowledge that can be used to bring about more actions to create what you desire.

Your actions sew a fabric into the life around you. What you do becomes part of your surroundings just as a thread becomes part of the fabric it is sewn into.

As you continually work to attain your goals, including by fumbling and making and learning from errors, and carrying on in determination, you will learn what you need to know to achieve your goals.

As you work toward what you want, the path toward the life you want will keep unfolding before you in a pattern relating to how you act, communicate, and lead your life, which is in accordance with the patterns of your thoughts.

"We are weaving character every day, and the way to weave the best character is to be kind and to be useful. Think right, act right; it is what we think and do that makes us who we are."
    – Elbert Hubbard

What you do each moment of every day creates a furrow. The seeds planted in that furrow consist of whatever you are nurturing through your thoughts, emotions, communication, and actions. Those thoughts and actions that are helpful and beautiful will continue to flower as you nurture them; the opposite thoughts and actions will result in negatives, and will need to be weeded out. Thus the longer you live, much of the reality surrounding you becomes part of your own making.

"We know what a person thinks not when he tells us what he thinks, but by his actions."
    – Isaac Bashevis Singer

Most people have likely heard of the concept that is, "As you sew, so shall ye reap." Usually attributed to The Bible (Galatians 6:7), it is not something limited to those who believe in the Bible. It is a fundamental law of life. Your actions and communication will most often bring about results in accordance with the communication and actions, which are the blossoms of your thoughts.

"No matter how small and unimportant what we are doing may seem, if we do it well, it may soon become the step that will lead us to better things."
    – Channing Pollock

Where you are right now is where you can begin using the knowledge you have to get you to where you want to be. The actions you take and communication you make will help bring you to and formulate your future.

"Any place that we love becomes our world."
    – Oscar Wilde

As artists use their imagination to create works of art, use your imagination to make your life into your art.

"'What are you?' someone asks. 'I am the story of my self,' comes the answer."
    – M. Scott Momady

# Resonational Inheritance

"Memories of our lives, of our works, and our deeds will continue in others."
– Rosa Parks

The resonation of others has an impact on you. The more closely you live in relation to someone the more of an influence you have on each other's thoughts, actions, communication, style, and lives.

Those who spend an abundance of time together, such as married couples, often not only start thinking the same, they also begin to resemble each other, express similar mannerisms and vocal patterns, and adapt to doing things in the same way.

Medical anthropologists at the University of Würzburg in Germany have discovered that when babies as young as three days old cry, they already imitate the melodic patterns of their mother's language. The study, published in the November 5, 2009 edition of the journal *Current Biology*, concluded that babies learn the melody patterns of the mother's language while still in the womb. Babies of French-speaking mothers were found to cry in a different melody than babies of German-speaking mothers. By three months, babies can mimic the vowel sounds in their parents' language.

"What you leave behind is not what is engraved in stone monuments, but what is woven into the lives of others."
– Pericles

Children often not only speak in tonal qualities similar to their parents, they also develop similar wants, appetites, emotional behaviors, concerns, and even breathing patterns. This is because they are exposed to the same patterns of thoughts, actions, communication, sounds, and nutrients.

Vibrational patterns can last generations. The subtleties involved with how your parents lived likely had to do with the life choices of their parents, grandparents, and other ancestors.

Scientists have discovered the presence of what are called "mirror neurons." This term is used to describe neurons within our brains and body tissues that respond to the way those around us conduct themselves.

To understand how mirror neurons work and how the brain wires itself in relation to what the person experiences is to understand that we can become wired in relation to what we see other people doing, hear them saying, and otherwise experiencing.

The simple act of continually being around someone helps to formulate our neural growth. In this way, we can inherit some of the neural growth patterns of the people we spend time around. Some of the neural growth patterns in us relate to what other people have been exposed to, and in how they respond and react to situations.

"Long after a deed is done, the trace or momentum of the intention left behind it remains as a seed, conditioning our future happiness, or unhappiness."
– Gil Fronsdal

The vibrational octaves of your ancestors are likely to keep flowing through you in thought processes, in habits, in choices of food, music, and lifestyle, and in how you communicate. Ancestral memories are expressed through your mannerisms, vocal tone, resonance, and inflection, the words you use, other forms of communication, and in other subtle ways.

The voice is a good example of how patterns developed in your ancestry continue through you. Vocal tone is one vibration that continues from generation to generation. Even a person who is adopted into a family will conform to the resonance, inflection, tone, and other voice qualities of the adopted family. The vibrations that travel through the parents and out through their voice boxes will tune the children's voices into the same vibration. This phenomenon represents that of energy influencing neural growth, tissue development, relationships, communication, and social interaction.

In addition to vocal tones, children absorb the energy vibrations of other parental expressions, including thought processes (which are also vibrations) expressed through words, actions, and attitudes (which are all tonal patterns). The thoughts alone create molecules of emotion, which carry vibrational patterns, and are emitted by all people, and subtly impact those around them.

"The past is never dead. It's not even past. All of us labor in webs spun long before we were born, webs of heredity and environment, of desire and consequence, of history and eternity. Haunted by wrong turns and roads not taken, we pursue images perceived as new but whose providence dates to the dim dramas of childhood, which are themselves but ripples of consequence echoing down the generations. The quotidian demands of life distract from this resonance of images and events, but some of us feel it always."
– William Faulkner

We are all tuning forks taking on the vibrations of what we are exposed to. By continually being around others, you are playing a role in tuning them. Be aware that you can send the vibrations of your thoughts and life into the lives of the people surrounding you, such as your family, friends, lovers, fellow students, neighbors, and co-workers.

The inciting incidents of your life also leave you with traits that are the evidence of your experiences. These traits are also vibrational tones expressed through body language, posture, facial movements, attitudes, communication, and lifestyle choices.

Unfortunately, you can carry on the negative and generally unhelpful energies carried by your ancestors and those you've spent time around.

For some, memories of their life are an echo of repulsion.

The good news is that you can readjust your being, retune your energy, and conduct yourself in more healthful ways that will build more helpful neural growth patterns.

"Don't seek to merely get rid of the negative things in your life. Instead, transform their energy into something of real positive value."
– Ralph Marston

Some of us have been lucky in that our ancestors and relationships have been relatively healthful. That does not mean we can't begin to make unwise choices bringing us into unhealthful patterns. Nor, if we came from an unfortunate background, does it

199

mean we need to continue participating in unhealthful patterns possibly resonating from our ancestry and associations.

We can recondition our conditions.

Every day and moment we can choose to saturate our lives with healthful behavior in harmony with a higher level of consciousness.

**"There is more hunger for love and appreciation in this world than for bread."**
— Mother Teresa

Some of us were born into families carrying a history of generations of brutal, drunken, poverty-stricken, depressed, angry, abused, uneducated, malnourished, unloving ancestors whose fractured lives were rife with some combination of addictions, homelessness, failure, petty crime, infighting, slander, dishonesty, unwise confrontations, and other forms of ruin. Often these sorts of family issues can be traced back several generations, and the pattern is the same – tragic or defeated lives that could have been otherwise, if people had used their power to change their state.

It can often be heard that we should honor our ancestors and the sacrifices they made. For some of us, this is noble and helps dignify our life. This is because we had ancestors who strived to become wonderful people and who did good things.

For some of us the strongest impressions we have of our ancestors are of the unfortunate decisions they had made. Under such conditions, being told we should honor them may take a leap of faith, and perhaps would be a step into the unwise den of denial.

Instead of feeling obligated to pay tribute to lives rife with ruinous behavior, we can at least live more healthfully for ourselves, for those around us, and simply perpetuate whatever beauty we can generate. By doing so we would be going forward out of blame and surpass the unhelpful activity of judging those who may no longer exist and whose mental conditions, injuries, trauma, life situations, and decisions we may never be able to understand.

Many families carry on unhealthful patterns developed over decades, and even centuries. Unwise family histories seem to saturate the lives of some people to such an extreme they are unable to function in society. It is as if they are intellectually paralyzed by the unfortunate choices of past generations, and as if they are the end of the tuning fork, which squeals with the heightened vibrations of whatever tonal qualities were experienced in the root of the fork.

Vibrational inheritance can be blazingly apparent in the frenzied lives of politicians. We can see this manifested in certain families that have had generations of political corruption infusing their business and personal lives. They are a crescendo of all the energy of greed, lies, hypocrisy, and corruption generated by their ancestors. It is a disconnection from and opposite to the healthful vibrancy of Nature wherein they become an enemy of Nature and wildlife. Many of the wealthiest, money-hoarding people resonate with this damaging energy. It is displayed in the lives of those who own and/or greedily benefit from companies doing great harm to the environment and wildlife, such as meat farming, and the GMO, toxic farm chemical, pharmaceutical, petroleum, coal, natural gas, plastics, nuclear energy, weaponry, and prison industries.

> "There is no king who has not had a slave among his ancestors, and no slave who has not had a king among his."
> – Helen Keller

Without placing blame, review your ancestry, life history, and family heritage. Explore what you find. Consider that the choices and behaviors of your ancestors are impacting your life.

> "Each difficult moment has the potential to open my eyes and open my heart."
> – Myla Kabat-Zinn

If your life is not working for you, recognize that you can become actively engaged in changing the vibrational patterns resonating through you so your energy is in tune with your potential of experiencing satisfaction, health, and love.

Behind your genetic makeup is the mechanism that is your spirit, or essence – your spiritual genetics. This mechanism formed your being, and it remains as a tool you can use to factor and reformulate your life. It functions better when you live more healthfully and use your better qualities. It can be clarified through wise life choices to work in tune with intellectual stimulation, a healthful diet, a daily exercise regimen, and intentional, goal-oriented actions to create an amazing life.

By living healthfully, you can retune your body cells and your spirit from a history of unhealthful ancestors. I suggest to the people who are interested in doing this to tune into the vibrations of Nature through eating a plant-based diet; being close to and protecting the wildlife of plants and animals; filling their mind with life-confirming and encouraging literature and music; developing talents, craft, and skills; working to have healthful, nurturing relationships; and filling their days with intentional, goal-oriented activities.

Following a diet consisting of high-quality, low-fat, and unprocessed plant-based foods while getting into the habit of daily morning exercise, priority review, and then intentionally engaging in activities throughout every day associated with goals are some of the most powerful steps you can take to break unhealthful intergenerational vibrations.

Living healthfully accesses the cryptic backup copy of your being to correct the damaging patterns that had been running through you. As you live more healthfully and engage in intentional, helpful actions and communication, your neurons will rewire to be in tune with the wiser lifestyle you lead.

"The greatest discovery of any generation is that human beings can alter their lives by altering the attitudes of their minds."
– Albert Schweitzer

Honor your life by moving onto a better path than the one that may have been created for you.

Be your own journey and remember that you may be helping to create the journey of those who walk beside you, and also who arrive after you.

"The quality and fullness of our lives is not measured in length, but in the love and examples we leave those we have left behind."
– Cindy Crawford

"Our greatest responsibility is to be good ancestors."
– Jonas Salk

# Knowledge Is Power

"Do not seek to follow in the footsteps of the wise. Seek what they sought."
— Matsuo Basho

"You can't always be happy, but you can almost always be profoundly aware and curious, and reap the psychological and physical benefits. Thankfully, curiosity is not a fixed characteristic. It's a strength we can develop and wield on the path to a more fulfilling life."
— Todd Kashdan

To increase the likelihood of becoming the best version of yourself, become proactive in stimulating your mind, intellect, instinct, talents, skills, craft, and your better qualities to learn, act, and grow into an expression of those qualities.

"Education is for improving the lives of others, and for leaving your community and world better than you found it."
— Marian Wright Edelman

"Whoever acquires knowledge but does not practice it, is as one who plows but does not sow."
— Saadi

Many people lead lives far beneath what they are capable of living. Many never voluntarily read a book, rarely experience local cultural events, and don't get involved in – or even know much about

– the region where they live. All this is representative of how they may never exercise their power outside of their most basic needs. Even while living their minimal life they may be slothful.

It is easy to disconnect from parts of life that have great impact on us, such as exercise, nutrition, and talents. Doing so may lead to results we do not wish to experience. Neglecting to use our talents, skills, craft, and intellect in any attempts to live up to our higher potential will likely also negatively impact the lives of others.

It may seem easy to ignore things we think don't matter, but which may matter more than anything else. What may seem easy may amount to neglect, and make life – and the lives of others – more difficult.

People often recognize too late that they had in fact neglected part of their life that might have offered much benefit – if they had given it more attention. Often they realize what they did focus on was far less important than things they could have been giving attention.

We live in an age in which information is constantly being spewed out of the media at a rate at which no one person can keep up. From books to newspapers, magazines, newsletters, and journals, to audio- and videotapes, to theatrical and documentary films, to radio and TV shows to blogs, podcasts, and the mix of helpful and distractive stuff on the Internet, and to live entertainment and educational seminars and classes, information today seems to be present everywhere.

Information overload has become an issue with those who spend their days tuned in to the mass media. While there is an enormous amount of information being presented by these outlets, much of it is useless and results in mind clutter, wasted time, and wasted life. But the information is often presented in a way making it appear as if it is especially important. The goal of commercial media is to keep you tuned in so you see advertising. The result is a junk mindset, a junk diet, unnecessary shopping, and debt – which are products of the predatory corporate mass media and its onslaught of advertising.

"The degree of one's emotions varies inversely with one's knowledge of the facts – the less you know the hotter you get."
– Bertrand Russell

The strongest message to obtain from the mass media is that paying attention to the mass media is likely to be a waste of your time, energy, and resources, and it fills your mind with useless trivia while encouraging you to go into debt to shop for stuff you don't need while eating the lowest-quality foods that dull and degrade you.

Just as there are people who can zap your focus, energy, time, resources, and better qualities, there are substances in commercial culture that can rob you of the same.

Just as it is beneficial to wisely choose the people you would like to spend time with, and with whom you would allow to influence you, it is also wise to select what sort of information you choose to listen to, read, and believe.

Whether you are aware of it or not, you are constantly being influenced, you are always learning, you are absorbing molecules and energy patterns, your mind is factoring your surroundings, and you are formulating questions, calculating answers, and making decisions based on the information you are exposed to – and your nerve cells are reacting to and forming in relation to all this. The good thing is that you have some control over this, can choose which information you will pay more attention to, and can decide which information to use for your benefit.

"He that to what he sees, adds observation, and to what he reads, reflection, is in the right road to knowledge."
– Caleb Colton

Information is like food. Just as you can choose the most healthful foods to nourish and build your physical structure, you can select which information you want, and then use it to help construct thoughts triggering actions, communication, nerve patterns, and habits that will formulate your life.

Fortunately, there is an amazing assortment of information you can use to learn what will trigger improvement in your life.

Learning is a part of health. It is just as important to feed your mind quality educational information as it is to feed your body vibrant nutrients. Just as your body can thrive when fed high-quality nutrients and combine that with exercise, so too can your mind – if you will give it what it needs to perform the tasks necessary to nurture and pilot your life in the direction you want it to go.

There are many stories of people who overcame amazing physical and mental feats and who later mention they got through the situation by focusing their mind on something specific. In the same way, you can choose to focus on what you need for guiding your self toward accomplishing a goal.

If you are leading an unsatisfying life, or are feeling stuck in your situation, focus your thoughts on what you want. You will go toward what you continually focus on, and will form neural connections and molecules of emotion in relation to your focus and its related thoughts, actions, and communication.

"When people go to work, they shouldn't have to leave their hearts at home."
— Betty Bender

You are unique, and have worthy beneficial qualities. Don't try to be someone else. Work with your better qualities to be the best version of you.

Work every day to place your self in a healthy situation aligned with a wise manner of living.

"The wisest mind has something yet to learn."
— George Santayana

"When I look back, I am so impressed again with the life-giving power of literature. If I were a young person today, trying to gain a sense of myself in the world, I would do that again by reading, just as I did when I was young."
— Maya Angelou

Explore books to find what will benefit you.

By studying what you desire to know about, focusing on what you desire to have, thinking of what you desire to think of, working toward what you desire to obtain, and doing things you desire to be doing, you will be a part of what you desire.

"Education is not the filling of a pail, but the lighting of a fire."
— William Butler Yeats

I find it unfortunate that many people do not read books. I know people who say, outside of what was assigned during school, they have never voluntarily read a book in their life. Over the past few decades, many bookstores and libraries have closed. Even schools are considering saving money by doing away with books and libraries. I don't know how people can receive a well-rounded education without reading a variety of books written throughout and about history, culture, society, the arts, theory, philosophy, and other matters. This issue brings up memories of a film I saw when I was young in which the main character finds himself in a future where books are ancient relics turning to dust, and nobody seems to care.

"We read to know we are not alone."
— C. S. Lewis

Awaken your brain with reading. Literature is food for the mind. People who regularly engage in reading are found to have healthier brains with a wider variety of neural activity.

"Always read something that will make you look good if you die in the middle of it."
– P. J. O'Rourke

There is wisdom in literature; thus, reading is a way to learn from those who have existed before you.

Use literature to gain knowledge to better utilize your power. Read about things having to do with what you want to do. Read about people who have succeeded in what you want to succeed in. Read what will nurture your thoughts to stay focused on your most healthful goals. Read inspirational things.

Read and plan and act and communicate and work and nurture yourself into owning more of the life you desire.

"I suggest that the only books that influence us are those for which we are ready, and which have gone a little farther down our particular path than we have yet got ourselves."
– E. M. Forster

As your thoughts, actions, and communication become more attuned with the life you want to lead you will be harvesting the fruits of your labors. You will associate yourself with thoughts, actions, and communication that – and people who – are more aligned with what you want. The mix of thought, action, and communication is part of the power of association that can be a positive force in all areas of your life.

Just as any person who is involved in a culture, and who associates with others in that culture, then becomes part of the culture, everything you do becomes a part of you.

"Sometimes we understand grace only in retrospect. If someone were to ask me what grace is, I would probably respond, 'It's all grace.'"
– Bo Lozoff

By nurturing your intellect, setting goals in association with your talents and skills, passionately working toward those goals using your resources, talents, and beneficial qualities, following a low-fat, plant-based diet rich in unprocessed fruits and vegetables, working to improve the conditions of Nature, and associating with those who are doing the same, you will connect with and participate in the awakening culture of health.

"It is in self-limitation that a master first shows himself."
– Johann Wolfgang von Goethe

"So often it's our anxiety that trips us up from being our best selves. The great bulk of my life is a war with my nervous system."
– Ethan Hawke

"I grew up doing gymnastics, and this is what it taught me: Keep your focus straight ahead, no matter what's going on, and you won't fall off the beam. And, no one cares when you whine – so it's not worth it. I apply that daily."
– Marti King Young

By following a healthful lifestyle, you will be helping to create a new paradigm within global culture. Please, see the documentaries *Seed: The Untold Story*, *A River of Waste*, *Blackfish*, *Forks Over Knives*, *CowSpiracy*, *What the Health*, *A Delicate Balance*, *The Corporation*, *Vegucated*, and *Earthlings*.

"In today's environment, hoarding knowledge ultimately erodes your power. If you know something very important, the way to get power is by actually sharing it."
– Joseph Badaracco

# Surpass Your Past

"In the past, oppressed peoples often resorted to violence in their struggle to be free. But visionaries such as Mahatma Gandhi and the Rev. Martin Luther King Jr. have shown us that successful changes can be brought about nonviolently. I believe that, at the basic human level, most of us wish to be peaceful. Deep down, we desire constructive, fruitful growth, and dislike destruction.

Many people today agree that we need to reduce violence in our society. If we are truly serious about this, we must deal with the roots of violence, particularly those that exist within each of us. We need to embrace 'inner disarmament,' reducing our own emotions of suspicion, hatred, and hostility toward our brothers and sisters."
– Dalai Lama

"Every adversity, every failure, every heartache carries with it the seed of an equal or greater benefit."
– Napoleon Hill

Some people don't get on with healing their life and moving on to create a more healthful and fulfilling life for themselves because they are too busy pointing fingers, placing blame, projecting guilt, and otherwise rehashing everything they consider wrong about their past relationships. Perhaps they are stuck in is a situation of post-traumatic suffering. Maybe it would be good to explore the possibility of it.

"Trauma is a psychological wound that people sustain."
– Gabor Maté

209

Some ongoing troubles are likely to be post-traumatic stress disorder. Such a situation can overwhelm someone, including in their dreams. They can be triggered by anything from songs and other sounds to colors and smells, lighting, foods, conversations, textures, shapes, and other things. Without help, the PTSD can continue to damage their life to ruinous levels. It can include seeking to escape their problems in unhealthful ways. If that is your situation, please investigate what might benefit you. What you find to be helpful might be something to share with others experiencing similar issues.

"Healing yourself is connected with healing others."
– Yoko Ono

"Hurt not others with that which pains yourself."
– Udanavarga 5:18

Some people allow themselves to be held back because they are permitting their thoughts to be filled with regrets, blame, shame, defeat, frustration, guilt, and sadness.

It is time to work your way out of regrets, blame, shame, guilt, defeat, frustration, and sadness, so they no longer confuse and distort your image, thoughts, relationships, talents, intellect, worth, or life.

Do what you can to prevent your past from halting your progression into a more healthful and satisfying life. Others have successfully done so. Believe you can – and work to – do the same.

"That which we do not confront in ourselves we will meet as fate."
– Carl Gustav Jung

How others are respond to life has to do with what they have experienced, sensed, learned, been told, and otherwise what life and their sensory experiences have conditioned them to think, do, and say.

Do your best to know that when someone is harsh, rude, or otherwise unhelpful, their communication and actions have more to do with their history and what they have experienced, and less to do with you. There is no sense in internalizing their choices in the form of your being offended. You are not them, and they are not you. Hopefully they will learn to make wiser choices, and not go through life harming others by taking out their past on other people.

"If you are irritated by every rub, how will you be polished?"
– Jalal ad-Din Rumi

Some of us have adapted to being overly sensitive to what we perceive as the mistreatment, harshness, unwelcoming tonal qualities, and askance glances of others. By taking the reactions, words, and behaviors of others personally, you assume they are reacting because of you. Instead, they are reacting because of what is going on in their mind based on their history. You can't control what their history was, and you don't have power of their mind. What you can do is think, act, and communicate in ways that are responsible and beneficial to your progression, your peace, your safety, and your community. You can do so without reducing yourself to destructive and aggressive behavior that negates and damages you.

"Bad things do happen; how I respond to them defines my character and the quality of my life. I can choose to sit in perpetual sadness, immobilized by the gravity of my loss, or I can choose to rise from the pain and treasure the most precious gift I have – life itself."
— Walter Anderson

"Never regret. If it's good, it's wonderful. If it's bad, it's experience."
— Victoria Holt

It is always time to put your childhood and other parts of your past into a healthful perspective, to live with the intention of accomplishing your goals using your better qualities, to learn from your experiences, and to use them to get on with improving your life.

"You can be the ripest, juiciest peach in the world, and there is still going to be somebody who hates peaches."
— Dita Von Teese

It is always time to remember that not everyone will like you, will welcome you, or will treat you with the best manners. The loving, or unloving, behavior of others is not your responsibility. This includes the people in your past, which you cannot change.

"The turning point in the process of growing up is when you discover the core strength within you that survives all hurt."
— Max Lerner

"Rudeness is a weak man's imitation of strength."
— Eric Hoffer

When someone says something rude to you it is about what is going on in their mind, and is not what is going on in yours. Allowing yourself to feel bad because of someone else's view of you is agreeing with their view, their concept, and their belief, and is

211

adapting to their views. It is okay to disagree with someone who has a negative view of you, and to disagree without telling them that you disagree, without explaining yourself, and without being defensive.

Understand that not everyone will like or accept you. You can progress in life without bothering to address everyone who does not favor you. You do not need to be validated through their approval.

Don't stop at every bump. Do not stall, move forward.

"The most beautiful people we have known are those who have known defeat, known suffering, known struggle, known loss, and have found their way out of the depths. These persons have an appreciation, a sensitivity, and an understanding of life that fills them with compassion, gentleness, and a deep loving concern. Beautiful people do not just happen."
    – Elizabeth Kubler Ross

Stop allowing yourself to be negatively impacted or distracted by what you perceive to be the bad treatment of others toward your person. Keep your calm, maintain your tone, integrity, and confidence, and refuse to roleplay into the drama, unfortunate choices, and negativity of others.

Part of growing up is learning to hold the wisdom to conduct yourself in a healthful manner, no matter what others choose to do.

"Children are the living messages we send to a time we will not see."
    – John W. Whitehead

Even if it is someone as important in life as your parents treating you badly, you still can choose to avoid going into a negative mindset. They also are not your thoughts, intellect, yearning, talents, skills, or craft. If they choose to behave badly, that is their choice. Don't make it yours, or carry it into the next generation.

There are likely things you don't know about your parents – especially if they are or were abusive or troubled. Maybe they blocked off certain memories as being too painful and difficult to consider. This is so even if those parts of their history dramatically altered their behaviors and the way they treat and communicate with people. Hopefully, they will get, or did get, the help they need or needed. Unfortunately, a great transition to better behavior doesn't happen with many abusive people.

Your parents were the physical gateway through which your spirit manifested itself into physical form. Maybe, as it relates to you, and especially if you are from an abusive childhood, you might think of that origin as the main purpose of your parents.

Of course it would be good for parents to also protect and nurture their children, but – for a vast variety of reasons, including personal history and health matters – many don't.

Instead of being parents in the traditional style, which is most helpful in bringing children into a situation where they can grow to live independently and healthfully with people they cherish, the unfortunate parents instill traditions of failure and ruin.

"You and I possess within ourselves, at every moment of our lives, under all circumstances, the power to transform the quality of our lives."
– Werner Erhard

Rather than dwelling on the fact that certain relatives – or others – were not exactly perfect examples of loving nurturers, consider making yourself into the person you hoped they would be. But in a self-realized form of a more healthful version of you.

You can endlessly twirl around thoughts of why certain people were various levels of awful to you, but this likely will not do you any good. It could keep you lost – and stuck – in the past.

You can't improve your life by focusing on the wasted energies and damaging memories of your past, or stuck in the muck of what likely was generations of unfortunate choices by people now gone, and who you will never be able to fully understand.

What you can do is to work beauty into your life by using the lessons of your past, and the energy and resources of the present in alignment with your better qualities to continually make wiser choices to build a more healthful life.

"Wisdom denotes the pursuit of the best ends by the best means."
– Francis Hutchenson

You may be living in the debris of a ruined life. Realize it, and get on with nurturing your life. Many of us have had to do this – to live toward our answer, to surpass our past and to rise out of it, orphaning ourselves from our past, and starting anew in fresh surroundings with goals we continually and intentionally engage in fulfilling through everyday actions. It takes work. Do the work.

"They always say time changes things, but you actually have to change them yourself."
– Andy Warhol

Because my childhood situation continued to be awful and dangerous, as I had suffered varieties of abuse, multiple nasal fractures, spinal and other injuries, and people chose to engage in substance abuse and threatening behavior, I disconnected from that sickly family. Checking in many years later didn't reveal much improvement. Bad behavior and ugly, belittling, dismissive responses continued. There are only so many times I can listen to someone tell me I should never have been born, my parents never wanted me, and that I was the one who brought shame on the family – even though I was among the youngest. Interesting words spoken by people older than me who continued being awful into adulthood. We were never close. It's not as if I felt a loss from not having contact with people with whom I had never developed good memories.

The brother a year older than me starved to death as an adult in the bedroom we were abused in when we were children. He had also been unwanted, neglected, disregarded, and treated like a burden. So, there is the awful history, which I cannot change.

My parents died many years ago. There have been many years of no contact with those older brothers. They are more like distant strangers. It's safer, and better, this way. There had been many years where I had helped to financially support them, but once the parents had died, I felt no reason to continue any support. Especially of people who treat me as if I am a sin, and unworthy of breathing.

Maybe disconnecting is something you will need to do, to protect yourself, and to live healthfully, and as your own person in a life you create. There are resources to help you work into realizing a full life, including psychologists (look up the Jungian-trained psychologists in your town), 12-step programs, college courses, clubs with members who have similar interests, and physical fitness, yoga retreats, arts, culinary arts, permaculture, wildlife, and community service programs, associations, and volunteer opportunities. Get involved in life. You will build your own network of friends and associates.

"Eventually everyone sits down to a banquet of consequences."
– Robert Louis Stevenson

Some of the debris of a ruined life may comprise your thought patterns, how you communicate, and the way you go about things. You also might have clutter that you would be better off selling, donating, giving away, or otherwise detaching from.

Unfortunately, many people have so much experience with living in households that were confrontational, possessive, verbally abusive, scandalous, and otherwise disrespectful and unkind that they end up in the habit of being in a hyperdefensive mode. They have been conditioned to be confrontational, accusatory, and to assume that people are eager to reveal their so-called flaws, to ridicule and belittle them, to take advantage of them, to dismiss their safety, to devalue their intellect, or otherwise to do them harm. Their common way of communicating tinges on the unhealthful experiences long since passed, and they continually respond to situations in ways that carry on the damage, which creates more.

Some of your thoughts and behaviors are what you developed to cope with situations in which you once existed.

It is the time to release thoughts and behaviors that may have drifted into the unhealthful, may not be best for your current situation, and may be continuing to deconstruct, neglect, and abuse your better qualities, and otherwise to violate, damage, or revictimize you.

"No problem can be solved from the same level of consciousness that created it."
– Albert Einstein

Sometimes talking about your childhood is helpful, and helps others. Especially with helping others to realize what they went through, and encouraging them to refocus and reimagine their life, and to get busy working a healthier life into reality. That is using your childhood as a learning and coaching tool, and a way to help people move forward in life. Helping others can also help you.

How are you using your childhood and past experiences as lessons, as wisdom, and as tools to help you progress into a more healthful version of yourself?

Some of us are so stuck in the past that we continually think about how our childhood was wasted and tragic. We tragically waste large chunks of our adulthood thinking about how our childhood was tragically wasted. We spend our time telling everyone who will listen about how much our childhood was wasted and tragic. We may be living as if our life is left petrified in the state of what happened to us, which is a tragic waste of life. The energy of the focus magnifies it.

"If you have time to whine and complain about something, then you have the time to do something about it."
– Anthony J. D'Angelo

Some of us who are products of unhealthful households get stuck in the past, choosing to believe that we are unworthy, and allowing ourselves to get buried by the problems we experienced. We choose to feed the critical voice within us, allowing the negative comments said to us to become so loud that the critical voice within becomes our dominating thought pattern. In this way we feed the negative, choose to dwell in despair, and assault ourselves through internalized shame and self-defeating behavior. Please, choose more healthful practices.

Some of us have gotten stuck in worrying about what others think of us, and continually adjust ourselves to what we perceive to be the critical views of and harsh statements of others. That is not healthy, and it negates our power, life, and joy.

"You probably wouldn't worry about what people think of you if you could know how seldom they do."
– Olin Miller

Some of us use various pills, forms of alcohol, and other substances in attempts to medicate away the psychological pain of our past, numbing our ability to learn to deal healthfully with life's issues. This continual escapism may lead to addictions, destroying us. If someone confronts us within concern for our well-being, we may cleverly rationalize into denial that their perceptions are unfounded, and that we are perfectly fine. Denial is a monster in itself.

"When a population becomes distracted by trivia, when cultural life is redefined as a perpetual round of entertainments, when serious public conversation becomes a form of baby-talk, when, in short, people become an audience, and their public business a vaudeville act, then a nation finds itself at risk; culture-death is a clear possibility."
– Neil Postman

In the modern-day, television, computer games, social media, and other technological instruments can become addictive, are used as escapism, and can lead to ruin through wasted time, resources, energy, neglected relationships, lack of exercise, and a withdrawal from an active, lively, healthful community in which we have sensory experiences to help develop us.

Instead of engaging in real life, in society, and in healthful relationships, many people are hooked into electronic toys, as if electronica will substitute for the sensual, healthful stimulation of face-to-face relationships with real humans.

"To be silent the whole day, see no newspaper, hear no radio, listen to no gossip, be thoroughly and completely lazy, thoroughly and completely indifferent to the fate of the world is the finest medicine a man can give himself."
– Henry Miller

216

Many people spend so much time with their electronic toys that their relationships and lives are falling apart around them while their eyes are focused on the technogadget screens. Social media and gaming and TV addiction will never give you the stimulation and sensory experience satisfaction of real human interaction free of screen technology. Yet, so many people are there, trying to rely on technology for what they are messing in their life. If that describes you, it is well past time to unplug, get outside, and live a more active life engaged with the better qualities of community and culture.

"There are two ways of exerting one's strength: one is pushing down, the other is pulling up."
– Booker T. Washington

Some of us have treated people wrongly, have thought ourselves better than others, have been haughty, snobby, dismissive, impatient, unmannerly, rude, unkind, self-absorbed, and self-righteous. The cynical crown we put on our royal heads may sparkle with grand jewels of delusion placing us under a continual burden of spiritual debt. We may have placed it there as a defensive measure as we were afraid of allowing others to see that we are no more than they, and we may have been afraid that we were less.

"I had gone through life thinking I was better than everyone else and at the same time, being afraid of everyone. I was afraid to be me."
– Dennis Wholey

"The keenest sorrow is to recognize ourselves as the sole cause of all our adversities."
– Sophocles

"When nobody around you seems to measure up, it's time to check your yardstick."
– Bill Lemley

This isn't to say that there are not people of whom it would be most helpful to steer clear, or that lowering our standards is raising them. It is meant to say that opening the mind to the possibilities of what may be helpful could lead us to discover things beneficial to us, and these may be things that we have ignored, and to which we may have been closed. It is also to say that reconsidering our situation may allow us to grow past our past, to reconfigure what matters and what is helpful, and to proceed with a renewed awareness while focusing on and working toward our goals.

"One must not hold one's self so divine as to be unwilling occasionally to make improvements in one's creations."
– Ludwig van Beethoven

"As youth fades and time brings changes, we may change many of our present opinions. O let us refrain from setting ourselves up as judge of the highest matters."
– Plato

Some of us carry on in one big foggy pit of life because we have not allowed ourselves to realize we may have been a large part of what became our problems. We may be lying in the shards of a shattered life, and, partially because of the way we choose to exist, the shards keep scraping our soul. When we feel the hurt we take it out on other people, perpetuating the damage – including damaging us. We may not have treated people in the best way, may have judged them harshly, caused harm to others, and chose actions and words that damaged our relationships.

We may have treated others badly because we believe they have treated us badly. Even if people have treated us badly, doing the same to them is like banging one's head against a wall of the pit in which we are dwelling.

If the previous paragraphs describe you, pull yourself from the stubborn hole. Forgive yourself, forgive others, forgive each other. Get on with life. Do it with more kindness, healthier communication, and greater aim toward realizing your better aspects, while not expecting others to be what you think they should be.

Forget about trying to change your experiences with others into something they cannot be. The past cannot be reformulated, but it can be refactored as lessons learned, and used to live more wisely.

Remember one thing about the past: it's over.

"What can we ever gain in forever looking back and blaming ourselves if our lives have not turned out quite as we might have wished?"
– Kazou Ishiguro

Instead of expecting the past to be something it wasn't, focus on making the future into something good it can be. That is: better.

"When I was a boy of fourteen, my father was so ignorant I could hardly stand to have the old man around. But when I got to be twenty-one, I was astonished at how much he had learned in seven years."
– Mark Twain

Once you have placed the past in its place, you may be amazed at how it can uplift you. If you are someone who once hated and despised certain people and their choices, you may be amazed by how much you don't hate them when you get on with moving forward into a better, healthier life.

"Shun idleness. It is a rust that attaches itself to the most brilliant of metals."
– François-Marie "Voltaire" Arouet

If you truly want to heal and change your life for the better, what will work is getting and staying busy with making it improve through more healthful and focused study, thoughts, goals, actions, practices communication, nutrition, and exercise.

Continually heal, work to build confidence, choose to nurture good things in all areas of your life; follow a nutritious, plant-based diet; get through the residues of your past, use your talents, develop your skills, create your craft, feed your intellect, accept the power of love, and move on into a more healthful expression of your better qualities.

"Yesterday has nothing to do with who you are, only who you thought you were."
– Neale Donald Walsch

All of us who lived in unhealthful household situations would be better off not allowing abuse, neglect, assault, and bad choices to define us. It would be beneficial to make certain never to let the mistreatment by anyone define us. Instead of continuing to allow ourselves to be damaged, set respectful boundaries, and respond smartly to unwise treatment and choices.

"That's what happens when you're angry at people. You make them part of your life."
– Garrison Keillor

"Perhaps all the dragons in our lives are princesses who are only waiting to see us act, just once, with beauty and courage. Perhaps everything that frightens us is, in its deepest essence, something helpless that wants our love."
– Rainer Maria Rilke

Do not scrape open old wounds and harm the child who has already felt the pain. Begin and stay engaged in the healing process. Do so, instead of spreading your hurt into the lives of others.

Do not be spiteful, angry, and otherwise discouraging toward yourself, or others.

By holding onto hurt, you are more likely to hurt others. As it is said, hurt people hurt people. Avoid perpetuating the scenario.

Extinguish the fire of unfortunate memories burning you. Focus on what is helpful. Let a list of goals and the practice of engaging in an intentional life of working to achieve the goals be your salve.

"A problem is a chance for you to do your best."
– Duke Ellington

Refuse to be a victim who limits yourself to the mental traps formed in your mind when you were dealing with your aggressors.

Break through the walls of conditional acceptance, the limiting thought patterns, the self-pity, the destructive forms of communication, and the post-traumatic behavior.

Refuse to dwell in victim mentality, slothful behavior, and poverty thought patterns of victimhood.

Live your life welcoming the blessings that arrive when you live a life ruled by your better qualities, living your true intellect, taking care of yourself, and flourishing in your talents.

"Loneliness is the way by which destiny endeavors to lead man to himself."
– Hermann Hesse

In breaking away from the past, you may find yourself feeling alone. Loneliness and sadness can be a sort of mourning for any sort of good you did, or hoped to experience. Instead of working to create a better way, in loneliness you may find yourself traveling down old paths, associating with old feelings, scanning your memories to over-analyze expired relationships, and consuming low-quality foods that dull you. In loneliness, you might end up communicating with people who did you harm, who may not have changed their ways, and who may continue to cause problems, including treating you badly, who don't respect you, and who are not trustworthy.

"Lying to ourselves is more deeply ingrained than lying to others."
– Fyodor Dostoyevsky

You can make the unhealthful choice of feeding your loneliness with nostalgia and by romanticizing the past into a fabrication of something it never was. In that state you may be revising your memories of bad situations by telling yourself they weren't so terrible. By doing so you can drift into formerly unhealthful relationships and thought patterns, shoving you in the same old rut.

Stop allowing yourself to repeatedly experience the same damaging consequences of unfortunate choices.

"To see your drama clearly is to be liberated from it."
– Ken Keyes

Identify when you are going into a mindset of negative feelings that distort your abilities, dismiss your intellect, distract you from your goals, and bring you to any conclusion leaving you in doubt, sadness, and despair.

If you are constantly allowing your mind to drift into the past, it is likely that you are fumbling, and will be stuck there.

Rather than focusing on the past you didn't like, bring yourself into the present, work on your goals, stay focused, live intentionally, use your talents and skills, and create a healthful future.

"I skate to where the puck is going to be, not where it has been."
– Wayne Gretzky

Think and behave in ways in alignment with health, satisfaction, and a life of intentionally improving your situation.

"You can't have a better tomorrow if you are thinking about yesterday all the time."
– Charles F. Kettering

"Your past is not who you are, it's who you were."
– James Ray

Bring yourself into the present, and create your better future.

Choose to recognize, connect with, practice, and participate in your talents, skills, craft, intellect, and beneficial qualities.

Command yourself to break out of negative thought patterns.

Force yourself into habits that are positive, life-affirming, and build upon your beauty.

"You've got to get up every morning with determination if you're going to go to bed with satisfaction."
– George Horace Lorimer

Stop living in the past.

Keep busy in the present creating the life you want by living intentionally with defined purpose as you work toward your future using the tools of actions and words.

"You're not the first person who was ever confused, frightened, and even sickened by human behavior. You're by no means alone on that score. Many, many men have been just as troubled morally and spiritually as you are right now. Happily, some of them kept records of their troubles. You'll learn from them – if you want to. Just as someday, if you have something to offer, someone will learn something from you. It's a beautiful reciprocal arrangement. And it isn't education. It's history. It's poetry."
– J.D. Salinger

If you need ideas on how you want to change your life, go to the library and use the resources of knowledge stored in books. Explore literature. Find what interests you, heals you, motivates you, moves you forward, helps you to focus on what benefits you, aids in your development, wakens you to your potential, connects you to and helps you use your skills and talents, and brings you into a better life.

"Reading was my escape and comfort, my consolation, my stimulant of choice: reading for the pure pleasure of it, for the beautiful stillness that surrounds you when you hear an author's words reverberating in your head."
– Paul Auster

Get busy planning, organizing, and taking actions to make your life improve. Other people have done it, including people who have experienced tremendously horrible situations. You can do it.

"The greatest glory in living lies not in never failing, but in rising every time you fail."
– Ralph Waldo Emerson

Again: focus on a short list of goals and priorities by writing them on paper in colored ink. Doing so will help to bring them into your consciousness. Rewrite them at the start of every day, and work to make them your reality.

"You will never be able to escape from your heart. So it is better to listen to what it has to say."
– Paul Coelho

Decide to create a solid and continual internal voice that heals, nurtures, motivates, loves, and propels you into a more healthful life.

"In the middle of difficulty lies opportunity."
– Albert Einstein

What if you allowed yourself to live your life guided by love?

# Clarity

For some people, it boils down to this: They have trouble moving forward, because they are unclear of their past, of their ancestral origins, of what they are about, and what they can do with the lessons from their past.

While many grew up in relatively healthy households that functioned as well as could be expected, and are not left with deeply disturbing issues, other people did grow up in greatly problematic households that left them troubled.

This isn't to say that people who grew up in healthy households don't also have some issues to deal with. No matter what your background, life can be somewhat of a roller coaster ride.

People who have babies aren't required to take classes to learn parenting skills. Instead, the task of parenting – which might be the most important of all – is largely left to guessing. It is also subjected to the manipulation of companies and those who make money from selling baby and child products, or providing some sort of service for childcare and children. Products marketed toward children are not always healthy. That is obvious when considering the junk food and mind-numbing technogadgets advertised to children. Greed – not health and wisdom – rules the child products market.

It is interesting how advertising shows and tells what children are to eat and how they are to spend their time. If it is being advertised to children as food, it likely is not healthy. Also, many of the toys revolve around screen entertainment. Anyone can look into the issues of what staring at a screen does to children's brains, and how it alters interaction with people, and impacts social, reasoning, and other life skills.

Children then spend many hours in school, where underpaid teachers are limited in what and how they can teach in underfunded systems. Classes might consist of the children sitting in front of screens. Often the foods served in the schools are unhealthy, and contain exactly what is not good for brain development, the hormonal system, or the cardiovascular, lymph, digestive, and other functions.

Meanwhile, the parents aren't getting the help they need, as in helpful advice about how to nurture the children, and how to build children into what can be responsible, mannerly, educated, excellent expressions of their better qualities.

Instead, some parents turn to churches to basically raise the children in the hours the children aren't in school. There, the children might learn prejudices, racism, and toxic masculinity, and be spiritually manipulated. They are potentially left with some level of scrupulosity. It is all from learning about some manipulative, guilt-inducing belief system that exists more for the power and wealth of few, and is some mix of superheroes, wishful thinking, revised history, false concepts, and antiquated, miraculous fiction.

The parents might have struggled through their childhoods, and are left with issues unfaced, multi-generational troubles, and the inability to cope with life in ways that are healthy for them, or for their children. The issues are transferred to another generation, and play out in the community, culture, society, and environment.

Some sort of escapism may be taking place in the home. This might involve multiple hours of staring at TV. It might be the social media addiction that is the spectator life of sitting and watching others live. It might be substance abuse. These issues exist while there is never enough money, there is undealt with work stress, there is the race to keep up with unmet wants, health and relationship issues, and unidentified yearnings, while there are children with unmet needs.

Parenting is not easy. At least, most would likely agree it is not. Somehow, there are some who say it is relatively easy.

Unfortunately, those who experience a childhood of troubles do carry those issues out to society, and into more generations. Hopefully, somehow, good things will intercede.

Many parents are the products of unhealthful households, and do not function well as parents. Before they realize that – if they ever do – they might also realize it is too late, because they already have one, two, or more children – and the trouble is already thick and complex.

There are so many issues with raising children that it is like a mine field. Depending on the economic and other situations, and the parent and child, it can be far more complicated to be the parent to one child than it is to be a parent to another one. Needs may vary.

Friends have told me they knew they were unplanned, and their parents had never considered having a child. I have been with them when they were sad and conflicted about their origins. One was treated as if he were a burden, mixed with other times of being treated as if he were the prince. One had parents who often mentioned they hadn't planned on him being there, and having him was so expensive they had to move to a less desirable and cheaper place to raise him.

One friend was an only child of a single mother and had no contact with her father. She felt as if she had to be prepared to behave a certain way as part of a package to help her mother find a sufficient partner.

In some ways, I don't know how it feels to be an only child with parents telling guilt tripping you with how they didn't plan on you, or they treat you as part of their package for finding romance.

My best friend of 23 years grew up as the oldest of several children. His mother died when he was in high school, and his father was basically a homeless alcoholic with so many problems he couldn't parent. In high school, my friend worked as a car mechanic to support his brothers and sister. He paid the rent, and kept them in school. As each became old enough, they worked after-school jobs to help fund the household. My friend worked his way through college, while continuing to parent his brothers and sister. He was heroic.

I didn't know what was like to be without parents. But having mentally troubled and unavailable parents, I know what that was like.

I can't blame my parents for their terribleness. Doing so would be unhelpful. Their rough childhoods, injuries, addictions, and a lack of help and of money played into the equation. It would make no sense to hate someone for being injured, handicapped, or poor.

My parents both were only children. I had no aunts, uncles, or cousins. My grandparents had died before I was born.

Both of my parents suffered personality-altering brain injuries when I was four years old. After the injuries, they were no longer the same people, and could not function in healthful ways. Brain injuries decades ago were even less understood than they are today.

Instead of getting the help they needed – which was not available – my parents were left on their own, sent home after hospital stays to deal with healing from their head injuries. There wasn't therapy or follow-up. It was the 60s.

After their head injuries, my parents seemed perplexed, somewhat stunned, overwhelmed by, and unable to deal with having eight children. There were not enough resources to provide what was needed. The drama of their head injuries played out in years of trouble, regret, frustration, and disaster. We were thrown into poverty. Dysfunction, abuse, neglect, filth, violent outbursts, and unfortunate, troubling, and damaging situations were normal.

The alcohol, horse gambling addiction, and mental unavailability issues of my father magnified the problems. After the head injury, it was rare that he spent time around us. At times, he got to the point of being confused by which one of the six boys was which. I never had a conversation with him. As far as I knew, he also never had a conversation with the brother a year older than me, who I shared a bedroom with. At least, I never once heard them talk with each other.

In one of the few times my father ever spoke to me one-on-one was when I was sixteen. He was drunk and/or hungover. He said that after I graduated from high school, he didn't want to see my face, hear my voice, or know anything about me, ever again. I said, "okay."

My mother was a "housewife," but often said she had no interest in it. The thought of being a housewife seemed like madness to her.

From the time I was a toddler, under her breath, my mother expressed that she lived in misery, and often mildly spoke grimly of wanting to die. I have no idea if she ever said those thoughts to my father, or who else heard the words.

My parents didn't seem to talk much. At least, I never heard them carry on much of what I would consider to be a discussion. She was quite aware that, after his head injury, she was married to a man who was intellectually less than who she had married.

At times, I heard her say she thought it would have been better if my father had died, saying the emergency workers should have known better when they saw him with his head cracked open.

It happened when he was driving drunk and crashed into a utility pole, sending him through the windshield, and into a lengthy hospital stay. When he finally returned to the house, I was told to stay away from him, and to not allow him to pick me up. When he saw me, he seemed to not only not know who I was, but appeared confused by what I was. He was no longer the happy dad who was friendly with the neighbors. Quick anger and ongoing frustration, disinterest, and total dismissal of us became his normal, as if he thought of us as useless irritants he regretted. It seemed that he knew how his life used to be, and very much did not like what it had become. His life was one of struggle, of low-paying industrial jobs, and of beer.

My mother's head injury happened only months after my father's.

The house started on fire late one night. She fell down the stairs, her head landing on concrete. She also landed in the hospital, for weeks. Then, she was sent home. As if healed. She never was.

She often stared, and also spent days sleeping, apparently unconcerned about and/or unable to deal with her children's lives.

She needed help, but never got it. It seems unlikely that someone so suicidal and troubled would live into old age – but she did.

Barely able to deal with life, my parents continued on – often making irrational, unhealthful, damaging choices that impacted all of us. It all continues to reverberate through the lives of their children who are still alive. So far, as far as I now know, two have died.

I was the youngest of six boys, with younger sisters. It was a brutal childhood, stuck in ruin, abuse, neglect, violence, lies, deception, and irrational behavior that couldn't be reasoned with.

I was told numerous times by my mother that I was not wanted, and they only had another child because they wanted a girl. Other people picked up on this, and repeated her views – to degrade, dismiss, belittle, and bully me. It was a view I had heard numerous times, until I got away from those people when I was a young adult.

I was an unsupervised child who was to stay out of sight, out of mind, and silent. That scenario made me susceptible to parasitical and predatory people. Many degrading, ugly, and sickly things happened.

Based on the behavior of my brothers, my becoming a troubled teenager was perhaps expected as being my normal trajectory.

From my earliest years, I did what and went where I wanted. I often stayed out late. Nobody asked what my days were like, who I was with, where I had gone, what I had done, or what was done to me. I was a different person outside of that house than how I was inside. From early on, I lead a double life, and held two personalities.

When I was fourteen years old, without first telling me, my parents tried to give me away to a married couple in another state. I only learned of the plan when the woman showed up to get me. She had known my mother from high school. It was freakishly uncomfortable, awkward, and disturbing. I wouldn't leave.

From then, even more, I felt as if I were an intruder in the house.

My parents never discussed anything with me. Interactions were brief, and more along the lines of being belittled, ridiculed, mocked, or completely ignored. Their behavior was mirrored by my brothers, who also never had conversations with me. Inside the house, their acknowledgement of me – when there was any – consisted of verbal or physical abuse. Outside of the house, I didn't exist to them –

including in school, or whenever they saw me. When asked, they denied being related to me. I solidly knew I was unwanted.

When I was sixteen, with a broken nose, facial bruises, scabs on my scalp, and limping from a back injury, all the result of being attacked for no apparent reason by brothers in their late teens and twenties as they were still living in that house, I went hitchhiking across the continent, which proved to be far safer than being at my parent's house. It opened my eyes to life beyond the horizon.

I graduated from high school ignorant about how to function in adult life. I eventually left Ohio, and have never returned.

So, yes, childhood can be a bit stressful, surreal, disturbing, perplexing, mysterious, painful, haunting, and all the rest of it.

It should be no surprise that I was a mess of a young adult. I made many, many unwise choices. Learning the hard way in the school of life was harsh, troubling, scary, and difficult.

I wrote this book and *Dream Another Dream* with the hope they will help people avoid the types of unfortunate decisions I had made.

I hope your life has been free of the sort of problems I experienced. And that you will be able to factor your life, even using any problems as ways of gaining wisdom and making smart choices.

Maybe you grew up in a household of being compared and valued according to your worth to the parents, or parent figures.

Within a household, away from the outside world, there can be so much of so many things, some to a lesser degree, and some to more. There might be good, indifference, bad, unfortunate, happiness, joy, appreciation, oppression, triangulation, comparison, manipulation, disregard, instability, oppression, shame, disgust, polarity, aggression, infantilization, disorder, accusations, gaslighting, odd transitions, avoidance, denial, grief, instability, co-dependency, strategizing, triggers, fury, emotional divorce, emotional coherence, aversion, selflessness, apprehension, distress, desperation, bating, habituation, narcissism, irresponsibility, trust issues, hyper and hypo situations, caretaking, defiance, arbitrary rules, inferiority complexes, abandonment, defaulting, anxiety, role playing, self-righteousness, esteem issues, disregard, outrage, revenge, compliance, refrain and neutral expression, infuriation, power struggles, intergenerational trauma, contempt, malnutrition, lack, melancholy, sorrow, dysmorphia, intolerance, neurodivergence, isolation, diminishment of basic human emotions, and so much other stuff on display within households throughout childhood that it can be continually overwhelming. Some of it will stick, and will be an issue for the person. Hopefully, it will be what the person uses as lessons and filters as wisdom to live more responsibly and healthfully.

Maybe there were so many problems that forgiveness is not a concept that enters into the equation, and reconciliation will never happen – as the family was truly shattered by horrible behavior. Especially so if the horrid behavior continued on for many years.

At some point, you have to realize what role you were playing in your family. It is likely that you were forced into a role.

It is time to figure out if the roles you have been playing are who you are – or if you need to recalculate who and what you are, and reform yourself in alignment with your better qualities. This could mean getting help through a qualified psychologist (do your research as to their education and specialty), group therapy, a 12-step program, exercise groups, art and music groups, and in other ways.

Avoid being self-consumed. Instead, be healthfully self-informed, and put your past in its place.

Some people grew up not being able to express themselves. Doing so could be considered a burden, magnify problems, and result in verbal or physical abuse. Perhaps some of it was about you unknowingly speaking what the parent was already unwilling to face. So then, as you bared uncomfortable thoughts, you were treated badly, and as if you need to stay quiet, behave, and conform to the assignment you are to carry within the household.

Perhaps you grew up in a household in which they did not care to hear about your grief, understanding, anticipation, needs, safety, concerns, or even love, joy, humor, interests, activities, plans, or achievements. As that indoor treatment continued, in public it is likely that your assignment was to be a good family spokesmodel, and to make the parents look good – no matter what.

Along with all of that, you could become so used to not expressing yourself that you avoid sharing as an adult, and you build up health problems in relation to the compacted, distorted, frustrated, confused, and unexpressed energy that alters your immune system.

As an adult, maybe you unknowingly seek the approval and validation you never got – or what you felt you deserved – as a child. This could play into who you choose as a partner, as that could become an abusive situation, which is your normal. You could be seeking approval and validation so badly that you do unwise things with and to yourself, and to or with others. Maybe to deal with all of that you engage in some sort of escapism. This could mean that you dive into addictions, emotional eating, gambling, screen obsession, dangerous situations, and/or obsessive religious practices.

"The shadow is the greatest teacher for how to come to the light."
 – Ram Dass

If you were living in an unhealthful household as a child, it is not your fault. Do not feel guilt or shame about it. Do not feel as if you are responsible for not changing the situation. You were a child. As a child you likely couldn't think of the words and/or didn't have the words in your vocabulary to describe the trauma, neglect, and abuse you experienced. Even if there were someone around who could have helped – if you were able to reach out to them – it is no fault of yours that you were unable to manage the situation better. You were a child and you factored and lived as a child. Now you are an adult and you can manage your life better and be proactive in getting the help you need, and in creating a healthful life for your self.

"Psychology is not only the study of weakness and damage, it is also the study of strength and virtue. Treatment is not only fixing what is broken, it is nurturing what is best within us."
 – Martin Seligman

Seek and participate in the help you need.

"Blood is not thicker than mental health.
Some people in your life are damaging your mental health. It's that bad. And you let it happen because they are family."
 – Paul Scanlon

Protect yourself. Work daily to create a better existence. Do what heals you. Don't be lazy about it. Intently heal and thrive in health.

"Please stop chasing uncommitted, aloof, unavailable people, and then telling yourself the story that you're always rejected and no one ever loves you."
 – Jillian Turecki

This book can't go into all of the situations that might have caused you trouble. I hope it helps you. Please, seek additional help.

"The mind and the body are inseparable. The emotional system and the immune system are part and parcel of the same apparatus. When you suppress the emotions, you're also suppressing the immune system. When you unbalance your emotions you are also unbalancing your immune system, and that's why those emotional traits of self-suppression also turn the immune system against you."
 – Gabor Maté

# Healing from Trauma

"Character is formed in the stormy billows of the world."
– Johann Wolfgang von Goethe

"We are kept from the experience of spirit because our inner world is cluttered with past traumas. As we begin to clear away this clutter, the energy of divine light and love begins to glow through our beings."
– Tomas Keating

As you clean your life you may find yourself dealing with suppressed issues. These may involve things you have not thought of in a while, such as feelings, relationships, emotional trauma, experiences you perceive of as failures, and unpleasant memories.

"Trauma is not what happens to us. People when they think of trauma usually think of catastrophic events, like a tsunami or our parents dying, or sexual – or of physical/emotional – abuse of a child. These events are traumatic, but they are not the trauma. The trauma is the psychic wound that we sustain, and our psychological traumas have lifelong impacts."
– Gabor Maté

Many people have found suppressed issues to be part of the cleansing that goes on when improving the diet. It seems that just as the body tissues detox as a person follows a junk-free diet, the emotions can go through somewhat of a detox stage as a person works to live a more healthful, fit, and intentionally goal-oriented life. This may be related to years spent emotionally eating, using food to shove down and bury feelings. Once the emotion-driven food feast ends, as weight and toxins decrease, an emotional purge begins.

"Failure should be our teacher, not our undertaker. Failure is delay, not defeat. It is a temporary detour, not a dead end. Failure is something we can avoid only by saying nothing, doing nothing, and being nothing."
– Denis Waitley

What you have faced in the past, however unpleasant it may have been, could be a most useful tool in getting what is right for you in the future.

The trials and problems as well as the happiness and successes you have experienced can be utilized as personal lessons to propel you into being a wiser, more skillful, and effective person.

"What lies behind us and what lies before us are tiny matters compared to what lies within us. And when we bring what is within out into the world, miracles happen."
– Ralph Waldo Emerson

While memories may bring up a lot of unpleasant emotions, try not to get caught up in the emotion of a memory, only the lesson of it.

Do not allow the past to hold you back or make you stumble.

Do not be afraid of – or troubled by – what you have already been through. Instead, take control by strategically working with the lessons of the events of your life to your advantage.

"Be not the slave of your own past – plunge into the sublime seas, dive deep, and swim far, so you shall come back with self-respect, with new power, with an advanced experience that shall explain and overlook the old."
– Ralph Waldo Emerson

Take the remnants of your past and weave a better life. Welcome it, deal with it, learn what you can from it, don't dwell on it, but do let go of it, and move on while looking forward to a better way of life taking actions to experience a more healthful future.

"Every man's memory is his private literature."
– Aldous Huxley

"Cancer is my secret because none of my rivals have been that close to death, and it makes you look at the world in a different light,

and that is a huge advantage."
— Lance Armstrong

Reinterpret your past as something to help you rather than something that harmed you. If it did harm you, then that is what happened. The history of harm doesn't mean you have to keep dwelling on it in a negative way that continues the flow of hurt through your life. It also doesn't mean you should keep using it as a crutch to keep wobbling around on the same path where you have already stumbled, fallen, been wounded, and felt pain.

"Sometimes we stare so long at a door that is closing that we see too late the one that is open."
— Alexander Graham Bell

"All healing is first a healing of the heart."
— Carl Townsend

Refuse to get caught in regrets or the reverberating energy of unfortunate incidents. If you are swimming in the rotting river of resentment, it's time to get out and clean off.

"If the world seems cold to you, kindle fires to warm it."
— Lucy Larcom

What may be helpful is to metaphorically compost the leftovers of your past into a nurturing soil. Root into it, grow from it, and rise above it. Shade it with the beauty consisting of the branches, leaves, and blossoms of a more healthful and satisfying existence you are in charge of factoring, nurturing, growing, and expressing.

"Often we allow ourselves to be upset by small things we should despise and forget. We lose many irreplaceable hours brooding over grievances that, in a year's time, will be forgotten by us and by everybody. Now, let us devote our life to worthwhile actions and feelings, to great thoughts, real affections, and enduring undertakings."
— Andre Maurois

"With all its sham, drudgery, and broken dreams, it is still a beautiful life."
— Max Ehrmann

"We consume our tomorrows fretting about our yesterdays."
— Persius

Stop brooding over your past, as that is an absolute waste of time, energy, and resources.

Formulate the now. Look and grow toward a better future from where you are, not from where you have been.

"The future depends on what we do in the present."
– Mahatma Gandhi

Be your solution. If you feel the waves of bad memories, which might trigger others, and magnify, instead focus on goal-oriented thoughts of the present that are more helpful and will move you into confident and uplifting thoughts. Become involved in planning or engaging in a healthful activity driven by thoughts based on what you do want, and not on what you do not – and did not – want.

"Although the world is full of suffering, it is also full of overcoming it."
– Helen Keller

Consider others who have succeeded and gotten past tremendously horrible life situations. Know that you too can bring yourself out of whatever rut you have been in. Choose to engage in the positive.

"In our society, psychological woundedness is very prevalent, and it is rather an illusion to believe some people are traumatized and others are not. I think there is a spectrum of trauma that crosses all layers and all segments of society. Naturally, it falls heavier on certain sections – on people of color, people with genders that are not fully accepted by society, people of economic inequality who suffer more from inequality – but the traumatization is pretty general in our culture."
– Gabor Maté

Understand this: It is up to you to form the thoughts, factor the solutions, and take the actions that formulate the changes to improve your life. Be your answer.

"The most authentic thing about us is our capacity to create, to overcome, to endure, to transform, to love, and to be greater than our suffering."
– Ben Okri

In one way or another, you are dealing with some sort of traumatic psychological wound. Anything from abuse, neglect, assault, bullying, rejection, dismissal, injury, terror, threat, grievance, and other matters cause some level of trauma. Your way of dealing with those wounds could be anything from laziness, overreactions, addictions, self-harm, denial, anger, frustration, anxiety, depression, emotional eating, being obsessive/compulsive, being a workaholic, neglecting your loved ones, resistance to change, the agreed inability to participate in healthful activities, miscommunication, aiming to be a perfectionist, ruinous levels of escapism, and obsessing over things even to the point of it causing trouble for you and for others.

Compassionately inquire with yourself about what sort of imprint trauma has on you. Research what might help you to be more healthfully self-realized and to be participating in your better qualities. Find ways of not "getting over it" with your issues, but discovering ways in which you use your knowledge, wisdom, and experiences to become a healthier version of you.

Perhaps you will benefit from visiting with a psychologist, or from participating in group therapy of some sort, or from attending a support group of people who are also working through similar issues.

Don't overlook the benefits and importance of exercise and nutrition as parts of your intentional healing adventure.

Work to eliminate those things from your life that are not in alignment with the life you want. This includes eliminating unhealthful and unhelpful patterns of thinking, eating, communicating, and behaving.

By constantly focusing your life away from what you don't want, and onto what you do want, you will naturally be drawn to things you do want. Freeing your life of those things you don't want allows you to make room for, to better accept, and to welcome that which you do want.

If you are in a situation of damaged and damaging relationships, plan and take action to improve – or to end – them. Recognize that damaging relationships often involve one person projecting shame, guilt, discouragement, or disgust on another with the goal of controlling that person. This is a combination of so many things, including weak, guilt-ridden, dysfunctional, and pathetic behavior.

If you are in an abusive situation, get out of it. Don't play the game in which you will always lose, and where there are no winners.

Do not allow yourself to be controlled by the negativity and ugly behavior of others. Stop hoping for their behavior to change.

Getting into a pattern of waiting for other people to change before your life can improve is being co-dependent, diminishes your power, and obliterates your chances of living a healthful life. Move forward into your goals, into healthful borders, and into self-respect.

Stop hoping for someone to change when it is up to that person to change. Everyone – including the adults who are not leading the life you think they should be leading – is responsible for their thoughts, actions, and communication. You can't control their mind, but you can take a large role in conducting your life.

Instead of participating in a relationship where you are being a people-pleaser, and where you may be stuck in a co-dependent relationship wherein you allow your emotions and quality of life to be controlled and dominated by the mood swings, whims, agendas, and mental states of others, get on with your life by using your intellect, yearning, talents, and power to improve your level of existence.

Stop hoping that things of the past were different, which is wasted hope. Stop being controlled by end results, which are of energy already spent. Work to create things that have more satisfying end results. Place hope in the now, in your self, in goal-oriented actions, in daily exercise and clean nutrition, and in the future.

"False hope is unnecessary pain."
– Rod Steiger

Do not focus on how you have been wronged, or on who did it.

Many people who perceive they have been wronged then proceed to entertain thoughts of revenge. This is a tremendous waste of time and energy, stagnates them, and it perpetuates any damage that may have been done to them.

"To be angry is to revenge the faults of others on ourselves."
– Alexander Pope

"An eye for eye only ends up making the whole world blind."
– Mahatma Gandhi

Do not take revenge on people. Instead, take responsibility to be more responsible and present in the now by spending your time and energy, and using your graces and resources to create a better future.

"The best form of revenge is success."
– Vanessa Williams

Avoid becoming a great, tattered, ramshackle display of someone who has been through a lousy situation, and remains in the trainwreck mindset of the victim. Some people get so caught up in analyzing their life, and in talking about it that they become a tedious bore to be around. Improving your life out of your past is not about burdening everyone around you by constantly talking about your difficulties.

Cast your life into the light of enlightenment, of working on a better future, and of moving into better health. Don't let your life stall or dwell in – or be in the shadow of – any sort of dark past.

"Complaining is not only hideously boring, but worse – it only increases the pain."
– Peter Megargee Brown

Many people who have been through tremendous difficulties have learned very well that it is best to move on into a smarter, focused, and intentional life in which they live in the present, not in the past.

The key to all this is to progress into healing, and to grow into a vibrantly healthful version of yourself in which you are following a well-rounded plant-based diet, setting goals and attaining them through intentional actions, and wisely and confidently living your intellect.

The sooner you go about creating a better life for your self with more healthful patterns, the better off you will be.

Continually thinking of what created stress in your life is not good for your brain, and can leave you dwelling in the energy of regret, sadness, and dissatisfaction, which can add to the damage that was done.

Daily stress creates stress chemicals that can kill brain cells, interferes with brain growth, increases tissue acidity and tension, and subtly restricts the flow of blood to the brain and other tissues.

Children who are continually exposed to bad situations may have experienced the type of stress that interferes with brain growth.

Long-term stress can play a role in heart disease, diabetes, back pain, disorders of the digestive system, muscle injuries, weight gain or loss, memory loss, and other problems.

Being continually exposed to situations that are dangerous, violent, and cause frantic emotions can result in an over-abundance of neurons forming in the locus coeruleus area of the brain stem. This is so because regularly being caught in situations of danger triggers the brain to release the fight-or-flight hormones, norepinephrine and adrenaline. This is conducive to the post-traumatic stress disorder (PTSD) common in people who have been exposed to dangerous, violent, and/or otherwise extremely upsetting situations.

In January 2010, researchers at the University of Minnesota and the Minneapolis VA Medical Center released a study they did of brain scans conducted on veterans of the Iraq and Afghanistan wars. They detected distinct patterns of activity within the brains of those suffering from PTSD. To conduct the study, they used an MEG (magnetoencephalography) brain scanner which captures electrical signals taking place every millisecond. By studying the scans of the electrical patterns within the soldier's brains, the researchers identified specific biomarkers as being common in 90 percent of the war veterans in the study diagnosed as suffering from PTSD.

Unfortunately, PTSD symptoms are seen in a variety of people who have been exposed to dangerous and extremely upsetting situations – including people who were abused as children. Luckily, the brain has some capacity to heal and reform itself as the formerly abused person learns how to cope and becomes more attuned to a healthful way of living.

Thinking plays a role in healing and maintaining a high level of health, or the opposite. There truly are toxic emotions that cause the body to create a damaging body chemistry.

In 1964, George Solomon and his team at UCLA coined the term *psychoimmunology*. He theorized that personality and the emotions play a part in people's health, and in what diseases and pain they may experience. His report "Emotions, Immunity, and Disease: A Speculative Theoretical Integration" remains landmark.

Luckily, we can learn to conduct our minds in a more healthful manner. Healthful thinking impacts the electrical circuitry of the body and helps to form healthful cells. As people heal and learn to conduct their being in a more healthful manner, the tissues throughout the body become attuned to creating more healthful molecules of emotion, known as peptides and ligands, which are messenger molecules.

Scientists have discovered how thoughts play into creating body chemicals, and how healthful thoughts both result in a more healthful body chemistry, and alter the electromagnetic field of the body. These are key to thought, senses, action, communication, and feeling.

The body creates chemicals in relation to what a person thinks. The chemicals are simultaneously created throughout the body, in the brain and other organs, and within everything from the blood, lymph, and hormonal systems, to the bones, and skin. This reveals that the mind exists not only in the brain, but throughout the body.

The cells in every part of the body feature receptor sites for the neuropeptide and ligand chemicals, which are the physical structures created by thought. When we conduct our thoughts in a certain way in combination with a healthful diet and exercise program, our body cells create more receptor sites that receive the peptides and ligands aligned with health, and the body creates more neuropeptides and ligands in alignment with how healthfully we are living. This process is why we feel emotions throughout our entire body, and not just in our brain, but also in our fingers and toes, our legs and arms, our back, chest, and tummy, and in our shoulders, neck, and cheeks.

Because certain parts of the body contain more receptor sites for certain neurochemicals, we feel some emotions stronger in certain areas of our body, such as stress in the stomach because there are more stress chemical receptors there, and the desire for sex in the sex organs because there are more receptors on the cells in those body parts to receive the chemicals in alignment with those feelings and emotions. However, sex hormones are not peptide-based, but are steroids, and interact within the nucleus of the cells. We also store memories throughout the body, and not only in the brain – which is why certain memories are also felt throughout the body.

Feeling is a whole-body experience because body chemistry and thinking do comprise of it.

The process of the membranes of our cells creating more receptor sites to receive the self-produced chemicals that make us feel good, including how the cell membranes can be consciously changed, is one of the miracles of healing. It can be assisted by a healthful, plant-based diet free of junk ingredients; intellectual stimulation; daily exercise; goal-oriented living, and nurturing relationships with healthful communication.

"Biochemicals are the physiological substrates of emotion, the molecular underpinnings of what we experience as feelings, sensations, thoughts, drives, perhaps even spirit or soul."
– Dr. Candace B. Pert, author of *The Molecules of Emotion*

The cellular processes continually happening in relation to thinking and activity, and how thoughts and actions alter both cell growth patterns and the production of chemicals within the body and brain reveal how people are always involved with helping to create their common level of health.

In response to thoughts and actions, human cells create mind-altering molecules called endogenous opioids, including neuropeptides and cannabinoids. The most commonly known are the endorphin opiate peptides associated with the euphoric *runner's high*. Cannabinoids cross the blood-brain barrier, are produced by the neurochemical endocannabinoid system, and may be more responsible for that elation. Exercise triggers the production of the chemicals, the body cell membranes to form endorphin receptors, and the brain and body cell membranes to form cannabinoid receptors. It is the same receptors that receive the cannabinoids found in cannabis, thus the *high* a person gets if they smoke or ingest marijuana. Exercise is the better choice for obtaining the natural high.

239

Acts of kindness produce pleasurable chemicals in the body. Among these are endogenous opioids, and hormones such as oxytocin, which triggers the blood cells to release nitric oxide, causing the dilation of the vessels, reducing blood pressure, decreasing stress, and lowering the presence of free radicals. These processes lead to a more relaxed mood and less acidic body chemistry. So again, an action, kindness, which is the result of thought processes, triggers a cellular response: the production, release, and reception of feel-good hormones and chemicals that improve health.

You can become accustomed to experiencing thoughts and actions that trigger the production of pleasurable chemicals just as much as you can become accustomed to experiencing those leading to the manufacture of body chemicals that make you feel lousy. Some of it is your choice.

There is communication between the conscious and subconscious functions of the body.

Neuroscientists have proved that the chemicals of emotion produced within the body are tied in with breathing, blood flow, salivation, gastrointestinal activity, body temperature, cellular replication, hormonal production, electrical fields, and even in what is eliminated by the body. This helps to reveal that we consciously play a role in our total health experience.

"If you think your body and mind are two, that is wrong; if you think that they are one, that is also wrong. Our body and mind are both two and one."
– Shunryu Suzuki

Even the immune system – including the lymph, spleen, bone marrow, and certain blood cells – is conducted with the exchange of various types of peptides between the immune cells and the endocrine system and nerve system – including the brain. In other words, in addition to genetics, environment, diet, relations, and exercise, your immune system is impacted by your thinking patterns. This is because your thoughts help trigger your cells to release some of the chemical cues that guide immune responses. This means: Your mind is part of your immune system.

Through high-quality thinking, diet, exercise, action, and communication choices, you can consciously create your own vitality and reformulate your body chemistry to be in alignment with all things healthy.

"Vitality shows not only in the ability to persist but in the ability to start over."
– F. Scott Fitzgerald

This understanding of how we, through thoughts, actions, communication, and diet, change our body chemistry, and the formation of our cell membranes should be helpful for getting people to also understand why it is helpful for them to stop doing the things damaging them, and to constantly be involved in living healthfully.

It is through thinking healthfully combined with healthful communication, actions, diet, and exercise that our cellular structures will heal from unhealthful experiences. The key is for us to actively and continually participate in making it happen.

"Focus more on your desire than on your doubt, and the dream will take care of itself. You may be surprised at how easily this happens. Your doubts are not as powerful as your desires, unless you make them so."
– Marcia Wieder

You are more likely to become the person you wish to become by conducting yourself in the way you wish to be. Thought, action, communication, diet, and exercise are how you create your paradigm.

Processes helpful for thinking healthfully include meditation and meditative exercises, such as yoga, jogging, hiking, biking, swimming, kayaking, canoeing, and cross country skiing.

In her book, *The Molecules of Emotion*, the late Candace B. Pert, whose life work was the study of peptides, wrote, "When stress prevents the molecules of emotion from flowing freely where needed, the largely autonomic processes that are regulated by peptide flow, such as breathing, blood flow, immunity, digestion, and elimination collapse down to a few simple feedback loops and upset the normal healing response. Meditation, by allowing long-buried thoughts and feelings to surface, is a way of getting the peptides flowing again, returning the body, and the emotions, to health."

The patterns of your thoughts and the type of health you are experiencing are an integration of your life. The state of your mind reflects the state of your immune system, which reflects the state of your fitness level, which reflects the state of your diet, which reflects the state of your happiness and satisfaction with being able to express your intellect, yearning, talents, and love.

"There is healing available to us and it can come through our imagination – if we honor ourselves and our situation, and if we keep

open to the potency of the universe, which is also the potency within us."
— Henry Seltzer

All of this information is in alignment with what I am speaking of throughout the book. It is that you can play a major role in healing your life. If you desire to experience vibrant health, you can. It is why I specifically approach a whole-life solution to healing. It also is why I include a fully plant-based diet and an active exercise program – such as by practicing yoga, calisthenics, and perhaps non-contact martial arts movement every morning – as part of true health maintenance. It is why I believe it would be most helpful that daily goal review, daily intellectual stimulation through study, and the daily practice of talent are included in healing.

If you were in a horrible situation while you were growing up, it is even more important for you to follow a nutritious plant-based diet, to eliminate all low-quality foods (see my book: *Plant-based Regenerative Nutrition*), to get daily exercise, to stimulate your mind with quality literature, to develop your intellect, to practice your talents, to improve your quality of communication, and to live intentionally creating a life in which you flourish in health.

Be aware that those who were raised in violent and abusive homes may have some form of post-traumatic stress disorder. One brain chemical found more prominently in those who have experienced traumatic, violent, and/or neglectful childhoods is cortical releasing factor (CRF). Those who go on to live more healthful lives, including children who are removed from violent and neglectful households, are found to experience a reduction of CRF to the state being of a healthful level. This is especially the case if they go on to experience nurturing relationships and constructive, uplifting, goal-oriented lives.

Perhaps more important than all relationships is the relationship of self, and nurturing the self to blossom into health – which will open you to others who are living more healthfully.

"Healing is not a matter of technique or mechanism; it is a work of spirit."
— Rachel Naomi Remen

Now is the time for you to heal from unfortunate experiences, to get out of the rut dug for or by you, to use your strengths and better qualities to rise above the past, and to purge your demons – without delay. That is, if you want to heal and experience health.

Many people know what it is like to be in a horrific situation. If you are one of them, know that you can rise out of it, that your life can be healthful, and that the person who can change it is you. Work for it to happen.

"Thought is the creative power, or the impelling force which causes the creative power to act; thinking in a certain way will bring riches to you, but you must not rely upon thought alone, paying no attention to personal action. That is the rock upon which many otherwise scientific metaphysical thinkers meet shipwreck – the failure to connect thought with personal action."
– Wallace D. Wattles

You are the rescuing spirit you have been waiting for. Allow your restorative spiritual genetics to kick into gear.

Begin now to live each day intentionally progressing to a more healthful and satisfying life.

"This is the way of peace: Overcome evil with good, falsehood with truth, and hatred with love."
– Mildred "Peace Pilgrim" Norman

Don't get caught in the bottomless whirlpool of thoughts centered on the fact that you were robbed of a nurturing, loving, safe childhood – or of other beneficial and good life experiences. Live your life as if your days are golden, and not stolen.

If you feel that you have more for which to be sorry than grateful, work every day to create the situation in which you do feel grateful.

"Perhaps our greatest gift is helping people choose truly loving family, what we here in Hawaii call 'ohana – literally the circle of those who breathe together."
– Richard Koob

If you spent time living in a home where lying, stealing, slander, deception, verbal abuse, mockery, and other damaging behaviors were common, it is likely that you have incorporated some of these unhealthful qualities into your adult behavior. If so, please learn to rid yourself of these habitual tendencies damaging to you and your relationships.

Make a personal, written declaration that you will heal your self from damaging tendencies.

Work to be a more trustworthy, sincere, kind, respectable, committed, hardworking individual, moving toward health, and who lives with a high degree of integrity.

Refrain from assaulting, insulting, mocking, belittling, degrading, undermining, or slandering others, and refrain from lying and from revenge. Work to treat others as you desire to be treated.

"I have never for one instant seen clearly within myself. How then would you have me judge the deeds of others?"
— Maurice Maeterlinck

So many times maybe the strife, contention, frustration, disappointment, and anger in relationships is about expectations. It is as if each person is expecting the other to behave like there are puppet strings attached to each, controlled by the other who gets upset if the one doesn't behave as the other expects. Refrain from reacting as if someone doesn't animate, express, and communicate in accordance with puppet strings that don't and never will exist.

"It is a bit embarrassing to have been concerned with the human problem all one's life and find at the end that one has no more to offer by way of advice than 'Try to be a little kinder.'"
— Aldous Huxley

Stop allowing the toxic energy of others to poison your life.

By focusing on the unhealthful energy of others, you are the person who is spreading the poison. Get out of that practice. One way to do so is to focus on your life and on your choices, on your goals, and on your future – not on your past, or on the choices of other people.

If you find yourself treating others badly, walk away from it. Refocus. Refactor. Reorganize your thoughts based on kindness and love – rather than on frustration, anxiety, spitefulness, ridicule, mockery, meanness, hate, or anger.

"Healing may not be so much about getting better, as about letting go of everything that isn't you – all of the expectations, all of the beliefs – and becoming who you are."
— Rachel Naomi Remen

In an unhealthful situation, not only will people hide their talents, but also assume a fake personage that is a complete roleplay of what they think is the most acceptable way to conduct themselves. They do this to avoid harsh comments. Doing so is abandoning authenticity.

"We forfeit three-fourths of ourselves in order to become like other people."
— Arthur Schopenhauer

If you lived in a terrible situation, consider that a part of you may have been abandoned. Not by someone else, but abandoned by you. It may have been done as a coping mechanism. As you grow out of the unhealthful situation and the mindset that were the results of consequences and your coping mechanism, it may help to figure out if that abandoned part of you is something that would be beneficial for you to reclaim.

Give yourself permission to grasp the parts of your intellect and talents that will help you to heal, to experience joy, to express the person you are, and to nurture love and beauty in your life.

"The people who get on in this world are the people who get up and look for the circumstances they want, and, if they can't find them, make them."
– George Bernard Shaw

Dignifying your life is accomplished by living intentionally, by valuing your intellect, by giving meaning to your actions, by conducting your self in a focused manner, and by fulfilling defined goals. Doing so will be a way to respect your intellect, talents, skills, time, energy, and resources, and those of others. It will help your life to flourish.

What you desire is likely already part of your intellect. Work to bring that forward.

The infinite power of the universe is what you are a part of. The strongest power in the universe is love.

Be aware of and enlightened to the fact that you have the energy to conduct yourself in ways that heal and transform your life into a healthful being.

"Turn pain into wisdom, mistakes into experience, and disempowering narratives into inspiring stories."
– J. Mike Fields

You are worthy of being loved, of experiencing love, and of loving.

Love your self – including by exercising every morning, following a plant-based diet free of junk food, using your intellect, practicing your talents, using your skills, and living intentionally guided by a set of daily goals and a personal written declaration. Doing so will magnify your power.

# Grief

Life has its ups and downs, and its tragedies.

Not everything in life is something that will make sense, no matter how much you want it to, or how hard you work for it.

The first time a death hit me hard was when a friend in grade school and his older brother were hit by a car, and died. It caused enormous grief for the family, friends, neighbors, and school mates. Nobody seemed to know that I was friends with the boy. We normally spent class recess together. That morning we were running around, laughing. During lunch hour, he and his brother were killed. I never spoke about him with anyone.

Several years later, a nice girl in my jr. high drowned in the summer. She was someone I thought was cute, and had joked around with her a little. Then, there was another girl I thought was pretty, and I wondered why she always seemed unhappy. She was older than me. It turned out she had been getting molested by her police officer father, and was left so distraught that she shot herself with his gun.

For a few years I had a casual friend. During the last summer I knew him he told me I was his best friend,. He was someone everyone looked up to. That winter, he was hit by a car and died. His funeral was held out of state. To me, it was as if it never happened, and he was only a memory. I never spoke about him with anyone, either. In my lack of having anyone to talk with about what I was experiencing prevented me from knowing what I felt. It was deep sadness, confusion about life, and – now I know – grief.

There are also other types of grief, which can happen when there is a different sort of loss that doesn't involve death.

My father had his life ruined when I was 4 and he was in the drunken accident that injured his brain, leaving him as a different person. He was not as vibrant, not as talkative, not as playful, not happy, and left unable to deal well with life. I was so young that I couldn't comprehend what he had been through, or how it was impacting me, or the rest of the family. It was the tragedy that pivoted the entire family in a different – and far more troubled – direction. None of us likely ever dealt with – or even knew how to handle – it.

As an adult, I've lost many people. What hit me the hardest was losing my best friend of 32 years. He drank too much vodka one night, and never woke up. We had just made plans to go to Europe to see his x-wife. We were also going to take trips to Costa Rica and Cuba. After being unable to reach him, his brother went to his house, and found him.

One friend, a brilliant musician known for having huge parties, died only two weeks after he was diagnosed with cancer. To honor him, hundreds of people had an all-night party he would have loved.

Another friend died of cancer several weeks after he found out. Another friend, who seemed so happy, hanged himself from a tree.

Another, who was strong and athletic, and avoided doctors, died from what he thought was a cold. It turned out to be a flu that went into pneumonia. He had waited so long to seek care that the pneumonia was so advance it was fatal.

One friend died in a car accident, when a car being chased by police slammed into her car.

All of those lives, and those of other people I've known, ended when they still had so much life to live, things to do, places to go, and people to spend time with.

I didn't expect to lose nearly every one of my best male friends, the ones I had traveled with, and spent years knowing. I had no reason to think at least some of them would be around for the long-haul, and we could continue having fun times, meaningful conversations, and a roller coaster of life experiences into old age. But they are gone.

**"Grief doesn't have a plot. It isn't smooth. There is no beginning, and middle, and end."**
– Ann Hood

I'm at a loss as to my brother's life. He was abused, neglected, and had a tragic life. He starved to death as an adult – in the same room where we were abused as children. I hadn't seen him in decades. I had left that brutal household after high school, and never returned. That sort of childhood leaves no treasure – other than lessons. I only have tragic and unfortunate memories of my brother.

"Grief is like wandering through a minefield, as my mother puts it: However carefully you tread, a sudden detonation can happen out of nowhere. A song played in a supermarket; an overheard phrase; someone in the distance who your mind cruelly suggests is your loved one for a fleeing moment."
– Owen Jones

Sometimes, I will see or hear someone who looks like someone I lost. Or, there is a song, a color, a fabric, a shape, a feeling, a lighting situation, a food, or a scent that brings on a pack of thoughts about someone from the past. The mind plays tricks, and for a second or more a flood of memories rush in, and I find myself having to refocus and re-arrive in the present, and to continue on.

There have been times where I've reached for the phone to call someone, only to remember they no longer exist. Or, I think of going to see someone, only to remember they are no longer.

I recently woke up to the sound of a dog barking, and it reminded me of my childhood dog. I was suddenly overwhelmed with missing her, in ways I had not experienced since she was killed.

"Grief starts to become indulgent, and it doesn't serve anyone, and it's painful. But if you transform it into remembrance, then you're magnifying the person you lost and also giving something of that person to other people, so they can experience something of that person."
– Patti Smith

It is likely that many of you relate to these sorts of grief situations. There are technical explanations about why the people in our lives have died. There is the description of how some things happened, and how they lead to other things happening. It doesn't cause the sadness, confusion, frustration, feelings of loss, or grief to go away. Maybe it all only dulls over the years as you push on, meet other people, and have other life experiences.

Grieving isn't unique to humans.

When a friend's cat died, his other cat would sleep every night on the spot in the middle of the floor where the other cat had died.

If you spent much time around dogs, you know they will grieve their friends, including cats they shared a household with. Dogs will also grieve if their human dies. Other animals known to grieve include dolphins, wolves, whales, swans, magpies, geese, monkeys, cows, pigs, goats, giraffes, and elephants.

Simply because non-human animals don't display the same physiological symptoms humans experience as they grieve doesn't mean the non-human animals don't go through some form of their own type of grieving. Many types of animals are known to gather when a member of their community passes away, and others display grief behaviors while alone. Some animals become so upset after the death of a companion that their health suffers.

"Finding others who have experienced a similar loss can be the only way to go. Support groups that have your specific kind of loss in common. I go to them, and I hold them for other bereaved parents at my home.

Nothing, absolutely NOTHING takes away the pain but finding support can sometimes help you to feel a little bit less alone."
– Lisa Marie Presley

Not everyone has the answers to certain things. For some things, there doesn't seem to be answers. There is only the way it is, and that it might never be something that will be in a place we are okay with. We can say life goes on. Some lives end earlier, and some lives end later. Some people live for minutes, others for hours, others for days, others for weeks. Some for months. Others for years, and decades, and some for more than a century. You can complicate things, but things end. Things move on. Each life rolls out differently. And that is all. We are human, and can't expect our story or the story of anyone else to play out into the sort of ending we'd expect.

There are still music, art, dance, literature, theater, film, museums, sport, craft, hobbies, classes, associations, and places to experience. There is Nature that consists of plants and animals and landscapes. There are gardens and trees and flowers to plant and tend to. There is food to grow and to be made, and people to feed and to help. There are things to see and stuff to enjoy and beauty to view and smiles to bring and kindness to spread and love to engage in.

"Grief knits two hearts in closer bonds than happiness ever can; and common sufferings are far stronger links than common joys."
– Alphonse de Lamartine

There are good things to do. There are volunteer opportunities for helping others, and for protecting and restoring the land, and for helping wildlife. There are ways of keeping busy and focusing on and doing what will keep you and your community and the Earth healthy.

Do things that create good memories, even if it is to go for a long walk, or to an art museum, a concert, a sports event, or for a swim, or to enjoy some sort of boating. Plant some trees. Grow and share food.

"My journey with grief, with learning how to grow through it, rather than get over it, will be a lifelong one."
– Zoe Buckman

I figure that grief isn't only limited to when someone dies. As it is with the situation of essentially losing my father's intellect and joy when I was four, grief could be the end of a relationship, the mess of someone doing something horrible, an event that massively changes your life so you are in a grieving mode for the person you used to be, the life you used to have, the relations you used to experience, the feelings you used to feel, and things you used to do.

"I think everyone understands grief, the journey it takes us on, whether it's the death of a loved one, the end of a relationship, a disappointment. Some people don't deal with it, the power of it. Some do. Some feel the weight of it and it informs their choices. I've had to open up to grief in different ways."
– Tori Amos

Probably some of the best art, music, poetry, literature, films, theater, and other works have been the creation of someone grieving, dealing with heavy situations, and wanting to express what they were feeling, and what they experienced. Art can be healing, and provide expression like nothing else does – or is capable of doing.

"Against eternal injustice, man must assert justice, and to protest against the universe of grief, he must create happiness."
– Albert Camus

Maybe you are one who will go through a great change because of grief, and it will spur you to become more of yourself, and less of the façade you had been living behind. Maybe it will motivate you in ways you had not expected, to go places and do advantageous and beneficial things you had never thought you would go and do.

Continue to be involved with what you are, your talents, your skills, your craft, your best qualities, and creating a life that is good and healthy for you, the people you love, and your community.

"Being reminded of your past doesn't' mean that you have to live with constant grief. It simply means that you have been given the opportunity to transform your past into something positive."
– Abby Johnson

Perhaps your grief will lead you to express things in ways helpful for you, and for others. This might be by becoming more involved in local culture, volunteering, building community, participating in group events, learning and doing new things, meeting and being involved with people intent on improving local conditions.

Get outside, engage in, and live life.

"Whatever you want to do, do it now. There are only so many tomorrows."
– Michael Landon

"If you don't have wrinkles, you haven't laughed enough."
– Phyllis Diller

"Enjoy the little things, for one day you may look back and realize they were the big things."
– Robert Brault

251

# The Forgiveness Concept

"Forgiveness is the fragrance the violet sheds on the heel that has crushed it."
– Mark Twain

"Never does the human soul appear so strong as when it forgoes revenge, and dares forgive an injury."
– Edwin Hubbel Chapin

If you are trying to move forward from a fractured life and into a more healthful existence, what may be beneficial to your progress is an understanding of forgiveness, or some form of moving on that is helpful to you. I say that, because forgiveness might be viewed as an antiquated and unrealistic concept some would say is lacking reality, and lost in pretend.

Maybe you don't need to "forgive" anyone. But being stuck dragging your mind in memories of what someone did is also unhealthful, and might be dragging you down, and keeping you stuck.

Even if you don't believe in the concept of forgiveness, consciously engaging in the endeavor to protect yourself – and to not be halted by whatever or whoever it is or was causing you harm or trouble – could be the healthful goal.

Some might agree with the following. Some will not.

"The weak can never forgive. Forgiveness is the attribute of the strong."
– Mahatma Gandhi

Maybe Gandhi's statement is too strong, and some would consider it to be unrealistic – and even insulting. Maybe it might be viewed as blaming, dismissive, and of the attitude of "get over it." Or, maybe it applies to you, and considering it might be helpful.

If you haven't already done so, sometime in your life you might have to deal with an ugly situation where someone did you wrong, caused you harm, violated your life, or otherwise left you feeling betrayed or victimized.

Maybe something has already happened, or is happening, and you have not yet recognized the harm being done to you. It could be a case of someone so enmeshed in your life to such an extent that the wrong they might be doing could not be obvious to you, and you are blind to the deception. Or, you don't want to acknowledge it – as doing so could be frightening and problematic. Eventually, you might realize how much damage was done, and then you will be left in a state of having to deal with the aftermath. I hope you are strong, make the more healthful and helpful choices, and are able to protect yourself from more harm.

Some of us have been betrayed, deceived, deprived, used, abused, or otherwise violated from those we should otherwise be able to trust. Those people are not healthy, and their situation is negating our life. Those situations can cause lifelong issues, and it is better to deal with them in the most helpful manner for us.

Perhaps you are one dealing with what *Mother Hunger* author Kelly McDaniel speaks of as the situation in which a parent does not provide the basic needs of protection, guidance, and nurturing, but instead causes harm. Maybe your parent or parental figure is so detached from your most basic needs that they too are damaged, is not facing their issues, and is causing more harm by their choices.

I know what it is like to have had people do horrible things to me. As someone from an abusive, neglectful childhood, from my earliest years, I experienced assault, in and outside of the household. The people I should have been able to turn to for help were deranged and doing wrong things to me, and to others. I grew up in a household where nobody ever had a conversation with me, and where my voice or opinions were not welcome or encouraged, but discouraged. I didn't know who to turn to, and wouldn't know the words to say – even if there were someone who could have helped me. My teenage years were filled with strife, unfortunate situations, and household brutality. Leaving that poverty childhood, and being completely unprepared for life, I was around people who were living in thoroughly unwise ways. As a young adult, some people once slipped

253

me drugs, and did wrong things. My trust was demolished, I didn't feel there was much of anyone to turn to. With that, and being overwhelmed by other health problems that complicated nearly everything, my life tanked. Digging through trash was one way to get by – including for food, and things to sell. I was shattered.

So, yes, I know what it is like to be left feeling like garbage, filled with frustration, anger, regret, and disgust, and to be emotionally dismantled to nearly the absolute bottom of ruinous depths.

After what I had been subjected to, it should be no surprise that I was a ramshackle mess of being a damaged, naïve, vulnerable, confused, disaster. I felt as if every cell, molecule, and subatomic particle of me was tainted, disfigured, mangled, or otherwise harmed.

If someone had told me when I was a young disaster that I would one day be writing books, having my own year-round vegetable garden, experiencing healthy relationships, running a screenwriting workshop, helping people polish screenplays, working in the film and TV industry, and doing other things in line with my better qualities, and that I would be out of back pain, and have undergone kidney surgery to fix that situation, and would not be in kidney pain, I would have thought they had an interesting and unrealistic imagination.

When the time comes, if you realize you had been wronged, you might be better to welcome the disillusion, and work with it as you seek and get the right help to improve your life, correct wrongs, build your boundaries and standards, live with more respect for your needs, and know that you are worthy of living a life that is right for you.

There are some things that can't be expressed to the people who did you wrong. Even trying to could be futile, might magnify the damage, and may put you in a situation of being vulnerable to more harm and ruin. Don't take revenge. Take steps to improve your life.

For some wrongs there are no words that could possibly describe the grotesqueness you feel. The legal system can also revictimize you, rob you of time and money, and leave you even more stranded. For some, mental health therapy might be elusive, unavailable, and financially unrealistic.

With some victimized people, they might have no understanding of how to go about seeking help. They might feel so incredibly wrecked that they are unable to understand the concept of what help for them could be. I am familiar with the situation.

I hope you are in a situation where you can seek out the help you need. That might involve therapy with a helpful psychologist. Study up on how to seek psychological help. Even if it means watching YouTube videos about recovering and rehabilitating your life.

Reading books relating to your situation can also help. (Even if only at the library, so anyone who is a problem for you might not know the books you are reading, the steps you are making to protect yourself, and what you are doing to better your situation.)

If you have health insurance, call the insurance company and ask what type of psychological therapy your insurance covers.

You might join a 12-step program, even if it is on MeetUp.com. There is likely to be one helpful for your history and situation.

One exercise in forgiveness some people have found useful in releasing toxic thoughts and in venting their anger toward someone in their past is to write the offender an undelivered letter expressing the anger. Key to this exercise is that the letter NOT be sent to the offender. Instead, it should be torn to pieces, or burned, or otherwise destroyed and disposed of immediately after it is written. The exercise is to explore your feelings, rather than to suppress them. In this way you are able to express anything you want to say to the person without the concern of harming anyone's feelings. It is important to destroy the letter, to not send it, and to get on with your life by immediately becoming involved with a specific activity aligned with a helpful priority or goal. This can help do away with unexpressed, pent-up anger.

Because emotions and thoughts influence the immune system, releasing toxic emotions can improve the immune system and allow the person to function more healthfully. The exercise of writing thoughts can be part of the process of moving on to better things.

**"Self-importance is our greatest enemy. Think about it – what weakens us is feeling offended by the deeds and misdeeds of our fellowmen. Our self-importance requires that we spend most of our lives offended by someone."**
– Carlos Castaneda

Another exercise in forgiveness involves recognizing the problems your perpetrators or offenders experienced. They also may have had difficulties in their life, including problems caused by others that led to their unfortunate choices. Perhaps they were abused, neglected, assaulted, or otherwise in a terrible situation when they were young. Maybe physical and psychological ailments caused them problems. These may not have been diagnosed, and never addressed. They may have been subjected to any number of problems and life difficulties that constricted their life, constructed their disaster, set them on a pattern of destruction, and played into their unwise lifestyle. Maybe they had it so badly that they lacked an

255

understanding of what they did, or did not have the resources, capacity, or ability to deal with it, to heal, or to overcome.

"Yet, taught by time, my heart has learned to glow for other's good, and melt at other's woe."
– Homer

"It is unwise to be too sure of one's own wisdom. It is healthy to be reminded that the strongest might weaken and the wisest might err."
– Mahatma Gandhi

"With a little time, and a little more insight, we begin to see both ourselves and our enemies in humbler profiles. We are not really as innocent as we felt when we were first hurt. And we do not usually have a gigantic monster to forgive; we have a weak, needy, and somewhat stupid human being. When you see your enemy and yourself in the weakness and silliness of the humanity you share, you will make the miracle of forgiving a little easier."
– Lewis B. Smedes

Those who did you wrong may never admit it, may deny it, may not be concerned about it, may not recognize it, and may continue doing unwise things to others.

Your healing does not depend on your perpetrators acknowledging anything. They are not your brain, mind, yearning, abilities, talents, craft, intellect, body, life, elegance, spirit, or future. They cannot guide your thoughts, set your goals, choose your actions or communication, conduct your relationships, lead your life, use your talents, develop your skills, or heal your wounds.

"Forgiveness, another word for letting go, is learned drip by drip, day by day, not as an act of altruism, but as a necessary cleaning of the past, a purification of our souls so we can live and function effectively in the now. The soul does not grow into its potential fullness when it harbors past hurt and turns it over and over. That is the way to grow bitterness, not soul."
– Matthew Fox

Focusing on unfortunate decisions and painful events depresses, frustrates, angers, distracts, stresses, and generally upsets and stumbles a person. It places people in a bottomless pit of being a victim of consequence, circumstance, and despair, and robs them of energy, power, talent, intellect, joy, and health.

"Darkness cannot drive out darkness; only light can do that. Hate cannot drive out hate; only love can do that."
– Martin Luther King, Jr.

Remaining focused on anger relating to what someone did to you, or on a mistake you made, swirls negative energy through you. This process triggers your cells to release stress hormones. Continually engaging in this process creates a pattern that is poison to your life. Changing how you think about the deceit, decision, action, mistake, or violation can change the energy of it within you.

Be compassionate to your self, and have compassion for others. You and all people make mistakes. Don't be a stick-in-the-mud unwilling to move, to change your opinions, to consider the opinions of others, to forgive, to learn new things, and to get on with better things – including with healing relationships, and with healing you.

"The man who never alters his opinion is like standing water, and breeds reptiles of the mind."
– William Blake

Begin to think and act in ways that heal, and move your life forward so you lead your life undefined by rotted relationships, or the damaging choices and actions of others, and any unfortunate events of your past.

Perhaps there is no perfect forgiveness, especially if extremely unfortunate decisions were made. But there are ways to live more presently so you can stop dwelling in the harm and stagnating in the negative energy of victimization, and then start getting on with your life so you are not your wounds, but are your intellect, talents, skills, and love.

Aim for a brighter future not constantly dimmed by focusing on unwanted and unpleasant memories.

Working for good things to happen is an essential nutrient for the soul that renews what might be called spiritual health. Do what benefits you. Engage in healthful thoughts, nutrition, activities, and true physical exercise to release stagnant energy. Doing so can help to release constraints, diminish your pain, relieve depression, disperse chronic anger, invigorate cellular structures, free blockages, melt fears, heal wounds, dissipate crippling tempers, end harshly defensive behavior, fractures hostility, move on from grief, enhance happiness, sweeten bitterness, open possibilities, and renew potential.

"A man who studieth revenge keeps his own wounds green."
– Francis Bacon

Getting rid of the burden of anger allows you to align with more helpful expressions of energy.

Forgiveness does not always mean reconciling with those who subjected you to their dishonesty, slander, anger, violence, or other damaging behaviors. It also does not mean unwisely allowing damaging relationships and situations to remain present in your life while pretending they are not.

"Forgiveness is letting go of all hope of a better past."
— Anne Lamont

"Forgiveness is freeing up and putting to better use the energy once consumed by holding grudges, harboring resentments, and nursing unhealed wounds. It is rediscovering the strengths we always had, and relocating our limitless capacity to understand and accept other people and ourselves."
— Sidney and Suzanne Simon

Move on toward a better future, and create a more healthful life. That is, rather than dwell in your past and/or continuing to passively exist in denial and dysfunction while engulfed in an unhealthful situation.

"Children begin by loving their parents; as they grow older they judge them; sometimes they forgive them."
— Oscar Wilde

What forgiveness sometimes does is stop you from placing blame on the wrong people. These are people you may have treated unfairly because someone else treated you badly, which means perpetuating the damaging energy you were served. Therefore, through forgiveness and behaving in a kinder and fair manner, you stop propagating harm.

It's helpful to keep in mind that people aren't perfect, including you. Relationships aren't perfect. Life is complex. We all do or say something to someone, if only to ourselves, that isn't the wisest choice.

Forgiveness may have to do with forgiving yourself, which can be a liberating act ridding a person of regret, self-hate, misery, anguish, and self-inflicted wounds. The wounds you may be inflicting on yourself out of anger and regret includes harming yourself with low-quality foods, thought processes, interactions, and activities – or lack of activity, which is wallowing in slothfulness.

Free yourself of the concepts of blame. The process of releasing blame is to free yourself of pointing your finger toward and focusing your mind on who and what you believe caused your problems.

Blame involves focusing on the past, and dwelling in things like regret, dissatisfaction, anger, suspicion, defeat, anger, hate, disgust, assumptions, and victimization.

"If you judge people, you have no time to love them."
– Mother Teresa

If you have been involved in repeatedly reminding people of what they may have done, perhaps consider the possibility you are carrying on the damage, and continuing to inflict the same wounds caused by the problem.

The skewers you put through people to roast them over the flames of shame and guilt are likely skewing your life as you carry the burden of focusing on them. By continuing to scratch open old wounds, you cause more harm to your relationships and self-worth, which means you are choosing to exist in the energy of victimization.

When you think you are making someone else appear to be terrible, maybe you are making yourself look bad.

Refrain from being the one who continually speaks of the perceived ugly behavior and supposed imperfections of others. What you might be doing is perpetuating the ugly things, fueling more damage, creating unhealthful energy, and encouraging hate.

"You can stand tall without standing on someone. You can be a victor without having victims."
– Harriet Woods

To counteract the practice of blame, work to intentionally live your life focused on what you need and want to do, and not on what unpleasantries have been done and what you don't want to re-experience.

Goal-oriented living is the opposite of blame. It is about focusing on what can be done for today and the future through actions and communication to improve things.

Let go of blame. Doing so relieves stress, strengthens the immune system, relaxes the arteries, improves blood flow, and helps lay the groundwork for better health.

"You want to place blame on people, but I don't think it's fair. You're dealt the cards that you're dealt. You can let that be your downfall, or a springboard to become something better. For me, I just thought, 'What a waste of time to be angry at my parents. What a waste of time to feel sorry for myself.' The best thing I can do is learn all the things I've learned from them, good and bad, have my

own family someday, and just keep on going. So many things are thrown at us as human beings, but you can't let any of them get you down, or you're just going to be defeated."
– Drew Barrymore

Just because you may have been raised around people who didn't express patience, kindness, nurturing love, and encouraging words doesn't mean you have to conduct yourself in the same unhelpful manner. You can continually choose to make wiser choices in your relationships than those choices others around you have made.

"Kindness is a language which the deaf can hear and the blind can see."
– Mark Twain

"People are lonely who build walls instead of bridges."
– Mark Buber

Get away from the bad forms of communicating and the continual assumptions of disgust you may have learned from living in an unhealthful household. Assumptions and damaging communication within families are like mold and fungus destroying in darkness.

Stop the destruction of your self. Learn to communicate healthfully, conduct your self with dignity, and recognize that your future can be more pleasing and healthful than your past.

Rid your self of negative thoughts and feelings. By thinking positively with an eagerness for and engagement in a more healthful life, you will create positive energy within you, which will create a beneficial body chemistry that will resonate from you and into your life, the lives of those around you, and your community.

"Respond intelligently even to unintelligent treatment."
– Lao-Tse

Many people who have experienced horrible things get stuck in the memory of the incidents and linger there for the rest of their lives, thus allowing their experience with negative events to define them. Many also continue to attract the same kind of drama, same types of damaging people, and same variety of problems into their lives while never seeming to learn their role of creating – or in not changing – the events.

You can be the creator of circumstance, or the victim of it. It partially has to do with what you choose to do with your mind.

We are all subjected to circumstance. You can choose how you react to it. You can make better choices. You can engage in thought patterns that result in more healthful ways of communicating and living.

"Every suffering is a seed, because suffering impels us to seek wisdom."
– Bodhidharma

While many of us have been subjected to negative, unpleasant, and damaging situations, we do not have to dwell on those situations, or in the energy surrounding those memories.

We can break free of the things that have stopped us from succeeding in life. This includes releasing the energy surrounding negative relationships; cruel comments and actions; unfortunate choices; laziness and slothful behavior; and low-quality, toxic, and damaging food choices.

We absolutely can be proactive in healing the festering wounds of our life and reform our thoughtscape, lifescape, and outlook.

"To forgive is to set a prisoner free and discover the prisoner was you."
– Unknown

To move on from a past that haunts you, tarnishes your view, holds you back, and dulls your drive, it may be beneficial to seek the help of a therapist, to attend group therapy, and to read books that help you understand ways of working through your issues. Do it. You are worth it.

"Friendship with oneself is all-important, because without it one cannot be friends with anyone else in the world."
– Eleanor Roosevelt

What will most likely change your life for the better is a specific written plan to improve your life mixed with parallel daily thoughts and continual actions and helpful communication all working to bring the plan into fruition.

"There is overwhelming evidence that the higher the level of self-esteem, the more likely one will treat others with respect, kindness, and generosity. People who do not experience self-love have little or no capacity to love others."
– Nathaniel Branden

You can stop thinking bad thoughts about those in your life. Instead, acknowledge the positive.

You can stop participating in things that bring you down.

You can stop rummaging around in the damage that was done to you, including what you might have played a role in through unhelpful communication and unwise actions.

"If you're in conflict with someone, and they're unaware, then you're in conflict with yourself."
– Meggan Roxanne

Be wise with your communication, including communication with your self.

"Self-doubt, regret, disappointment, and embarrassment are instruction manuals for learning. The goal isn't to dwell on what went wrong yesterday. It is to discover what you can do better now."
– Adam M. Grant

How you value yourself is revealed in what you do and say. It is revealed in how you treat and communicate with others. How much you value others reveals how much you value yourself. The amount of wisdom you express in governing your existence balances with your participation in life, and with your community and society.

"Self-love is about slipping up, having the bad day, and loving ourselves despite them, forgiving ourselves, and, most importantly, having compassion for ourselves and how we are feeling. So, give yourself permission to fall, but don't give yourself permission to stay there."
– Saskia Lightstar

Most often, the person to go to for help is yourself, that includes reaching out and seeking the help you need to healthfully move forward into a better existence.

You can be wiser with your time, energy, resources, and words.

You can consume a more balanced diet of the most highly nutritious foods available to you – while avoiding foods that are damaging, dulling, and unhealthful.

You can take better care of your body and mind through exercise and education.

You can communicate better, choose gracious manners, and nurture healthful relationships.

Doing these things is liberating, empowering, healing, nurturing, and loving.

"Man's goodness is the flame that can never be extinguished."
– Nelson Mandela

# Vivid Consciousness

"My position concerning God is that of an agnostic. I am convinced that a vivid consciousness of the primary importance of moral principles for the betterment and ennoblement of life does not need the idea of a law-giver, especially a law-giver who works on the basis of reward and punishment."
– Albert Einstein

If someone is looking to me for information about which religion to align with, they likely won't find the answer they are looking for. Or, at least not what they might expect. I view religions as guessing games filled with pretend, wishful, magical, and convenient thinking, greed, twisted logic, epistemology, and a hunt for power.

As far as the idea of a God person who many view as a glorified being, I had attended Catholic school for my first four years of schooling, I was vaguely taught the mysterious concept. Even then, it seemed fictional to the point of cartoonish pretend.

I have no idea what my parents believed, other than they often went to church during my first several years, and then less and less, until they stopped by the time I was nine.

I was left not knowing what to believe in, and had looked around a bit in my early 20s. I went around to various places of worship, and considered everything from Buddhism to Hare Krishna, Jewish to Muslim, various Christian denominations, and other cults, including Scientology and Mormonism. For a while, I was involved with Mormonism, but found it to be absurd, racist, deceptive, sexist,

263

homophobic, spiritually brutalizing, limiting, based on an incredible amount of lies, and a global financial scam. (See: *The C.E.S. Letter.*)

I pretty much have the same view of all organized religions: They make money for some people, and give them control and power over people who they deceive. I see them as hucksters. Now, there are the "prosperity gospel" types who believe God blesses the believers with extreme wealth. That belief consists of even more impossibilities.

I have belief that there is some sort of what some people might define as a spirit energy. What that means isn't something I can define in exact terms. I don't think much of or focus on it. I figure it is still going to exist, whether I believe it, or not.

There is power and energy and chemistry and magnetism and light and a variety of other things working together somehow to form things that live and die, and arranges things in ways that work together, such as what is seen in the stars, planets, moons, and other arrangements that are in space, and also deep within all Earth life.

I will forgo attempting to define this energy, and only leave it open to whatever it is the reader's understanding is, or is not.

I mean to refer only to an energy of sorts that is far beyond our present comprehension, but that is clearly within our impression that is so very limited to whatever it is we are. Call it whatever you want.

As I see it, what we call spiritual beliefs and practices – along the lines of living healthfully taking care of our body and the planet – are in tune with the natural masterful pattern evident in the way things formulate and function, such as in cellular structures, electromagnetic fields, chemistry, molecules, atoms, particles, light, dark, and so forth.

It is interesting that, just as the stars, planets, and moons do not touch, and do not appear to be physically connected, but exist in some pattern relating to forms of energy, so too do our cells, molecules, and the substances that make up us also not connect. Just as there is space between the stars, planets, and moons, there is also space between our molecules and particles. Amazingly, it somehow all works in sync.

"You are not just a meaningless fragment in an alien universe, briefly suspended between life and death, allowed a few short-lived pleasures followed by pain and ultimate annihilation. Underneath your outer form, you are connected with something so vast, so immeasurable and sacred, that it cannot be spoken of."
– Eckhart Tolle

"Quantum physics tells us that the space between the molecules is not nothing, but rather is energy. And that energy is the same in all things. Everything, everyone, contains this same energy – God! But it

is when we focus on something with our consciousness that we actually merge with it, become one with it somehow, or rather become more conscious of this common energy of which we are all part – that our energies join and the boundaries diminish. Therefore, if I focus on my uniqueness, I become more myself. If I focus on someone else, I become more like them. And if I focus on the God in me, I become more like the God in me!"
– Jinjee Talifero

Clearly, there is an energy miraculously orchestrating us. Once that energy leaves, we "die" and our physical tissues degrade. If it is left exposed to the elements, a deceased human becomes part of the soil, the plants, and other wildlife, and the air and water. In that way, I understand the beliefs told to me by my indigenous American friends. They say the land, plants, wildlife, water, air, the clouds, and rain are all our ancestors. Substances once part of humans are now throughout Nature and the terrain, soil, water, air, animals, plants, fungi, bacteria, and the whole environment. Are their "spirits," too?

Just as miraculous as our decomposition is, our composition while alive has some somewhat predictable behaviors. Through living more in tune with Nature, especially through a plant-based diet free from junk food, it appears that we live more in tune with the powers of the energy that rules a healthy Nature. Through a healthful, highly nutritious plant-based diet that is of Nature and contains the unaltered substances from Nature in the form of fruits, vegetables, nuts, seeds, and seaweeds, the substances in foods feed our physical structure, and our body functions more healthfully.

Humans are meant to consume a natural diet, and not one of processed junk containing synthetic chemicals, highly heated and rancid oils, extracts, and highly fired foods. Eating animals contributes to and increases the incidence of cardiovascular disease, and of cancers, and autoimmune disorders, including common degenerative and chronic conditions. So, why even kill animals and eat them, when eating plants doesn't cause those health problems?

By eating a natural, plant-based diet, we invite the amazing power of Nature into our tissues.

"You are not a human being in search of a spiritual experience. You are a spiritual being immersed in a human experience."
– Pierre Teilhard de Chardin

People ask me if I believe in religion, but they have their own classification of what they mean by religion. Maybe they will

265

consider my beliefs as some sort of religion. Clearly, I'm not in alignment with organized religions, don't support them, don't attend them, and don't conform to their belief systems. My understating of what religion is and what other people mean by religion could be two very different things, and very much likely is.

**"I'm not into isms and asms. There isn't a Catholic moon and a Baptist sun. I know that universal God is universal. I feel that the same God-force that is the mother and father of the pope is also the mother and father of the loneliest man on the planet."**
**– Dick Gregory**

Someone once asked me if I believe in creationism, evolution, or intelligent design. My answer is "Yes, we are here." Maybe it wasn't the answer they wanted as agreeing to one or another. I'm not here to confirm, validate, or collapse their belief, or to conform to their logic.

No matter what belief someone conforms to, they are still of their own belief. Nobody could possibly agree on all and every concept of one religion. Get them in separate rooms, and ask people of the same religion what they believe in, and you will find they all don't agree to the same exact concept of what they believe in. It's all a mix of feelings and concepts and learned and indoctrinated systems of belief. In that way, I figure there are as many "religions" as there are people. Everyone is observing, factoring, and wishing as they go through life.

I avoid engaging in what often turns into some form of a debate or gentle argument about religious topics. Often the discussions have to do with people wanting others to agree with their concept, as if they need to be validated in their opinion of what it all means.

We are here, which stands as enough evidence for me. I can leave the details of how it all happened up to something we may possibly understand at the next stage in the juncture. I do believe our energy carries on, in some way or another. I've had my experiences in life that all tend to reveal there is something more to it all, other than this concept of life we are living as humans on Earth. There is a much larger something going on, including planets and stars and space matter and energy and dark and light – all beyond our understanding.

While discussions may be helpful in sharing understandings, and to formulate opinions, any sort of argument about it all to get people to agree to one idea seems to be a nonsensical waste of time.

I often hear people say that certain religions are "weird." It is often said in a tone implying that the speaker's religion is not weird. Is one religion less weird than the other, or more antiquated, important, cartoonish, awkward, bizarre, cultish, or less believable? Is one person less of a person, or less important because they believe in one way of twisted logic, and not the other illogical belief system? Are they foolish, normal, or more important if they believe their gods resemble them, or a dog, a cow, a tree, a belly dancer, a supermodel, their favorite superhero, the mysteries of Nature, or nothing at all?

Conversations and debates about religion could go on forever with no two people agreeing on the same principles or concepts. It isn't important to me which religion someone espouses. What matters more to me is that people live to do what is the best they know how in the best way, and to respect each other, wildlife, and the environment, even with consideration for future generations of wildlife.

This is what I know: We are made up of a variety of substances, and there is an energy holding these substances together in a form that we define as us. There are things we can do to help us function better, and other things that cause us to function negatively, sickly, and tragically. Everything beyond that knowledge is what people tend to argue about – which is what I am not interested in doing. I'm working to live in a way that gets me to function better, and preferably more in tune with Nature, which I think is best for all, including for wildlife. Otherwise, I wouldn't be doing it. More than sometimes, like probably everyone, I am very much not the best at being in alignment with better behavior and wise choices. We can't expect anyone to be perfect, including ourselves. I am very much far from perfect.

"The cosmos is a vast living body, of which we are still parts. The Sun is a great heart whose tremors run through our smallest veins. The moon is a great nerve-center from which we quiver forever. Who knows the power that Saturn has over us, or Venus? But it is a vital power, rippling exquisitely through us all the time."
– D. H. Lawrence

People ask me if I believe in astrology. I am not a person who seeks out information about my astrological impressions. My exposure to astrology has been from reading a little about it and randomly meeting people who seem to be somewhat knowledgeable about astrology. Sometimes these people say things that interest me. Sometimes they don't. Sometimes they are interesting to listen to simply because of their conviction and theatrical delivery. Some have attempted to explain it all to me, or their understanding of it, but I don't dwell on it. However, as the moon and stars affect the tide that is the water of the sea, so too are we, who largely consist of water, affected by the electromagnetic and other structures, energetic wavelengths, and intricacies of what are called "the heavens."

267

"The truths – those surprising, amazing, unforeseen truths –
which our descendants will discover, are even now all around us,
staring us in the eyes, and yet we do not see them."
– Paramhansa Yogananda

What we do always plays into natural laws existing in patterns,
and even within what people refer to as *sacred fractal geometry*. We
are either doing what is in tune with patterns that build health, or we
are doing what is in tune with the opposite. In that way we are in tune
or out of tune with what will benefit us. In that way our decisions
impact us so that when we make choices that don't coincide with
what is best we often get what is in sync with our bad choices.
Somewhere within that is my concept of right and wrong, or what
some may call their religion.

No matter what religion a person is, it seems to me that the main
thing is to know oneself, and to understand something deeply about
your soul in a way that you will be committed to leading a life that
aims for the best you can be while using your talents, intellect, and
better qualities. And to do so in peace with others while living a life
that respects Earth and protects animals. Everything else seems
secondary and trivial.

"He who knows others is wise; he who knows himself is
enlightened."
– Lao Tzu

I believe that Nature is the manifestation of what some people
might call the beauty of divine spirit energy. As formulations of spirit
energies, we can help manifest the beauty of Nature in cooperation
with a more glorious and glorified existence with which we may one
day be more aware of on an enlightened spiritual level – and that we
are continually interacting with on some level – which is always what
can be called "spiritual" in one way or another.

When we live closer to Nature, respect wildlife, and follow a
plant-based diet, we build a stronger relationship with our loving,
spiritual side. I believe that enlightenment has to do with respecting
Earth and protecting animals (including by not killing them).

I also know that we are territorial, and will do things to protect
ourselves, which might mean against fungi, bacteria, viruses, certain
bugs, and against illness and danger.

"A knowledge of the existence of something we cannot
penetrate, of the manifestations of the profoundest reason and the
most radiant beauty, which are only accessible to our reason in their

most elementary forms – it is this knowledge and this emotion that constitute the truly religious attitude; in this sense, and in this alone, I am a deeply religious man."
– Albert Einstein

Too often it appears "religions" focus on shame and guilt, limit potential, and drive people to lose the beauty and originality of their individuality – all while working money out of people's pockets to support self-serving ministers and unsustainable church infrastructures. Much of it is done with the undercurrent of telling people they should live as told, or risk experiencing some sort of vague and unpleasant eternal something-or-other that is used as a subtle threat – spiritual brutality – to get them to obey, and to donate their time, and – especially – their money. Or else.

"When I do good, I feel good; when I do bad, I feel bad, and that is my religion."
– Abraham Lincoln

A preacher once asked me, "Son, don't you fear God?" I asked him, "Why would I fear God?" He said something about how, if I feared God, I would live more righteously. I told him that I think people can live righteously without being fearful.

I don't want to be motivated by shame, guilt, or fear. I also don't feel it is helpful to use those conditions as a way to get people to act in alignment with what gives power to some grifter who calls themself a minister, preacher, or otherwise some so-called person favored of God. Scam artists dominate religions. As Stephen Hawking said, "I don't fear God, I fear his believers."

Not that I am anything close to being an example of any righteous virtue, but I think it is better to be motivated by beauty and love.

I feel no connection to churches projecting shame, guilt, and fear as motivational factors for leading a good and honest life. I also have no interest in ministers, preachers, and other religious leaders telling me what is going to happen to me after I die. I think it would be better to motivate people to focus on and live in the present while creating a beautiful life.

To me it seems you will have a better chance of becoming a world-renowned artist by attending truck-driving school than you will of becoming closer to a God by associating with the churches that are "in business." I do not consider these money-grabbing churches to be associated with the teachings of their so-called idealized Divinity of choice, or whatever distorted image of it they have conceptualized.

Some of these churches may as well be worshipping cartoon characters. If their members considered how their idealized person actually lived, they would likely find the person to be someone who lived naturally, and far distant from how the so-called church leaders are living with their greed, self-righteousness, projections of shame, manipulative spiritual brutality, expensive clothing, material possessions, and rituals that are pure, complete theatrical nonsense.

"Peace I leave with you, my peace I give unto you: not as the world giveth, give I unto you. Let not your heart be troubled, neither let it be afraid."
– attributed to Jesus in a book written several decades after his apparent death

If I were asked if I am a certain religion, and if I were to answer "yes," people would naturally apply their own definition of their concept of that belief to my answer. But their definition of that belief is likely very far removed from what I believe. If they find out I follow a vegan diet, then they mix in their assumptions about that, too. Then some think of me as less.

Perhaps nobody is beyond assuming things about a person's religious or spiritual beliefs. Are we less or more than examples of our beliefs? Nobody could be so rigid in their thoughts, actions, and communication to be the perfect example of a belief system.

Many churches appear to be organized to feed off people who have given up, or who never have taken hold of their power. The money-making endeavors of these churches blend in perfectly well with the companies exploiting every possible religious holiday by manufacturing and selling various products in connection with those holidays. Most of what religion has become seems to be a big marketing sham to get money from the so-called pilgrims in every which way possible. To me – while the related music and theatrics may involve major expressions of talent and creativity – Christmas and other mass-marketed holidays have as much to do with God and spirituality as bricks and boulders have to do with soft.

"A clergyman earns his living by assuring idiots that he can save them from an imaginary hell."
– Henry Louis Mencken

Many churches glorify not in what is best for the people, but in what can make the church bigger and grander. There is no way to explain their brash techniques, other than to recognize their main goal as being to get money from people by manipulating them. Their leaders dress in elaborate clothing to represent their man-given titles and engage in man-invented mystical and theatrical rituals. None of their activities have anything to do with Divinity, but have more to do with traditions driven by megalomania. The leaders self-glorify and validate their vanity by gaining the favor of people. They speak as if they know every nuance of the thoughts of Divinity, as they lead unsustainable lives out of tune with Nature. They project shame and guilt when it would be greatly more beneficial to build and nurture intellect, talents, and gifts of the spirit while advocating a sustainable diet and lifestyle.

"Being a Baptist won't keep you from sinning, but it'll sure as hell keep you from enjoying it."
– James Dean

Many churches condemn people for being outside the robotic and extremely limiting standards that the churches have defined as the acceptable forms of behavior. It seems to me that those who most adamantly promote such teachings are dealing with projecting their own form of self-hate, repression, neglect, and denial.

"Whoever undertakes to set himself up as judge of truth and knowledge is shipwrecked by the laughter of the gods."
– Albert Einstein

Isn't it interesting that some of those most fervent in preaching against moral issues are found to be leading secretive double lives completely out of tune with what they so strongly preached against?

To understand what some people are struggling with in the shadows of their minds, sometimes all you have to do is listen to what they confess to hate. Especially so in relation to other genders.

"Stories serve the purpose of consolidating whatever gains people or their leaders have made or imagine they have made in their existing journey through the world."
– Chinua Achebe

We live on a planet with cultures and countries dominated by various religions and their leaders declaring how people are to live in obedience to them, often to a point of tragic consequences – including murders, suicides, and wars. Many beliefs are of distorted concepts originating in poetry, lyrics, parables, fables, metaphors, tribal legends, ancient myths, and wishful thinking mixed with bigotry, sexism, racism, revised history, and miraculous, romanticized, and fancified tales of patriarchal superheroes. It's written in antiquated, vague styles continually debated and reinterpreted. Many scriptural

271

stories are lessons using outlandish claims set in fiction. Some are mistranslations – often of plagiarized and restyled stories used by clever narcissists driven by the agenda of gaining power and wealth. It's time for people to disconnect from that nonsense. (See the book: *God: An Anatomy*, by Francesca Stavrakopoulou.)

"The greatness of a nation and its moral progress can be judged by the way its animals are treated."
– Mahatma Gandhi

It seems to me that the humble people described in many of the various scriptural texts wouldn't relate to a vast majority of those who claim to be living in tune with "scriptural teachings," and whose daily food intake involves many of the most life damaging foods ever created. Many people who also confess to leading their lives according to scriptural teachings also seem to overlook the number of characters in the texts who are murderers, slave owners, rapists, and otherwise engage in all sorts of ruinous behavior.

Many churches teach people to reject others and encourage remote attitudes, cold-heartedness, and the denial of the obvious, leading to pain in the hearts of the two-spirited who are simply born that way. Many churches teach people to be afraid of themselves and shameful of what could be enjoyable relationships that would otherwise be loving if expressed respectfully between two adult people in a committed, nurturing relationship. But many of the church teachings nurture denial, dysfunction, self-hate, and family fights. Narrow-minded church teachings have brought about such restraint in some people that it leads to double and high-risk hidden lives that harm and ruin what would otherwise be those living safe, monogamous lives, accepting who they are while living in communities that would otherwise be welcoming of diversity.

"Our Western institutional religious tradition has essentially repressed and distorted the sexual instinct and thereby created a variety of personal and social pathologies. In so doing it has also effectively removed sexuality from its spiritual foundation."
– Gunther Weil

In his book, *The Hidden Spirituality of Men*, Matthew Fox writes, "So often religion seems more bent on controlling sex than on mining it for its spiritual power," and that, "In the West, we prefer linking sex to shame rather than to the sacred."

Rather than being inspirational, much of what I see in some churches are lessons in greed, narrow-mindedness, unkindness, sexism, racism, and hate. Their actions speak much louder than their words. They create problems, teach people to reject anything other than what the megalomaniac church leaders say, and get people to shut down what may be the best parts of themselves.

"What it comes down to is the churches are not operating like instruments of love. They're hate machines. They're ignorance factories."
– Sean Penn

You don't have to belong to a religious organization, or be a follower of some sort of so-called spiritual leader, minister, priest, or other figure to be inspired, and to live rightly for you.

You can receive your own inspiration, without giving your money or power to anyone, or by having to believe in antiquated concepts.

"If we cannot see how what we are doing or not doing is contributing to things being the way that they are, then logically we have no basis at all, zero leverage, for changing the way things are – except from the outside, by persuasion or force."
– Adam Kahane

"Where questions of religion are concerned, people are guilty of every possible sort of dishonesty and intellectual misdemeanor."
– Sigmund Freud

"From the beginning men used God to justify the unjustifiable."
– Salman Rushdie

Many people who consider themselves religious often espouse political views that are pro-war; live selfishly in opulent homes; support politicians who vote to spend more money on prisons than on schools; support officials who allocate more money for the military and corporate welfare (which can be the same thing) than on protecting the environment and wildlife; and appear to live with the attitude expressed through their diet and lifestyle that Earth and wildlife are here for us to exploit, violate, plunder, and destroy.

While the prior paragraph unfortunately describes many people, there are other people who are living lives disconnected from religions, and who find inspiration in a variety of things and in a number of ways not necessarily associated with what some people consider to be a religion.

"Every day people are straying away from church and going back to God."
– Lenny Bruce

Some people find inspiration to be a better person by creating music, poetry, paintings, functional sculptures, and other forms of art. Others find inspiration to be a better person by spending quality time with family, friends, neighbors, and lovers. Others find it in making and/or growing food and sharing it with others, including the less fortunate. Some find it in working with the disabled, working with those who are troubled, or working with rescued animals.

"Connection with gardens, even small ones, even potted plants, can become windows to the inner life. The simple act of stopping and looking at the beauty around us can be prayer."
– Patricia R. Barret

Some find inspiration to be a better person in the wilds of Nature, in surfing, in hiking through forests and among other landscapes, in kayaking, in planting and maintaining culinary gardens, in nurturing wild edible native plants, and in working to clean, restore, and protect wildlands, and in helping wildlife and improving the habitat needed to sustain it. I understand how people can relate more to these types of activities than to sitting in a building listening to a preacher tell them about life. Working to build strong human bonds and to protect Nature are more beneficial to both the planet and the person than sitting in church while listening to someone talk about how to live.

Go outside, live, and help life. Including local wildlife.

"Anything else you're interested in is not going to happen if you can't breathe the air and drink the water. Don't sit this one out. Do something. You are by accident of fate alive at an absolutely critical moment in the history of our planet."
– Carl Sagan

Imagine how many millions of acres of pristine wildlands have been bulldozed to build churches, synagogues, temples, and other places of worship, and the accompanying parking lots.

Imagine how much damage has been done to Earth to provide all the materials used to build all those religious buildings and parking lots.

Imagine how much energy in fossil fuels is used to light, heat, and otherwise run and manage the religious facilities, and how much damage is continually being done to Earth to access these resources and turn them into religious buildings and products.

"Show by your lives that religion does not mean words, or names, or sects, but that it means spiritual realization."
– Sri Ramakrishna

"Don't be content in your life just to do no wrong. Be prepared every day to try and do some good."
– Nicolas Winton

"Everybody needs beauty as well as bread, places to play in and pray in, where nature may heal and give strength to body and soul."
– John Muir

"I am I, plus my surroundings, and if I do not preserve the latter, I do not preserve myself."
– Jose Ortega Y Gasset

Imagine how much better the world would be if instead of sitting in church for hours every week, the congregants went out and did environmental service; if instead of donating money to churches they donated money to groups restoring and protecting forests, rivers, and wildlife habitat, such as the Natural Resources Defense Council, Earth Island Institute, Earth First, Sea Shepherd, and the Green World Campaign; and if instead of church buildings and parking lots covering millions of acres of land, there were millions of acres of wildlife habitat protected and held as havens of Nature and natural sanctuaries for worship.

"I believe in Spinoza's God, who reveals Himself in the lawful harmony of the world, not in a God who concerns Himself with the fate and the doings of mankind."
– Albert Einstein

"A morning-glory at my window satisfies me more than the metaphysics of books."
– Walt Whitman

A friend once asked me what provides me with my inspiration. I answered that some people look in books to try to find the mysteries and magic things of life. I see the miracles and mysteries in the plants, wild animals, soil, rivers, lakes, ocean, and sky.

Later, my friend sent me the following quotation:

"In music, in the sea, in a flower, in a leaf, in an act of kindness. I see what people call God in all these things."
– Pablo Casals

It would be nice if churches, which are tax-free and major land owners on every continent, would stop building parking lots and buildings, which are destroying the planet by paving over paradise; discontinue investing money in commercial real estate sprawl, which is destroying the planet; and in investing in the companies that are destroying the planet. (Yes, churches invest their money in stocks and companies and real estate.) Instead, it would be good if they became more involved in aggressively protecting the sanctuary of Nature that is this wonderful planet created by the God they profess to worship.

"Our intellect has achieved the most tremendous things, but in the meantime our spiritual dwelling has fallen into disrepair."
– Carl Gustav Jung

It is interesting that churches function under for-profit business plans with investment portfolios while claiming to be nonprofit. It is unfortunate that churches are working out of huge, high-maintenance structures contributing to urban sprawl, and are accompanied by parking lots. It all plays into the destruction of the creation of the Divinity the church members confess to believe. All of it is robbing the land of beauty, creating toxic air, and ruining many millions of acres of land that should have been left as wildlife habitat on every region of the planet – a planet with wildlife that is going extinct specifically because of the use of fossil fuels, unwise food choices, plastic and pharmaceutical and chemical pollution, and the destruction of habitat.

People may say that churches are needed to provide social support. It is true that churches provide some obvious social benefits, including structure for people who are struggling, and some provide shelter for those who are destitute. Studies have concluded that gathering with people in a nurturing environment is healthful on many levels.

It is known that isolation from human contact can cause depression and increase the chances of dementia in old age. In this way, churches provide something many people might not otherwise get: a social structure where they are exposed to a variety of people with various interests.

However, churches are not the only solution for providing social stimulation. Continuing education, participation in volunteer work, being involved in environmental causes, going to a yoga and other fitness classes, and being a member of sports, arts, gardening, culinary, music, hobby, professional, and community organizations also provide social involvement providing the sensory experiences that stimulate the neural pathways of the brain.

"Dogs give unconditional love. For me they are the role model for being alive."
– Gilda Radner

Interestingly, science has shown that interacting with animals provides some of the brain stimulation a person can get from interacting with people. This stands as another reason why we need to take care of the animals and protect wildlife and the environment.

"The human race is challenged more than ever before to demonstrate our mastery, not over nature but of ourselves."
– Rachel Carson

Churches throughout history have played a role in the arts, including music, painting, sculpture, architecture, and craftsmanship. Much of this has been to enrich the churches disproportionate to the benefits to the worshippers. Many churches own art, land, jewels, gold, and other belongings gathered from people in various ways, and often deceptively, sometimes violently, or otherwise unrighteously. The Catholic church especially has a history of plundering and robbing the poor. The Vatican stores many stolen belongings.

"We have the money, the power, the medical understanding, the scientific know-how, the love, and the community to produce a kind of human paradise. Yet we're led by the least among us – the least intelligent, the least noble, the least visionary. We are led by the least among us, and we do not fight back against the dehumanizing values that are handed down as control icons."
– Terence McKenna

We are living in amazing times. While so much needs to be done to transform society to protect the planet, it seems the main focus of many governments is on war; on providing welfare for the most environmentally damaging industries and corporations; on making the rich more wealthy; on catering to commercialism; on passing laws that cage more of the poor in tremendous prisons while government administrators slash funding for childcare, the arts, libraries, and education; and in building structures that both cause terrific damage to the planet and provide venues for Earth-damaging activities.

"In wildness is the preservation of the world."
– Henry David Thoreau

"The world is charged with the grandeur of God."
– Gerard Manley Hopkins

"The more closely we can focus our attention on the wonders and realities of the universe about us, the less taste we shall have for destruction."
– Rachel Carson

I believe we have a sacred responsibility to take care of Earth and the delicate web of Nature. I believe that if we are to gather and unite for an ongoing human concern it would be most helpful to tune each other into more environmentally sustainable beings actively involved in protecting and restoring wildlife habitat. That is the mastery I believe would be most helpful for all of us to be working on and striving for.

"Religious people must do more than offer prayers if the world is to become a better place to live."
– Dalai Lama

For those who say churches must exist, and who are involved in creating churches, to them I say: Consider meeting in the cathedral of Nature that is a forest, or under a large canopy of sorts to protect the people from the elements. Or in any of the many structures that already exist, rather than by building new structures. Consider building no new parking lots or structures that destroy meadows, woodlands, wetlands, hillsides, or any other wildlife habitat, or otherwise fallow or wild land. Existing structures could be converted to be more sustainable.

"Community means strength that joins our strength to do the work that needs to be done. Arms to hold us when we falter. A circle of healing. A circle of friends. Someplace where we can be free."
– Starhawk

"If more of us valued food and cheer and song above hoarded gold, it would be a merrier world."
– J. R. R. Tolkien

"It is no use walking anywhere to preach, unless our walking is our preaching."
– St. Francis of Assisi

It can be considered that churches squash individuality and harm Nature, including by way of holding unsustainable lifestyles as an ideal. Ways of engaging in the opposite would be building a community that works to improve wildlife habitat, including by unpaving land, planting more trees and native plants, and creating lasting good that can play into a healthier planet. Replant paradise.

"Almost anybody can learn to think or believe or know, but not a single human being can be taught to feel. Why? Because whenever

278

you think or you believe or you know, you're a lot of other people; but the moment you feel, you're nobody-but-yourself.

To be nobody-but-yourself – in a world which is doing its best, night and day, to make you everybody else – means to fight the hardest battle which any human being can fight; and never stop fighting."
– E. E. Cummings

"In the life of the Indian there is only one inevitable duty – the duty of prayer – the daily recognition of the Unseen and Eternal. He sees no need for setting apart one day in seven as a holy day, since to him all days are God's."
– Santee Dakota Ohiyesa

To everyone's benefit, there are many people in all religions who are becoming involved in environmental issues by working on protecting wildlife, on restoring forests, on living more sustainably, and on following a diet that is more respectful of the treasures of Nature. There are vegan groups in many religions, and others are forming.

On January 1, 2010, which marks the annual World Peace Day, members of the Catholic Church were told by Pope Benedict that, "Respect for creation is of immense consequence, not least because creation is the beginning and the foundation of all God's works, and its preservation has now become essential for the pacific coexistence of mankind." He added, "It is imperative that mankind renew and strengthen that covenant between human beings and the environment, which should mirror the creative love of God, from whom we come and toward whom we are journeying." It would be excellent if people took action in tune with that advice. Following a plant-based diet free of synthetic chemicals would be a good place to start, as food is the number one way in which we interact with Earth and wildlife.

There are also some of the money-collecting churches doing a good job of accepting a broad variety of personalities, including those who have been rejected by other churches based on color, nationality, and gender. Instead of projecting shame, punishment, fear, and guilt, and teaching about sin and apostasy, these churches are encouraging and nurturing people with the intention of bringing out their talents, intellect, and individual beauty. Instead of pointing to two adults and forbidding them to be together, they say, let them be and let them love. Some offer social activity or otherwise fellowship programs that include dance, art, music, song, poetry, literature, environmental responsibility, yoga, and plant-based nutrition.

279

Do good for what we all need: a healthy natural environment in which wildlife thrives. Consider belonging to – or organizing – an environmental group involved in restoring and protecting local wildlife habitat. As Madalyn Murray O'Hair said, "Two hands working can do more than a thousand clasped in prayer."

"I don't believe that the solutions in society will come from the left or the right or the north or the south. They will come from islands within those organizations, islands of people with integrity who want to do something."
– Karl-Henrik Robert

"I do not believe in a personal God and I have never denied this but have expressed it clearly. If something is in me which can be called religious then it is the unbounded admiration for the structure of the world so far as our science can reveal it."
– Albert Einstein

If you are going to church to find inspiration to live your life, but all you are doing is sitting around trying to get inspired, how much inspiration are you truly getting? If you are not being inspired to use your talent, intellect, skill, and other better qualities to become busy creating a better world, then what are you being inspired to do?

"The eye with which I see God is the same eye with which God sees me."
– Meister Eckhart

Your thoughts are the sources driven by your spiritual force that will bring you to do what you want to do with your life.

Be an inspiration to yourself. Manifest inspiration through your words, actions, foods, and lifestyle to awaken the beauty within.

"We do not destroy religion by destroying superstition."
– Marcus Tullius Cicero

"I have learned so much from God that I no longer call myself a Christian, a Hindu, a Muslim, a Buddhist, a Jew. The truth has shared so much of itself with me that I can no longer call myself a man, a woman, an angel, or even pure soul. Love has befriended Hafiz so completely, it has turned to ash and freed me of every concept and image my mind has ever known."
– Hafiz

"Always remember that you belong to no one, and no one belongs to you. Reflect that someday you will suddenly have to leave

everything in this world – so make the acquaintanceship of God now."
 – Paramhansa Yogananda

"Why should I respect a capricious, mean-minded, stupid god who creates a world so full of injustice and pain?"
 – Stephen Fry

"I think of a little child in east Africa with a worm burrowing through his eyeball. The worm cannot live in any other way, except by burrowing through eyeballs. I find that hard to reconcile with the notion of a divine and benevolent creator."
 – David Attenborough

"Can any rational person believe that the Bible is anything but a human document? We now know pretty well where the various books came from, and about when they were written. We know that they were written by human beings who had no knowledge of science, little knowledge of life, and were influenced by the barbarous morality of primitive times, and were grossly ignorant of most things that men know today."
 – Clarence Darrow

"You don't have to be religious to have a soul; everybody has one. You don't have to be religious to perfect your soul; I have found saintliness in avowed atheists."
 – Harold Kushner

"Spirituality is about joy, fun, creating, and playing. It is absolutely not rigid, full of rules, or judgmental. It is about freedom, love, and laughter."
 – Karen Bishop

"My religion is kindness."
 – Dalai Lama

"Humanity and divinity will be identical when we recognize divinity in humanity."
 – Ernest Holmes

"Our task is to say holy yes to the real things of our life."
 – Natalie Goldberg

"The way is not in the sky. The way is in the heart."
 – Buddha

# Love

"Love is the greatest refreshment in life."
– Pablo Picasso

Similar to the other aspects of a person, what people call "the soul" can experience illness. An ailing soul manifests its ailment in low-quality choices. A sign that a person is suffering is that they are harming themselves, or others, and/or Nature.

"It is hard for me to understand a culture that not only hates and fights his brothers, but even attacks Nature and abuses her. Man must love all creation, or he will love none of it. Love is something you and I must have. We must have it, because our spirit feeds upon it. Without love, our self-esteem weakens. Without it, our courage fails. Without love, we can no longer look out confidently at the world. Instead, we turn inwardly and begin to feed upon our own personalities and little-by-little we destroy ourselves."
– Chief Dan George

Perhaps the health of the soul is the most important of all. It is the root of the person, and their connection to their better qualities. One healing agent is that of love.

"The story of a love is not important – what is important is that one is capable of love. It is perhaps the only glimpse we are permitted of eternity."
– Helen Hayes

After age four, love is not on the list of things I would say I experienced while growing up. Hate was. Eventually, I have felt better when I had what I perceived to be love in my life.

"Neither a lofty degree of intelligence nor imagination nor both together go to the making of genius. Love, love, love, that is the soul of genius."
– Wolfgang Amadeus Mozart

The importance of loving everyone is a concept I would like to believe in. However, I have not been so successful at this. Other people seem to be doing their best at shattering the possibility of the concept of being loving to everyone from becoming reality.

In addition to being a healing agent, love could be considered an essential nutrient. It needs to be both synthesized within us and obtained from outside sources. Love is a nutrient that helps us to experience and infuse healing energy.

"Love is a force that connects us to every strand of the universe, an unconditional state that characterizes human nature, a form of knowledge that is always there for us if only we can open ourselves to it."
– Emily Hilburn Sell

Perhaps, for some, if they don't receive nurturing, loving interaction when they are young, their brain does not develop the receptors that respond to kindness and to related pleasurable feelings and emotions. This is one of the tragedies of child neglect and abuse.

Because the society in which we grow up also helps our brain to develop, the children growing up under the stressful conditions of war-torn regions and poverty-stricken situations are also not being given the opportunity to develop healthful brains. This is one level of the horrors of war and poverty, and damage caused by ill-advised, power-hungry politicians, and the wealthy who manipulate them.

"Whether one believes in a religion or not, and whether one believes in rebirth or not, there isn't anyone who doesn't appreciate kindness and compassion."
– Dalai Lama

No matter how we have lived, or what we have experienced, I believe we can choose to live in a way that heals us.

Luckily, the brain continues to form and rewire itself throughout life, thus living healthfully at any stage of life allows us to become more healthful.

To heal our brains from unfortunate experiences, the healing energy of love is helpful. Even better if this love is combined with the best-quality foods available to us, intellectual stimulation, daily exercise, the use of talents and intellect, and intentionally goal-oriented living, while being with people we care about.

"As the body needs food to survive and grow, the soul needs love. Love instills a strength and vitality that even mother's milk cannot provide. All of us live and long for real love. We are born and die searching for such love. Children, love each other and unite in pure love."
— Mata Amritanandamayl "Amma" Devi

Love is the most positive, life-affirming energy a person can feel. It permeates us, is the strongest power, and can be considered to be the domineering superpower. Because it can be generated from within, love is available to us at all times.

"There is no remedy for love, but to love more."
— Henry David Thoreau

Love is the song inside you that gently and compassionately encourages you to tune into your spirit and express your intellect and better qualities through healthful living.

"What else is the world interested in? What else do we all want, each one of us, except to love and be loved, in our families, in our work, in all our relationships?"
— Dorothy Day

Love is the nutrient of and gift from the spirit. When love is present, people communicate, learn, heal, play, think, feel, and sleep better. Loving thoughts are uplifting, kind, patient, healing, bring solutions, and result in good works.

"When we love, we release our thought energy and transpose it to the recipient of our love. Our primary responsibility is to love."
— Marcel Vogel

The problems of the human world are strongly related to the fact that humans refuse to love one another and to act lovingly toward the other sentient beings with whom we share this amazing planet.

Many people have suffered tragedies, experienced failure, been subjected to the harsh treatment of damaged and disturbed people, and have gotten caught in the energy of failure, ruin, defeat, and deception. All of these have brought them to dwell in the bottomless pit of disappointment, anger, depression, sadness, and psychological and spiritual pain. These can become their normal and most common feelings. They may get to the point where they don't know anything closely resembling joy, and feel as if they are descending. Anything outside this pain can cause them to feel uncomfortable. They can be so focused on and attached to this draining energy of suffering that they become lost in it and dwell in the martyr energy. They can get to the point where they lack an understanding that they have energy resonating inside them that can help them change their situation. This energy is the healing and ascending energy of love.

Love is necessary for a life to be healthful. Love uplifts and brightens. It helps those who are sad to become happy. It helps those who are ailing to heal. It seems thriving in love in their communities is how the animals of the land, sky, and water function.

Sigmund Freud philosophized that happiness is obtained through work and love. The nurturing energy of love brings people to prosper by uplifting them and getting them to use their intellect, talents, abilities, and better qualities.

"We love because it is the only true adventure."
– Nikki Giovanni

To bring love into your life, be sure to first love your self. Love for self includes taking care of and respecting your physical being. Love for self includes believing that your essence is worthy of love. Knowing that you are worthy of love, of being loved, and of loving will drive you to improve your life, and help others experience the same.

"To love oneself is the beginning of a lifelong romance."
– Oscar Wilde

When you carry love and work to rule your self by love, you are working to be a holder of the higher consciousness.

Emotions and expressions in alignment with love include kindness, forgiveness, patience, encouragement of good, and respect for the safety, talents, skills, intellect, and health of others.

"Too often we underestimate the power of touch, a smile, a kind word, a listening ear, an honest compliment, or the smallest act of caring, all of which have the potential to turn a life around."
– Leo Buscaglia

Loving someone does not mean doing everything for them that they are capable of doing for themselves – as that would encourage laziness, spur weakness, and prevent them from learning. Instead, love in a relationship means respect while nurturing a life together.

"First – If you are in love – that's a good thing – that's about the best thing that can happen to anyone. Don't let anyone make it small or light to you.

Second – There are several kinds of love. One is a selfish, mean, grasping, egotistical thing which uses love for self-importance. This is the ugly and crippling kind. The other is an outpouring of everything good in you – of kindness and consideration and respect – not only the social respect of manners, but the greater respect which is recognition of another person as unique and valuable. The first kind can make you sick and small and weak, but the second can relish in you strength, and courage, and goodness, and even wisdom you didn't know you had.

You say this is not puppy love. If you feel so deeply – of course it isn't puppy love.

But I don't think you were asking me what you feel. You know better than anyone. What you wanted me to help you with is what to do about it – and I can tell you.

Glory in it for one thing and be very glad and grateful for it.

The object of love is the best and most beautiful. Try to live up to it.

If you love someone – there is no possible harm in saying so – only you must remember that some people are very shy and sometimes the saying must take that shyness into consideration.

Girls have a way of knowing or feeling what you feel, but they usually like to hear it also.

It sometimes happens that what you feel is not returned for one reason or another – but that does not make your feelings less valuable and good."

– John Steinbeck, to his son

Things attract complementary things. All good things are in alignment with the energy of good, which is of the energy of love. If you want good in your life, you must align yourself with the energy of love.

"Everything in the future will improve if you are making a spiritual effort now."

– Paramhansa Yogananda

With the energy of love, you can perceive yourself, others, and everything around you in an entirely different way.

Where the person people call Jesus is quoted in the Bible (written many decades later) advising people to not allow their hearts to be troubled or to be afraid, I believe that it – whoever wrote it – is addressing the topic of toxic thought patterns. Allowing yourself to feel troubled and afraid is damaging to you, creates stress, and harms your body tissues. Being troubled and afraid is the opposite of love.

By allowing yourself to be ruled by love, to act out of love, to project love, and to promote love, you are participating in the strongest energy of all. It is the energy of bliss, of euphoria, of nirvana, of the power of Nature, the resonance of the best feelings, and the frequency to aim for and tune into.

"Once you begin to acknowledge random acts of kindness – both the ones you have received and the ones you have given – you can no longer believe that what you do does not matter."
– Dawna Markova

Sometimes you may find the concept of loving everyone difficult to practice, especially because of the way certain people conduct themselves, and what they have done – and continue to do. Loving everyone doesn't mean trusting them, or not protecting yourself from people who make unfortunate and unwise and harmful decisions.

"The essence of nonviolence is love. Out of love and the willingness to act selflessly, strategies, tactics, and techniques for a nonviolent struggle arise naturally. Nonviolence is not a dogma; it is a process."
– Thich Nhat Hanh

"Nonviolence means avoiding not only external physical violence but also internal violence of spirit. You not only refuse to shoot a man, but you refuse to hate him."
– Martin Luther King, Jr.

Just because others select words, actions, and expressions that are opposite of love does not mean you have to participate in the same behavior or posture, or to communicate in the same manner.

"Love lights more fires than hate extinguishes."
– Ella Wheeler Wilcox

People often act violently out of fear. Work against this by piloting your self more by love than by fear.

Choose to take the higher road. Whatever you do, don't forget to do it with love. Love for yourself, and love for those around you, including the animals.

287

Love is in alignment with magnetizing your life to attract health, to be in loving relationships, and to treat animals and wildlife with respect.

Demonstrate your love for yourself by nurturing and using your talents and intellect, getting daily exercise, following a plant-based diet, stimulating your mind with high-quality and inspiring material and activities, doing something to improve the state of wildlife in your region, and in living intentionally to fulfill your goals.

"Teach only love for that is what you are."
– Marianne Williamson

"The moment you have in your heart this extraordinary thing called love and feel the depth, the delight, the ecstasy of it, you will discover that for you the world is transformed."
– Jiddu Krishnamurti

"Like the in breath and the out breath. You gather the light and then you give it out. That's just the way it works."
– Nancy Rivard

"Dare to reach out your hand into the darkness, to pull another hand into the light."
– Norman B. Rice

What would love do?

"The purpose of life is to express love in all its manifestations."
– Count Lev Nikolayevich Tolstoy

As for you, consider that it is up to you to tune into the frequency of love.

"Our entire biological system, the brain, and the Earth itself, work on the same frequencies."
– Nikola Tesla

# What are You Attracting?

"It's not what you are that holds you back, it's what you think you are not."
– Denis Waitley

There are things you are capable of doing, participating in, experiencing, and feeling. They remain so, no matter what your thoughts are of whether or not you can do all of those.

A person isn't incapable of being a painter if they don't paint. Their skills may atrophy and become less masterful from lack of experience and practice, but they still can become the artist they are capable of being, if they would participate in the process.

A person who is capable of being a singer but who never sings isn't incapable of being a singer. As with the painter, their skills atrophy from lack of use, and by not participating in the practice.

"All things appear and disappear because of the concurrence of causes and conditions. Nothing ever exists entirely alone; everything is in relation to everything else."
– Buddha

Participating in the life you want has to do with your thoughts, as in using them in actions, communication, skills, craft, and talents.

"Vision isn't enough unless combined with venture. It's not enough to stare up the steps unless we also step up the stairs."
– Vance Havner

So many people languish in their disbelief. They yearn for something, but never make the moves to make it appear in their reality. Their inaction and non-participation is likely the chief thing holding them back. Their inaction feeds upon itself.

Of course, there are certain things some people will never do. Someone who has certain physical or other limitations simply can't do some things. There are other things they can do, and they will do well – IF they engage in the practice process of improving in the skills by regularly doing them. It's up to the person.

"Do not sit down and try to attract the thing you want to you; but begin to move toward the thing you want, and you will find it coming to meet you. Action and reaction are equal; and the person who steadily and purposefully moves forward with one thing in view, becomes a center toward which the thing he seeks is drawn with irresistible power."
– Wallace D. Wattles

What you are attracting in life has much to do with what you choose to do with your participation in life.

"I am certain that nobody can always be responsible for what other people are. You can only be responsible for who you are."
– Paul Newman

Many people seem to want an abundance of luxury, as if that will validate them. Why that is so is perplexing, just as much as it is that they think they will have those things without doing and saying what is necessary to get those things. Abundance is accompanied by complications, including the time and means necessary to keep them maintained, in functioning order, and safe.

"Abundance comes not from stuff. In fact, stuff is an indication of non-abundance. Abundance is in the sacred; it's in the connection of love. We will find abundance through hard times when we find each other."
– Rebecca Adamson

Refrain from participating in the wanting mind that is irrational and irresponsible in its desires to have things not worth the price, time, and energy you will pay to have them. What appears attractive from the distance might be far from what you imagine it to be.

"There are many things in life that will catch your eye, but only a few will catch your heart. Pursue those."
– Michael Nolan

What you are thinking, doing, and saying is somehow attracting something or another in ways you might not be aware of. Your expectations mixed with yearning and desire play into it, and might lead you astray.

Be careful of not only what you wish for, but of what you are working for, and of what you are attracting. Simply because you want it does not mean it is a wise thing for you to have. What you also might do is spend your life pursuing things you cannot have, will never be in your reality, and also aren't wise for you to have.

"Our limitations and success will be based, most often, on our own expectations for ourselves. What the mind dwells upon, the body acts upon."
– Denis Waitely

Your defeat of not attaining what you think you want, including what you will never have, might only be the self-perpetuating disaster you built for yourself as you focused on non-important goals.

"There is no defeat except from within, no really insurmountable barrier save our own inherent weakness of purpose."
– Elbert Hubbard

There are things you are capable of, and things you can attain, and things you can experience. Be realistic in your goals, but also work in tune with those goals to make them your reality.

Be the person who sets realistic goals, and works hard and with purpose and vision to attain the satisfaction you desire.

"This life is yours. Take the power to choose what you want to do and do it well. Take the power to love what you want in life and love it honestly. Take the power to walk in the forest and be a part of Nature. Take the power to control your own life. No one else can do it for you. Take the power to make your life happy."
– Susan Polis Schutz

Many people get so caught up in what they see as the big prize that they pay a large price, and neglect the little things in life that matter. Living with such focus can be helpful in certain ways, but damaging in other ways. It is often the case with someone who neglected their family, and then when they felt the need to have family, their family had already grown away and developed their own lives in ways that no longer include that person who ignored, neglected, or abused them.

Be sure to take the time for the things that matter in the long run.

"You develop courage by doing small things, just like as if you wouldn't want to pick up a 100-pound weight without preparing."
– Maya Angelou

While coaching yourself to be the success you hope to experience can be all well and good, consider what it would mean to have a full life in which you participate in healthy relationships with the people of your community, and the planet and wildlife you depend on.

"Your ultimate goal in life is to become your best self. Your immediate goal is to get on the path that will lead you there."
– David Viscott

Using your craft and skill and talent and intellect is important, and self-development and fitness and excellent nutrition are all good to have as part of your plan. Hopefully, have someone to share your adventure with, perhaps family, friends, and associates.

Humans are social beings, and they enjoy companionship, touch, and safe and encouraging interaction. One way of having those in your life is to participate in the culture of the arts, of music, of theater, of dance, and other ways of interacting with people in your community, including invigorating action and sports of some sort.

"Visualize this thing you want. See it, feel it, believe in it. Make your mental blueprint, and begin."
– Robert Collier

Have the blueprint, not only of the building, but include the landscaping, relationships, health, and social life in there, too.

"One ship drives east and the other drives west by the self-same winds that blow. It's the set of the sails and not the gales that determines the way they go."
– Ella Wheeler Wilcox

Maybe you try and try again, and come up empty handed. You won't be the first person who has not attained a goal. Even if you feel you have done everything right, put in the work, practiced, and sharpened the skills, there still may not be satisfaction in attaining what you want. That can be a drag. But do know that the path to getting there is also part of life, and can also include satisfaction, healthy relations, and a variety of experiences worth having.

"Don't let life discourage you; everyone who got where he is had to begin where he was."
– R. L. Evans

Steer your life away from that which holds you back. Aim your thoughts and actions toward health, happiness, nurturing relationships, and satisfaction.

Some people complicate everything, which could mean overpreparation, getting upset at little things that shouldn't matter, treating people in ways that are not helpful, accumulating things they will never need for experiencing what they desire, and getting lost in technicalities.

"The ability to simplify means to eliminate the unnecessary so that the necessary may speak."
– Hans Hofmann

Clarify your life, and eliminate the unnecessary that complicates and clutters things, stalls you, blurs your focus, and halts you from experiencing some sort of joy.

"Life is not easy for any of us. But what of that? We must have perseverance and above all confidence in ourselves. We must believe that we are gifted for something and that this thing must be attained."
– Marie Curie

Continually develop and prepare yourself to receive the situations you want. Do it through healthful nutrition of the highest quality available to you; through physical preparation of exercise and a confident stance and composure; through mental awareness, knowledge, focus, visualization, and rationalization; and through using your intellect, talents, skills, abilities, graces, and resources to set the stage for magnetizing your life to draw in the life you desire.

"Gardens are not made by singing 'Oh, how beautiful,' and sitting in the shade."
– Rudyard Kipling

Get busy and stay active with creating the life you wish for, including healthy relationships, and physical health.

You cannot continue to eat a degenerating diet and expect to generate health. In the same way, you cannot think negative thoughts and expect positive actions out of your being.

Be your own solution.

"Most people search high and wide for the keys to success. If they only knew, the key to their dreams lies within."
– George Washington Carver

293

Rather than being a replicant of everyone else, explore who you are, your strengths, your potential, your talents, your intellect, and what it is about you that might fit you into a life that is authentically yours.

What you think, do, and communicate are more likely than less likely to play a role in the life you wish to have.

"If you want to be respected by others the great thing is to respect yourself. Only by that, only by self-respect will you compel others to respect you."
– Fyodor Dostoyevsky

Part of respecting yourself is doing what is needed to take care of your body and mind, respecting your time and energy, studying what will benefit you, focusing on a set of worthy goals, treating others with respect, protecting yourself, being a benefit to your community, and absolutely working hard to be your solution. With all of that, you will be more likely to attract what is right for you.

Get and remain busy and engaged with formulating the life you desire to own.

# People

"Consider the following. We humans are social beings. We come into the world as the result of others' actions. We survive here in dependence on others. Whether we like it or not, there is hardly a moment of our lives when we do not benefit from others' activities. For this reason it is hardly surprising that most of our happiness arises in the context of our relationships with others."
– Dalai Lama

The people around you are power sources emitting energy through thoughts, communication, actions, and molecules of emotion that can alter your energy, thoughts, communication, actions, and molecules. Our brains react to seeing, touching, smelling, hearing, reading the words of, listening to the music of, observing the creations of, and otherwise interacting with other people and the things they formulate.

The study of mirror neurons has revealed that the people around you play a part in how some of the neurons in your brain form, connect, and function, which plays a role in what you think, say, and do, and what sorts of molecules your body is producing in relationship to these activities.

Just as there are foods that are more nourishing and foods that are less nourishing, there are people who are nurturing and those who are at various levels of being the opposite – or who could nurture or alter you in ways you don't want to be.

"It takes a variety of people to challenge us, encourage us, promote us, and most of all, help us to achieve a broader dimension of ourselves."
– Glenn Van Ekeren

Some people are wonderful to be around because they propel themselves toward creating an amazing life for themselves. They are well connected to their beneficial attributes and their presence can invigorate, enlighten, uplift, and nurture others in better ways.

Some people are their own worst enemy. This may be so because they don't live up to their power while allowing themselves to be influenced by the negative energy of others. They may fail to face the truth, and instead choose to live in denial so deep that their life becomes one of laziness and self-deception. They may fall so far below their potential for doing good they drift into darkness, and carry others down with them.

"Power is strength and the ability to see yourself through your own eyes and not through the eyes of another. It is being able to place a circle of power at your own feet and not take power from someone else's circle."
– Agnes Whistling Elk

Explore the role you play in each of your relationships. Are your relationships healthful and nurturing in ways that influence your better qualities? Do you feed off others, or do others feed off you? Do you play a role as an enabler who allows – and even encourages – others to participate in damaging behavior? Are you an underminer who continually slanders, belittles, and says negative things of and breaks down others? Or are you inspired and inspiring? Do you feel loved and are you loving?

If you don't like what you find in the assessment of the people in your life, without projecting blame, shame, or accusations, take action to change things. This may include working to improve your relationships, being more cautious of, taking a break from, or even simply not staying in touch with certain people.

"The best measure of a human being is in how we treat the people who love us, and the people who we love."
– Lynda Carter

Sometimes the best parts of people get lost in relationships as they may abandon their true selves to maintain a certain level of a relationship that may not be worth the price they are paying.

If all you are doing is roleplaying in your relationships, you might benefit by considering on what your relationships are based – other than a personage you have developed as a sort of character in a theatrical presentation. It would likely be beneficial for you to stop roleplaying in your relationships in ways that stifle your spirit, bury your talents, or otherwise hold you back from experiencing a better life in which you flourish in your better qualities.

Roleplaying is normal. It occurs within families, in relationships, among friends, at work, in social interactions on all levels of society, and among all people. It happens when a person conforms to a particular set of values and/or expectations to adjust to the role they are assuming to communicate with the person or persons they are with. It has to do with why people conduct their mannerisms in consideration of the people in their presence. Much of it is allowing only one side of their personality to be exposed in a way that works for them, or for what they perceive is being expected of them by the people in their presence. Some of it is healthful, and a wise way to conduct yourself, according to what you are engaged with.

Sometimes roleplaying patterns of behavior can be less than helpful as they can stunt a person's social, emotional, creative, spiritual, and other areas of development. In an abusive or neglectful relationship, roleplaying can be most harmful as the person conforms to the downtrodden underling as they become the victim of whatever abuse or neglect is occurring.

The way you carry yourself, the actions you take, the words you choose to use, and the attitude you express toward others through your body language has an influence on those around you, on how they think of you, and in what gets accomplished.

At work many people have to roleplay to associate on a "professional level," which means a veil of vagueness is cast over some of their real emotions, and over their private life. There is a healthful level of roleplaying at work that is best for the tasks being done, and to maintain a professional relationship. However, this can carry over to other areas of life to the point that people are always living undercover and trying to portray themselves in a certain way they have somehow agreed to as acceptable, even when it may not necessarily be helpful, or healthful.

"The beginning of love is to let those we love be perfectly themselves, and not to twist them to fit our own image. Otherwise we love only the reflection of ourselves we find in them."
– Thomas Merton

Many people get so caught up in trying to present a certain image that the most unique and admirable aspects of their character become hidden. This can lead to people becoming lost in trying to build the façade of what they consider to be the most acceptable way to present themselves. In this situation they may spend their money shopping for things they don't need with the goal of impressing people they don't know. When they finally do try to associate with people, they may work to reach some level of intoxication before they feel comfortable expressing themselves.

"Our deepest fear is not that we are inadequate. Our deepest fear is that we are powerful beyond measure. It is our light not our darkness that most frightens us. We ask ourselves, who am I to be brilliant, gorgeous, talented and fabulous? Actually, who are you not to be?

You are a child of God. Your playing small does not serve the world. There's nothing enlightened about shrinking so that other people won't feel insecure around you.

We were born to make manifest the glory of God that is within us. It's not just in some of us; it's in everyone. And as we let our own light shine, we unconsciously give other people permission to do the same. As we are liberated from our own fear, our presence automatically liberates others."
– Marianne Williamson

You may know of people who have many talents, skills, and high levels of intellect, and who do nothing with these attributes. They likely are involved in self-destructive behavior, or mindless activities, such as spending vast amounts of time staring at the television and/or the Internet, or hanging out with other people whose lives are wasteful or are tragedies. Perhaps you see some of your traits in them. Maybe they are some of the people who are closest to you.

"To live is so startling it leaves little time for anything else."
– Emily Dickinson

If your life is highly unsatisfactory to you, it is likely that you are surrounding yourself with similar people. This has likely become your normal, but it is not your natural, and it never can be.

If that last paragraph describes you and your most prominent relationships, you are due for a major life overhaul – including through thought patterns, plans, actions, communication, exercise, diet, time management, focus, sleep schedule, intention, and the daily practices relating to all of it.

"To free us from the expectations of others, to give us back to ourselves – there lies the great, singular power of self-respect."
– Joan Didion

Some of the people who have been zapping your energy will be able to deal with your actions to take control of your life. They may recognize their low-quality behavior, improve their ways, and choose to conduct themselves with respect to your life in a way that greatly benefits both of you. Others may get upset and respond like spoiled children as you work to stop allowing them to continue what is your unhealthful relationship with them. Others may feel overwhelmed by the change they see in you and become a nuisance and a problem to you. This can be taken as a red flag indicating that you need to disassociate yourself from them.

"By acknowledging your own fears and insecurities and corruptions, you start to have a much more gentle and profound sense of where they come from in other people."
– Andrew Harvey

Some people walk around spreading toxic thoughts by criticizing and belittling those around them. Sometimes it appears they are expecting others to be doing things in ways they themselves aren't doing. It seems they think of themselves as the ones making the better choices when they may be making the lowest-quality choices, including those devaluing the lives of those around them.

It is interesting how certain people conduct themselves in relation to how they expect others around them to respond. They may be so accustomed to using other people as crutches that they feel lost when their subordinate role-player is not available. They may have based much of their identity and daily agenda on continuing their unhealthful treatment of others.

"I have been through some terrible things in my life, some of which actually happened."
– Mark Twain

Some people continually choose to participate in and/or create the most dramatic events they can possibly involve themselves in as a way of feeling validated. It seems they feel more important if they are successful in eliciting dramatic responses from other people. What they may not realize is the things they think matter are pure nonsense.

Some people feed off one-night stands that turn into one-night scandals. They spew the story to anyone who will listen while embellishing the story with flavor and spice. The better their delivery, which often involves trying to make the other characters appear as fools, and the more of a rise they get from the listener who agrees with them, the more they feel satisfied and validated by their pathetic behavior.

Some people always seek to be viewed as making the best decisions, often on the shoulders of others while working to surround themselves with people who will agree with them.

"Self-righteousness is a loud din raised to drown the voice of guilt within us."
– Eric Hoffer

This all goes along with the age-old question: How is it that people think they can point out what they perceive to see as the flaws in others if they have not worked to correct their own?

"Behavior is a mirror in which everyone displays his own image."
– Johann Wolfgang von Goethe

What many humans seem to do best is to display their issues and flaws. Often you can listen to a person who is criticizing another and understand that they are unknowingly displaying their own issue. This scenario may be why the issue is foremost in their mind. They are engaging in transference as they are seeing their own traits in others, and they may be completely unaware of it. The issues they are noticing in others may be something they themselves have struggled with, or had their life affected by. It may be some aspect of their being that they may be uncomfortable about, and especially something with which they would never want to be associated. It is true that when someone points a finger at another person, there are (usually) three fingers pointing back at them.

"The judgment of others does not change who I am. Quite the opposite is true. It reveals who they are. Those who deem me unworthy at a glance and pass me by, have my blessing to keep walking, for they have a long way to go. They have not reached the point where they are able to see and appreciate me for who I am."
– Terri McPherson

There are also other reasons people may belittle others. This aspect of undermining has to do with control. If they can keep others down, they can continue to walk all over them. They may want to take into consideration that their low-level treatment may have to do with a lower level of self-esteem.

"As long as you keep a person down, some part of you has to be

down there to hold him down, so it means you cannot soar as you otherwise might."
– Marion Anderson

There are so many combinations of personalities out there that it can sometimes be a mine field of characters to deal with. There are healthy – or somewhat healthy – people who do manage life well, and can be a blessing in life. There are people who are experiencing troubles and complications that could be a trial for you, and for them, or together. There are other people who might, through no fault of their own making, be dealing with personality disorders that can complicate matters. This is especially so within families, in work and school environments, and in neighborhoods and other situations. Personality disorders can include anankastic (also called obsessive/compulsive neurosis), avoidant and defensive, bipolar, borderline unstable, dependent dissocial, histrionic, impulsive narcissistic, paranoid, and schizotypal (detailed in the *Diagnostic Statistics Manual of Mental Disorders*, and sometimes unwisely tossed around as labels to blame and shame). Add in substance abuse, financial stress, medical issues, unhinged urges, education level, manners, personal and family history, culture, and other matters, and you can be faced with a wide variety of people to deal with.

Some people leach off the energy of the people around them by using them, taking whatever they can get, and drawing others into their problems and drama. They choose to be endlessly needy, are takers, and basically function as energy parasites, or energy vampires, and are dependent on others to continue their unhealthful behavior.

People who live off the energy of others may be so accustomed to doing so that they lead their lives through other people. They may appear strong and in control, but they are likely weak and unable to carry themselves on their own energy. It is the enabler relationship that allows them to continue. When they have no one from whom to leach, they flail about in life, and may become desperate, grasping for someone to dominate.

Don't allow parasitic people to rely on you to continue their unhealthful ways.

**"The wrongdoer is more unfortunate than the man wronged."**
– Democritus

Be aware of your influence on other people. Just as a dog becomes fine-tuned to, relies on, and responds to the emotions of its caretaker, the people around you are responding to your emotions –

and vice versa. Just as resting musical instruments, such as drums and guitars, vibrate by the sound waves hitting them from another instrument being played in the room, the vibrations, or emotions, of a person affect the vibrations of the other people around them and with whom they come into contact.

"You can understand and relate to most people better if you look at them – no matter how old or impressive they may be – as if they are children. For most of us never really grow up or mature all that much – we simply grow taller. Oh, to be sure, we laugh less and play less and wear uncomfortable disguises like adults, but beneath the costume is the child we always are, whose needs are simple, whose daily life is still best described by fairy tales."
– Leo Rosten

Maybe it is better to simply be and let be, and that means be yourself. Be kind to yourself while being active and engaged to accomplish the life you hope for.

Connect with your intellect, yearning, and better qualities, and work to be healthful, without damaging others. Be your most healthful self, in relation to what you have to work with.

"We are not here to fit in, be well balanced, or provide examples for others. We are here to be eccentric, different, perhaps strange, perhaps merely to add our small piece, or little clunky, chunky selves, to the great mosaic of being. As the gods intended, we are here to become more and more ourselves. We, too, must enjoy amazement at what unfolds from within us while our multiplicitous selves continue to incarnate in the world, contribute, and confound."
– James Hollis

"Be not forgetful to entertain strangers for thereby some have entertained angels unawares."
– Paul of Tarsus

# Bridging Over the Underminers

"Always in life an idea starts small, it is only a sapling idea, but the vines will come and they will try to choke your idea so it cannot grow and it will die and you will never know you had a big idea, an idea so big it could have grown thirty meters through the dark canopy of leaves and touched the face of the sky."
– Bryce Courtenay

Recognize those people who may be takers of your time, energy, resources, and talents. You may recognize the takers placing an unreasonable amount of dependence on others. This may be done to the extent they keep others under control by working on deconstructing their self-esteem. There may be negative comments instead of compliments, impatience instead of patience, insults instead of kindness, cutting down instead of building up, demeaning cynicism, and general undermining comments that work to confirm their superiority complex while belittling those around them. Maybe the behavior is reflective of the household they grew up in, and relationships they have been in.

Once you have recognized these people in your life you will be able to start putting a stop to their vacuuming of your energy, and resources. Not setting and maintaining your boundaries is enabling them to continue their actions, cheating yourself out of your life force, neglecting your needs, dismissing your concerns, disregarding your interests, devaluing your life, and undermining your strengths.

303

Not making changes to improve your life by not disconnecting from parasitical people will be contributing to your victimization and an underutilization of your potential.

Many people have become conditioned to allowing themselves to be treated as if they are inferior to others; don't use their power to get ahead in life; and are stuck in a circular motion of self-deceit. Many people have been in these types of degrading, people-pleasing, belittled, undermining situations their entire life. The dysfunction has become their normal. Anything outside what is normal to them may become uncomfortable – even if it is more healthful. Even when they are faced with the truth, and at a point where they can make a healthful decision, they may react dismissively, harshly, or angrily at the prospect. Their response may have to do with their unwillingness to accept that they were wronged by people they had been deluded into considering as admirable.

Many people are caught in a circle of compulsive behaviors they formed as a way to cope with their undesirable situations. Often the way they spend their time is more of an escapism mechanism than a coping mechanism. Under these situations they become their own underminer. For instance, for many people, TV watching (staring) becomes a coping mechanism, and is a way to escape from thinking about how empty and disappointing they have allowed their lives to become. This escapism also may have to do with self-hate, being uncomfortable with their life, looking for a way out, not dealing with their issues, and not believing in their ability to change and improve, while focusing on scandalous, self-important celebrities, or the variety of fictional characters constantly presented in the mass media.

**"Real generosity toward the future lies in giving all to the present."**
– Albert Camus

Wake up and both be more self-aware and self-propelled on a trajectory toward improvement and better health.

If you want to improve your life, stop wasting your time. Turn off the TV, get away from the Internet obsession, stop paying attention to celebrity culture and the gossip consciousness, don't buy into commercial nonsense, and stop trying to replicate corporate imagery in your life. Those are all things in the classification of underminers.

It is up to you to stop the undermining people, activities, and surroundings from undermining you, your potential, strengths, and best qualities. Stop the undermining elements from taking up residence in your life, and from stealing your intellect and power.

Avoid always placing blame on other people. It is unproductive to blame others for your situation, and it focuses on energy that has already been spent. Focusing on blame is of the victimhood mentality. This is not to say you are or are not a victim, or have not been harmed by others. Instead, it is about using your power and resources to move onward toward better, safer experiences, and a brighter future.

When you are overly critical of others, and accusing others of shortcomings, you may be accusing yourself of the very same – while undermining the lives of others.

Instead of focusing on what others may have done wrong, move forward out of the train wreck and spend your intellect, time, energy, and resources on what you can do to improve your existence.

Recognize that you may be your own underminer. This might be because you have allowed your life to be overtaken by the lives of others who drag you down; went into debt to replicate commercial imagery; made choices with the thought that you will only be happy if your life resembles corporate idealism; used excuses and denial to rationalize slothful behavior; consumed health-degrading, processed, and junk foods; not maintained your fitness; and/or allowed your true self to be buried beneath various layers of unhealthful activities, behaviors, and relations.

**"Be careful the environment you choose for it will shape you; be careful the friends you choose for you will become like them."**
– W. Clement Stone

Take an assessment of the people in your life. Identify the relationships that are wearing you down, which may be of your own making. Also, identify the relationships in your life that are healthful.

Work to create more healthful relationships by either healing those that are damaged, ending those that are damaging, and beginning some that are nurturing and enriching – including a healthful relationship with self.

Spend some time alone and/or with your significant other to organize your life to better reflect what it is you are striving for.

What many people do when they end one unhealthful relationship is they jump into another. Often they exhibit an amazing ability to find and associate with those who are at a certain level of dysfunction in tune with the same low qualities they've been wallowing in. Their new relationship will resemble those of the past, with similar difficulties – but with a different face and name.

If you have constantly been around people who put you down – or who otherwise undermine your life – it is likely that you have low self-esteem. Be aware that low self-esteem can be just as debilitating as an addiction to drugs or alcohol.

You may be dealing with psychological wounds. These are trauma from awful experiences and lousy relationships. Factor if that is so, and do what it takes to heal, to move on into a more healthful way of living, and to realize who you have the potential of becoming as you continually engage with your better qualities.

> "Your time is limited, so don't waste it living someone else's life."
> – Steve Jobs

Living a life conforming to the projections of others is one way to limit yourself to a small fraction of what you can be.

If you have continually been around people who project negativity toward you – including through overly critical comments, name-calling, toxic sarcasm, mockery, ridicule, belittlement, racism, sexism, and unhinged or unrighteous dominion – it is likely you may not be living anywhere near your potential for satisfaction. It is likely that your talents and intellect have been muted. It is a strong indication that you have work to do to get and stay on a better path.

> "I don't want everyone to like me; I should think less of myself if some people did."
> – Henry James

You may be the type of person who has kept adjusting yourself to try to be what you think is most acceptable, to gain the favor of someone impossible to please – and/or to be the example of someone who is perceived as having it together – all so you gain favor with others, exist as the charming spectacle, or are considered to be the life of the party. You will never be liked by everyone. Stop trying to compete for being the most popular. Popularity contests ended in high school – where they were also ridiculous. They also feed into the sort of roleplaying you don't want to engage in – to satisfy people who will never be satisfied with you, no matter what you do. That isn't a healthy way to live. It's a way to be undermined, and weak.

> "The willingness to accept responsibility for one's own life is the source from which self-respect springs."
> – Joan Didion

You may be playing a part in supporting someone else's life by subjecting yourself to their visions and dreams while living little – or none – of your own. If that is the way you want to live, it is your right. Maybe it works for you. But maybe you are cheating yourself, underestimating your abilities, and denying yourself the expression of your talents, skills, craft, intellect, and beauty.

By conforming to the lives of others, what you may be doing is setting yourself up for deep regret when you realize you have not established and worked toward the expression of your talents, abilities, and intellect. These feelings can be greatly compounded if or when the person you lived for is found to have deceived you, used you as a stepping stone, and/or drops you from their life.

Stop allowing others to steal your life. Stop permitting yourself to be influenced by those who undermine you and pull you down. Stop thinking about the damage their words and actions may have done to you. Instead, get busy in the present making the changes in your life to improve your existence.

"It is not because things are difficult that we do not dare; it is because we do not dare that they are difficult."
– Lucius Annaeus Seneca

Improving your life may be as difficult or as easy as you make it, or allow it to be. But it is better to use your energy to achieve your goals and live your life – rather than to cheat yourself by allowing others to rob you of the better life you could experience and own.

"We should not judge a man's merit by his great abilities, but by the use he makes of them."
– François de la Rochefoucauld

Don't waste time trying to tell others what you are capable of doing. It is always more empowering to plan, work for, and accomplish goals. Whether others do or do not recognize your achievements does not devalue your work. Don't expect praise. Keep moving along toward accomplishment.

"I was told, 'You can be anything you want, kid.' When you hear that often enough, you believe it."
– Ed Bradley

Getting through life is sometimes like walking down a street. When the dogs bark at you, don't stop to listen. Simply keep moving along.

Rather than permitting the negativity of others to undermine your life, allow the good of others to affect you. Reject the negative. Accept the positive. Acknowledge the helpful. Nurture beneficial qualities. Create situations leading to satisfaction.

"Life has been your art. You have set yourself to music. Your days are your sonnets."
– Oscar Wilde

It is not productive to expect others to improve your life. Doing so weakens your power.

It is up to you to make the changes in your life you want to experience. Of course, having supportive relationships can play an important role in helping you to attain goals. But ideal relationship structures don't have to exist for you to advance in your life.

Maybe you have not made the best choices and have been key to damaging your relationships and in getting people to lose trust and faith in you. You may find that you will have to go it alone for a time because – for any number of reasons – including those due to your unfortunate choices, you simply have no one in your life who nurtures you. Whatever the case, it is invigorating to make positive changes in your life. The sooner you do it, the better. As mentioned elsewhere, a psychologist and attending a 12-step program might be of help.

"Trust in yourself, then you will know how to live."
– Johann Wolfgang von Goethe

Again, it is up to you to improve your life. Don't wait for anyone to do it for you, or give you permission to do it. You will learn and gain strength as you go, and will validate your self as you do.

"It's all really very simple. You don't have to choose between being kind to yourself and others. It's one and the same."
– Piero Ferrucci

Refuse to be an underminer of others, or of yourself. That means refusing to think lousy things about yourself, or to say nasty things to other people. Do the opposite. Nurture good in yourself.

"One kind word can warm three winter months."
– Japanese proverb

"I've learned that people will forget what you said, people will forget what you did, but people will never forget how you made them feel."
– Maya Angelou

"The ideals that have lighted my way, and time after time have given me new courage to face life cheerfully, have been kindness, beauty, and truth."
– Albert Einstein

"Life is short and we have never too much time for gladdening the hearts of those who are traveling the dark journey with us. Oh be swift to love, make haste to be kind."
   – Henri-Frederic Amiel

"I expect to pass through this world but once; any good thing therefore that I can do, or any kindness that I can show to any fellow creature, let me do it now; let me not defer or neglect it, for I shall not pass this way again."
   – Etienne de Grellet

"I seek constantly to improve my manners and graces, for they are the sugar to which all are attracted."
   – Og Mandino

"When I was young, I used to admire intelligent people; as I grow older, I admire kind people."
   – Abraham Joshua Heschel

**Instead of doing these things:**
Negate
Criticize
Be mean
Insult
Belittle
Call names
Undermine
Devalue

**Do these things:**
Uplift
Compliment
Be kind
Nurture improvement
Acknowledge good
Encourage good
Induce motivation and positive-thinking
Recognize the beauty in people, including in you.

"No kind action ever stops with itself. One kind action leads to another. Good example is followed. A single act of kindness throws out roots in all directions, and the roots spring up and make new trees. The greatest work that kindness does to others is that it makes them kind themselves."
   – Amelia Earhart

"Leave each person you meet a little better than when you found them."
— Robin Sharma

"A compliment is verbal sunshine."
— Robert Orben

"When you are kind to others, it not only changes you, it changes the world."
— Harold Kushner

"Each of us has a spark of life inside us, and our highest aspiration ought to be to set off that spark in one another."
— Mark Albion

# Unison

"Love is a form of prejudice. You love what you need, you love what makes you feel good, you love what is convenient. How can you say you love one person when there are ten thousand people in the world who you would love more, if you ever met them? But you'll never meet them. All right, so we do the best we can. Granted. But we must still realize that love is just the result of a chance encounter."
– Charles Bukowski

Can anything be more complicated for humans than human relationships? Especially considering how many genders there are, and the situation of some being more monogamous, others being polyamorous, some being asexual, and some simply being sexually ambiguous, elusive, and other varieties of desires and preferences, and non-desires and preferences. Then, there are racial issues, sexism issues, mental health issues, ageism, religious and scrupulosity issues, relative and in-law issues, tradition issues, toxic patriarchy or matriarchy issues, addiction and sobriety issues, abuse and neglect issues, personality issues, materialism and financial issues, and sexually transmitted infections. And sexual imagery is so commonly flaunted, and shoved around in the media to entice, market, stimulate, and play with emotions and attention spans. It's no wonder why double lives, mental affairs, cheating issues, porn issues, and divorce, are so common.

With all that, humans are still social creatures.

"Life without love is like a tree without blossom and fruit."
– Kahlil Gibran

"Love is always open arms. If you close your arms about love you will find that you are left holding only yourself."
– Leo Buscaglia

"We're never so vulnerable as when we trust someone – but paradoxically, if we cannot trust, neither can we find love or joy."
– Walter Anderson

"Every man needs love, guys like romance. I do anyway."
– Paul McCartney

"Three keys to more abundant living: caring about others, daring for others, sharing with others."
– William A. Ward

"The scientific search for the basic building blocks of life has revealed a startling fact: there are none. The deeper that physicists peer into the nature of reality, the only thing they find is relationships. Even subatomic particles do not exist alone. One physicist described neutrons, electrons, etc. as '...a set of relationships that reach outward to other things.' Although physicists still name them as separate, these particles aren't ever visible until they're in relationship with other particles. Everything in the Universe is composed of these 'bundles of potentiality' that only manifest their potential in relationship."
– Margaret J. Wheatley

"Before I can live with other folks I've got to live with myself. The one thing that doesn't abide by majority rule is a person's conscience."
– Harper Lee

"I can live alone, if self-respect, and circumstances require me to do so. I need not sell my soul to buy bliss. I have an inward treasure born with me, which can keep me alive if all extraneous delights should be withheld, or offered only at a price I cannot afford to give."
– Charlotte Brontë

If any species is to carry on, there has to be relationship. Because we rely on other forms of life to keep living, all life on Earth is interconnected relationship. Just as a plant cannot exist without water, we could not exist if it were not for other people. None of us would exist if it weren't for relationships.

"Difference must be not merely tolerated, but seen as a fund of necessary polarities between which our creativity can spark like a dialectic. Only then does the necessity for interdependency become unthreatening. Only within that interdependency of different strengths, acknowledged and equal, can power to seek new ways of being in the world generate, as well as the courage and sustenance to act where there are no charters."
– Audre Lorde

"It is in the shelter of each other that the people live."
– Irish Proverb

"Do you know what people really want? Everyone, I mean. Everybody in the world is thinking: I wish there was just one other person I could really talk to, who could really understand me, who'd be kind to me. That's what people really want, if they're telling the truth."
– Doris Lessing

Science has shown that the interaction with others impacts our brain neuron growth patterns and function, our hormone levels, and the function of our tissues – including the heart. Even our brains function better if we are in a healthful relationship. It very much appears that we are wired to be in a close, intimate relationship with another person. The more complete, functional, nurturing, and satisfying that relationship is, the better it is for our health.

"Only through our connectedness to others can we really know and enhance the self. And only through working on the self can we begin to enhance our connectedness to others."
– Harriet Goldhor Lerner

On the other hand, an unhealthful relationship can do the opposite, increasing our stress, resulting in unhappiness, physical ailments, and trauma wounds to our consciousness that play out in all sorts of unfortunate, damaging ways – including unwise escapism.

In an unhappy relationship, everything good that can be present in a happy relationship can exist in the direct opposite form.

It seems that one of the most common elements of unhealthful relationships consists of assumptions.

"Assumptions are the termites of relationships."
– Henry Franklin Winkler

Some of us have been around those who assume in ways that are confrontational, accusational, degrading, undermining, and fully

313

unhealthful. This is the projection of guilt, and it commonly has to do with the guilt and dysfunction of the people making the accusations, their lack of healthful communications skills, and their history of being in dysfunctional relationships where their trust was broken, was brutalized, or didn't exist. They have decided that, rather than assuming good, they are going to assume bad. Rather than give compliments, they will be cynical, belittle, or be dismissively silent. Rather than saying what is pleasant, they are going to mutter guilt, disdain, and darkness. Rather than uplift, they are going to put down. Rather than accept individuality, they are going to be unaccepting – and close their mind to acceptance. Rather than offer solutions, they are going to refuse to help, or will create problems. Rather than provide nurturing, they are going to project shame or indifference. Instead of being helpful in the relationship, they create damage.

"Much of the conflict of our lives can be explained by one simple but unhappy fact: We don't really listen to each other."
– Michael P. Nichols

"The greatest compliment that was ever paid me was when one asked what I thought, and attended to my answer."
– Henry David Thoreau

"So when you are listening to somebody, completely, attentively, then you are listening not only to the words, but also to the feeling of what is being conveyed, to the whole of it, not part of it."
– Jiddu Krishnamurti

People experiencing dissatisfaction in relationships often mention that their partner does not listen to them. In that situation the basic form of communication may have broken down to where every other part of the relationship is in disrepair. But the relationship doesn't have to remain in that condition.

"Listening is such a simple act. It requires us to be present, and that takes practice, but we don't have to do anything else. We don't have to advise, or coach, or sound wise. We just have to be willing to sit there and listen."
– Margaret J. Wheatley

For healthful communication in a relationship, there needs to be active participants listening, sharing thoughts, and taking actions to move forward into improvement.

"Only that in you which is me can hear what I'm saying."
– Ram Dass

"If someone listens, or stretches out a hand, or whispers a kind word of encouragement, or attempts to understand a lonely person, extraordinary things begin to happen."
– Loretta Girzatlis

"An elementary particle is not an independently existing, unanalyzable entity. It is, in essence, a set of relationships that reach outward to other things."
– H. P. Stapp

Often one person in a dysfunctional relationship has an issue with selfish, narcissistic, or other damaging behavior. Usually, it is likely that each side of the relationship isn't functioning well. Concerns may focus on how everything should work in one person's favor, regardless of the needs of the other. Family conditioning may exist, wherein the underling person has been permitted to only display a certain aspect of their being. They have to hide others sides of themselves in ways that might have to do with adjusting to shame, denial, fear, and being subjected to more of what they don't want.

"Narcissism thus involves a withdrawal of instinctual energy and an investment of libido in the ego. This investment in the ego implies that the person is unable to love or relate with others, and is self-absorbed."
– Carl Gustav Jung

"We're afraid of a lot of things in life. It's part of the human condition. What do we fear? Love? Failure? Telling the truth about ourselves? I think we don't show people all we truly are because we're afraid that if they actually know everything about us, they won't love us. I'm as guilty of that as anyone."
– Kevin Costner

"When you are in a state of nonacceptance, it's difficult to learn. A clenched fist cannot receive a gift, and a clenched psyche – grasped tightly against the reality of what must not be accepted – cannot easily receive a lesson."
– Roger John

"People travel to faraway places to watch, in fascination, the kind of people they ignore at home."
– Dagobert D. Runes

"We let go of one phase, one aspect of love, and enter another. Passion dies and is brought back. Pain is chased away and surfaces another time. To love means to embrace and at the same time to

withstand many endings, and many many beginnings – all in the same relationship."
– Clarissa Pinkola Estes

An easy way to determine if communication in a relationship is breaking down, or is kaput, is when people stop spending time together, make opposing plans, and are not interested in any sort of compromise or joint venture. Is that healthy, or toxic?

"Real relationships tend to change rather than to remain static."
– Carl Rogers

It is interesting how certain people conduct themselves in their relationships. Much of what they decide to do in a relationship may be related to behaviors they learned from childhood. Other decisions they make relating to how they treat their companion have to do with peer pressure, or what they interpret their relationship should be according to what they see in TV shows, commercials, other media, and in celebrity culture, and in antiquated religious teachings. They can get so hung up in how their relationship is supposed to appear according to the pop media and teachings, they lose touch with what it is, and in how they can play a part in making it better.

"Remember, we all stumble, every one of us. That's why it's a comfort to go hand-in-hand."
– Emily Kimbrough

Often people move to be separate from their partner when their partner isn't falling into a mold formed by peer, family, religion, and societal pressures. One little mistake, or what is perceived as a flaw, can be the determining factor of whether or not the relationship ends. Under such conditions perhaps the relationship likely wasn't healthful, helpful, solid, or loving from the start – but was an act.

"We often discover what will do, by finding out what will not do; and probably he who never made a mistake never made a discovery."
– Samuel Smiles

All of us have made unwise decisions. All of us have issues. Simply because someone has made bad choices, or has what you choose to define as flaws, is no reason to discard them like rubbish.

"Whenever catching sight of others, look on them with an open, loving heart."
– Patrul Rinpoche

Some people are truly a mess, and they need to spend some time getting their life together before they, and their problems, become a part of the life of someone else. Some may need a helping hand, a guide, a confidante, an advisor, a mentor, a sponsor, a life coach, and a patient, kind, and forgiving someone to show them a better path in a way they may never have experienced. They may benefit from meeting with others in a support group who are also working to change from slothfully dysfunctional to intentionally healthful.

"Men's willingness to downplay weakness and pain is so great that it has been named as a factor in their shorter life span. The ten years of difference in longevity between men and women turns out to have little to do with genes. Men wait longer to get help, and once they get treatment do not comply with it as well as women do."
– Terrence Real

Some people find help by turning to psychologists, joining support groups, attending retreats, and reading books by authors who have been through similar situations, or books by authors who specialize in helping people work through their issues.

"For a chunk of my life, I avoided shy people, assuming they had nothing to say. Then one day I realized that if I quit blabbering for a minute, they'd often utter something that would blow my mind."
– Tara Somerville

"People can only hear you when they are moving toward you, and they are not likely to when your words are pursuing them. Even the choicest words lose their power when they are used to overpower. Attitudes are the real figures of speech."
– Edwin H. Friedman

All too often relationship storms turn into a blame game, with one topping the other. When there is a lack of love, gratitude, appreciation, and caring, the relationship becomes like an unfounded structure that will eventually tumble as the weight added to it lacks a solid base.

"The meeting of two personalities is like the contact of two chemical substances. If there is any reaction both are transformed."
– Carl Gustav Jung

A sign that a relationship is starting to heal is that people start listening to each other, don't try to tell the other how to think, consider the other's point-of-view, and stop dictating the other person's life and feelings. When relationships heal, the caring, gratitude, listening, and appreciation return.

"To learn through listening, practice it naively and actively. Naively means that you listen openly, ready to learn something, as opposed to listening defensively, ready to rebut. Listening actively means you acknowledge what you heard and act accordingly."
– Betsy Sanders

Quality of communication is a determining factor of the health of a relationship. The expression of the individuals through words is just one level of communication. People also communicate through body language, facial expressions, eye movements, activities, and thoughts – and through the chemicals they emit in tune with their thoughts.

"A wonderful fact to reflect upon, that every human creature is constituted to be that profound secret and mystery to every other."
– Antoine de Saint-Exupéry

People also communicate by not communicating. It may be that one person simply came to a realization in their life, and their companion is no longer part of it.

"People change and forget to tell each other."
– Lillian Hellman

One basic fact about people is that they tend to change. And they do so on many levels. Sometimes together, sometimes in ways that bring them closer, sometimes in ways that move them apart.

"Have a heart that never hardens, a temper that never tires, and a touch that never hurts."
– Charles Dickens

In healthful relationships, there is a dance between the people, how they change, and how the other person goes with it, against it, supports it, or otherwise adapts to it.

In controlling relationships, at least one of the partners expects the other to conform to a particular role. This is also where conflict can exist, and much of it in ways that can destroy happiness, self-expression, intellectual stimulation, social exchange, and sensual satisfaction.

"Indeed, this need of individuals to be right is so great that they are willing to sacrifice themselves, their relationships, and even love for it."
– Reuel Howe

What a certain level of unhappiness – or certain types of relationship traps – can lead to is escapism.

Escapism may be through drugs, food issues, secretive behavior, double lives, obsessive fanaticism, TV staring, gambling, what can be the fake satisfaction and weakening and degrading influence of pornography, and through cheating and lies.

Unfortunately, cheating, affairs, and anonymous sex can bring sexually transmitted infections into the mix.

Under the conditions of a broken relationship, people would likely benefit by getting together and figuring out if the relationship is salvageable, or if kindly ending it would be the best maneuver. Carrying on with indifference to each other could be nothing but a waste of two lives that would be more satisfied in experiencing joy.

"All the art of living lies in a fine mingling of letting go, and holding on."
– Havelock Ellis

"If only I could throw away the urge to trace my patterns in your heart I could really see you."
– David Brandon

"Out beyond ideas of wrong-doing and right-doing, there is a field. I'll meet you there."
– Jalal ad-Din Rumi

Discovering the strengths and/or weaknesses of your relationship may come about when discussing what you both want from life, what makes you feel satisfied, and what areas you would like to change. Some are revealed through living, interacting, and everyday activities.

Actions speak louder than words – especially in relationships.

"Seldom – or perhaps never – does a marriage develop into an individual relationship smoothly and without crisis; there is no coming to consciousness without pain."
– Carl Gustav Jung

I have heard people say they had to rediscover the person they were after their relationship became committed, and they also had to rediscover their partner. When the courting ends and the home life begins, each may discover many issues and traits about the other they had not considered, may not have noticed, and may have ignored or overlooked. When this new discovery is made, a whole new level of the relationship can get underway – and with it, a level of openness and adjustment. Otherwise the closed-mindedness and stubbornness is bound to close doors, and bring about relationship traps, dysfunction, escapism, and unhappiness.

"There is no greater weakness than stubbornness. If you cannot yield, if you cannot learn that there must be compromise in life – you lose."
– Maxwell Maltz

Stubbornness and closed-mindedness introduce conflict. One person in the relationship may like the way things are going, and does not conceive of changing – even if the suggested changes will bring about a more healthful life. They also may have felt overrun, may not want to participate in the ideas and life concepts of others, and are uncomfortable with change – even when they are encouraged to participate in designing the changes.

"By mutual confidence and mutual aid great deeds are done, and great discoveries made."
– Homer

Work to create healthful relationships where respect and love are present. Listen to each other and collaborate on projects, giving one another a turn at what they do best. Allow others their opportunities to learn, express, and grow – including alone time for their hobbies, learning, talents, and friends.

"It takes more courage to reveal insecurities than to hide them, more strength to relate to people than to dominate them, more 'manhood' to abide by thought-out principles rather than blind reflex. Toughness is in the soul and spirit, not in muscles and an immature mind."
– Alex Karras

Some of the people in your life may have played key parts in events that were not your best experiences. You may need to heal those relationships. One way of doing so is to recommit to each other to improve both of your conditions, nurturing a better future for both of you. It might involve couples therapy, group therapy, a support group, and things like working out together, making food together, growing food together, volunteering together, and other activities.

"For him who confesses, shams are over and realities have begun; he has exteriorized his rottenness. If he has not actually got rid of it, he at least no longer smears it over with a hypocritical show of virtue."
– William James

"The fragrance always remains on the hand that gives the rose."
– Mahatma Gandhi

When the clouds of contentious behaviors have passed over and forgiveness – or otherwise regained commitment – has set in, that is when people have learned, and a renewed kindness and nurturing can begin – perhaps beyond what it had ever been. That is when relationships can be wonderful, strengthening, nurturing, and loving, in the good times, as well as the trials.

"Shared joy is double joy, and shared sorrow is half-sorrow."
– Swedish proverb

"The meeting of two personalities is like the contact of two chemical substances. If there is any reaction, both are transformed."
– Carl Gustav Jung

There are times where persons in your life will shine brighter. But if relationships are to be healthful, it is more likely that they will be based on nurturing and respecting each other, and not on who is more prominent. Without a plant, the beautiful flower never grows. The plant and the flower are part of a whole.

"There are two ways of spreading light; to be the candle, or the mirror that reflects it."
– Edith Wharton

"Maybe love is like luck. You have to go all the way to find it."
– Robert Mitchum

"I hold this to be the highest task for a bond between two people: that each protect the solitude of the other."
– Rainer Maria Rilke

Synergy in a relationship can be a tremendous force in accomplishing goals, in unburdening your life from clutter and conformity, in unlearning and detaching from toxic and harmful religious and other antiquated cultural teachings, and contributing to persistence in working toward a better life for both of you.

"In my friend, I find a second self."
– Isabel Norton

"Friendship is the marriage of the soul."
– François-Marie "Voltaire" Arouet

"It is not a lack of love, but a lack of friendship that makes unhappy marriages."
– Friedrich Wilhelm Nietzsche

"The best way to inspire people to superior performance is to convince them by everything you do and by your everyday attitude that you are wholeheartedly supporting them."
– Harold S. Geneen

When you have a partner, and you are both following a healthful diet and getting daily exercise, you can become attuned to the same frequencies. Even couples that are not living healthfully often are able to finish each other's sentences, and may end up taking on the same physical characteristics. This is because they are living in sync, subsisting on the same nutrients, and often engaging in the same physical, sexual, and sleeping patterns.

When two people are living healthfully, the bond can become strong, including through high-quality nutrition, the function of mirror neurons, and the production of similar molecules of emotion.

"Look at sex realistically and in a light mood. Sexual energy is needed to upgrade your brain cells. Sex, sweetness, and intimacy are good but you must also have a functional brain."
– Choa Kok Sui

When other areas of the relationship complement each other, the intimacy will also likely become more aligned. The simple act of intimacy relieves stress, triggers similar hormonal changes, creates mirrored neural connections, forms molecules of emotion, induces and releases fantasy, and adds to the healing and nurturing qualities of the relationship.

Be with each other sexually in relationship.

"Sexuality is one of the biggest parts of who we are."
– Carla Gugino

Just as some types of wood will support four times the amount of weight if two beams are joined together, so also will a couple be able to become many times stronger living in unison than if they lived separately. The vibrational frequency of the couple will be tuned into much of the same energy. Thoughts, ideas, hopes, desires, and dreams harmonize. A synchronicity happens that can both astound and strengthen. When following a healthful diet, getting regular exercise, and set in healthy patterns of expression and communication, a couple can become an amazing expression of synchronized energy.

"We are one, after all, you and I. Together we suffer, together exist, and forever will recreate each other."
– Pierre Teilhard de Chardin

Studies have shown that couples will follow and maintain an exercise regimen more regularly if they join each other in their agenda to become physically fit. Not that they have to be directly next to each other doing the same exercise, but simply knowing their partner is involved in improving their health is a motivating factor in improving their own.

"We are each of us angels with only one wing, and we can only fly embracing each other."
– Luciano de Crescenzo

Equally, similar to succeeding at an exercise program, maintaining a healthful diet can be an easier goal to accomplish if you do so with the accompaniment of a lover, relative, or friend. In this way you can motivate each other to maintain the goal of eating healthfully, share in each other's experiences with recipes, and in locating and trying out unfamiliar foods, places, events, and activities. All of this can help bind a relationship.

"The objectives of two lovers is almost always the same: to find meaning in their individual lives and in their life together."
– Paul Pearsall

No matter how you are living, it could be an interesting exercise to make a list of things you want, things you want to do, and things you need to do to bring about the life you would like to have. Ideally you would be able to work on this with the person with whom you are in a relationship, and then collaborate to align your goals, priorities, needs, and wants. Then work together to attain those things.

"Love lasts when the relationship comes first."
– Abraham Lincoln

"Being in love shows a person who they should be."
– Anton Chekhov

"To love someone is to see a miracle invisible to others."
– François Mauriac

"Love doesn't just sit there, like a stone; it has to be made, like bread, remade all the time, made new."
– Ursula K. Le Guin

"A positive attitude is perhaps more important at home than anywhere else. As spouses and parents, one of our most vital roles is to help those we love feel good about themselves."
– Keith Harrell

"Underneath all the twists and turns of relationships, love is the only and ultimate truth between souls."
– Kathy Hearn

"Things derive their being and nature by mutual dependence and are nothing in themselves."
– Natgarjuna

You help set the tone, mood, energy, and movement for yourself, as well as those around you. If you are feeling a lack of good in your relationship, it is likely others are also feeling it. What you think, factor, say, and do can be part of the solution.

"The unique personality which is the real life in me, I cannot gain unless I search for the real life, the spiritual quality, in others. I am myself spiritually dead unless I reach out to the fine quality dormant in others. For it is only with the god enthroned in the innermost shrine of the other, that the god hidden in me, will consent to appear."
– Felix Adler

"The world we live in will be either better or worse, depending on whether we become better or worse. And that's where the power of love comes in. Because when we love, we always strive to become better than we are."
– Paulo Coelho

"The time to be happy is now. The place to be happy is here. The way to be happy is to make others so."
– Robert Green Ingersoll

"Let us be grateful to people who make us happy; they are the charming gardeners who make our souls blossom."
– Marcel Proust

"Relationship is surely the mirror in which you discover yourself."
– Jiddu Krishnamurti

"When we share, that is poetry in the prose of life."
– Sigmund Freud

"To live in this world you must be able to do three things, to love what is mortal, to hold it against your bones knowing your own life depends on it, and, when the time comes to let it go, let it go."
– Mary Oliver

# Tell A Vision: Screen Addiction

"Ralph Waldo Emerson once asked what we would do if the stars only came out once every thousand years. No one would sleep that night, of course. The world would become religious overnight. We would be ecstatic, delirious, made rapturous by the glory of God. Instead the stars come out every night, and we watch television."
– Paul Hawkin

"When people are free to do as they choose, they usually imitate each other."
– Eric Hoffer

"Time is a companion that goes with us on a journey. It reminds us to cherish each moment, because it will never come again. What we leave behind is not as important as how we have lived."
– Jean Luc Picard

All of us have the same amount of time in our days. Some of us spend it wisely. Others of us give it away to frivolity. People in modern society most often waste their time away from jobs they dislike, and avoid relationships and lives in need of healing by lounging into escapism. Often they are the very same people who complain about their jobs, are dissatisfied with their relationships, don't like their lives, and wish they could be experiencing more joy.

Most common ways people waste time include by spending it in front of a television, game monitor, the Web, or social media. They would be better off if they spent this wasted time getting their life, relations, home, diet, and fitness in order, and creating a better life.

"If you read a lot of books you are considered well read. But if you watch a lot of TV, you're not considered well viewed."
– Lily Tomlin

"When a person can't find a deep sense of meaning, they distract themselves with pleasure."
– Viktor Frankl

Television programming largely focuses on that which is energetically dark, such as greed, vanity, corruption, deception, crime, punishment, mistreatment, ridicule, and brash or vulgarized sexuality, and cheating. By focusing your attention on this form of "entertainment" you are absorbing this energy into your thoughts, life, and atmosphere.

"You can tell the ideals of a nation by its advertisements."
– Norman Douglass

TV programming is designed to keep you watching for as long as possible so that you watch as many commercials as possible with the goal of getting you to spend money on the advertised products.

Screen advertising is the best way companies have found to sell low-quality, mass-produced, trendy products. It is also why municipalities have to spend so much money on trash management. The trash largely is created by all the stuff people purchase. (Research: "Fast fashion pollution." It's a tremendous problem.)

"The bitter taste of poor quality lingers long after the sweetness of low price is forgotten."
– John Ruskin

"Television is the first truly democratic culture – the first culture available to everybody and entirely governed by what the people want. The most terrifying thing is what people do want."
– Clive Barnes

The same thing can be said about social media, and its madness of encapsulation in "following" only what you agree with or obsess about. On social media, misinformation, distortion, and unresearched information is spread globally, within seconds.

Never have humans spent so much time not moving, and doing so while their eyes stare at screens. Social media and electronic games have massively increased the amount of time humans spend nearly

motionless, and often while being presented content that is limited –
and limiting, while encouraging consumption, spending, and debt.

Many TV shows and film productions contain products
companies have paid producers to feature. This is called *product
placement* and *product integration*, and has to do with products being
obvious in a scene or part of a show or storyline. It may be as simple
as having an actor hold a can of soda (product placement), or as
involved as designing a certain type of car that will first be seen in a
major movie production, such as cars used in the Bond films (product
integration). It is a subtle form of advertising, but is effective enough
to interest more and more companies in paying large sums of money
to production companies to place products in TV episodes, films, and
music videos. Sometimes the cost of producing film or TV show can
be paid for by product placement or integration.

**"Don't you wish there were a knob on the TV to turn up the
intelligence? There's one marked 'brightness,' but it doesn't work."**
– Leo Anthony Gallagher

In addition to TV advertising and the product placement and
product integration seen in film and TV productions, the similar
practices taking place on social media are exposing people to more
and more products, often in ways that are both subtle and suggestive.
"Social media influencers" have gotten quite skilled in integrating
products into their "content." Additionally, there is product placement
in that content, and full endorsements and demonstrations. It has
made many influencers multi-millionaires, which has allowed many
of them to then purchase mansions and expensive cars, which they
then flaunt in their social media – as if it validated their existence and
greed. How they portray themselves on screen is often fiction.

I have dealt with a social media influencer, and she has been paid
simply to say the names of products. The companies know that if she
even so much as mentions the products, it increases sales. She is
continually sent cases of products, with the companies hoping she
will show, mention, or feature the products in her screen content.

Many people give no mind to saving for the future. Many spend
their money on whimsy. All too many spend every penny as fast as
they get it, and usually on purchases that do not hold a lasting value
for the purchaser or the planet, but that make them appear more like
the characters they see in advertisements, and especially the
characters on TV commercials, and the influencers.

Unfortunately, many people use TV as a babysitter, which the
advertising agencies are well aware of. While advertising aimed

toward children is most present during daytime TV shows watched by children, some of it also airs during shows aimed toward adults. This is because advertisers know children are watching TV at all hours of the day.

Commercials portray parents buying certain products for their children. Children seeing the commercials who then do not get those products from their parents, even after asking and begging, can reason that they are being denied, neglected, or mistreated. They see others with the products, and therefore feel entitled to also have them. In this way, commercials play into the guilt and shame factor, and the sense of fitting in, and being part of the cool scene. It's indoctrinated competition manipulating values and tarnishing relations.

Many parents who use the TV as a babysitter say they don't know what else to do with their children. Perhaps they'd like to consider that TV has been around only since the mid-1900s, and that babies have been around for unknown numbers of years. What do they think people did before TV? Having calm time, including reading, talent practice, and exercise is better than continually exposing the young minds to the frantic distortions of life featured on screen technology.

Some parents keep their babies and toddlers in front of TVs with the belief that watching television will educate their children and/or develop their intelligence. I'm certain Albert Einstein, Leonardo da Vinci, Artemisia Gentileschi, Camille Saint-Saens, and Jalal ad-Din Rumi were as smart as they were because they spent their developing years staring at television shows while consuming junk and processed foods. Obviously, they were not.

A study published in the August 2007 issue of *Pediatrics*, conducted by researchers at the University of Washington and the Seattle Children's Hospital Research Institute, concluded that infants who watched the most baby educational videos knew fewer words than children who did not watch educational videos.

According to a study published in the March 1, 2009 issue of *Pediatrics*, and conducted by researchers at Boston's Children's Hospital and Harvard Medical School, having babies and toddlers watch educational DVDs and videos does not make them smarter. The study's authors wrote, "Contrary to parents' perceptions that TV viewing is beneficial to their children's brain development, we found no evidence of cognitive benefit from watching TV during the first two years of life." The study, which monitored more than 800 babies for their first three years of life, concluded that DVDs and videos tailored for children as young as three months had no benefits. By age three, the study subjects who watched the most TV scored lower on tests for language and visual motor skills.

The American Academy of Pediatrics advises parents to avoid exposing children under the age of two to TV or "screen media," which includes video games and computer screens.

The more children watch TV the more likely they are of having short attention spans and to eat unhealthful foods. Maybe that has something to do with the fact that an American watching the average amount of TV sees dozens of junk food commercials, every day.

Advertised food is most commonly the most unhealthful. A 2007 study conducted by researchers at Indiana University and the Kaiser Family Foundation reviewed over 8,000 TV advertisements and found none of them to be for fresh fruits or vegetables.

When it is taken into consideration that about the only thing many people know about nutrition is what they hear in the mass media, it is no wonder that obesity, diabetes, colon cancer, kidney stones, ED, heart disease, and other commonly diet-related health conditions keep increasing in commercialized society.

On average, people who watch TV are heavier and less healthy than those who don't watch TV. The more TV people watch the more likely they are to consume low-quality foods, fast foods, and junk foods, such as those containing synthetic chemical dyes, preservatives, flavors, scents, and sweeteners; processed salt; monosodium glutamate (MSG); fried and sauteed oils; trans fats; cholesterol; gluten grains; and sugar extracts, including sickeningly sweet and health-degrading corn syrup, rice syrup, and agave.

"As long as people will accept crap, it will be financially profitable to dispense of it."
– Dick Cavett

"You can fool too much of the people too much of the time."
– James Thurber

TV was once the king of the media-saturated and commercial-driven celebrity culture. Social media likely has replaced it, including because cell phones make it possible for people to click onto social media numerous times per day. The more screen material adults watch the more likely they are to be in financial debt. It is not difficult to figure that the debt has something to do with the constant messages people get from screen technology encouraging them to spend money on the advertised, placed, and integrated, and otherwise promoted products they don't need.

By watching screen content you are removed from relating with people. This is especially true within families. There are people who consider quality time with their family to be watching TV and social media together. They may become more emotionally connected to the characters on the screens than they are with the people in their lives. As a family activity they spend their weekends wasting money shopping for the advertised and promoted stuff they saw on the screens. They also eat at massively advertised chain restaurants selling the lowest-quality foods that degrade health and dull their life. This scenario puts the people further into debt, which means they have to rely more on the job they dislike so that they can attempt to keep up with their credit card payments that are the result of spending sprees to purchase all the unnecessary stuff they shove into their garages, closets, attics, basements, rented storage units, and mouths.

"You are here to live, not to sit on the couch."
– Jon Krakauer

By watching screen "entertainment" you are removed from your self. When you are tuned-in to a screen, you are not using your talents, you are not developing your skills, you are not practicing your craft, you are not exercising, you are not having meaningful conversations with the people in your life, and you are not involved in improving your life.

When the screen entertainment is turned on, your life is turned off.

Stop being a spectator. If you have a TV, turn it off. Unplug from social media.

Watching screens is watching other people lead their lives. It is a waste of time and a waste of life.

If you own a TV, put it in a place that is out of the way, or place a cloth over it. Also, remove the batteries from the remote and store it away.

If you don't have a TV, don't get one.

By avoiding TV, you are excluding the invasive sensationalism and commercialism of television from your days and nights.

"If you wish to achieve worthwhile things in your personal and career life, you must become a worthwhile person in your own self-development."
– Brian Tracy

Make sure that the sensationalism and commercialism of screen entertainment does not rule your emotions or relationships.

Stop trying to live your life as if you are stuck in an advertisement. Instead, focus on living an authentic life. Realize that your life is worth living, your talents are worth developing, your intellect is worth stimulating and using, and your relationships are more important than what is happening on screens.

Maybe the television is telling your vision too much, and you need to stop it.

Consider that your life may be much better off without watching *tell a vision*, and without social media, and instead, working to create your own vision with people you love.

Many people have spent so much of their time watching screen entertainment throughout their life that their thought patterns are in lock-step with the patterns of nonsense spewing out of their screen. They have been paying so much attention to screen content that their thoughts are no longer their own, but are the products of Hollywood, Silicon Valley, Madison Avenue, and Wall Street.

"Turn off the TV, don't read the newspapers, listen to your own heart, and listen very tenderly to the hearts of those people who are within your circle of care and affection."
– John Robbins

Instead of watching TV, spend time on and take actions aligned with developing your talents, skills, craft, and intellect to improve your life, surroundings, and relationships.

Refuse to get caught up in pop nonsense and celebrity gossip, especially the garbage constantly flowing from the electronic media, which is always an example of a distortion of values. Celebrity culture consciousness gives you a spiritual lobotomy.

Click out of the Kardashian consciousness. Live your life.

"It's how we spend our time here and now, that really matters. If you are fed up with the way you have come to interact with time, change it."
– Marcia Wieder

Make your life real and based on your talents, abilities and intellect, and not on a commercially- and celebrity-obsessed culture.

Set goals. Exercise every morning. Follow a low-fat, vibrant plant-based diet rich in raw fruits and vegetables.

Make your life beautiful.

"Be glad of life because it gives you the chance to love and to work and to play and to look up at the stars."
– Henry Van Dyke

# If You Are Going to Get It

"Most people never run far enough on their first wind to find out they've got a second. Give your dreams all you've got and you'll be amazed at the energy that comes out of you."
– William James

If you are going to get what you want, you need to be absolutely proactive in getting it.

You are more likely to become what you wish to be by simply and continually becoming attuned to the change you want, and working every day through action and communication to manifest it.

"Even the most deeply implanted habits of the heart learned in childhood can be reshaped. Emotional learning is lifelong."
– Daniel Goleman

"Happiness is not achieved by the conscious pursuit of happiness; it is generally the by-product of other activities."
– Aldous Huxley

Whatever it is that you are reflects the common patterns of your behavior, which are the patterns you have developed throughout your life according to what you have permitted, combined with your intellect and to what you are naturally drawn.

Your common patterns of thought and behavior are your self-traditions. They determine where you go, what you do, what you agree to, and how you communicate. Luckily, if they aren't working for you, you can change your patterns, and develop new traditions.

"Character is the basis of happiness and happiness the sanction of character."
– George Santayana

Changing your life starts with the way you think and with what you conclude your life needs in relation to what you want it to be.

"We must gain our strength and our values from self-growth and self-discovery. Against all odds, against all handicaps, against the chamber of horrors we call history, man has continued to dream and to depict its opposite. That is what we have to do. We do not escape into philosophy, psychology, and art – we go there to restore our shattered selves into whole ones."
– Anais Nin

Once you understand the source of what has formed your life into what it is, you can begin to put the unhelpful things out of your life, and/or organize them in a way beneficial to you.

In your mind you can dispose of the clutter and damage forming the wall blocking you from experiencing the thoughts fueling the actions to create a better life.

To improve your physical health and promote healing, you can follow a more healthful diet, and you can exercise every morning.

"Extreme measures are very appropriate for extreme disease."
– Hippocrates

When the tissues of the body heal, they need nutrients. The better-quality of nutrients consumed, the better the tissues can heal and function. In a similar manner, if you are healing your life from one that has injured your spirit, mind, and body, you need to feed your life with those things helpful for healing, for rehabilitation, and for functioning on a healthful level.

Maybe the reason your life has not turned out the way you want it to be is because you have allowed others to take it over, or have thought others would create a good life for you. Under these conditions, you have given up your power as you lean on others.

"Caring means doing."
– Andre Agassi

If you want your life to improve, you need to care about it. Your caring becomes evident through confidently taking intentional actions to take charge of your life. Your caring is evident in what you permit yourself to participate in, and in how you communicate – including how you communicate with your self.

It is you who can improve your life, you who can make it function, and you who can transform it to become more of the way you wish it to be. If you don't do it, nobody will do it for you. You are your rescuer, and your source of power to fuel your change.

"Nothing is more revealing than movement. Actions do speak."
– Martha Graham

How your life evolves largely depends on what you are permitting yourself to think, do, communicate, and ingest.

As negative thoughts lead to negative emotions, so too do positive thoughts lead to positive actions and helpful communication. Think about that while considering what you most desire to have in your life.

"Be careful with the present you are creating – it should look like the future you dream of."
– Mujeres Creando

Do you want positive emotions? Then continually focus on thoughts that will uplift you. This will illuminate your life because thinking positively changes the electric charges throughout your cells, enlivens your tissues, and alters your tension, hormones, molecules of emotion, and expression.

You can't be focused on damaging thoughts as you are working to nurture thoughts to bring positive change. By continuously entertaining intentional, goal-oriented, health-affirming thoughts, you are bathing your cells in positive energy and positive-thought chemicals that create positive emotions. Act in alignment with them.

"Live your life and forget your age."
– Norman Vincent Peale

Do away with revolving thoughts that create negative emotions.

Do not get caught up in regrets, which are an enormous waste of time and energy – and do not create anything worthwhile. Instead, focus on more healthful and helpful thoughts to bring about improvement in your life through intentional, goal-oriented actions and communication in tune with goals.

"Let everything happen to you. Beauty and terror. Just keep going. No feeling is final."
– Rainer Maria Rilke

334

As you work intentionally to set goals and attain them, you will learn to better control your thoughts to focus on the positive. As you do so you will notice positive changes in your life.

"By thinking and acting affirmatively in this minute, you will influence the hour, the day, and the time, your entire life."
– Denis Waitley

Replace thoughts of unfortunate memories with those of planning for a better future. Replace thoughts that make you feel drained with those that create good feelings. Choose to think of the life you want to have, instead of thinking of the life you had – or the life you may feel you had missed out on. By working the power of your mind this way, you can bring positive thoughts to fuel your life trajectory.

"The important thing is not being afraid to take a chance. Remember, the greatest failure is to not try. Once you find something you love to do, be the best at doing it."
– Debbi Fields

By continually harboring the thoughts that are in alignment with the goals you set and the life you want, you are planting the seeds to grow into the actions and communication to create the life you want.

"Go confidently in the direction of your dreams! Live the life you've imagined. As you simplify your life, the laws of the universe will be simpler; solitude will not be solitude, poverty will not be poverty, nor weakness weakness."
– Henry David Thoreau

Those who are well nurtured, are encouraged, get adequate physical activity, have access to healthful food, and are provided for when they are growing up are more likely to succeed than those who experience a childhood of abuse, neglect, dismissal, denial, ridicule, belittlement, and assault. This is where the power of suggestion is evident. This does not mean you will be a failure if you grew up in a harsh environment, were not well nurtured, or were mistreated.

At any time you can shed your past and begin to provide the nurturing you need – not only to change your life, but to radically transform it into something amazing. Many people from awful backgrounds have done this, and have succeeded far beyond what anyone would have predicted.

When I was growing up in a violent household stricken by poverty, saturated with the defeated, frustrated, anxiety-ridden alcoholism mindset, and overshadowed by many misfortunes, and where neglect, abuse, and assault were common, I still had the feeling that I could formulate a sort of life more in alignment with my better qualities. Even though I couldn't retain what I read until I was in $8^{th}$ grade, received lousy grades all through school, was continually told I was stupid, an idiot, useless, and many other degrading things, and was brutalized by people, including the people I otherwise should have been able to trust the most, I still had the feeling I would one day write books and do something worthwhile with my life. For that to happen, it was up to one person: me. And so, it is.

"It is not the strongest of the species that survive, nor the most intelligent, but the most responsive to change."
– Charles Darwin

You can work to deal with what the universe flows your way. Instead of fighting it, work with it. Use it. Reformulate it. Treat it as lessons and your teacher. Gain the wisdom, regroup and refactor yourself, and continue to aim and work for your better life to happen.

Take your trials and work with them as strengthening tools to use to get you where you want to be. Do so in the same way that a sailor works with the wind to get a boat to its destination.

"Any change, any loss, does not make us victims. Others can shake you, surprise you, disappoint you, but they can't prevent you from acting, from taking the situation you're presented with and moving on. No matter where you are in life, no matter what your situation, you can always do something. You always have a choice and the choice can be power."
– Blaine Lee

What may assist you in bringing your life onto the level you wish to experience is the law of substitution.

Many people mention the law of substitution as a concept written about by Brian Tracy in his book *Maximum Achievement*. The law of substitution works to exercise your mind so it holds positive instead of negative thoughts in ways that crowd out the negative.

Because your mind is always working, make it work in the best way to suit your desire to create a beautiful life.

This is the start of tuning your power to guide your life. Use your power to drive you to think, act, plan, and communicate more positively. To build upon this you will need to provide your body with what it needs to grow more healthfully. This means the best nutrients available to you while avoiding low-quality foods; exercising your intellect by learning about and practicing new things;

setting goals, structuring priorities, and acting on them every day; and by getting exercise every morning to make your body generate health, balance hormones, and release stagnant and damaging energy. All these actions will work in symphony to drive your life forward toward what you intentionally focus on manifesting.

"Happiness does not lie in happiness, but in the achievement of it."
– Fyodor Dostoyevsky

No matter what happened in the past, what you become from now on is very specifically up to one person. That person is: you.

Focus on your goals, not obstacles. Focus on the present, not the past. Do not engage in slothfulness. Instead, remain active in doing what will create a healthful life in which your better qualities thrive.

As you conduct your life in a more proactive, intentional, and goal-oriented manner, there is no more blaming others, there is no more self-loathing and droning on and on about the past. Instead, when living intentionally with continual actions and communication aligned with your goals, there will be the creation of positive change in your existence.

"Deep, unspeakable suffering may well be called a baptism, a regeneration, the initiation into a new state."
– George Eliot

Things will happen that you will not like. Whether you like it or not, they still are going to happen. You may as well deal with them in ways that bring some benefit to you.

Be agile. Even when you feel as if you are taking a beating, look for ways to learn and grow while relentlessly remaining engaged in actions to bring about creating your higher vision.

Take every situation you are presented with and somehow make it work as a benefit to you. That is the secret of persevering.

"If we had no winter, the spring would not be so pleasant: if we did not sometimes taste of adversity, prosperity would not be so welcome."
– Anne Bradstreet

"Better to do something imperfectly than to do nothing flawlessly."
– Robert H. Schuller

What you think of as your greatest failure may turn out to be your greatest success, or a doorway to it.

You can take charge of your life and force positive change to take place. You can change your character from one who is unhealthful to one who generates health.

No matter what happens, persevere!

"You must be willing to do the things today others don't do in order to have the things tomorrow others won't have."
– Les Brown

Keep using your intellect, talent, skills, energy, yearning, resources, spirit, nutrition, exercise, and the power of your thoughts to work toward creating the healthier life you desire.

"I think that where you go wrong is that you imagine that your reasons for living ought to fall on you, ready-made from heaven, whereas we have to find them for ourselves."
– Simone de Beauvoir

Write yourself a note of declaration every morning to both remind and contract with yourself to be actively involved in working and communicating to improve your life that day.

"I'd rather be a could-be if I cannot be an are; because a could-be is a maybe who is reaching for a star. I'd rather be a has-been than a might-have-been, by far; for a might-have-been has never been, but a has was once an are."
– Milton Berle

Positive change happens at the present, and can be made in the future. Not in the past.

Positive life change comes through motivational, inspired thoughts eliciting intentional, goal-aligned actions and related communication, not in depressing thoughts that focus on the drama of former disastrous relationships, that create mental decay, and that bask in laziness, defeat, frustration, regret, and failure.

Positive life change comes through providing the nutrients the body needs to function at a high level. These are the nutrients available in vibrant, richly-colored fruits and vegetables containing the power of Nature. Some are available in soaked raw grains and nuts. Some are available in germinated and/or soaked and boiled legumes. They are not available in a diet of deadened, microwaved, commercialized, corporatized, overly processed, and otherwise junk foods containing fried oils, bleached grains, processed salts and sugars, MSG, and synthetic chemicals. Select foods from the more than 30,000 varieties of edible plants, not from the deadness of carcasses, or from animal milk meant for non-human babies, or from bird eggs that are essentially what you don't want to think of.

Positive life change comes through working toward established goals and from organized priorities set to guide a person toward betterment. Not in disorganized randomness.

"Our responsibility is to consciously dwell both in surrender and effort. What cannot be changed demands unconditional acceptance, and what requires change needs unceasing action. So the whole idea of life is to live in a fine balance."
– Rabb Jyat

Positive life change comes through daily exercise to enliven and strengthen the body. Not in sedentary slothfulness spent in front of a television, playing endless video games, in surfing the Internet, or hanging with others who are wasting their time, energy, resources, intellect, talents, and skills.

Positive life change comes by taking charge of your choices, which happens in your mind. It is the mind you need to change if you are going to change your life.

"He not busy being born is busy dying."
– Bob Dylan

Use your imagination to help you formulate a realistic life plan.

"You can't depend on your eyes when your imagination is out of focus."
– Mark Twain

Focus on and do what you need to do to get into the life you want to experience.

"If opportunity doesn't knock, build a door."
– Milton Berle

"I didn't get lucky. I got inspired. I got focused. I got informed. I got skilled. I got busy. I got consistent. I got productive. I got experienced. I got excellent. I got positioned. Then, I got rewarded."
– Ben Johnson

# Awakening

"When one realizes one is asleep, at that moment one is already half-awake."
– P. D. Ouspensky

First, you learn it is okay to breathe. Hopefully you learn how nice it is to be cuddled, feel safe, and hear kind and loving words. You learn about movement and the senses. Then, you learn about the satisfaction of nourishment. You learn that when you cry you get attention. You learn that your vocal tones get you certain things. You learn that your physical structure can be worked to get you things. From that point onward, you learn all sorts of stuff, some of which may be beneficial and help you thrive in health, and other stuff that can put you in a state of despair, regret, and other unfortunate situations.

As you become an adult, you will know at all moments that you are the one who decides the healthful directions for you.

"One's mind, once stretched by a new idea, never regains its original dimensions."
– Oliver Wendell Holmes

Teachings and teachers do not give you intellect, talents, or instinct. What you learn can only work with, awaken, and adjust what you already possess.

As you make your way through life, you will learn more, because you can't learn less, but you can use less of what you learn.

"I do not believe that the same God who has endowed us with sense, reason, and intellect has intended us to forgo their use."
– Galileo Galilei

It is easy to recognize those who are not living up to their better potential. Look around you and see that there may be people in your everyday life who are living mundanely – stuck in a lifestyle of complication clusters they most likely would not have chosen. Also recognize that there are people who have allowed themselves to be positioned in a pattern of habitually going about their days in a perpetual path to dullness that is far beneath the level of life they could be living IF they otherwise were proactive in creating a better life. Don't neglect to consider that you may be one of them.

"We do not see things as they are. We see them as we are."
– The Talmud

Consider that the most important thing you need for changing your life is the version of you continually focused on and learning of and engaging in actions which create the life you wish to live.

"Let us become the change we seek in this world."
– Mohandas Gandhi

Just as some people were able to develop their talents and skills in their childhood, unless you are in some unfortunate position, it is possible at any stage in life to begin working with whatever strengths and resources existing within your fabric to change your life.

"I'll match my flops with anybody's, but I wouldn't have missed them. Flops are a part of life's menu, and I've never been one to miss out on any of the courses."
– Rosalind Russell

You have things to learn from your past.
Using one single piece of paper, make a list of each year of your life since age ten. Using few words, list each thing you have done and/or each realization you had in each of those years that most impressed and/or changed you. Maybe some of the years will be blank, which is okay.
Recognize if there are any patterns of behavior in your life that brought about more satisfaction or less satisfaction. Realize that if something had not happened in your life that you wished for, you can still work to make things happen that you yearn for.
Make a short list of things that would satisfy you if they were regularly present in your life. The simple act of writing these words

341

can help plant the seeds leading to the actions and communication helping to manifesting your wishes.

"All the flowers of tomorrow are in the seeds of today."
– Unknown

"Use every letter you write, every conversation you have, every meeting you attend, to express your fundamental beliefs and dreams. Affirm to others the vision of the world you want. You are a free, immensely powerful source of life and goodness. Affirm it. Spread it. Radiate it. Think day and night about it and you will see a miracle happen: the greatness of our own life."
– Robert Muller

As you awaken each morning, read through the list of things you want to achieve. Remind yourself that you are worthy and capable of attaining these things as well as the health and life you desire.

Nurture the seeds of attaining your goals by continually engaging in actions to achieve their manifestation.

"People often say that motivation doesn't last. Well, neither does bathing – that's why we recommend it daily."
– Zig Ziglar

Reading your list of goals every morning is like fertilizing your thoughts, actions, and communication with focus and intention.

"Every day we are engaged in a miracle which we don't even recognize: a blue sky, white clouds, green leaves, the curious eyes of a child – our own two eyes. All is a miracle."
– Thich Nhat Hanh

Life is like a vine that can be trained to grow in a certain pattern. The way your life grows starts within your mind and continues into what you do with thoughts propelling actions, words, and choices.

You can train your mind to think more healthfully just as you can train your body to perform certain tasks. Provide the right seed thoughts that blossom into a complete set of manageable ideas to guide your actions and communication. How your body works can be guided with the best nutrients combined with daily morning exercise. How your mind performs in conjunction with your actions depends on how you train it. It all has to do with practice.

As an athlete practices every day to win, be so engaged in training your mind with motivational thoughts that they form into actions manifesting the sport-like triumphant satisfaction in your life.

Awaken your life from any slumber. Arise and be actively and continually engaged in making your life one of health and satisfaction.

"The temptation to quit will be greatest just before you are about to succeed."
– Chinese proverb

"Our greatest glory is not in never falling, but in rising every time we fall."
– Confucius

"I will waste not even a precious second today in anger, or hate, or jealousy, or selfishness. I know that the seeds I sow I will harvest, because every action, good or bad, is always followed by an equal reaction. I will plant only good seeds this day."
– Og Mandino

# Practice Improvement

"Everybody is nine years old."
– Jerry Lewis

As schooled children, dancers, athletes, artists, and musicians repeatedly do the same tasks, they learn them from a molecular biological base impacting their nerve and muscle growth and function. The way to learn how to do things well is by repeatedly doing them. It is through the practice of principles and action that the muscles, nerves, brain, and mind learn to perform. By repeatedly practicing a craft, skill, or art, a master is built.

Just as a painter creates a picture with repeated brush strokes of colors that can be either dark, medium, or bright, so too can you create your life with repeated motivational thoughts that bring about goal-oriented, intentional actions.

"Life is painting a picture, not doing a sum."
– Oliver Wendell Holmes, Jr.

Think of your thoughts as a constant movie playing in your mind and you are the screenwriter, the producer, the set designer and decorator, the wardrobe department, the lighting gaffer, the camera operator, the sound mixer, the soundtrack composer, the script supervisor, director, editor, colorist, and actor. You can write the script any way you wish. Begin writing the script of your life the way you want it by thinking about ways you desire things to happen. Then, act it out to build your skills, craft, and life.

"Write the story you want told when you are gone."
— McCaul Lombardi

Your mind is the choreographer of your life. Think about your life circumstances continually arranging around you in ways that would best suit your needs, talents, skills, intellect, desires, and love.

"To know what you prefer instead of humbly saying 'amen' to what the world tells you what you ought to prefer, is to have kept your soul alive."
— Robert Louis Stevenson

Prefer to focus on the things you want in your life, not on the things you don't desire.

Recognize the substances of character you like to see in other people, and do not focus on the qualities you don't like.

Train yourself to be what you wish to be by continually being engaged in activities that formulate your life into what you want it to be.

Always engage in thoughts, education, goal setting, and activities using your better qualities that make your life prosper so you can be the better version of yourself for those you love, your community, and yourself.

"Education is the movement from darkness to light."
— Allan Bloom

The power of believing is evident when little children get slightly hurt. They often will stop crying and seem to feel better once their parent says, "It's all better now." Nothing changed with the injury. The only change was the child's state of mind as it was guided by the power of suggestion to believe.

"It's no accident that things are more likely to go your way when you stop worrying about whether you're going to win or lose, and focus your full attention on what is happening right this moment."
— Phil Jackson

Perhaps your normal way of thinking is negatively. Negative thoughts create pathways leading to more negativity. You cannot experience positive growth if you are going to constantly entertain negative thoughts, which create negative emotions, which affect your actions, relations, atmosphere, and results.

If you want to improve your life, it is always time to make your normal way of thinking a positive pathway, and to keep engaged in what is parallel to achieving to your goals.

"The problem is never how to get new, innovative thoughts into your mind, but how to get old ones out. Every mind is a building filled with archaic furniture. Clean out a corner of your mind and creativity will instantly fill it."
– Dee Hock

No longer allow your way of thinking to destroy your potential of living the life you want to own.

It is understandable that there are things in your life controlled by factors other than your thoughts and actions. However, it is most likely that the life you have been leading is partly the result of your thought patterns.

To create different results, think differently from the way you have been thinking. To take yourself out of the life you have been living, and into the life you want, think and do things differently from the ways you have thought and done.

Think of any object or event created by humans. If someone did not think it up, it would not exist. If ancient people did not think of building pyramids, the pyramids would not exist. If people did not think up war, there would not be war.

"All that we are is the result of what we have thought."
– Buddha

Investigate the possibility your life is what it is simply because of the way you have thought, and the actions you have taken in alignment with those thoughts.

If you are not satisfied with your life, ponder the likelihood you have behaved in ways that have blocked you from potentially experiencing a more satisfying life.

"Find the seed at the bottom of your heart and bring forth a flower."
– Shigenori Kameoka

It is not easy to recognize the colors and beauty of a flower that has not bloomed. Your beauty is manifested by working to use your talents and living up to your capabilities through taking care of yourself while working to achieve your goals.

Open your life to your intellect and talents. Draw on the substances available to you to restructure your life. Look at yourself as capable, teachable, workable, and able.

Believe and know you can be better at what you do, and can be more healthful and more satisfied with a stronger presence of health and love in your life.

346

"The art of awareness is the art of learning how to wake up to the eternal miracle of life with its limitless possibilities."
– Wilfred Peterson

Consider that your problems are your opportunities and lessons to learn what can be done better in your life.

Observe and consider what you perceive to be your disadvantages, and then work with them to your advantage.

"Opportunities to find deeper powers within ourselves come when life seems most challenging."
– Joseph Campbell

Use your energy to build your strengths to break through any boundaries between how you are living and how you want to live.

Use your talents, intellect, skills, instinct, intuition, and power to create the life you want. Do so regardless of obstacles landing in your way. Get around them.

"To maintain a skillful balance between the inner and outer aspects of our lives is an enormously challenging and continuously changing process. The objective is not to dogmatically live with less, but is a more demanding intention of living with balance in order to find a life of greater purpose, fulfillment, and satisfaction."
– Duane Elgin

One of the first steps in building a beautiful life is to eliminate what prevents such an existence from becoming your reality. This could mean doing away with clutter in the living space, clearing up, healing, or ending fractured relationships. Do so while heightening your education, improving your nutrition and fitness, practicing your skills and talents, communicating healthfully, and working daily to bring into your life what it is you will need to attain a more satisfying state in which you can thrive.

"Take away the cause, and the effect ceases."
– Miguel de Cervantes

One of the most powerful things people can do to improve their life is to identify and fix or eliminate that which is problematic – including by thinking more helpfully, eating cleaner and more nutritionally, getting rid of cutter, refusing to be slothful, getting daily morning exercise, and living out loud continually with days filled with actions in alignment with goals.

Without blaming, belittling, or confronting others, as they are dealing with their own life matters that might be what you don't know

– and don't need to know – about, identify what may be stopping you from personal advancement.

Cautiously, responsibly, and strategically arrange your situation, and adjust your style of communicating in ways that will be most helpful in propelling your life forward.

The key words in that last paragraph are *cautiously* and *responsibly*. Depending on the current life condition, it will take more time, energy, effort, focus, skill, and patience for some than for others to attain a more desirable state.

"If saying the truth ends a relationship, then it is probably a relationship that needed to end."
– Jenette McCurdy

Practice safety, respect, and responsibility when dealing with what may need to be aligned in your relationship to attain a more healthful life – especially when your choices may impact the lives of others.

"We don't receive wisdom; we must discover it for ourselves after a journey that no one can take for us or spare us."
– Marcel Proust

While creating a healthful life involves truths that are universal, because of life complexities, each person may be dealing differently with them. While one person's life may be relatively easy to transform, others' may be far more complex. Because of consequences too numerous to mention here, people will have to tally their own resources and factor the solutions right for them.

It is through observation, examination, study, consideration, decisions, actions, interactions, and experience that wisdom is built.

A challenge is to bravely deal with the issues, situations, and objects in beneficial ways.

Be smart in dealing with your circumstances in ways that will improve – not damage – your condition and relations. Your first thoughts on what to do may not be the most appreciated or helpful. If a relationship has always been so damaged that it is like a rotted house, maybe it was time to end it, anyway. Even knowing that, caution and responsibility in strategies, communication, and actions are keys. Don't cause more damage or harm to someone.

"The secret of health for both mind and body is not to mourn for the past, worry about the future, or anticipate troubles but to live in the present moment wisely and earnestly."
– Buddha

Even people who are leading the life appearing to be most desirable to others must also deal with the constant influx of things the universe presents to them.

"Never give up, for that is just the place and time that the tide will turn."
– Harriet Beecher Stowe

Be diligent, brave, wise, and use any other trait, ability, and attribute needed to transform your life into more of what you wish it to be so you can be best for your loved ones, community, society, and environment.

"Do you know what a big shot is? A little shot who keeps shooting."
– Norman Vincent Peale

Improving your life includes doing so for other life forms.

Help create the healthier world, including by reversing the mistakes of humanity.

Plant trees in which wildlife can thrive.

Detach from antiquated, ignorant forms of culinary choices that are damaging to you, wildlife, and the planet.

Food is the number one way in which you naturally interact with Earth. Turn to a more natural, plant-based diet that is less harmful to the environment and the nonhuman creatures on this planet. Where possible, grow some of your own food. Identify local native fruiting trees and bushes, and plant some of those – including to help local wildlife to thrive.

# Break Free

"One concept we often impose on our experience is an assumption of permanence, which can put us at odds with the impermanence of all natural processes."
– Gil Fronsdale

"To ignore the power of paradigms to influence your judgment is to put yourself at risk when exploring the future. To be able to shape your future, you have to be ready to change your paradigm."
– Joel Arthur Barker

Those who discover an improved way of living may have to push themselves to eliminate stubborn patterns of thought, behavior, and communication, as well as low-grade nutrition, and lack of exercise. The level of their change likely will not only be driven by how badly they want it, but also by how much they don't want their former life. Their self-improvement will likely also be driven by how strongly they grasp and engage with the knowledge that they are responsible for making the improvements they want to see and experience.

"Such is the irresistible nature of truth, that all it asks, and all it wants, is the liberty of appearing."
– Thomas Paine

"Don't feel stupid if you don't like what everyone else pretends to love."
– Emma Watson

There may be many things that people new to healthful living have to deal with when following a new path. Behaviors and thought processes they may be expressing could appear as odd to those familiar with them. They may be vulnerable to a whole new variety of observations, which may in the form of criticism and belittlement from those who lack belief in themselves, or who are afraid to break away from conformity, mundanity, or the stagnation of being stuck.

"Let them judge you. Let them misunderstand you. Let them gossip about you. Their opinions are not your problems. You stay kind, committed to love, and free in your authenticity. No matter what they do or say, don't you doubt your worth or the beauty of your truth. Simply keep shining like you always do."
– Scott Stabile

The more the person sticks to their truth, the more they will see the benefits through experiencing a life of health and satisfaction. The more they experience the benefits, the more others are likely to recognize the improvement. The more they experience improvement, the less likely they are to give consideration to the naysayers, critics, ridiculers, and anyone who speaks undermining comments.

"Nothing would be done at all if a man waited until he could do it so well that no one could find fault with it."
– John Henry Newman

People often expect things to happen in a certain way according to their concepts, history, education, experiences, relations, beliefs, and preferences. They may do this deliberately, or may be unaware of their expectations. Anything outside the boundaries of what they are anticipating – or what they are accustomed to seeing – may cause them to display surprise, laughter, bliss, perplexity, guffaws, regret, dismay, offense, ridicule, mockery, protest, or even violence.

"When you judge another, you do not define them, you define yourself."
– Wayne Dyer

"You can think up all the wild ideas you want, about me. But darling, they will only give you more insight into yourself, than anything close to who I am."
– Stacie Martin

Those who try a new way of living – even if it is a much more healthful way than what is being lived by the people around them – are often criticized for their new way – even when the benefits are

351

obvious. They may experience some undesirable attention from those around them who are not accustomed to seeing someone conduct themselves in a certain manner.

"We seldom realize that our most private thoughts and emotions are not actually our own. For we think in terms of languages and images, which we did not invent, but which were given to us by our society."
– Alan Watts

Criticism can be what hampers many from attaining the advantages of living more healthfully. It is peer pressure and it can play a role in the way you agree to conduct yourself to conform to what your local society considers to be normal and acceptable, but not necessarily the most healthful.

"Don't be distracted by criticism. Remember the only taste of success some people have is when they take a bite out of you."
– Zig Ziglar

"You must constantly ask yourself these questions: Who am I around? What are they doing to me? What have they got me reading? What have they got me saying? Where do they have me going? What do they have me thinking? And most important, what do they have me becoming? Then ask yourself the big question: Is that okay?"
– E. James Rohn

Those who discover a better way often find they need to break free of peer pressure, which is often based on negativity, unfair criticism, disbelief, societal pressures, antiquated concepts, and low self-esteem. This depends on what is going on in the minds of the peers. The critics may think those who are working to improve their lives consider themselves to be better than others. More than anything, this exposes the closed mindset of the critic.

Words reveal the concepts in the mind, and if that mind dwells in a system of personality disorder, which adds a whole other level to what a person says about and how they treat others.

What you might be dealing with when you are experiencing bullying is what I detail in my book *Dream Another Dream*. It is personality disorders that can include anankastic (also called obsessive/compulsive neurosis), avoidant and defensive, bipolar, borderline unstable, dependent, dissocial, histrionic, impulsive, narcissistic, paranoid, and schizotypal (detailed in the *Diagnostic Statistics Manual of Mental Disorders*, and sometimes unwisely tossed around as labels to blame and shame). Add substance abuse, financial stress, medical issues, unhinged urges, bad manners, and other matters, and you can be faced with a variety of problems.

"Great spirits have always encountered violent opposition from mediocre minds."
— Albert Einstein

Those who spend their time doubting others likely are doubting themselves. Those who do not believe in the capabilities of others likely do not believe their own capabilities. Those who focus on the negative things build on the negatives in their own life. Those who do such things shut down the opportunity for achieving good in their life, as the flow of muck that is of doubtful nudniks spewing criticism creates an atmosphere of destruction and failure, of fear-based stagnation and defeat, and of conforming to the mundane.

"The truth is that there is nothing noble in being superior to somebody else. The only real nobility is in being superior to your former self."
— Whitney Young

Improving your life is not about considering yourself to be better than other people, for we are all reliant on and made of the same substances. It is not about comparing yourself to others, for we are all unique. It is not about competing with others, for there is no competition. It is about you, and not about anyone else, because you can only be you.

"Life is what we make of it, always has been, always will be."
— Anna Mary Robertson "Grandma" Moses

Improving your life is about thinking and working to be more healthful and satisfied in ways that complement your talents, intellect, skills, intuition, wisdom, and other beneficial qualities.

"The greatest danger for most of us is not that our aim is too high and we miss it, but that it is too low and we reach it."
— Michelangelo di Lodovico Buonarroti Simoni

People may misinterpret your self-improvement, and think you are judging and detaching from them. What you might be detaching from is slothfulness, stagnation, defeat, obstruction, bleakness, suffering, conformity, and from not living up to what you are capable of being. What you are doing by living healthfully, and engaging daily in intentional, goal-oriented living, regular exercise, improved nutrition, and better habits, is that you are changing your personal resonance to be more in tune with what you healthfully yearn for.

When you are improving your life you are attaching to your higher potential, elegance, and beauty.

"I have spent a good many years since – too many, I think – being ashamed about what I write. I think I was forty before I realized that almost every writer of fiction or poetry who has ever published a line has been accused by someone of wasting his or her God-given talent. If you write (or paint, or dance, or sculpt, or sing, I suppose), someone will try to make you feel lousy about it, that's all."
– Stephen King

Consider those you find to be your strongest critics. If they are the people keeping you in an unhealthful situation, realize that the louder their criticism becomes may be a sign that they are not dealing with their own life in the best way. Consider the possibility that you may have agreed to allow them to keep you down. The agreement shows through in your roleplaying, behaving in ways corresponding to being harshly criticized, giving into the criticism, allowing belittling comments to define and limit you, and being shaded by low self-esteem that can be as damaging as substance addiction.

"Tell not your dreams, but to your intimate friend."
– George Washington

Not only should you be careful about with whom you associate, you should also be careful about with whom you share your goals. This isn't because you are trying to be secretive or to hide something about yourself. It also isn't about competition. It is about your energy, setting your boundaries, and not allowing others to damage you.

"Do not reveal your thoughts to everyone, lest you drive away your good luck."
– Apocrypha, Ecclesiasticus 8:19

Explaining your goals to people disperses energy. It can also get those who don't believe in you to infuse you with their invasive discouragement and/or otherwise work against you.

People who don't like you, who don't believe you are capable of succeeding, or who simply are negative, can consciously or subconsciously develop thought patterns that result in words and actions not in your favor. It falls under the definition of discouragement; it also has more to do with their thoughts, beliefs, and esteem, their control issues, their cynicism, their mania and life concept, and little to nothing to do with you. Thus, ignore discouragement that would stop you from being more healthful and that would halt your life from advancing to a better path.

"A man who trims himself to suit everybody will soon whittle himself away."
– Charles Schwab

Don't feel as if you need to explain yourself to everyone who criticizes you. That type of defensive behavior disperses energy, robs you of your drive, weakens you, and is an absolute waste of time and energy.

Those running a race do not slow down to explain their goals to the spectators. They simply stay focused on and remain confident in running the race the best they can.

"You have to believe in yourself when no one else does. That's what makes you a winner."
– Venus Williams

"Example is always more efficacious than precept."
– Samuel Johnson

I strongly suggest that you do this: Instead of slowing down to explain yourself, simply stay on course and live your life aiming toward improvement in all areas. Allow your healthful life, and not your words, to stand as the explanation you do not need to voice.

"Well done is better than well said."
– Benjamin Franklin

"What you do speaks so loudly that no one will ever hear a word you are saying."
– Ralph Waldo Emerson

"I think one's feelings waste themselves in words; they ought all to be distilled into actions which bring results."
– Florence Nightingale

Through achievement you will experience satisfaction, self-validation, skills, wisdom, and insight.

When you live more healthfully, and distance yourself from the life you had been living, you may realize how unhealthful you were. You also may recognize how sensitive and susceptible you had been to the influence of peer pressure. You may also realize how you may have spent time trying to conform to the expectations of others. You will likely experience a great relief by freeing yourself from all of the nonsense you were accepting and trying to adjust to.

"When patterns are broken, new worlds emerge."
– Tuli Kupferberg

"All the world's a stage, and all the men and women merely players: they have their exits and their entrances; and one man in his time plays many parts."
– William Shakespeare

People are sensitive to the expectations of those around them. They often get caught up in roleplaying into what they are expected to do and say – or what they perceive as being what they are expected to do and say. This type of behavior may also lead to not living up to their higher potential. Some people call this living an undercover life.

People go undercover to assimilate into their perceptions of what is socially acceptable. Under the conditions of being undercover, they may never break free of the shadow they permit to be cast on them by the expectations of others. They may never lead their own lives to experience the beauty they can be.

"If you do not express your own original ideas, if you do not listen to your own being, you will have betrayed yourself."
– Rollo May

There are many stories of those who planned to make something of themselves in ways nobody else had done, to go places nobody else had gone, to discover things nobody else had found, and to bring things about that others had not made happen. Often these people were doubted, laughed at, disowned, mocked, assaulted, or worse.

"Keep away from people who try to belittle your ambitions. Small people always do that, but the really great make you feel that you, too, can become great."
– Mark Twain

You do not need to tune into the negative, degrading, dismissive, damaging commentary, and attitudes of others. Instead, tune them out.

Choose to focus on those thoughts, people, activities, and things that will uplift you and help you to reach your goals.

"Wanting to be someone you're not is a waste of the person you are."
– Kurt Cobain

Conforming to the lives of others is a sure way to fail when it ignores who you are, and is less than what would bring out your best.

Remain aware that choosing less vibrant foods, choosing to not exercise and take care of yourself, and making choices that don't sustain the quality of life you desire puts you on the path to getting what you don't want.

Continually break free of that which holds you back. Stop compromising your self-awareness, your intellect, your experience, your wisdom, your talents, and your better qualities.

Wake up from the personalities you created to assimilate into the perceived society in which you are living undercover.

"Be who you are and say what you feel because those who mind don't matter and those who matter don't mind."
– Theodore Geisel

Be who you are, not the personality you created to assimilate into a life that is not yours, and not the personage you may have pretended to be to avoid criticism of what your beauty can be.

Open up your constricted perception. Get closer to your truths. Advance in the ways you yearn for.

Enable yourself to become fluent in your higher consciousness and to maximize the manifestations of your life within that energy.

Work to secure your connection to the spirit of your intuition, talents, intellect, and wisdom.

Amplify the beauty of your soul.

Aim to experience your life out loud.

"My father didn't tell me how to live; he lived, and let me watch him do it."
– Clarence Budington Kelland

Understand that to improve the condition of your life you need to keep making better choices.

As you remain on the path to self-improvement not only are you more likely to meet and associate with others who are doing the same, but you are likely to inspire others to better themselves. It is a process of benefitting not only you, but the people around you, and your community.

By living your life securely within the composition of your goals and true needs, you may find that you are an inspiration for those who haven't been inspired, who have not had a role model, and who have not otherwise tuned into what they can achieve by utilizing their most valuable aspects.

357

"We're here for a reason. I believe a bit of the reason is to throw little torches out to lead people through the dark."
— Whoopi Goldberg

"Life is a blank canvas, and you need to throw all the paint on it you can."
— Danny Kaye

# Bring It On, Stronger

"Adversity introduces a man to himself."
— Unknown

An elderly woman once told me that wisdom comes with age because throughout life you learn from experience. She added, "Especially from the unfortunate experiences."

"We don't receive wisdom; we must discover it for ourselves after a journey that no one can take for us or spare us."
— Marcel Proust

"Let us not look back in anger, nor forward in fear, but around in awareness."
— James Thurber

We can constantly choose to take the unfortunate experiences and make them work for us.

"Smooth seas do not create skillful sailors."
— Unknown

This brings me to suggest a mental exercise I've heard more than one person suggest. As the mind is like a garden where good thoughts can grow, it also, like a garden, has weeds that need to be tended to and combined in a compost pit where they can transform into fertile soil.

"Heaven never helps the man who will not act."
— Sophocles

359

Many of the problems of your life are not likely to simply vanish. You will benefit by facing them and dealing with them. Not doing so is similar to having an invisible force working against you, holding you back, and preventing you from dealing with the task of taking care of whatever your life problem may be.

If you have a rotting sack of garbage in your home it will not go away until you dispose of it.

"Not everything that is faced can be changed. But nothing can be changed until it is faced."
– James Baldwin

Rather than ignore a problem, deal with the issue, then proceed to do what it takes to fix it so that the mind can be freed to think about more helpful things while using the wisdom gained from experience.

"What we plant in the soil of contemplation, we shall reap in the harvest of action.
– Meister Eckhart

Part of the issue at hand when people are not taking care of their life stems from thinking they are not strong enough or worthy enough to have such a life free of whatever problems they are not dealing with. They may be dwelling in shame, pity, and guilt, and in the ever-damaging issues of self-hate and self-defeat, which all might be residues of a variety of unfortunate experiences and interactions, including if they had spent time in abusive households, toxic relationships, and degrading environments. These all can be most dreadful habits they are not aware of, and keep them down.

"Life cannot give me joy and peace, it is up to me to will it. Life just gives me time and space, it is up to me to fill it."
– William James

When people grasp the concept that they don't have to settle for having problems overtake their life, and they are worthy and strong enough to deal with their issues, they begin to factor solutions, they stop procrastinating, and they take the actions necessary to manage whatever it is they need to do to improve their situation.

"A good indignation brings out all one's powers."
– Ralph Waldo Emerson

Allow yourself to realize you can take actions necessary to fix your life and rid it of the fractured and tarnished things. It is likely that you will find your problems easier to deal with than you had thought, and will find dealing with them to be well worth the time, energy, and resources spent doing so.

"Appreciate your learning process, for it is of equal value to have realized there is a need for change as for the change itself."
– Beth Johnson

One mental exercise that can be practiced to help you prepare for cleaning your life is to perform a task that clears your life in a smaller way. A way to do this is to get rid of something – or things – that you do not need. This may include giving something away to someone who can get better use from it, or putting it somewhere it can be found and reused, or simply cleaning and organizing your home. Identify what is clutter, and rid yourself of it. Use this as a representation of what your mind must be like with thoughts that are disorganized because you have not cleaned up other areas of your life – and this other clutter in your life is cluttering your mind.

"Simplicity is the ultimate sophistication."
– Leonardo da Vinci

A similar exercise is to rid your body of clutter. This could mean excess weight, and foods that dull and degrade you.

Unhealthful foods leave behind residues and intercellular plaque that slow your cellular function, including your brain function, and add to ailments holding you back from experiencing vibrant health. Clean your diet of the unhealthful, dulling, deadening, processed, and heavy foods. (See my book: *Plant-based Regenerative Nutrition*.)

"If humans clear inner pollution, then they will also cease to create outer pollution."
– Eckhart Tolle

Go into your kitchen. Get rid of the unhealthful foods and ingredients. Dispose of any foods containing artificial preservatives, dyes, flavorings, scents, and sweeteners. Eliminate all foods containing monosodium glutamate (MSG). Look for items containing white flour, white rice, white bread, corn syrup (and other clarified sweeteners, including white sugar, rice syrup, and agave), corn oil, margarine, shortening, and lard. You are not a baby cow or bull. Eliminate dairy products (milk, butter, cheese, cream, ice cream, yogurt, kefir, casein, and whey). Get rid of eggs (including mayonnaise). Identify foods containing gelatin, which is made from animal bones and cartilage. Do away with any foods containing cooked oil. Get rid of all fried and sautéed food. Commit to keeping your body free of all these nonfood and dulling, low-quality foods that inflame the tissues, and play into chronic and degenerative health problems.

Have your diet consist of fruits, vegetables, nuts, seeds, herbs, natural spices, whole grains, and water vegetables. If you desire cooked foods, chiefly choose boiled or steamed foods, as they are free of heat-generated chemicals formed when foods are highly heated.

I encourage people to stop consuming dairy. If you consume dairy, avoid dairy from factory farms, pasteurized dairy, dairy containing additives, homogenized dairy, and heated dairy. Research xanthine-oxidase, oxidized cholesterol, neurotoxic amino acids, and casomorphins in dairy. If you consume dairy, choose unpasteurized, raw, organic dairy. One example is organic raw goats' milk kefir. Find dairy from local organic farmers, or natural foods co-ops. Learn about how dairy increases the incidence of diabetes, osteoporosis, Alzheimer's, MS, skin issues, varicose veins, cardiovascular disease, and cancers of the brain, other organs, and blood. Dairy contains the Neu5GC molecule, which is found on cancer cells. Dairy cows are eventually slaughtered for meat. Baby bulls are useless to the dairy industry, are killed, their muscle is sold as veil, and their stomach lining is sold as rennet used to curdle cheese – which is why it smells like vomit. Learn about the amount of land, water, and fuel used to support the dairy industry, and what it does to wildlife, the oceans, lakes, land, and climate. Humans don't need to consume cow milk.

"Just as the material of the body that is ready for life has need of the psyche in order to be capable of life, so psyche presupposes the living body in order that its images may live."
– Carl Gustav Jung

Follow through on your commitment to improve your life, on ridding it of clutter, on getting daily exercise, on consuming the highest-quality foods available to you, on focusing on the positive, on reading your priority list every morning, on taking goal-oriented actions, on nurturing your talents and intellect, and on communicating more healthfully. It will help you deal with challenges.

Seek out books and documentaries inspiring a more sustainable life, including a plant-based diet.

Please, where possible, get involved in growing some of your food. Also, support your regional organic produce farmers.

Learn about organic culinary gardening, community supported agriculture (CSA), feral wild gardening (planting wild berry plants and fruiting tree forests), wild food foraging, and permaculture.

# Collective Mind, Environment, and Society

"We are like islands in the seas, separate on the surface, but connected in the deep."
— William James

"We don't accomplish anything in this world alone. And whatever happens is the result of the whole tapestry of one's life and all the weavings of individual threads from one to another that creates something."
— Sandra Day O'Connor

"The life I touch for good or ill will touch another life, and that in turn another, until who knows where the trembling stops or in what far place my touch will be felt."
— Frederick Buechner

"Let go of your attachment to being right, and suddenly your mind is more open. You're able to benefit from the unique viewpoints of others, without being crippled by your own judgment."
— Ralph Marston

"A hundred times every day I remind myself that my inner and outer life are based on the labor of others, living and dead, and that I must exert myself in order to give in the same measure as I have received and am receiving."
— Albert Einstein

363

Look to those who surround you as part of your collective mind.

"Act as if what you do makes a difference. It does."
– William James

"Life is divine, life is an extraordinary, incredible, miraculous phenomenon, our most precious gift. We must grow a global brain, a global heart, and global soul. That is our most pressing current evolutionary task."
– Robert Muller

Not only are your thoughts part of a flow of the thoughts of others, the substances of you are part of the collective substances in the environment. This includes those of the people, animals, plants, soil, terrain, microorganisms, gasses, liquids, and objects around you.

There are a number of materials and energies continually flowing in, out, and about you. These include liquids, solids, gasses, bacteria, magnetic fields, molecules of emotion, and atomic particles. Each vibrates at different frequencies. In this way the substances and energies making up you are continually communicating with your environment and community, on many levels. Quantum physics and sacred geometry provide an understanding of these things.

The thoughts and actions of others often influence your thoughts and actions. In this way you are being tuned by the vibrational energy patterns carried by the minds of others. This is part of how you are a participant in the collective mind, community, society, and culture.

"I have inherited a belief in community, the promise that a gathering of the spirit can both create and change culture. In the desert, change is nurtured even in stone by wind, by water, through time."
– Terry Tempest Williams

"I am of the opinion that my life belongs to the community, and as long as I live it is my privilege to do for it whatever I can."
– George Bernard Shaw

What you think about and how you live your life helps to guide the direction of society. The way each person lives also impacts the environment, from organisms of the soil to the birds in the sky, from the wilds of the mountains to the bottoms of the seas.

Collectively how each of us chooses to live carries more weight and is of a much greater influence than the small number of politicians and other so-called world leaders. That is why it is important to participate in making good things happen. Get involved in environmental, wildlife, and wild land protection groups, as those are what will help keep Earth, Nature, and us healthy.

"Every man is more than just himself; he also represents the unique, the very special and always significant and remarkable point at which the world's phenomena intersect, only once in this way, and never again."
– Hermann Hesse

"The whole idea of compassion is based on a keen awareness of the interdependence of all these living beings, which are all part of one another, and all involved in one another."
– Thomas Merton

"Every action in our lives touches on some chord that will vibrate in eternity."
– Edwin Hubbel Chapin

The collective mind is made up of the people in the society and region of the world where you live. It ripples with influence into distant communities and cultures. The collective mind plays a role in the thoughts of people around the planet. Because of the electronic and mass media, the collective mind is accelerating in its thought processes – unfortunately, not always in an ascending manner.

The collective mind, much like yours, can also be changed. For example, at one time a large number of people thought racial segregation and the killing of various types of people for petty or fabricated reasons were okay. As people became enlightened and began to understand the wrongs taking place, the attitude changed and society no longer accepted the former barbaric actions. The collective mind changed. However, as is clear, there is still much work to do, and there are helpful changes to be made, and standards to heighten.

"One little person, giving all of her time to peace, makes news. Many people, giving some of their time, can make history."
– Mildred "Peace Pilgrim" Norman

Another example of how the collective mind is changing is in the way many people are becoming aware of environmental issues, and that small decisions they make to improve their environment make larger differences. For instance, millions of people have finally become aware of how much environmental damage is being done by the global community using billions of plastic bags and bottles every month. Many people are now choosing to use reusable fabric bags, and reusable drinking bottles.

"Nothing is more powerful than an individual acting out of his conscience, thus helping to bring the collective conscience to life."
– Norman Cousins

You are a part of the collective mind, environment, culture, and society in which you live. What you think about and the actions you take and words you speak matter. You matter and your choices are important to the health, standards, practices, and temperament of society. What you do impacts the environment, and wildlife.

"Perhaps the most basic challenge humanity faces is to awaken our capacity for collective knowing, and conscious action so that we can respond successfully to the immense social and ecological difficulties that now confront us."
– Duane Elgin

"We ourselves feel that what we are doing is just a drop in the ocean. But the ocean would be less because of that missing drop."
– Mother Teresa

If you want society to improve and to become more environmentally sustainable, you need to improve and to live a more environmentally sustainable life. If you want there to be less pollution, you have to pollute less. If you want there to be fewer toxic chemicals and a world safer for wildlife, you have to use fewer toxic chemicals and work to protect wildlife and to restore wildlife habitat.

If you want people to be more healthful, you have to be more healthful.

If you want people to be positive and to be part of the solution, you have to be more positive and you must be part of the solution.

"The people's good is the highest law."
– Marcus Tullius Cicero

Just as a rotten berry can ruin a box of berries, a person with a negative and damaging attitude can spread their energy among the people around them. Similarly, just as one pebble can change the flow of a stream to transform a landscape, the positive attitude of just one person can sway an entire group of people toward a better way.

The process of influence also works on an individual level. Slight changes in your thought pattern can lead you to a completely different situation from the one you were in if you had you not taken control of your thoughts guiding your actions and communication.

If you notice that a situation you are in is on a course you don't like, know that you can play a part in changing the current.

"As human beings we all want to be happy and free from misery. We have learned that the key to happiness is inner peace. The greatest obstacles to inner peace are disturbing emotions such as anger and attachment, fear and suspicion – while love and compassion, a sense of universal responsibility are the sources of peace and happiness."
– Dalai Lama

Group dynamics can be an interesting phenomenon, given that the attitude of everyone in a group can be altered by the expressions of one person.

When you are around a group of people you may notice one or two who are focused on what they don't like about someone else in the group. They may begin to say degrading, belittling, dismissive, and otherwise slanderous things about that person, spreading the negative thoughts into others within the group. They offer no solutions while they centralize their thoughts on the negative things they consider to be about the person, instead of on the positive, helpful, and nurturing.

"When you speak of someone or about someone, you should speak as though they were in the room with you. The ears that you speak to today are attached to the mouth that could relay the message tomorrow."
– William Biddy Allen

The energy resonating from someone in a position of power can be especially communicable within – and spread throughout – an organization. This works either positively or negatively. In the same way, the people who are not in the top positions of an organization can also be a major influence in creating change.

Many people have experienced gossipy, alarmist, tyrannical, contentious, or otherwise unpleasant bosses. A boss can wreak havoc on the nerves of the staff – creating an unfavorable work environment, leading to stress in the lives of the employees – all the way into their personal lives, relationships, health, and life trajectory.

People who coach sporting teams work every day to guide the collective mind of the group of people for which they are responsible. Wise coaches know their attitude can quickly spread throughout the team and have a huge impact on their success. Therefore, a coach will constantly work to recognize when anything other than an attitude of success is present in the team, and work to adjust the views of anyone who is not being helpful.

There may be times when you will need to advise someone to be cautious of another person, but there is a tender balance between advising caution and promoting unfair attitudes and judgments, between warning and slandering, between helpful and hateful, and between advising and requiring or expecting.

"If we encourage and uphold our essential goodness and capacity for loving connection, we can nurture a society of people who are healthy and whole and whose lives will bring healing, peace, and joy to those they touch."
– John Robbins

While you may not always be successful at it, work to be patient, kind, and forgiving. By doing so, it is more likely that others will be likely to conduct themselves in a similar manner.

Bring a good energy with you wherever you go. By holding positive energy, you are a positive influence on people around you.

By being confident, you can help those around you to become more confident.

By working hard, you will likely inspire others to do the same.

"Of all the things I have learned in my lifetime – the one with the greatest value – is that unexpected kindness is the most powerful, least costly, and most underrated agent of human change."
– Bob Kerrey

Uplift, compliment, nurture, encourage, and guide people toward better choices. Treat others as you like to be treated. Watch it spread as if you are conducting the matter around you – because, you are.

Your actions cause reaction – often in the most subtle ways.

"Even if it's a little thing, do something for those who have need of help. Something for which you get no pay but the privilege of doing it."
– Albert Schweitzer

"Few people know that they have the power to bless life. We bless the life in each other far more than we realize. Many simple, ordinary things that we do can affect those around us in profound ways."
– Rachel Naomi Remen

Just as your mental health is important to your physical health, and your physical health is important to your spiritual health, and your diet is important to your body and environment, and the quality of your environment is important to your ability to live healthfully, you and all of the people around you are important to the wellbeing of each other. You are part of the link in the chain of influence.

"The greatest good you can do for another is not just to share your riches but to reveal to him his own."
– Benjamin Disraeli

Recognize that your thoughts and words can help reveal the best qualities of people. Nurture the things you like about people.

Complimenting, encouraging, and nurturing good in others is doing the same for yourself. Expressing gratitude for the little things people do is one way to bring about more of the same.

"Those who bring sunshine into the lives of others cannot keep it from themselves."
– James M. Barrie

"Some of the most significant problems of humankind can only be fundamentally approached as matters of conscience, commitments of the human spirit, and endeavors of whole communities, local and global."
– Thomas S. Inui

"Gratitude is something of which none of us can give too much. For on the smiles, the thanks we give, our little gestures of appreciation, our neighbors build their philosophy of life."
– A. J. Cronin

"This ongoing journey requires faith in the power of a single lamp to hold the darkness at bay. It demands confidence in the power of humble actions to act as an inspiration, or a magnet, and draw in greater energies. There is also a need for a certain agility and strategic planning that puts these positive energies a few steps ahead of the negative trends. And, above all, we need a constant awareness that the 'other' is not really different from the 'self.'"
– Rajni Bakshi

Treating others in a way that respects their intellect, talents, and abilities is mutually beneficial, as it creates an atmosphere of respect within you. This is why it is good to acknowledge the positive aspects of those around you. It is in alignment with the concept that you should treat others as you like to be treated.

How you are treating others is how you are treating your self.

When considering molecules of emotion, body electrical fields, and body language, and how people are partially controlled by mirror neurons that are influenced by and influencing the actions, reactions, and other expressions of others, what you put out is what you may receive. On every level.

"Happiness is a perfume you cannot pour on others without getting a few drops on yourself."
– Ralph Waldo Emerson

Your energy is swayed by the energy of those with whom you choose to associate.

If you want to be more positive and successful, associate with those who are in alignment with those conditions. By conducting yourself in a certain manner you are more likely to meet and associate with others who are doing the same.

"It is one of the most beautiful compensations of this life that no one can sincerely try to help another without helping himself."
– Ralph Waldo Emerson

"We cannot live only for ourselves. A thousand fibers connect us with our fellow men."
– Herman Melville

"Kindness is the golden chain by which society is bound."
– Johann Wolfgang von Goethe

By first conducting ourselves in the best way we know how, and doing what is right while learning to do even better, we are becoming enlightened and allowing others in our realm to benefit from our enlightenment.

"Each time a person stands up for an ideal, or acts to improve the lot of others, or strikes out against injustice, he sends forth a tiny ripple of hope, and crossing each other from a million different centers of energy and daring, these ripples build a current that can sweep down the mightiest walls of oppression and resistance."
– Robert F. Kennedy

When you are involved in improving the situation of the environment, of wildlife, and of the human condition, such as by creating a more sustainable culture, you will find the impact you have can be magnified greatly when you join others who are involved in doing the same. That is a community you want to be a part of.

It is by strengthening ourselves, our resolves to do better, and our words and actions to create a more healthful planet that we strengthen others, our culture, our society, and create a better future for both ourselves and those who are born after us.

It is by learning and doing that you influence others. In it, you can become a beacon of light to guide others to a better way of living.

More people are awakening to the global environmental and wildlife travesties created by humans, and are choosing lives involved with correcting the wrongs of humanity, and making better decisions to bring better results than what we have been experiencing.

Many people are involved in protecting the environment, and improving the conditions of wildlife. Please, be one of them.

Many are excluding toxic foods from their diet, and choosing to follow plant-based diets free of harmful ingredients. In turn, they are increasing the demand for better quality foods that are safer for Earth.

Many are becoming involved in growing food using organic methods, and in supporting regional organic farmers.

Those actions are a testament to the changing collective mind.

"So divinely is the world organized that every one of us, in our place and time, is in balance with everything else."
– Johann Wolfgang von Goethe

As mentioned, by doing what you like to do, and going where you like to go, you are likely to meet others who share your interests, goals, and activities, and are on the same educational path.

"People are longing to rediscover true community. We have had enough of loneliness, independence, and competition."
– Jean Vanier

At this time, it is particularly important to be involved with improving the conditions of wildlife terrain, wildlife existence, and wild Nature on Earth.

At this stage, it is crucial to the continuation of all species that everyone participate in building a more sustainable culture that is protecting and restoring forests, wildlands, and wildlife habitat.

As the situation for wildlife and the health of Earth improve, so too will the conditions of humanity.

"It is worth reminding ourselves that what brings us the greatest joy and satisfaction in life are those actions we undertake out of concern for others. Indeed we can go further. For whereas the fundamental questions of human existence, such as why we are here, where we are going, and whether the universe had a beginning, have each elicited different responses in different philosophical traditions, it is self-evident that a generous heart and wholesome actions lead to greater peace."
– Dalai Lama

371

"With every deed you are sowing a seed, though the harvest you may not see."
— Ella Wheeler Wilcox

"If I have been of service, if I have glimpsed more of the nature and essence of ultimate good, if I am inspired to reach wider horizons of thought and action, if I am at peace with myself, it has been a successful day."
— Alex Nobel

Choose to be part of the solution to improve Nature, and help connect with and build a generation of people doing the same.

"Sometimes it falls upon a generation to be great."
— Nelson Mandela

"The greatest discovery of my generation is that we are unique. The greatest discovery of the next generation, I pray, is that we are one."
— Thomas Leonard

"What you leave behind is not what is engraved in stone monuments, but what is woven into the lives of others."
— Pericles

"We have all known the long loneliness and we have learned that the only solution is love, and that love comes with community."
— Dorothy Day

"Today we are faced with the preeminent fact that, if civilization is to survive, we must cultivate the science of human relationships — the ability of all people, of all kinds, to live together and work together, in the same world at peace."
— Franklin D. Roosevelt

"So many people walk around with a meaningless life. They seem half-asleep, even when they're busy doing things they think are important. This is because they're chasing the wrong things. The way you get meaning into your life is to devote yourself to loving others, devote yourself to your community around you, and devote yourself to creating something that gives you purpose and meaning."
— Morrie Schwartz

"On this shrunken globe, men can no longer live as strangers."
— Adlai E. Stevenson

Be aware that your thoughts, actions, communication, food choices, and results help to guide those of others.

Always remember you can change the course of your community toward solutions, and it is you who can change your world.

"We are participants in a vast communion of being, and if we open ourselves to its guidance, we can learn anew how to live in this great and gracious community of truth."
– Parker Palmer

"To appreciate beauty; to give of one's self, to leave the world a bit better, whether by a healthy child, a garden patch, or a redeemed social condition; to have played and laughed with enthusiasm, and sung with exultation; to know even one life has breathed easier because you have lived – that is to have succeeded."
– Ralph Waldo Emerson

"We have a calling. We are the people who know what we need. What we need surrounds us. What we need is each other. And when we act together, we will find our way."
– John McKnight

"We are earth people on a spiritual journey to the stars. Our quest, our earth walk, is to look within, to know who we are, to see that we are connected to all things."
– Lakota seer

One way we are all connected to all of humanity and to wild animals and plant life is through breathing. The oxygen we all need is produced by plants. What we exhale is what plants take in. Help yourself, everyone else, and wildlife by planting more trees, bushes, and other plants native to your region. It helps provide oxygen, sequesters greenhouse gasses, improves the soil, protects the water, provides homes to wildlife, and makes Earth a nicer place to be.

Working to improve that state of Nature is one way to help end anthropocentrism practices, which stage humans as more moral and more worthy than – and superior to – other animals and wildlife. (Research: biocentrism and ecocentrism, compared to anthropocentrism.)

For a healthier collective mind, community, society, culture, environment, and you, get involved with permaculture, with your local environmental and wildlife organizations, and with growing food, and with supporting your local and regional organic produce farmers. Follow a plant-based diet.

Get involved in replanting paradise. Plant native trees, native bushes, and other native plants.

# Artists

"The creative individual has the capacity to free himself from the web of social pressures in which the rest of us are caught. He is capable of questioning the assumptions that the rest of us accept."
– John W. Gardener

"A musician must make music, an artist must paint, a poet must write, if they are to be ultimately at peace with themselves. What a man can be, he must be."
– Abraham Maslow

"To the artist is sometimes granted a sudden, transient insight which serves in this matter for experience. A flash, and where previously the brain held a dead fact, the soul grasps a living truth! At moments we are all artists."
– Arnold Bennett

"An artist worthy of the name should express all the truth of nature, not only the exterior truth, but also, and above all, the inner truth."
– Auguste Rodin

"Every artist dips his brush in his own soul, and paints his own nature into his pictures."
– Henry Ward Beecher

Artists are often open-minded, exploratory, and willing to consider unconventional possibilities. They might find themselves having to sneak through the closed-mindedness of those around them to create their art, to accomplish their goals, and to experience satisfaction. Doing so can display their creativity, yearning, and determination to express their intellect.

"Art is literacy of the heart."
– Elliot Eisner

Artists often fall into the classifications of nonconformity. How they handle being so can make or break them. This is especially so in the earlier parts of their lives.

Artists are often sensitive to and can be susceptible to losing themselves in and to being entrapped by peer pressure and conformity. This might be done to protect against harsh criticism. When this happens they can become engulfed by self-deceptive and destructive behavior, and in living inauthentic undercover lives lost in the conformity in which their creativity is stagnated.

People who don't follow society's norms might be considered odd or eccentric. If this is expressed or detected in childhood, the child might be misunderstood. Instead of recognizing and working with the attributes of the child, the unconventional child might too quickly be given pharmaceutical drugs to conform. This is so they are more likely to fit in with what is considered normative behavior of children who can sit for hours doing math and English lessons, memorizing trivial things, and giving rehearsed answers to test questions. This systematic failure and chemically-induced conformity can be a recipe for personal disaster, and it fails society.

"Artmaking is making the invisible, visible."
– Marcel Duchamp

Society suggests that we live our lives in certain patterns, wearing particularly acceptable styles of clothing and hair arrangements, eating common foods, listening to and watching common entertainment, and living in structures of a popular standard of design.

What much of society has transitioned into is the "norm" that is intellectually stifling and talent-strangling mundanity.

You aren't supposed to stain your hair with beet juice, turmeric, and henna, and you aren't supposed to wear clothes that don't look like the mass-manufactured wardrobe everyone else wears as they replicate commercial imagery. You are supposed to conform to standard styles of highly polluting fast fashion. Goodness help you if you should paint your house anything other than bland colors to blend in with the neighborhood landscaped with flowers, bushes, and trees approved by the homeowners' association.

"Be daring, be different, be impractical, be anything that will assert integrity of purpose and imaginative vision against the play-it-safers, the creatures of the commonplace, the slaves of the ordinary."
– Cecil Beaton

In 1997 author, artist, and educator Sandra Cisneros went against the grain of the San Antonio, Texas, neighborhood where she lived and painted her house traditional Tejano colors, including violet.

"Color is a power which directly influences the soul."
– Wassily Kandinsky

"The chief function of color should be to serve expression."
– Henry Matisse

People reacted to Cisneros' choices as if she had committed a crime. News cameras and people swarmed her home to take photos. Her story made the international news.

Cisneros was out-of-line with homeowners who had painted their homes the approved, dull shades of beige, grey, brown, green, or blue.

The so-called rebellious act of Cisneros became the focus of the Historic Design and Review Committee, which gave her the option of repainting her home, or going about the process of proving that her choice in colors for her home were historically appropriate.

Cisneros argued that the Tejano people who formerly lived in the area did paint their homes in similar colors to those she chose for her house, and they didn't have architects and review committees determining the colors of their homes. The Tejano history had been erased, their homes demolished, and their humble villages replaced by the modern city with its parking lots, government buildings, freeways, shopping centers, gas stations, convenience stores, and homes with colors and designs approved by committees.

In arguing her case, Cisneros wisely responded, "Color is a language. In essence, I am being asked to translate this language. For some who enter my home, these colors need no translation. However, why am I translating to the historical professionals? If they're not visually bilingual, what are they doing holding a historical post in a city with San Antonio's demographics?"

Cisneros won her case. After several years, the violet house faded in the sun to a blue. She then painted it Mexican pink with a backyard office painted marigold.

"The core psychology of a social entrepreneur is someone who cannot come to rest, in a very deep sense, until he or she has changed the pattern in an area of social concern all across society."
– Bill Drayton

Artists help define how people feel and communicate, what a community is, and what society becomes. Don't underestimate the influence of artists on your life. Be aware of the good they do.

Closed minded people who don't consider the influence of artists may want to consider everything made by humans that is on, over, under, and around them. All human-made things were designed by someone, in essence: artists.

"Anyone who loves art knows that psychoanalysis has no monopoly on the power to heal. Art and poetry have always been altering our ways of sensing and feeling – that is to say, altering the human body."
– Norman O. Brown

We have often heard someone start a sentence by saying, "That movie (or book, song, etc.) made me feel…" Those who create things spread their energy into other people through design, and this process influences other expression, and guides society.

Artistic expression is communication. It is language.

"Acknowledge all those who gave their lives in pursuit of the great human service, the service of the artist, transforming the sometimes unbearable discrepancy between the way things are and the way they ought to be, into something that makes us want to dance."
– Richard Berger

In the spring of 1968 there were riots and demonstrations in the streets of Paris, and later in other parts of France. This happened after the French minister of culture tried to oust Henri Langlois and to close the Cinematheque Française run by Langlois. The crowds and well-known persons of the international film community rallied behind Langlois.

Langlois considered film to be its own country. He was famous for endless screenings of films he had spent decades collecting from all over the world, including from war-torn countries. His theatre reigned over a large part of the art community of Paris. It was because of Langlois that the Cinematheque existed, and it is because of his dedication that many films from throughout the world have been preserved.

Among those attending Cinematheque Française was a group of passionate film fans and creators known as "the Rats of Cinematheque" or "Children of the Cinematheque." The Rats, including New Wave film directors, such as Jean-Luc Godard, Francois Truffaut, and Jacques Rivette, spent many hours at the theatre and in social settings passionately discussing the films they watched at the Cinematheque.

The knowledge shared at Cinematheque altered the film world. It strengthened the concept that film is a form of art, and a way for filmmakers, and society in general, to express and to be expressed.

The energy of the Rats of Cinematheque continues to vibrate through the international film community. As film helps to formulate the thoughts of people around the world, this part of film history is an example of how little things can affect much larger things.

I have an appreciation for Langlois. I have spent many years running a film and TV screenplay incubation workshop to help writers. I write screenplays. I wrote a screenwriting book used as a text in film schools, and I polish scripts for producers.

**"Respect yourself and others will respect you."**
– Confucius

Society has a lack of value and respect for artists and creative types, often dismissing them as meaningless, yet there is a large dependency on artists to create the appearance, function, and trajectory of society. Artists help determine the types of clothing people wear, the type of structures they work in, live in, and are transported on, in, and through, and what they experience through all forms of entertainment.

No matter what stage of life you are in, it is never too late to recognize and engage in your talents, and to practice your art.

**"It is later in the dark of life that you see forms, constellations. And it is the constellations that are philosophy."**
– Robert Frost

**"I am always doing that which I cannot do in order that I may learn how to do it."**
– Pablo Picasso

Some of those who have been considered to be the greatest artists went through decades of learning about and/or misunderstanding themselves – and experienced the turbulence of being misunderstood, and perhaps treated badly because of those misunderstandings – before they created their most celebrated works.

"There are some truths about life that can be expressed only as stories, or songs, or images. Art delights, instructs, consoles. It educates our emotions."
— Dana Gioia

There are many examples of artists who created landmark works in their later years. For instance, Louise Bourgeois didn't create her famous steel and marble Maman spider sculpture until she was 87 years old. Another example is Anna Mary Robertson "Grandma Moses," who didn't start painting until she was in her seventies. In the acting community, there are people like Estelle Parsons, who, at age 82 was on a national tour starring in the play, "August: Osage County," in which she appeared on Broadway when it won both the 2008 Tony Award and Pulitzer Prize for Best Play.

"At the deepest level, the creative process and the healing process arise from a single source. When you are an artist, you are a healer; a wordless trust of the same mystery is the foundation of your work and its integrity."
— Rachel Naomi Remen

"It has been said that art is a tryst, for in the joy of it maker and beholder meet."
— Kojiro Tomita

Art influences people to feel energies within their body tissues, which result in thoughts and emotions, and both molecules of emotion and electrical responses in tune with the thoughts and emotions.

Films, television, plays, literature, music, and design create various forms of energy, which then influence culture. Including the culture of art.

"It is incontestable that music induces in us a sense of the infinite and the contemplation of the invisible."
— Victor de LaPrade

"Healing is communication; and music, in its universal nature, is total communication. In the deepest mysteries of music are the inspirations, the pathways, and the healing which lead to one-ness and unity."
— Olivea Dewhurst-Maddock

"Music is the language of the spirit. It opens the secret of life bringing peace, abolishing strife."
— Kahlil Gibran

"I experience a period of frightening clarity in those moments

when nature is so beautiful. I am no longer sure of myself, and the paintings appear as in a dream. An artist, under pain of oblivion, must have confidence in himself, and listen only to his real master: Nature."
– Auguste Renoir

Artists are sometimes eccentric types with the potential of both being misunderstood and mistreated. Because of their sensitive nature artists may experience things on deeper levels, including mental pain – which can become overwhelming and lead to unwise choices of how to relieve it. Maybe the strife can lead to better things, as that is how many deal with it. Not that anyone needs to contribute to the pain. As others do, artists need a nurturing and safe environment; and to steer their creativity into useful, helpful, and healthful projects. Just like everyone else, they need love and dignity.

"When I'm trusting and being myself, everything in my life reflects this by falling into place easily, often miraculously."
– Shakti Gawain

Today we need a whole new set of artists dedicated to designing all levels of society to establish a more environmentally healthful and sustainable culture.

"The painter of the future will be a colorist such as has never been seen."
– Vincent Van Gogh

"I think raising consciousness, helping people see and understand how they're connected to these larger systems in the world around us, is an incredibly important thing. I think art can do this in ways that are provocative, meaningful and inspirational, deeply moving, beautiful, connected with history and culture and resonant. I think that's a big part of it. There's another part of it where I think artists have the opportunity to more than call attention to problems and preach, to really help solve problems. To help create things that work better, that are just more beautiful and right."
– Sam Bower

"Obstacles cannot crush me. Every obstacle yields to stern resolve. He who is fixed to a star does not change his mind."
– Leonardo da Vinci

"When we make a conscious decision to create – to make a painting for instance – we are opening the door to the pure source energy flowing through us and asking that we become able to

interpret it in a way that we and others may understand it. Fasting is the greatest way that I know of to achieve ultimate clarity in this process – to tap directly into the source in order to bring back information via visual language that will inspire growth and awareness in others. Art is free to all without rules – how can anyone pass that up? Art is our responsibility – it is the essential catalyst for universal shift."
  – Zito

"Live your life from your heart. Share from your heart. And your story will touch and heal people's souls."
  – Melody Beattie

"Where the needs of the world and your talents cross, there lies your vocation."
  – Aristotle

If you are an artist, please become a part of the movement to create a more healthful, environmentally sustainable society that protects Nature and wildlife. Infuse yourself with Nature through a plant-based diet, be healthy, and let that be a creative fuel.

"At the deepest level, the creative process and the healing process arise from a single source. When you are an artist, you are a healer; a wordless trust of the same mystery is the foundation of your work and its integrity."
  – Rachel Naomi Remen

"An artist is not a special kind of a person – every person is a special kind of an artist."
  – Ananda Coomaraswami

"Every man's work, whether it be literature or music or pictures or architecture or anything else, is always a portrait of himself."
  – Samuel Butler

"In art the hand can never execute anything higher than the heart can inspire."
  – Ralph Waldo Emerson

"My art has led me into deeper relationship with the Earth. When I am outside painting the landscape I often feel part of it – not just a spectator, but a participant. Perception is participation. The more we perceive, the more we participate. The more we participate, the more we are connected. With connection comes caring."
  – Adam Wolpert

"All children are artists. The problem is how to remain an artist once he grows up."
– Pablo Picasso

"The distribution of talents in this world should not be our concern. Our responsibility is to take the talents we have and ardently parlay them to the highest possible achievement."
– Alan Loy McGinnis

"No matter how old you get, if you can keep the desire to be creative, you're keeping the man-child alive."
– John Cassavetes

"I do know that craft, if you pursue craft, will return you again and again to this creative state. To pursue the craft means to endeavor to bring together the intention of the mind to the hand, and an invitation to feeling – an invitation to a new kind of feeling."
– Nicholas Hlobeczy

"There are no days in life so memorable as those which vibrated to some stroke of the imagination."
– Ralph Waldo Emerson

"Every artist makes herself born. You must bring the artist into the world yourself."
– Willa Cather

"When you do things from your soul, you feel a river moving in you, a joy."
– Jalal ad-Din Rumi

"Your life is a work of art. You are the designer of your life, the paint brush is in your hands and with every beautiful picture you paint and every opportunity you cease, will one day form into your masterpiece."
– Adam Taste

# Brain Plasticity

A key tool for creating a more healthful life, and being part of the solution to matters facing humanity, is a well-functioning brain.

Brain nutrition begins before birth as hundreds of millions of brain cells form and divide. Women who are planning on becoming pregnant, and those who are pregnant, would benefit their babies by choosing the most highly nutritious foods available to them, especially in the form of a variety of raw fruits and vegetables, and other plant matter.

Excellent prenatal nutrition is beneficial in numerous ways. Women who consume a variety of fresh fruits and vegetables during pregnancy are found to have babies with more healthful lung, heart, kidney, liver, and autoimmune functions, and with less susceptibility to experience asthma, diabetes, and other autoimmune issues.

Substances in fresh fruits and vegetables are particularly beneficial to brain function.

The neurotransmitter acetylcholine is key to cell communication and a healthful memory. This brain chemical tends to decline with age. Antioxidants in raw, dark-colored fruits and vegetables, and especially in apples, apricots, broccoli, cantaloupe, chard, kale, mangos, blueberries, goji berries, spinach, and watermelon help maintain a healthful level of acetylcholine.

Low-quality nutrition prevents the tissues from being able to function at the most healthful level. On a junk food diet, the brain does not function anywhere near its higher potential.

383

Many people are consuming such unhealthful foods while leading slothful and unsustainable lives their brains are neglected, and in a state of dysfunction to the point of injury. By living so far below their potential to be part of the solution to societal and environmental problems they are embedded in being part of the problems.

The brain especially needs raw plant substances containing a variety of high-quality nutrients. But the type of foods many people are consuming contain overly processed substances no longer resembling what is found in Nature. They are consuming highly heated, processed, and otherwise low-quality fats, such as lard, mayonnaise, shortening, pasteurized dairy, unhealthful salad dressings, trans fats, and oils that have been heated for frying and sautéing. None of those fats are what the brain or body need. Those heat-damaged fats are so unhealthful to ingest that they cause tissue dysfunction, including altering nerve and other cellular communication, and causing inflammation. Toxic, damaged oils pave the way for and fuel disease, including of the cardiovascular system.

To be clear: Following a low-quality diet of junk and toxic foods is degrading to all areas of a person's health – including brain, skin, kidney, heart, liver, lungs, and other organ function, muscle and immune system function, neural growth, and cellular communication. All of it plays into life function, ability, creativity, and potential.

"The food you eat can either be the safest and most powerful form of medicine, or the slowest form of poison."
– Ann Wigmore

Health suffers when a person follows a diet lacking in fresh fruits and vegetables while following a diet consisting of fried and sautéed foods, bleached grains, junk foods, and even more if rich in meat, dairy, and eggs – especially if from horrid factory farms.

"If I were to remain silent, I'd be guilty of complicity."
– Albert Einstein

Mass bred farm animals live unhealthful lives of incarceration while fed awful diets, and treated with drugs. They never experience the sounds, smells, sights, feelings, or nutrients of what would be in their natural habitat. The animals live without knowing life outside of confinement. They don't experience loving families. Factory farming and the animal meat and dairy industries are anthropocentric practices based on antiquated human dominion theories, and need to end.

Factory farmed animals are sickly, and are filled with stress chemicals, molecules of harsh emotions, and residues of farming chemicals and pharmaceutical drugs. Consuming their flesh, tissues, milk, and eggs is putting illness into your body.

One malady triggered by the unhealthy processed foods and toxic proteins and fats people are eating is obesity.

According to the National Institutes of Health, in the U.S. obesity increased in 23 states in 2008, and lowered in none. In 2000, 42.4% of the U.S. population was considered obese. In 2022, it was 41.9%. Obesity increases a variety of health problems, including cancer, arthritis, cardiovascular and kidney disease, and diabetes.

Obesity has increased since refrigeration increased meat and dairy consumption. Obesogenic chemicals in meat stimulate adipose tissue growth, especially during gestation. Epigenetic studies reveal that the more meat a pregnant woman eats (prenatal obesogen exposure), the greater chances are her child will experience obesity. The weight issues can continue to the next generation. Exercise and a plant-based diet rich in diversity are important for expectant mothers.

Not only do people suffer from a number of common ailments when they become obese, their brains are also altered.

According to a study published in the August, 2009 edition of the journal *Human Brain Mapping*, and funded by the National Institute on Aging, National Institute of Biomedical Imaging and Bioengineering, National Center for Research Resources, and the American Heart Association, the brains of obese people contain eight percent less brain tissue, and appear 16 years older than people of a healthful weight. The study considered the brains of 94 people in their seventies. The lead author of the study, Paul Thompson, a UCLA professor of neurology, was clear to explain that obesity interferes with cognitive function and increases the risk of Alzheimer's and other brain diseases. Brain scans detected that the brains of the overweight study subjects appeared to have lost brain tissue, including in the frontal and temporal lobes (which control memory and strategy), anterior cingulate gyrus (controls attention and executive functions), hippocampus (controls long-term memory), parietal lobe (controls senses), and basal ganglia (controls movement). The brains of obese people also had a reduction in white matter composed of axons.

An unhealthful diet, lack of exercise, and being overweight interferes with brain function, shrinks the brain, dulls the senses, increases the likelihood of stroke, heart attack, Alzheimer's, MS, diabetes, kidney disease, osteoporosis, arthritis, dental issues, and cancer, reduces neural activity and sex drive, and simply is detrimental to health.

According to the World Health Organization, hundreds of millions of people on the planet are classified as obese, and another billion are overweight.

It's not only the basic unhealthful foods that trigger health problems, it is the chemicals often found in those foods. This includes synthetic dyes, preservatives, flavorings, and the chemicals used on the farms, which can include pesticides, miticides, fungicides, and the chemicals in the plastics and packaging – including the chemicals in bottles and cans, fast food wrappers, and microwave food product containers, including popcorn bags. They are also in pet food bags and packaging. Then, there are the chemicals in kitchen pots and pans, especially in those with non-stick coatings (Teflon). Some of the chemicals are called "forever chemicals," because – according to scientists – the chemicals can take thousands of years to degrade.

"They are often referred to as 'forever chemicals' because they don't break down easily in nature, and can build up in the body over time. PFAS have been linked to thyroid problems, immune system issues, decreased birth weights, and various types of cancer."
– Web MD

"A study published in the journal *Water Research* and led by Johns Hopkins University researchers detected PFAS in 38 out of more than 100 bottle waters tested, in some cases at levels deemed concerning by water quality experts."
– Consumer Reports

PFAS (per and polyfluorinated alkyl substances) accumulate in your body. Research it.

A study from 2007 by the US Centers for Disease Control and Prevention estimated that PFAS were detected in 98% of the U.S. population.

Health problems found to be related to – or made worse by – PFAS include birth defects, decreased fertility, fatty liver, high cholesterol, hormone suppression, kidney cancer, obesity, pregnancy-induced hypertension, rectal cancer, testicular cancer, thyroid disease, and ulcerative colitis.

In other words, aim for an organic diet, decrease or eliminate foods in toxic packaging. Aim to buy in the bulk section of your natural grocer, and from farmers' markets. Preferably, grow some of your own foods while using organic methods.

Many people who feel they are not functioning healthfully go to an allopathic doctor who is likely to prescribe chemical drugs and/or surgery. There is no doubt that a growing number of surgeons are making money from an increasingly obese population. A scan of today's media will turn up a number of advertisements seeking overweight people willing to undergo stomach reduction and fat reduction surgery. The advertisements often give the impression that surgery is simple, and practically risk-free.

Anyone who knows anything about surgery knows that even simple surgeries can lead to serious complications caused by anesthesia, clotting, infection, nerve damage, and healing issues. What would be better for obese people is for them to stop eating junk food, to follow a fresh-food, plant-based diet, and to get adequate daily physical activity. Surgery can't replace those.

Not that everyone will naturally be a certain body fat percentage. Some people hold onto more weight, and some people don't. Whatever the case, it's never okay to make fun of someone's body shape, or to ridicule or bully a person in relation to their shape.

In addition to obesity, as the popularity of junk food has risen, so has the use of prescription antidepressant medications. Every year in America there are tens of millions of prescriptions written for antidepressants. In 2018, over 13% of Americans over 18 took antidepressants.

Those who experience mood swings, depression, emotional instability, and/or general fatigue would likely benefit by eliminating all unhealthful fats, fried and sautéed fats, bleached grains, processed and clarified sugars, processed salts, synthetic food chemicals, and MSG from their diet. Then, follow a plant-based diet naturally rich in antioxidants, anti-inflammatories, fiber, and other beneficial substances. While remaining on a diet free of junk while getting daily exercise and maintaining a regular sleeping pattern, they will likely experience a more stable state of mind.

I don't typically advise people to take supplements. However, to overcome depression, and especially if someone is transitioning from an unhealthful lifestyle and low-quality diet, there are certain supplements and foods that can help fuel the change toward better brain and neural function. This is why, in addition to following a plant-based diet rich in green vegetables; getting daily morning exercise; following a list of goals; and getting into a habit of positive-thinking and intentional living, I encourage those with a history of depression to research the following natural amino acids, berries, herbs, mushrooms, oils, foods, supplements, and vitamins to identify those that may be of benefit: ashwagandha herb; methylcobalamin B-12 (from vegetarian sources); chlorella (freshwater vegetable); lichen-based vitamin D-3 (vegan supplement); digestive enzymes (in vegetarian supplement form); essential fatty acids (they are in raw vegetables, fruits, berries, nuts, seeds, and water plants, [hemp seeds, germinated buckwheat and chia seeds are often mentioned as sources]); 5-hydroxytryptophan, also known as 5-HTP (in veg caps); gamma-aminobutyric acid (also known as GABA); all edible berries; hemp seeds (raw and organically grown); kelp and dulse (seaweeds); l-glutamine; lions mane mushrooms; mesquite powder; MSM powder; mucana prureins; phenylamine; pomegranate, probiotic powder (from vegan source); pumpkin seeds (raw, organic); red cabbage; sesame seeds (raw, organic); spirulina; taurine; and tyrosine. Also, consider adding a green powder to your daily intake, such as Infinity Greens.

By a plant-based diet, I mean one that consists of fruits, vegetables, and berries, sprouts, soaked raw nuts and seeds, seaweeds, and absolutely no meat, dairy, eggs, processed sugars (including corn syrup, rice syrup, and agave); processed salts; synthetic food chemicals, fried food, or MSG.

If there is anything people don't eat enough of, it is fresh fruits, berries, and vegetables – especially green leafy vegetables.

It can be especially helpful to those suffering from depression to follow a lower-fat diet, with little or no bottled oils, and few nuts. Any fat should also be raw (unheated), from plant sources, and preferably organic, such as unheated organic walnuts, hemp seeds, sesame seeds, soaked raw almonds, seeded grapes, raw pumpkin seeds, sunflower sprouts, germinated buckwheat and chia seeds, and other high-quality sources of botanical fat, including raw green vegetables (all plant cells have fat).

As I write this there are millions of people taking prescription medications for sleep, mood, and psychological disorders while they are at the same time consuming the lowest-quality foods and trying to get more energy by consuming coffee, cola, soda, and caffeinated "energy drinks." To experience better psychological health, get the diet in order while following a daily exercise regimen and regular sleep pattern.

How is society supposed to progress to a more healthful state if the brains of the people can't function at a high level because they are eating health-depleting, brain-numbing junk food, and popping prescription chemical pills at every turn of the day to control their brain function while they waste their lives staring at some form of escapism brain numbing screen nonsense they call "entertainment"?

Your body and brain run on fuel. If your brain is bogged down by useless thought processes, stagnation, and clutter, you are not going to be able to function at your highest level. With the wrong brain and body fuel you will have limited use of your power. If you follow the typical lifestyle of low-quality foods and junk media thoughts you will not be able to accomplish the goals through intentional living that you would otherwise be capable of accomplishing if you thought, exercised, ate, communicated, and participated in life better.

The brain grows in a way consistent with the quality of our thoughts and actions, communication, rest, and the nutrients in our food choices. As a person remains focused on a certain thought or action over a period of time, the brain grows more neurons in the area of the brain being used more often. What a person does, says, sees, and otherwise experiences, yearns for, and anticipates creates patterns of thoughts, which result in patterns of connections between neurons. The nerve reaction plays a role in the production of related body chemicals called molecules of emotion.

The processes involved with thoughts and actions trigger certain genes in the brain and other neurons to be turned on or off. The patterns of activities conducted among the brain's hundred billion or so neurons, including how the synaptic connections between the neurons take place within the heart (which has its own set of nerve factoring mechanisms sharing information with the brain) and throughout the body, are what we call "thinking."

While not all of your thinking can be controlled by you, a significant amount of it can be. You can think on a higher level, if you feed your brain better-quality nutrients and engage in activities that train your brain to act and respond more to your liking.

What you do, say, see, hear, smell, feel, taste, and yearn for, affects the neurons in your nerve centers: the brain, heart, intestines, stomach, brain stem, and vagal nerves. You are always either engaging already formed nerve synapses, or creating new ones.

Activity, social interaction, and intellectual stimulation are good for the nerves. Slothfulness is not. People who stare at the television, screen games, or Internet, and/or do not engage in daily activities that utilize their skills, talents, intellect, and muscles are doing their brain, heart, and other nerve centers no favors. Isolating from social, intellectual, and physical sensory stimulation atrophies you.

Vigorous exercise is beneficial to the nerve centers, because it increases the flow of information through the neurons while also increasing blood flow and releasing endorphins, which relieve stress.

Exercise works the brain to produce more cells, especially in the hippocampus region of the brain, which helps to manage retention and organization of information.

Exercise helps maintain gray matter in the brain, and protects against age-related brain degeneration.

Anxiety and psychological stress negatively affect the brain. Exercise and quality nutrition help to reduce stress and anxiety.

Physical activity along with intellectual and social stimulation engages the brain in ways that stimulates it to form new neural pathways. It also triggers the brain to release neurotrophin, which is beneficial to maintaining cellular health.

Those who want to maintain brain health would benefit by remaining active on several levels, including physically, socially, intellectually, and educationally while following a diet rich in fruits and vegetables, and free of "junk food."

Everything you do and eat has an impact on the brain. If one part of the brain is not used as often, the activities of that part of the brain will diminish, and a certain amount of atrophy will take place. Like a muscle, the brain needs activity combined with quality nutrients to stay strong and engaged.

A diet rich in raw plant matter is also rich in biophotons. These tiny fields of light play a role in cell communication. The brain is rich in photoreceptor proteins, which work as light sensors in the cells.

"Each of us has that right, that possibility, to invent ourselves daily. If a person does not invent herself, she will be invented. So, to be bodacious enough to invent ourselves is wise."
– Maya Angelou

You are continually forming new brain cells while also, through your thoughts, actions, relationships, and nutrition helping to form the way the brain is wired and rewired.

You have some control over how your brain forms. You can build neural pathways corresponding to what you do want to think, feel, do, and otherwise experience. Or you can build neural pathways corresponding to what you don't want. For these reasons, it is important to be involved with what you love – every day.

The brain and heart are connected through the vagal nerves of the parasympathetic nervous system – an involuntary network. The heart has an intrinsic nervous system which detects, factors, and sends information to the brain. Those messages impact the way we perceive, factor, feel, react to, and participate in life. Your heart has both long- and short-term memory, and tells you things. The heart is a thinking device and can trigger the production of molecules of emotion. In some matters of life, it is best to follow your heart.

# Sleeping and Arising

"Within you right now is the power to do things you never dreamed possible. This power becomes available to you just as you can change your beliefs."
– Maxwell Maltz

Considering that your brain, heart, stomach, intestines, and other nerve centers become wired in correspondence with what you think, the intentions you agree to, the words you speak, the actions you take, the relations you make, and the nutrients you consume, it is easy to understand how important it is to be engaged in doing what you want to do while following a diet of the best nutrients available to you.

To get your brain to function in tune with the life you desire, do things corresponding with what you ideally hope to be doing; teach yourself about the things you need to learn to live the life you want to have; physically do things relating to what you see yourself doing; and eliminate brain-numbing, low-quality foods from your diet.

Align yourself with what you want. Whatever it is you want to do, learn about it, and do it. Read books about it. Think about doing it. Plan on doing it. Do it mentally and physically. Doing so will develop habits of behavior and thoughts constructing physical and mental pathways, body chemistry, molecules of emotion, and energy patterns in tune with the life you want to have.

"Finish each day and be done with it. You have done what you could. Some blunders and absurdities no doubt crept in; forget them

as soon as you can. Tomorrow is a new day, you shall begin it well and serenely, and with too high a spirit to be encumbered with your old nonsense."
 – Ralph Waldo Emerson

"When you arise in the morning, think of what a privilege it is to be alive: to breathe, to think, to enjoy, to love."
 – Marcus Aurelius

Two things you can do to help manifest your goals is to introduce thoughts and learning processes into your mind at the two times of day that highly influence your existence. They are: in the morning when you awake, and at night before you sleep.

Adjusting your mind by guiding your thoughts and energy just before and after sleep will help steer your life in the direction you want to go. These are the two times each day when your mind is in the alpha-wave zone. It is when your mind is open to suggestion and motivation. It is when your mind can be tuned in a way helping you to continue your thought processes toward attaining your goals. It is the time to plug into your power and get your gears moving in the desired direction.

"There are only two ways to live your life. One is as though nothing is a miracle. The other is as though everything is a miracle."
 – Albert Einstein

Saturate your mind with that which is aligned with the life you want.

Upon awakening, spend time engaged in reading, studying, writing, drawing, or otherwise thinking about things that inspire you to attain your goals. Exercise as you focus on the intentions. Continue the intention through daily actions, communication, and choices.

"The secret of discipline is motivation. When a man is sufficiently motivated, discipline will take care of itself."
 – Alexander Paterson

Keep your list of goals and priorities near your bed so you can review them every morning. This is a tool in getting you to create the life you want. It will help tune your mind and heart and nerve energy to it.

"There is between sleep and us something like a pact, a treaty with no secret clauses, and according to this convention it is agreed that, far from being a dangerous, bewitching force, sleep will become

domesticated and serve as an instrument of our power to act. We surrender to sleep, but in the way that the master entrusts himself to the slave who serves him."
– Maurice Blanchot

About one-third of your life is spent sleeping. High-quality sleep is important in maintaining vibrant health, balancing the hormones, raising growth hormone levels, resting the adrenal glands, stress relief, and in improving and maintaining focus.

One thing that happens during healthful sleep is the occurrence of rapid eye movement (REM). Before and during REM the system experiences ponto-geniculo-occipital (PGO) spikes. During these REM/PGO phases the brain and body produce chemicals that counteract or work in alignment with and balance other chemicals the body has produced in sync with what has been experienced while awake. In other words, everything you experience, whether you are awake or asleep, produces some sort of chemical reaction in the cells throughout your body.

Sleep helps you produce chemicals that balance your chemistry, including hormones, blood sugar, digestive enzymes, and neurotransmitters, and these all factor into your mood, focus, stamina, strength, and immune function.

Diet, exercise, and what you do with your time, energy, intellect, and talents are also important parts of the body chemistry equation.

During sleep, and whether a person remembers or not, dreaming happens – and especially during the REM/PGO phase of sleep – which is when the most vivid dreams may occur.

Dreams can help a person deal with unmet expectations, often through metaphorical imagery and thought patterns, helping to relieve stress and pent-up thoughts. The brain is always active in factoring solutions, including during sleep.

During sleep, the neural pathways go through testing patterns, and develop connections in tune with what people need for how they are choosing to spend their time and energy, and in how they are deciding to express their thoughts, talents, intellect, and desires.

When a person does not get high-quality sleep, there is a buildup of stress and anxiety, which impacts health. Both sleep and exercise help relieve stress. Vigorous exercise helps a person sleep better, and good quality sleep helps the body and brain perform.

Sleep, exercise, and diet all impact the function of the digestive tract, which is where many neurotransmitter chemicals are produced.

The neurotransmitters are needed for a healthful nerve system, including within the brain, brain stem, heart, stomach, and intestines.

It has been found that children who sleep in dark rooms sleep better, experience fewer mood swings, and get better grades. Sleeping in the dark also helps maintain healthful neural growth in the brain. This is one reason why babies born prematurely have dark eye masks put on them. Their brain development benefits from the darkness. At all ages, sleeping in a dark room – or with the eyes covered – also helps to maintain healthful hormone levels.

The sensors within the eyes are light sensitive and play a role in controlling the body's internal clock. About two percent of the cells in the retina contain sensors that detect the presence and level of light. The molecule in the sensors is called a melanopsin. This molecule is active even in the eyes of those who have lost their vision. This is why sleeping in a dark room is also beneficial for blind people.

Billions of dollars are spent every year on sleep aid medications. This reveals that many people are searching for better sleep.

Rather than drugs, there are other ways of getting better sleep.

Avoiding coffee and caffeinated and stimulating drinks is key to better sleep. Also, not eating for at least a few hours before sleep will allow the body to close down for the night and relax. Chocolate, spicy foods, and fried and sautéed foods interfere with sleep.

Foods containing tyramine inhibit the body's natural neurochemicals, such as norepinephrine, and cause restless sleep or insomnia. These foods include bacon, cheese, chocolate, ham, potatoes, tomatoes, and sausage. For better sleep, eliminate all fried food, sautéed food, meat, colas, and processed chocolate from the diet.

Even raw, organic, vegan, natural chocolate can interfere with sleep.

If people are seeking the antioxidants and other nutrients in raw chocolate, it would be helpful to consume it early in the day. While some people tend to eat an abundance of chocolate, I tend to stay away from it – because it makes my heart race and interferes with sleep. But I'm not pure, and do randomly eat some chocolate. I have found that carob is an excellent replacement for chocolate. While chocolate is stimulating, carob is calming – and also contains its own spectrum of nutrients.

One of the many things sleep does is balance the body's level of leptin, a hormone that plays a role in signaling the brain when you have eaten enough. Those who get quality sleep have been found to be of a more healthful weight. Being a healthful weight plays a part in all levels of wellbeing, including cardiovascular, kidney, lung, bone and joint health, and healthful levels of blood sugar and hormones.

Those who typically sleep during the day, such as people who work at jobs requiring them to be awake during the dark hours, benefit from sleeping in a darkened room or wearing a dark eye mask to block light from their eyes.

One of the best things you can do for yourself is to create a sleeping environment that is pleasant, restful, organized, and clean. This is because what you are doing when you are in rest helps to determine what you will be doing when you are in motion.

Consider keeping a potted plant in your bedroom, such as mothers-in-law tongue, which is a plant that produces oxygen at night, and absorbs our exhaled gasses. Other houseplants, including the money tree plant, provide healthful air in the bedroom while absorbing pollutants. These plants will do better if they are exposed to outside air and sunlight. Rotating them outside and inside every few days so they have some exposure to sun can help them grow.

"Keep the peace within yourself. Then you can also bring peace to others."
– Thomas A. Kempis

Pay attention to what things you put into your mind before you sleep.

Visualization before sleep helps guide your dreams. It can be a powerful tool in accelerating the accomplishment of your goals. But at night, be sure to be calming and assuring rather than motivating and enlivening. Serenely drift into sleep with confidence that you are capable of obtaining the life you envision.

You can guide your sleep into calmness by thinking pleasant thoughts and imagery as you drift into sleep.

"Music washes away from the soul the dust of everyday life."
– Berthold Auerbach

If any music is listened to before, during, or immediately after sleep choose what is pleasant, and kind.

"Joy, sorrow, tears, lamentation, laughter – to all these music gives voice, but in such a way that we are transported from the world of unrest to a world of peace, and see reality in a new way, as if we were sitting by a mountain lake and contemplating hills and woods and clouds in the tranquil and fathomless water."
– Albert Schweitzer

Avoid waking to loud, frantic sounds; to commercials; to the crass and exploitative attitudes often expressed on talk radio; and to news that immediately introduces your waking mind to negative stories that project fear and worry – which is often done by the commercial media for someone's political and/or financial gain.

"Music has the capacity to touch the innermost reaches of the soul and music gives flight to the imagination."
– Plato

The music you wake to, the thoughts you choose to have when you awake, your movements upon awaking, and the information you take in during the beginning of your day help tune your thoughts and energy patterns for the rest of the day. Bring it on stronger by reading things that inspire you, writing an intention that motivates you, writing a declaration for the day, exercising to tone you and balance body chemistry, and eating foods that nurture you at the highest level (or, get into skipping breakfast and continuing your nighttime fast, ingesting nothing but water until mid-day).

"Take the breath of the new dawn and make it part of you. It will give you strength."
– Hopi saying

Out of all the things you take on every morning, your attitude is the most important.

The attitude you carry throughout the day can be established by what you tune your thoughts into during your waking moments.

"Today is the tomorrow that you worried about yesterday."
– Dale Carnegie

Take a bit of time each morning to settle, meditate, and tune into the energy of your spirit. A good way to do this is by starting your day with meditative and intentional stretching, calisthenics, yoga, and things like cord exercises, and bo staff spinning.

Watching the way an animal awakens can be interesting. Take for instance the typical house pet, a cat or dog. When these animals awaken, they often take a few moments to stretch their limbs in a way resembling yoga poses. Awaking is a whole body experience. Do it gently and intentionally – taking time to feel the stretch, and to feel your muscles, joints, and body tissues awaken.

"Make friends with your shower. If inspired to sing, maybe the song has an idea in it for you."
– Albert Einstein

396

After waking, take a few moments to review your list of priorities. This will help you tune your mind, and will place purpose and intention into the actions, communication, and choices of the day. Make a separate list of things you want to accomplish that day. This way you will give your day a purpose with goals you intend to achieve, before you return to bed at the end of the day.

"Give to us clear vision that we may know where to stand and what to stand for – because unless we stand for something, we shall fall for anything."
– Peter Marshall

To further empower your intention, sometime during each morning write a short one-sentence, empowering, intentional belief statement or declaration. It doesn't matter if it is nearly the same as the statement you wrote the previous day, of for many days in-a-row. The goal is to keep your mind and actions focused on your intentions of creating the life you want through helpful actions and communication.

"Compose yourself in stillness, draw your attention inward and devote your mind to the Self. The wisdom you seek lies within."
– Bhagavad Gita

Be determined to awaken and start your day on a positive note. Begin by thinking and saying words that uplift, encourage good, and build belief in your talents, skills, and intellect. Tune into the positive energy of love and choose to keep it with you throughout the day.

Focus on uplifting not only your mind through positive thoughts and actions, but also those around you through encouragement, compliments, and words that uplift and build confidence – rather than those that discourage, degrade, belittle, bully, doubt, criticize, slander, and deconstruct.

By choosing to align with and keeping in a positive groove you will spread good energy. It may be rejected by some, but that is their decision to accept it or reject it – just as it is your choice to focus either on the positive or the negative.

It is up to you to live a better life.

Today and every day you can position yourself closer to where you wish to be.

In all of your actions each day, make it a habit to strive in bringing your life closer to a sustainable, healthful existence.

"Each day comes bearing its own gifts. Untie the ribbons."
– Ruth Ann Schabacker

# Dreaming

"A man's dreams are an index to his greatness."
– Zadok Rabinowitz

Sleep is equally as important to brain health as physical activity, nutrition, intellectual stimulation, and social interaction.

On many levels, sleep is important for the health of all body tissues, including by providing time to rest the digestive tract, where many mood chemicals form. Sleep is also the time for the body and brain to regroup and recharge. With the body at rest, it can tend to the processes of repair and cleaning, including by releasing toxins from the cell structures and intercellular pathways.

"Dreams are the touchstones of our character."
– Henry David Thoreau

As you sleep, you dream. Your mind is used during dreams, and is tuned by them.

The thought-related chemicals your body produces when you are awake do not stop when you are asleep. The chemicals keep sharing information, including that which deals with feelings you are experiencing in your dreams. In this way, dreams can be quite real for you in that you physically experience them as your body chemistry responds to the dreams. It is why an intense dream can make you sweat, lose your breath, and feel panic related to molecular changes.

Your communication system is involved with your dreams. The difference between when you are awake and when you are asleep is that different levels of chemicals are being produced, and maybe at more healthful levels than when you are awake.

Perhaps sleep also helps you to organize and file thoughts and memories into a more manageable arrangement while rewiring the brain to deal with things according to what you are focusing on in your life.

During sleep the neural pathways of the brain seem to go through testing patterns, rewiring, and reparation. This brings us to dream of things from the past and present, and often mixing these into some sort of random story strung across our yearning and other feelings, thus the theatre of dreaming reflects our past and present, our imagination, creativity, hopes, fantasy, and reality, and our spiritual, physical, and sexual nature.

"Dreams digest the meals that are our days."
— Astrid Alauda

"Let's not forget that the little emotions are the great captains of our lives and we obey them without realizing it."
— Vincent Van Gogh

Because your body can store emotional energy from various experiences you have had, some of what you are experiencing in your dreams may replicate the emotions from past experiences and expectations being released. This is why some dreams can be as intense as when you originally experienced the events in your awake life – possibly even more intensely.

"A dream is a microscope through which we look at the hidden occurrences in our soul."
— Erich Fromm

"Yet it is in our idleness, in our dreams, that the submerged truth sometimes comes to the top."
— Virginia Woolf

Paying attention to your dreams might help you to heal.

Just as talk or art therapy can help you to release pent-up thoughts from life situations and deal with those situations, just as sex can help you to release built-up sexual emotions and develop a close and healthful relationship, and just as exercise can help you to release stress emotions and build a stronger body, dreams may help you to release clogged emotions that can play a part in your situations, relationships, ailments, healing, and motives.

Your soul writes in dreams. Without being fanatical about it, write down some of your sleep dreams. Describe some of the colors, textures, and tonal qualities of things you saw in your dreams – as well as the feelings you had during the dreams. There may be a message in there for you. It may not be something you can fully – or even partially – interpret for many years. The longer you maintain the habit of writing down your dreams, the better you may become at understanding the language of your dreams.

"Judge of your natural character by what you do in your dreams."
– Ralph Waldo Emerson

"Dreams are illustrations from the book your soul is writing about you."
– Marsha Norman

The study and interpretation of dreams and what humans may learn from them is ancient practice.

Dreams have influenced all areas of human expression, including the artistic expressions of dance, storytelling, theatre, writing, music, painting, drawing, film, and structural arts. Religious writings often mention dreams. Dreams and the fantasies and concepts springing from them help sculpt our lives, community, and culture.

Because of what is going on with your brain during sleep, it is healthful to end your day by reading a calming book, drawing a picture, writing an intentional statement, listening to gentle music, doing mild yoga, and kindly loving who you are with.

Some people will wake in the middle of the night and watch trash TV, doom scroll on social media, play video games, fall down the internet slime hole, and/or listen to crass talk radio. If you engage in activities when you awake in the middle of the night, work on accruing information that is more in tune with what you want in your life – instead of the people and characters on TV, the net, and radio that are representative of society's ills, and what you do not want.

Don't underestimate the importance of a healthful and regular sleeping pattern. Regular sleep is key to restoring, maintaining, and building a healthful brain. Sleep also helps preserve the health of all body tissues, regulates hormones and body chemistry, and balances the emotions and blood sugars.

As mentioned, when combined with a life of intention to create the satisfaction you want, quality sleep is as important as diet and exercise in maintaining vibrant health.

"Dreams pass into the reality of action. From the actions stems the dream again; and this interdependence produces the highest form of living."
– Anais Nin

While I was writing this chapter, I considered what the dreams of animals might be. It is obvious that cats, dogs, and horses dream – because they often physically engage or get fidgety while they sleep. I wondered what other animals dream about, including those living far out in the wild. As I considered what bugs and insects dream about, I wondered what butterflies dream about. Later that day, I found this quotation:

"I dreamed I was a butterfly, flitting around in the sky; then I awoke. Now I wonder: Am I a man who dreamt of being a butterfly, or am I a butterfly dreaming that I am a man?"
– Zhuangzi

Perhaps your awake life is just as important to your sleep life in revealing and creating what and who you are, and how you will present and express yourself, and experience and participate in life.

"Sleep is the single most effective thing we can do to rest our brain and physical health each day. Atop of sleep, dreaming provides essential emotional first aid, and a unique form of informational alchemy. If we wish to be as healthy, happy, and creative as possible, these are facts well worthy waking up to.
– Matthew Walker

There are many interesting studies and books about sleep.
Matthew Walker's book *Why We Sleep: Unlocking the Power of Sleep and Dreams* might be of interest. He's a Professor of Neuroscience at UC Berkeley.

"Evidence points toward an important function of dreams: to help us take the sting out of our painful emotional experiences during the hours we are asleep, so that we can learn from them and carry on with our lives."
– Matthew Walker

# Exercise

"I find, by experience, that the mind and the body are more than married, for they are most intimately united; and when one suffers, the other sympathizes."
– Philip Dormer Stanhope

Movement plays a part in health. Similar to thoughts, food, and relationships, and even entertainment, movement can also be healing or damaging.

"Take care of your body. It's the only place you have to live."
– E. James Rohn

Ailments are often related to bad diet, stressful working and living conditions, unhealthful relationships, lack of love, substance abuse, a history of neglect, abuse, assault, ridicule, belittlement, belligerent cynicism, and destructive patterns of thought.

Illness can also be attributed to insufficient exercise, which results in pent-up, unreleased energy and stress working against the person. Lack of movement and exercise also plays a role in the accumulation of toxins and plaque in the tissues, muscle atrophy, decreased lung and cardiovascular capacity, imbalanced hormone and blood sugar levels, and increased fat. Those degenerate the body.

Reasons it is good to exercise every morning include because it creates a pattern of releasing stress, and it improves brain, heart, lung, kidney, and other organ function, and balances chemistry. Combined with a healthy, plant-based diet, exercise helps the tissues to become less acidic, more alkaline, less inflamed, and more attuned to experiencing health, which is in tune with happiness and satisfaction.

"The body is a sacred garment. It's your first and last garment; it is what you enter life in, and what you depart life with – and it should be treated with honor."
– Martha Graham

Take care of your physical structure by getting daily exercise, such as swimming, running, biking, or doing yoga, calisthenics, cord exercises, sports, and outside activities – and working with skills that require physical activity that also engages the mind.

Daily exercise is essential to maintaining the health of body, mind, and spirit. It helps to maintain the health of the various systems, from the blood, lymph, hormonal, and immune systems to the brain, digestive organs, bones, muscles, tendons, skin, and heart. It also improves sleep.

"Take care of your body with steadfast fidelity. The soul must see through these eyes alone, and if they are dim, the whole world is clouded."
– Johann Wolfgang von Goethe

A 1986 study conducted by Ralph S. Paffenbarger at the Stanford University School of Medicine is often mentioned as key to proving that exercise boosts longevity. Paffenbarger's College Alumni Health Study tracked the exercise patterns of 52,000 men who attended Harvard and the University of Pennsylvania between 1916 and 1950. His study found that those who exercised vigorously lived longer and experienced better health than those who did not engage in regular exercise. Those who did not engage in exercise had a higher incidence of heart disease, and what are considered to be age-related disorders. The study has been used to form guidelines issued by both the Centers for Disease Control and Prevention, and the American College of Sports Medicine. While Paffenbarger was conducting the study, he took up jogging at the age of 45 because he recognized that exercise produces health benefits at any age. He went on to run the Boston Marathon 22 times, and participated in 150 marathons.

"The body is the soul's house. Shouldn't we therefore take care of our house so that it doesn't fall into ruin?"
– Philo Judaeus

It has been shown that those who exercise regularly have a clearer memory, a higher level of attention, have better decision-making and learning abilities, and are better at multitasking. They are less likely to experience depression, are more likely to be of a healthful body weight, are more likely to have a strong immune system, and are more likely to have healthful lung, brain, and neural function, and balanced hormones.

Getting daily exercise induces positive physical feelings that work in conjunction with positive thoughts.

Exercise increases the neurotransmitters serotonin, epinephrine, and dopamine, helping to maintain a brighter outlook on life.

Being physically fit increases the likelihood of experiencing elation, euphoria, exhilaration, delight, and bliss.

"You cannot devalue the body and value the soul – or value anything else. The isolation of the body sets it into direct conflict with everything else in creation."
– Wendell Berry

Those who exercise regularly have healthier tissues in every area of the body. Exercise helps both blood vessel and neuron growth (neurogenesis) within the brain because it boosts growth chemicals that nurture new nerve cells. Exercise also helps the brain to work more efficiently and adapt to both mental challenges and new experiences.

Health professionals continually promote daily exercise, discourage overeating, advocate intellectual stimulation, and encourage people to deal with their daily stress by working to better manage and organize their days, improve their relationships, follow a plant-based diet, and get adequate sleep. This is because a large number of people do eat too much, don't eat enough fruits or vegetables, don't get enough exercise, and don't face their problems.

Managing your life involves not only eating healthfully, but also dealing with those four issues: movement, quality caloric intake equal to need, stress relief, and healthful sleep.

"If exercise could be packaged into a pill, it would be the single most prescribed and beneficial medicine in the nation."
– Robert Butler, M.D.

Not only does exercise help you to relieve stress, it also allows your mind to free itself and to concentrate on attaining workout goals – to run the extra mile, practice longer, bike or paddle at a brisker pace, swim more laps, or to move with the yoga pose more intentionally and in tune with the breath. This focus on goals during exercise trains your mind into attaining goals in your daily life.

For those who are less physically active, working in a garden can do some of the same things as exercise, because gardening involves both physical movement and the attainment of goals. That is, goals to maintain and build a garden that produces in abundance.

Other benefits of exercise are that it works the physical system, increases the heart rate, triggers faster and deeper breathing, helps detoxify the system, and strengthens muscles and neural connections throughout the body while improving cellular function and the production of a variety of healthful body chemicals.

When you are breathing deeply your lungs are moving the digestive organs in a way similar to giving them a massage. This assists the organs in releasing sediment, waste, and plaque.

The deeper breathing happening during exercise helps you to lose weight. This situation was clarified by Australian researchers Andrew Brown and Ruben Meerman of the University of New South Wales.

Largely, weight loss happens by way of exhaled carbon dioxide and water vapor. Through the process of oxidation, fats break down into the atoms carbon, hydrogen, and oxygen. Breathing in oxygen helps to oxidize the fats. The oxidation process produces more carbon dioxide than it does water. The carbon dioxide and some of that water leaves the body through the lungs. Additional weight is lost as water by way of sweat, urine, and feces.

The increased heart rate during exercise improves the flow of nutrients traveling through the tissues, while helping to collect and release waste products from the system.

The rise in body temperature experienced during exercise helps to detox the system through sweat, and through the need and ingestion of water to replace the water that is lost – thus helping to flush out toxins and waste products.

When you get regular exercise you are releasing stressful, acidic tensions from your system while strengthening bones and muscles – including the heart.

An alkaline diet prevents acidic conditions.

Meat, milk, and eggs promote an acidic condition. This weakens bones because it triggers the formation of osteoclast cells, which remove calcium from the bones to make the blood more alkaline. This increases the likelihood of experiencing osteoporosis, a condition involving weakened bones subject to fracture. Osteoporosis is often what causes decreased height and a humped, bent-over back to form in older age.

A plant-based diet rich in unprocessed fruits, vegetables, and seaweeds promotes an alkaline condition, which strengthens bones

405

because it triggers the production of osteoblasts, which are cells involved in bone growth and strengthening, this also improves the blood.

A plant-based diet is specifically helpful to the kidneys, which play a role in the production of red blood cells. The kidneys produce the erythropoietin (EPO) hormone, which works as a chemical messenger triggering the bone marrow to produce red blood cells. This is something I learned from the various doctors I have had to deal with in relation to being born with malformed, defective kidneys.

People with malfunctioning kidneys are prone to being anemic.

To help avoid experiencing anemia, please, follow a plant-based diet – which will help your kidney function. (See my book *Plant-based Regenerative Nutrition.*)

While I've been following a vegan diet for more than half of my life, it has only been in the past several years that the kidney doctors have also been telling me to follow a plant-based/vegan diet. They are always pleasantly impressed to learn how long I have been following a vegan diet. They say it is what has kept me alive with functioning kidneys, without undergoing a kidney transplant.

The combination of following a plant-based alkaline diet rich in green vegetables, along with a daily exercise routine, will tune your body and brain in ways benefitting other areas of your life. More about this in the next chapter.

When maintaining a regular exercise schedule with an alkaline diet, you will notice differences in your body, mood, energy, posture, confidence, relationships, and in how you approach tasks, and life in general.

The advantages you will experience when you improve your levels of nutrition and fitness will prove that it is up to you to improve your life. This philosophy will carry over to how you address other issues in your life that are in need of attention.

# The Most Natural Diet

Humans experience more diseases than their nonhuman counterparts. More and more humans also eat a diet that is more diverse and far removed from the natural diets of animals living in the wild. Consider the connection.

Many have compared the products sold in supermarkets and restaurants as being equivalent to garbage. The products are so processed, preserved, and with saturated with synthetic chemicals that they say the foods are "plasticized."

When nutrient requirements are taken into consideration, what is being sold as food is not quite food, but filler. It might fill the stomach, but quality nutrition simply is not in many commercialized "foods" – while health-damaging substances are.

Regionally, humans who follow a certain diet experience health conditions at rates not seen in areas where that type of diet is not followed. Those living in regions where meat and dairy consumption are highest also experience the most elevated rates of heart disease, heart attacks, strokes, colon cancer, arthritis, diabetes, osteoporosis, certain types of kidney disease, and other chronic and degenerative maladies at rates not experienced among people living in areas of the world where meat and dairy consumption is lowest.

People in North America who consume the most meat are also more likely to consume the most pasteurized dairy, synthetic food chemicals, fried foods, oil extracts, and processed foods, and the most corn syrup and other clarified sugars. These are the same people who are most likely to eat junk food, to be obese, and to experience conditions common among those in similar situations.

This isn't meant to body shame, which is cruel. You never know what someone has gone through in life – including what sorts of health problems and life trials they have experienced. Mean, rude, invasive comments about appearance are not acceptable.

"To eat is a necessity, but to eat intelligently is an art."
– François de la Rochefoucauld

When choosing a low-fat diet rich in raw fruits and vegetables, you are likely to experience health in relation to that nourishing diet. If you previously followed a horrible diet, and switched to a clean, unprocessed, plant-based, low-fat diet free of processed, clarified, and chemical ingredients, and free of highly heated oils, your health can go through profound improvement.

As you change your life and become different from what you used to be, you may find yourself getting attention you had not been accustomed to receiving.

When people are accustomed to seeing you maintain a certain lifestyle and appear a certain way, and they then see you have physically transformed, they also may feel uncomfortable. You will be breaking from the role you had been playing. People will have to re-cast you in their mind as no longer being the person they thought you were – and perhaps the person they thought you could never be.

Completely changing your diet to the most healthful way available to you – especially one rich in raw fruits and vegetables, and free of junk – will make a huge difference in your life. When provided with high-quality nutrition, the body will change to a state in tune with those nutrients. It is even better with daily exercise.

The body has the power to heal, to detoxify the cells, to reform the tissues, and to reconfigure the shape of the organs. Providing the body with a clean diet rich in vibrant, raw fruits and vegetables can fuel the power.

"You can't turn back the clock. But you can wind it up again."
– Bonnie Prudden

When you become more healthful, people notice. Your skin, shape, and movement change. Your confidence and energy improve. It is then that people may be interested in what you had been doing to change.

Those who are used to experiencing health problems, and who then switch to a clean, unprocessed vegan diet can undergo such a change in health that they will need to reconsider the medications and other "medical" treatments they might have been undergoing. Their blood pressure, cholesterol, and blood sugar levels will improve. Their weight likely will change. If they had been taking prescription drugs, their medical provider will have to be informed. It is likely that medications will need to be adjusted, or halted.

As you follow a fresh food diet your health and life will change. This is especially true if you had been eating devitalized, deadening, fried, and otherwise processed foods. Opportunities will arise you may never have considered. Things will happen that you didn't think were a possibility, and even not in your concept of how things could happen. You will feel and think differently from the way you had been. Perceptions will change, and senses and nerves will enliven. Foods, music, and designs may seem different to you. Activities in which you had never thought of participating in may draw your attention. The way you eat, dress, think, and play, and the general way you participate in life may go through radical changes. The higher frequency you tune into by eating more vibrant foods can ignite your passions in intense ways you never considered possible.

**"Through our soul is our contact with heaven."**
– Sholem Asch

The power of your being is what formulated your tissues and is what animates you. It is making you think. It is making your heart beat and your lungs breathe. It is making your cells function. It is what is making you want and seek opportunities to express your desires. It is pushing you to constantly work out your yearning into actions. You can make it work for you. It is your power source. Honor it with self-respect, helpful actions, healthful communication, exercise, and a clean diet rich in vibrant fruits and vegetables.

**"The brain gives the heart its sight. The heart gives the brain its vision."**
– Rob Kall

When you follow a clean, balanced diet, like the rest of your organs and tissues, the pineal gland, which is located at the center of your brain, functions at a higher level, as does your heart and brain.

Cells of the pineal gland resemble the photoreceptor cells in the eyes. A low-quality diet leads to degeneration of the eyes. Similarly, a low-quality diet degrades the function of the pineal gland.

Early French philosopher and scientist René Descartes called the pineal gland *the seat of the soul*.

While the cells of the eyes allow you to see and interact with structures, it is said that the cells of the pineal gland allow you to interact with spirit, inspiration, energy, and what motivates you in your yearning and visualizations. For these reasons, the pineal gland is often referred to as *the third eye*.

The pineal gland is not walled off behind the blood brain barrier. It receives large amounts of blood, and is connected to the function and feelings of the heart.

"When you start using senses you neglected, your reward is to see the world with completely fresh eyes."
– Barbara Sher

A healthful diet and daily exercise will assist your intestines, liver, kidneys, lungs, heart, brain, and other organs, and the pineal gland to function at a higher level. It will improve your immune system, lymph system, digestive system, nerve system, and blood system. It will help the rest of your life function at an elevated level.

Do not pollute your body and brain with low-quality and junk foods. Pretty much any food that is advertised is likely processed, and not of the nutrient-rich, health-infusing, highly vibrant quality you want or need.

Learn about making foods from scratch. One good source of recipes for healthful, low-fat, plant-based meals is the site ForksOverKnives.com.

To learn the science behind plant-based nutrition, read the articles and watch the videos on NutritionFacts.org.

Do not eat deadened or otherwise processed and junk foods. They dull you, lower your frequency, and leave residues of toxins in your tissues, clogging your system, slowing you, and paving the way for disease.

Follow a diet of high-quality foods that enliven your body, bring about the vibrant beauty of health, and improve your focus, energy, and level of consciousness.

Partake in the living power of Nature contained in vibrantly alive, organic fruits, vegetables, sprouts, seeds, and seaweeds.

Let a clean diet help to ignite your health, passions, intellect, talents, confidence, and love.

See my book *Plant-based Regenerative Nutrition*.

"And the time came when the risk to remain tight in a bud was more painful than the risk it took to blossom."
– Anais Nin

# State of Your Being

"The pursuit of truth and beauty is a sphere of activity in which we are permitted to remain children all our lives."
– Albert Einstein

"Now I truly believe that we in this generation must come to terms with Nature, and I think we are challenged, as mankind has never been challenged before, to prove our maturity and our mastery, not of Nature but of ourselves."
– Rachel Carson

Your thoughts lead to actions and communication creating an atmosphere influenced by what it is you have been thinking.

As you think in a way that is respectful and compassionate of life, you likely will be more of the same for your life. You will place more value in the person you truly are, including your intellect, instinct, talents, skills, and other qualities. Bring your state of being into one that uses them, experiences them, and benefits from them.

Do what it takes to live a full life, in whatever way that means for you, without comparing yourself to – or competing with – others.

"Our culture has become hooked on the quick-fix, the life hack, efficiency. Everyone is on the hunt for that simple action algorithm that nets maximum profit with the least amount of effort. There's no denying this attitude may get you some of the trappings of success, if you're lucky, but it will not lead to a calloused mind or self-mastery."
– David Goggins

When you participate in life while using your better qualities, you are likely to attract and interact with others aligned with the energy you conduct through your mind, words, and actions.

Be willing to be vulnerable, to live, to allow yourself to love, and to free yourself of that which has disallowed you from living your life the way you wish.

In their quest to feel better, many people get lost in the escapism of drugs. What they may not realize is the drug may be bringing out something they already have, a mind capable of working in a way that makes them feel and live better in alignment with their liking. There are ways to work through their blockages so that they can experience the splendor of life they are trying to discover through drugs.

It isn't only street drugs people seek in a quest to feel better. Consider that in 2006 there was an average of more than one new corporate pharmacy opening in the U.S. every day. There was a slowdown, but more pharmacies continued to open. From 2017 to 2020, over 1,000 new pharmacies opened, for a total of 27,561. The figure does not take into account the number of pharmacies within hospitals and large care facilities, or prescriptions filled through Internet pharmacies. This provides an idea of how many people are taking prescription drugs to try to improve or maintain some aspect of their health. A large number of these very same people are consuming low-quality foods that dull and damage health. In the same way, people consuming harsh street drugs are leading themselves to experience less vibrant health, and often horrible health problems.

Many of the so-called "legal" drugs are used in an attempt to feel better. Instead of improving their diet and relationships, and getting into the practice of daily exercise, regular sleeping patterns, and goal-oriented living in which they use their intellect and talent, they rely on some form of mass-marketed chemical drug in an attempt to feel better. It's a fantastic situation – for pharmaceutical company profits.

A large number of the drugs people take have to do with trying to get to a more comfortable state of mind. Their lives are so off-kilter that they think pills will be some sort of answer to their problems. Pills will offer a type of answer for some. But there is a possibility that many are also cheating themselves by not changing their diet, and improving their activities and lifestyle to experience better health.

The body naturally creates consciousness-altering substances. These self-produced, natural psychoactive drugs are manufactured within the cells of the brain and body. Perhaps the most commonly known of these substances is the endorphin peptide that produces the "runner's high" people experience when they regularly exercise.

These chemicals produced within the tissues of a healthful person are called _endogenous drugs_. When these are produced, they are received on the receptors of cell membranes, altering the function of the cells. This happens both in the brain and throughout the body, and it involves many millions of chemical reactions throughout the brain, heart, intestines, and other areas of body – every split second.

The type of reaction endogenous drugs produce can occur when a person takes street or prescription drugs, which are _exogenous drugs_. The synthetic drugs are treated by the body in much the same manner as the drugs the body naturally produces. The drug molecules bind with the receptors on cell membranes.

Over time, the body system can be weakened and damaged by synthetic drugs as they compete for receptors with which the body's own chemicals dock. When there is an overabundance of chemicals that dock with the cell membrane receptors, the cells may start to produce fewer receptors. The opposite may also be true, wherein the body cells start to produce more receptors to deal with the onslaught of chemicals. Either of these situations can throw the body out of balance – especially when a synthetic drug prevents the body from producing chemicals that naturally dock with cell receptors that also connect with the synthetic chemicals. Addictions and body tissue damage can occur, including in the brain, brain stem, organs, and within all parts of the body. Use of certain drugs can result in organ malfunction, and organ failure, and death.

The longer a former drug abuser stays away from the substance and follows a healthful diet and exercise regimen and sleep pattern combined with goal-oriented living while working to have healthful relationships, the better their health will be. As the person stops taking the drugs and lives more healthfully, the liver begins to produce a healthful amount of enzymes, and the person's physical and psychological/emotional health improves. Depending on the level of abuse and addiction experienced, it can take some time for the cell structures throughout the body to come back into balance with producing a healthful amount of receptors and peptides.

If you are a person with a history of drug abuse, I encourage you to follow a plant-based diet that is free of fried and sautéed oils, bleached grains, processed salt, white sugar, corn syrup, rice syrup, agave, and other processed sugars, and that is completely free of MSG, and artificial dyes, flavors, scents, and sweeteners. Follow a diet containing an abundance and variety of fresh, unheated green vegetables along with raw fruits, sprouts, and some seaweeds. Look into the benefits of soaking things like raw beans, nuts, rices, quinoa, and even oats, before cooking. Soaking improves nutrition, and reduces allergens and inflammatories. Where possible, grow some of your own food, and/or get your food from farmers' markets, regional organic farms, and natural foods stores. Follow more of a low-fat, organic, whole foods diet. Get regular daily exercise, especially at the start of your day. Work to stimulate your mind with study, literature, and music, and by practicing your talent and craft. The goal is to function completely without the drug stimulation, and allow the body's natural chemistry to come into play.

While some people randomly use drugs for recreational or personal discovery purposes (see pages 183-184), other people take and abuse mind-altering substances to deal with issues or situations they otherwise don't feel they can deal with. These emotions may involve trauma, unhealed relationships, anger, fear, disgust, frustration, sadness, regret, and other factors. In other words, drugs can help us to ignore our feelings, remain in denial, fool us, dull us, weaken us, and halt personal progression and healing.

"The feelings that hurt most, the emotions that sting most, are those that are absurd – the longing for impossible things, precisely because they are impossible; nostalgia for what never was; the desire for what could have been; regret over not being someone else; dissatisfaction with the world's existence."
– Fernando Pessoa

What would be beneficial is for people to stop ingesting artificial food and damaging drugs, and to eat a more natural, plant-based diet while getting in shape so their bodies and brains function better. When your body and brain function better, so too does your life.

It is amazing how much sedation is going on among people in Western society. Many millions of people are taking sedatives their doctors claim will help them. They feel eager or anxious, unable to suppress their urge for something they can't define. Their body is trying to tell them something, trying to get a message across. But instead of working through and discovering what the message is, they suppress it by using some sort of drug from which pharmaceutical companies are making millions and billions by selling them through drug businesses we call "the drug store."

"We have become so drug-oriented, that the idea of changing anything just through diet is kind of preposterous to a lot of people. It's almost like old medicine, like a witch doctor."
– Morgan Spurlock

Doctors often prescribe medications without sufficient information on patient health, and without knowing what other drugs a patient may be taking that could counteract the prescription drug, or may interact with another drug the patient is taking – which might cause the patient to suffer long-term, or even grave consequences. We also don't know how many of these prescription drugs react with the variety of synthetic chemicals found in mass-marketed foods, or when those chemicals are combined and heated in cooking processes.

When a person goes to a pharmacy to have a prescription filled, the person they deal with may be an employee with no formal medical training and who may be as young as 16. There is an ongoing problem of misfiled prescriptions resulting in patient injuries, which have led to overdoses, comas, strokes, and deaths.

Prescription drugs carry serious risks – even when taken as directed. Thousands of patients die or suffer horrible consequences after being misdiagnosed, or after taking misprescribed drugs, or a mix of conflicting medications. Many more die or are left disabled by surgeries that should never have taken place.

One clue to the level of health wisdom contained in a typical pharmacy is on the shelves. In the U.S., the pharmacy is often at the back of a store filled with aisles containing products damaging to health. They sell candy, milk chocolate, fried chips, bleached grain snacks, junk foods, sodas, artificial sweeteners, and those destroyers of health: cigarettes and brewed and distilled alcohol. What is it that these pharmacies are promoting? It isn't health.

Many people suffer from disease because they live unhealthfully on many levels. They are filled with toxic thoughts, tarnished emotions, and have an acidic system fed with low-quality foods clogging them with fried oils, synthetic chemicals, and degrading food residues. They aren't getting adequate exercise, eating fresh fruits and vegetables, drinking water, or sleeping well.

An acidic body can be alkalized by a diet consisting largely of unheated leafy green vegetables, sprouts, some sea vegetables, and fruit, and raw beans, seeds, grains, and nuts that were germinated.

An alkaline diet and daily exercise brings the system more in tune with a healthful frequency. It is the good part of the high people strive to experience with drugs.

"We lift ourselves by our thought. If you want to enlarge your life, you must first enlarge your thought of it and of yourself. Hold the ideal of yourself as you long to be, always everywhere."
– Orison Swett Marden

To be the healthful, satisfied person you wish to be, begin to act the part. Work to be in alignment with the quality of life you wish to have. Think in a way that nurtures actions that use your talents to bring satisfaction. Carry yourself with an attitude and posture of confidence. Follow a diet and exercise regimen more likely to bring about health. Communicate in a way that is respectful, clear, nurtures loving relationships, and encourages growth toward good. Breathe in a way that calms your spirit and mind, but that energizes you to fulfill your intentions. Flow your intentions into your words, hands, feet, and life as you visualize and work for manifesting what you desire to be.

This may all sound pleasant and nice, but you also have to live in the community of humans with whom you must interact, and many might not be living healthfully. However, it can be surprising how people respond better to when others behave in a respectful way, focused on being part of the solution.

Not allowing the damaged emotions and unhinged drama of others to control your thought patterns, or to affect your state of being, can build confidence and respect – both within yourself and within others. Staying focused when others are upset can bring a spirit of dignity into any situation.

"Each person has inside a basic decency and goodness. If he listens to it and acts on it, he is giving a great deal of what it is the world needs most. It is not complicated but it takes courage. It takes courage for a person to listen to his own goodness and to act on it."
– Pablo Casals

You are worthy of vibrant health. You are worthy of love. Your intellect and talents are worthy of being developed and used. Your life and the lives of those around you are worthy of being respected and nurtured. You deserve and are capable of maintaining a healthful diet and of working to improve your life.

"Never forget the importance of living with unbridled exhilaration. Never neglect to see the exquisite beauty in all living things. Today, and this very moment, is a gift. Stay focused on your purpose."
– Robin Sharma

Whatever you do, do it well. Be the best example of yourself at that time in whatever it is you choose to be. Wherever you are and whatever you are doing, work to bring out your best qualities. Doing so will build and strengthen your abilities and skills.

416

"Start by doing what's necessary; then do what's possible; and suddenly you are doing the impossible."
– St. Francis of Assisi

Do whatever it takes to self-coach your transition into a more healthful, satisfying life.

Feed your mind with intellectually stimulating information to nurture your life to improve.

Feed your body with a biophoton-rich fresh plant-based diet rich in raw greens and that will generate vibrancy.

Have faith in the power of your mind, in the power of a clean diet, in the power of daily exercise and a regular sleeping pattern, in the power of intentional, goal-oriented living focused on accomplishment, and in the power of tuning into the frequency of Nature.

"There is a basic law that like attracts like. Negative-thinking definitely attracts negative results. Conversely, if a person habitually thinks optimistically and hopefully his positive-thinking sets in motion creative forces – and success instead of eluding him flows toward him."
– Norman Vincent Peale

Believe in the power of your intellect and talents. Believe you can use them to formulate your life the way you would like it to be. You can do this in the same way your spirit formed your physical structure. This power can be accessed by rejecting the damaging, and by doing away with non-nurturing thoughts, non-nutritious foods, and activities that waste your time, energy, resources, health, and love.

"Aging is an extraordinary process where you become the person you always should have been."
– David Bowie

Become a being in tune with vibrant health, with your better qualities, with learning and improving, with your higher intellect, with your goals, and with being part of the solution.

"Keep your dreams alive. Understand to achieve anything requires faith and belief in yourself, vision, hard work, determination, and dedication. Remember all things are possible for those who believe."
– Gail Devers

"Life is a gift of Nature; but beautiful living is the gift of wisdom."
– Greek adage

# The Self Revolution

"A great revolution in just one single individual will help achieve a change in the destiny of a society and, further, will enable a change in the destiny of humankind."
– Daisaku Ikeda

"It is indulgent to sink down into states in which your own vibration and healing power is diminished. With it, your own capacity to act with exuberance, vitality, creativity, and passion and joy is also drained. What is needed is for a lot of us to become more fully alive."
– John Robbins

"I am only one; but still I am one. I cannot do everything, but still I can do something; I will not refuse to do something I can do."
– Helen Keller

We are all playing a role here on Earth. Some are more aware of it, while others are not.

Some people work to participate in a way that uplifts others.

Some people seem to be completely unaware of their power, and spend life sloppily taking care of only the most basic necessities.

Some people work in a selfish way by doing nothing for anyone – while living selfishly and unsustainably.

Some people bring down others through demeaning, belittling, and otherwise undermining words and actions.

Selfishness is one of the most destructive things, in the long run it works against the person, and against everyone.

The opposite of being selfish is being selfless, being so engaged in generating good and helpful things that there is no room for anything else.

"Life is a gift, and it offers us the privilege, opportunity, and responsibility to give something back by becoming more.
– Anthony Robbins

When we do what is good for us, by following a plant-based diet, by being fit through daily exercise, by keeping our thoughts, actions, and communication focused on improvement, by using our intellect and practicing our natural talents and abilities, by living more sustainably, and by working to protect the planet and animals, we are doing what is good for all, and are not living selfishly.

"Happiness depends, as Nature shows, less on exterior things than most suppose."
– William Cowper

"The best things in life aren't things."
– Art Buchwald

Selfish behavior may involve having the biggest, and so-called "best," and living by the false concept of competition.

It is likely that we all know someone who works to have more than anyone else – as if that validates them. Based on wealthy people I've known, the game of "who has the most toys wins" tells its own story. If anything, the people who are obsessed with wealth are likely to carry a lack of satisfaction, and even a particular sadness. Being caught up in accumulating things is likely to be more of a spiritually disintegrating indulgence than anything that ever benefits the person, or brings them true happiness.

"It was possible, no doubt, to imagine a society in which wealth, in the sense of personal possessions and luxuries, should be evenly distributed, while power remained in the hands of a small privileged caste. But in practice such a society could not long remain stable. For if leisure and security were enjoyed by all alike, the great mass of human beings who are normally stupefied by poverty would become literate and would learn to think for themselves; and when once they had done this, they would sooner or later realize that the privileged minority had no function, and they would sweep it away. In the long run, a hierarchical society was only possible on a basis of poverty and ignorance."
– George Orwell

"It all depends on whether you have things, or they have you."
– Robert Cook

Just as drugs, alcohol, and poverty can distort a person's view of life, so can wealth. The whole concept that wealth equals happiness is a distortion.

Some people place so much focus on wealth, on getting wealthy, and on projecting the image of being wealthy, that it is practically their religion. This is all so telling in a day when the banks and governments controlling money are in buildings resembling temples.

"The country is governed for the richest, for the corporations, the bankers, the land speculators, and for the exploiters of labor. The majority of mankind are working people. The majority of mankind is ground down by industrial oppression in order that the small remnant may live in ease."
– Helen Keller

In ancient times, the larger buildings were for ceremonial purposes to honor life and Divinity. In today's commercial society, the stores are the larger buildings, and it seems that buying stuff and accumulating things to replicate advertised imagery has taken the place of living simple, honorable, authentic, respectful lives. In being commercial replicants, people have lost touch with their instinct, intellect, talent, power, uniqueness, needs, and their very nature.

"The whole culture is one unified field of bought, sold, market researched everything. It used to be that people fermented their own culture. It took hundreds of years and it evolved over time. That's gone in America. People now don't have any concept that there ever was a culture outside this thing that's created to make money. Whatever is the biggest, latest thing, they're into it. You just get disgusted after a while for not having more of a kind of like intellectual curiosity about what's behind all this jive bullshit."
– Robert Dennis Crumb

Large numbers of people lead spiritually impotent lives in which they have given up their hope and replaced it with monetary desires. Many have given up on goals and lead lives in which they rely on the surrogates of TV personalities to define their desired successes. Instead of practicing talents or engaging in hobby, in craft, or in volunteering for worthwhile causes, people spend their time watching TV programs, playing screen games, and buying stuff. The items they accumulate are a congealment of their wasted energy that could have been spent doing something worthwhile for the planet. Their strongest belief appears to be one of trusting in the seductive distortions of advertising. They have been programmed to watch and shop. The people they know most about are of the delusionally self-important celebrities in the media. An activity that a growing number of people are most engaged in is working to pay off debts created by shopping to replicate commercial imagery, an activity that produces a wasted life of nonsense. The program is greed.

"The more we accumulate wealth, the more it leads to a breakdown of community."
– Mark Boyle

While riding my bike I was shouted at by a man driving a big SUV. He told me I should stay off the road. I was riding on the area marked as a bike path. But that didn't appear good enough for him. It was as if he believed he had more rights than I because he was driving a gas-guzzling monstrosity – likely owned by a finance company he was making monthly payments to. Many of the very same types of dissatisfied and controlling people work jobs they dislike, but which they need, if they are to pay off the parasitic debts they have allowed themselves to accumulate. The largest part of their days are spent counting the minutes before they can go home for the day. Their jobs do not nurture them, their deadened and processed diets do not provide high-quality nutrition, many of their relationships are as shallow as skin, and their lives do not fulfill them. Everything they do not like and that dissatisfies them is the other person's fault. Personal responsibility for the state of degradation they are lost in is a concept not under consideration as they are too busy working to appear hip and cool, as if they are still working to be the center of attention at the high school dance.

"Know thyself? If I knew myself, I'd run away."
– Johann Wolfgang von Goethe

An astounding number of people are caught up in the image parade. They have become lost in the concept that the accumulation of the latest trendy things validates their lives. They fit in with the others who have conformed to the advertising imagery. Many of them have gone into debt to maintain the façade. Their lives are inauthentic and they have become lost in the power of greed and covetousness. They've bought into and have become slaves to the corporate system of working, buying things, and paying debt. They keep rolling with it, digging themselves deeper into the system by buying things and buying more things, but seem to lack an understanding that nothing they purchase can fill the void of a life in which their most beneficial qualities are being ignored to the point of atrophy.

"Realize that true happiness lies within you. Waste no time and effort searching for peace and contentment and joy in the world outside. Remember that there is no happiness in having or in getting, but only in giving. Reach out. Share. Smile. Hug."
 – Og Mandino

Don't wait for others to make you content, or fulfilled. Take what you have and work with it to make your life more content, and fulfilled, without feeling as if you are competing.

"I always wondered why somebody doesn't do something about that. Then, I realized I was somebody."
 – Lily Tomlin

No matter our financial status, we all have abilities, talents, and intellect that can bring us to participate in improving our situation, and in being a part of the solution to the issues facing our communities, culture, and society, wildlife, and Earth.

The more natural way in which we live, the more naturally our natural instincts will become pronounced in our life. As we do so, we become closer to the way we are naturally meant to live. That is: more in tune with Nature.

"Happiness is a continuously creative activity."
 – Baba Amte

"If you want your life to be a magnificent story, then begin by realizing that you are the author and every day you have the opportunity to write a new page."
 – Mark Houlahan

We all are capable in some manner of uplifting our lives as well as the lives of others; capable of achieving something good; and capable of learning from and using the substances and energies to gain the knowledge we need to improve our situation. What we have to do is tune into this process and act on it.

"The heart is the chief feature of a functioning mind."
 – Frank Lloyd Wright

Everyone is capable of participating in a lifestyle that is more respectful to the web of life on Earth. At least, to be more concerned with and getting away from the less respectful, Nature-damaging way many of us have been living. (Research: The extinction crisis.)

"If you expect the best, you will be the best. Learn to use one of the most powerful laws in this world; change your mental habits to belief instead of disbelief. Learn to expect, not to doubt. In so doing, you bring everything into the realm of possibility."
– Norman Vincent Peale

Like seeds, thoughts create after their own kind. Thoughts, words, and actions are seeds. The more that people are active in thinking and working toward living in a natural way, the more it plants the seeds for and others to live naturally. By living more naturally we are living in greater kindness for our fellow beings, for Earth, and for ourselves.

"Don't ask what the world needs. Ask what makes you come alive, and go do it. Because what the world needs is people who have come alive."
– Howard Thurman

"He who lives in harmony with himself lives in harmony with the universe."
– Marcus Aurelius

Many people speak of a feeling within themselves they know has something to do with what they desire to be doing and how they yearn to live. They may not know what it is, and they may fluctuate in life while not knowing how to satisfy this feeling. But once they find its meaning, it is powerful and drives them to focus on accomplishing what they feel they should be doing.

I don't think it is necessarily one thing most people can do or feel satisfied in doing. It can be a variety of things within a range of a certain occupation, talent, skill, ability, hobby, craft, or interest.

"Every decision you make – every decision – is not a decision about what to do. It's a decision about who you are. When you see this, when you understand it, everything changes. You begin to see life in a new way. All events, occurrences, and situations turn into opportunities to do what you came here to do."
– Neale Donald Walsch

"If you don't live it, it won't come out of your horn."
– Charlie Parker

Some people get caught up in trying to find the meaning to their life by focusing on things outside themselves. Perhaps they would be better off to simply live their life with intention driving their intellect, talents, and passions into their actions to accomplish set goals, then they will find their lives inside themselves.

"I've come to believe that each of us has a personal calling that's as unique as a fingerprint – and that the best way to succeed is to discover what you love and then find a way to offer it to others in the form of service, working hard, and also allowing the energy of the universe to lead you."
– Oprah Winfrey

Instead of listening to discouragement, listen to encouragement. As you do so, realize the value of each, and that encouragement is the more helpful, valuable, worthwhile, and powerful of the two.

The world is full of discouragement, which stumbles many on their way to succeed at using their intellect, in practicing their talents, in exercising their skills, and in loving those around them.

"Creativity is a flower that praise brings to bloom, but discouragement often nips in the bud."
– Alex F. Osborn

"My mother has always been unhappy with what I do. She would much rather I do something nice, like be a bricklayer.
– Mick Jagger

Much of the discouragement you experience may come directly from the people who should be encouraging you the most. Some of this may be that they are afraid you are wasting your time, and they believe you should be looking to succeed in something else. Or they may think you are incapable of succeeding in anything, which may be a case of not believing in their own power, and could be a display of their devalued self-worth. It may have something to do with their refusal to open their mind to the possibilities and beauty of life. It may have to do with their wanting you to remain playing the same role they are accustomed to seeing you play, which may allow them to carry on certain low-grade behaviors – thus using you as their enabler and crutch. This may be because they are typically underminers, takers, users, and abusers.

I grew up in a sickly household of older people mocking, ridiculing, abusing, and attacking me, and saying ugly things about me. As if their grotesque views were to be my truth, and my reality.

The words of others have more to do with what they have been fed, how they've been treated, what is in their thoughts, how they feel about themselves, and about their world view, and has less to do with who you are. Don't mistake who you are for who they are.

"Only by having faith in ourselves can we be faithful to others."
– Erich Fromm

Listening to discouragement, including from others and from ourselves, may have to do with not wanting to go outside our familiar comfort zones. Perhaps our comfort zones are the things making us uncomfortable, holding us down, and stagnating us.

Perhaps it is time to cast yourself in a new role with a whole new cast of supporting characters.

"It takes a lot of courage to release the familiar and seemingly secure, to embrace the new. But there is no real security in what is no longer meaningful. There is more security in the adventurous and exciting, for in movement there is life, and in change there is power."
– Alan Cohen

In any situation, believe in your power and manifest the life you desire through intentional thoughts, planning, beneficial actions, and helpful communication.

"Ability is what you're capable of doing. Motivation determines what you do. Attitude determines how well you do it."
– Lou Holtz

You may talk about leading a better life, and talking can make a lot of noise. Sitting around talking about it also squanders the energy that would be more helpful for you to spend on accomplishing your goals. Instead, do this: Don't be lazy and stuck in wishing. Work.

Taking continual daily actions to improve your life is what will break you out of the fantasy of doing it, and into the reality of creating and experiencing it.

"Don't be afraid to take a big step when one is indicated. You can't cross a chasm in two small jumps."
– Richard Buckminster Fuller

"Every worthwhile accomplishment has a price tag attached to it. The question is always whether you are willing to pay the price to attain it – in hard work, sacrifice, patience, faith, and endurance."
– John C. Maxwell

People may not be able to believe in your words, but they can believe in your accomplishments. Don't waste your time in explaining to others that you are capable of doing something. It is always more empowering to go out and accomplish your goals. Then you will recognize that you are capable of accomplishment.

It is through your accomplishments that you will feel satisfaction, and you can allow yourself to feel and enjoy it regardless of the response – or lack thereof – you get from those around you.

"Every production of genius must be the production of enthusiasm."
– Benjamin Disraeli

If the people around you are not providing you with the encouragement you need to hear, use your own encouraging thoughts and goal setting to motivate your actions. Do so every day, with clarity and intention, starting at the moment you awake.

If you want to hear encouraging words from others, perhaps what you will find helpful is to encourage them. The energy of this will likely produce more of the same.

"Most people live, whether physically, intellectually or morally, in a very restricted circle of their potential being. They make very small use of their possible consciousness, and of their soul's resources in general, much like a man who, out of his whole bodily organism, should get into a habit of using and moving only his little finger."
– William James

People who are catering to a healthful mind will be constantly working to improve their situation without degrading their family, friends, co-workers, neighbors, associates, or acquaintances. They will dwell in an energy that is both nurturing to them while also being encouraging and uplifting to those around them.

"To accomplish great things, we must not only act but also dream, not only plan but also believe."
– Anatole France

There is power in knowing you have talents and abilities to use to improve your life.

There is power in recognizing your spiritual essence and yearning that can guide you toward doing what is right for you.

There is power in creating and using motivational thoughts to trigger goal-setting and intentional actions of self-improvement.

There is inspiration to be gained by succeeding in taking actions to turn your goals into accomplishments.

"Change and growth take place when a person has risked himself and dares to become involved with experimenting with his own life."
– Herbert Otto

Everyone has a spiritual tool that helps them to realize when they are spending their time and energy wisely. While some people may choose to ignore this, they still have it. Recognizing it and using it to guide you to do what is right is a good thing. The tool may be best described as your inner compass. It is controlled by an invisible field of energy that has formulated your physical structure, and with which you can connect for creating the thoughts leading to the actions to build the life you desire.

"The mind should dance with the body, and the whole universe is your stage. Try to feel that whatever you are doing is the most beautiful thing, the prettiest dance, because you are dancing with the whole universe. Don't resent anything. Let your heart guide you, free of all regimentation."
– Yogi Bhajan

If you are not actively working toward improving your life, you either are stagnant, are stumbling, or are going backward.

"One's destination is never a place, but a new way of seeing things."
– Henry Miller

"Life is a pilgrimage. The wise man does not rest by the roadside inns. He marches direct to the illimitable domain of eternal bliss, his ultimate destination."
– Oscar Wilde

You can start today to use all the tools naturally available to you for improving your life. This includes writing down your goals and making a daily priority list to work out how you are going to make your goals come true. It involves waking up and writing a daily declaration. It involves eating healthfully, exercising daily, communicating helpfully, organizing your life, avoiding the accumulation of things you don't need, and approaching your life with thoughts of intention to drive your actions.

"Victory is won not in miles but in inches. Win a little now, hold your ground, and later win a little more."
– Louis L'Amour

One of the key ways to improve your life is to do what comes naturally in regard to your better talents and abilities. Figure out, recognize, and work with the good that comes naturally to you.

"There are only three colors, ten digits, and seven notes; it's what we do with them that's important."
– Ruth Ross

If you are not constructing your life with your better qualities, you are out of harmony with your spirit – and you likely have a strong feeling this is happening. This shows up in frustration, in anxiety, in dissatisfaction, in regret, in depression, in choosing low-quality foods, in unhelpful communication, in dysfunctional and damaged relationships, in lack of love, and perhaps as anger and misspoken thoughts, and in an unfulfilling, unsatisfying life.

"A thought is an act of creation. It is what we are here for, to create, to bring into being ourself by means of thinking."
 – Marcel Vogel

"I like projecting positivity. I believe that we are all fields of energy and you have the choice whether to be a positive or negative field of energy. I know that sounds hippie-ish but it's what I believe fundamentally. So you could be a bag of toxicity, or you could be a happy, good person who spreads joy. I believe in spreading joy."
 – Drew Barrymore

Nurture your life with good things. Recognize that you are worthy and capable of improving your life.

Use visualization techniques to understand what you want.

Keep a journal to help you build and journey toward a better life.

Act daily to achieve your set list of goals.

Do the work to bring satisfaction.

Use your intellect, talents, abilities, and energy to work for you.

Associate with the music, literature, food, and people that will work to uplift, enliven, and propel you into a better life.

Experience joy, respect, satisfaction, kindness, and love in your life. Let this be your normal comfort zone.

Read books that motivate and teach you.

Listen music that inspires and energizes you.

Plant the thoughts in your mind that activate positive change. Put in what you want to get out.

Create a piloting consciousness that glides you to self-manifest the goals you set.

I did that to create my books out of my mind. And so, they are.

"Books are the carriers of civilization. Without books, history is silent, literature dumb, science crippled, thought and speculation at a standstill."
 – Barbara Tuchman

"Education is not the piling on of learning, information, data, facts, skills, or abilities – that's training or instruction – but is rather making visible what is hidden as a seed."
 – Thomas Moore

"Nobody can go back and start a new beginning, but anyone can start today and make a new ending."
– Maria Robinson

"Every moment of every day we can bring this consciousness to our choices about our money, our time, and our talents to take a stand for what we believe in."
– Lynne Twist

Be brave in taking control of your talents and intellect. Take command of what you think about and what you do. Force yourself to prosper in ways that bring about health and happiness at levels you had not experienced.

"Things may come to those who wait, but only the things left by those who hustle."
– Abraham Lincoln

"If there is one thing I say to those who use me as their example, it's that if you ever get a second chance in life, you've got to go all the way."
– Lance Armstrong

Improving your life can become so desirable to you that it will be the driving force behind self-discipline. Your desire can become stronger as you learn the benefits of working to create satisfaction. You will be willing to pay the price of living healthfully. The fee is giving up unhealthful foods, thoughts, words, and activities while living intentionally. It will be a fee well spent.

"Happiness is the meaning and the purpose of life, the whole aim and end of human existence."
– Aristotle

Work to change your life while believing you can do it.

Conceptualize and know that your mind power, talents, and what you can learn through study can bring about the changes you like.

Bring all the useful tools into your life to make the changes in tune with what you desire.

Improve your learning. Improve your way of thinking. Improve your diet. Improve your physical structure. Improve your atmosphere. Improve the way you spend your time. Improve the way you think of yourself as well as the way you think of others.

Believe in your power and that you can shape your future into one of brilliant health, sustainable living, and satisfaction.

429

"Live with intention. Walk to the edge. Listen hard. Practice wellness. Play with abandon. Laugh. Choose with no regret. Appreciate your friends. Continue to learn. Do what you love. Live as if this is all there is."
– Mary Ann Radmacher

Do away with negative-thinking. Dispose of unkind words. Avoid slander. Communicate better with those around you.

Conquer any tendencies preventing you from organizing your life into the best it can be.

Build a nurturing environment that propagates health, respect, kindness, and love for you, those you love, and your community.

"Kindness is more important than wisdom, and the recognition of this is the beginning of wisdom."
– Theodore Isaac Rubin

Refuse to detach from your strengths. Continually take action to propel yourself toward happiness.

Respond in the direction of health and command through your thoughts, actions, and food choices that health be present in your life.

"The height of your accomplishments will equal the depth of your convictions."
– William F. Scolavino

"It's time for greatness – not for greed. It's a time for idealism – not ideology. It is a time not just for compassionate words, but compassionate action."
– Marian Wright Edelman

Think, visualize, plan, act, live, grow, and love toward the solution.

Provide the terrain and atmosphere, the illumination and the enlightenment, the nutrients and the activity, and the intention and drive for a better life.

Commit to breaking the limits under which you lived.

Realize that your limits may have been of your making as you dwelled in a lack of faith in your abilities, talents, and intellect, and especially in a lack in your power of love.

Recognize and be your universe, your galaxy, and your star systems of thought energy guided by your power and yearning and desire for what specifically is healthful and good for you.

Gain access to your power, connect with and be conscious of it. It is what you are. That is, a powerful work of art forming through thoughts, actions, communication, and your relationship with people, objects, the arts, terrain, and atmosphere.

Envision yourself engaging in the life you want to lead. Propel yourself into the realization of it.

Choose to be around people who believe in you, nurture you, and uplift you.

Choose to listen to music, read literature, and have things around you that inspire you.

Organize your surroundings so they better suit what you want.

Make all of your being play a part in the manifestation of a healthier you.

"The energy in space is not trivial, there's a lot of it and we can actually calculate how much energy there is in that space, and that realty might actually come out of it. Everything we see is actually emerging from this space."
– Nassim Haramein

Perhaps the most prominent part of your being is the part you cannot see, not your physical structure, but your ether, and the energy playing out within and of it. It is not only part of you, but is part of what you have been and what you will be. It plays out in how what happens in it alters all of you. It is your quantum phenomenon dimension in which your photons and electrons play and weave you into what you will be.

"All perceptible matter comes from a primary substance, or tenuity beyond conception, filling all space, the akasha, or luminiferous ether, which is acted upon by the life-giving prana or creative force, calling into existence, in never-ending cycles, all things and phenomena."
– Nikola Tesla

Dip into your fifth element, that is the ether of your life, your spirit that plays into the gravitational field of your power velocity, to settle your mind and place yourself more in tune with your talents, and with what you can achieve.

Sharpen your self into an instrument that will weave the fabric of your existence into a beautiful symphony in tune with Nature, health, and self-awareness.

"Health is a state of complete physical, mental, and social well-being and not merely the absence of disease or infirmity."
– World Health Organization

"In terms of being late or not starting at all, then it's never too late."
– Alison Headley

Respect your life. Do it by refusing to allow junk foods and damaging substances into your system. Do it by allowing your body detoxify the residues of unhealthful foods you have eaten. Do it by recognizing you are an amazing and beautiful being. Do it by revealing that your life has value. Do it by allowing yourself to become more healthful. Do it by following a high-quality, low-fat, plant-based diet rich in raw fruits and vegetables. Start now to visualize the power of Nature and nutrients of those biophoton-rich living foods streaming through all of your cells and infusing you with health as you engage in goal-oriented activities.

"Do the things you want to see."
– Russell Simmons

"Fear is what prevents the flowering of the mind."
– Jiddu Krishnamurti

Know you are worthy of love. Understand it is healthier to continually live accompanied by love and not by fear.

Know that love is the strongest power on, in, and through the universe. Rule and blossom your life by and through love.

"When we are motivated by goals that have deep meaning, by dreams that need completion, by pure love that needs expressing – then we truly live life."
– Greg Anderson

Focus your mind on what you want.
Enliven your powers and transform your situation.

"Be happy. It's one way of being wise."
– Sidonie-Gabrielle Colette

"Personal transformation can and does have global affects. As we go, so goes the world, for the world is us. The revolution that will save the world is ultimately a personal one."
– Marianne Williamson

Make every day noble with the elegance of your spirit.
Become fluent in the language of the love within your heart.

"There is no moment of delight in any pilgrimage like the beginning of it."
– Charles Dudley Warner

"Dreams are something you have to believe in."
– Ke Huy Quan

"We live in a wonderful world that is full of beauty, charm and adventure. There is no end to the adventures that we can have if only we seek them with our eyes open."
– Jawaharlal Nehru

"Start living now. Stop saving the good China for that special occasion. Stop withholding your love until that special person materializes. Every day you are alive is a special occasion.
– Mary Manin Morrisse

"When you reach the heart of life, you shall find beauty in all things."
– Kahlil Gibran

# The Symphony of Self

"The world is not to be put in order; the world is order incarnate. It is for us to harmonize with this order."
– Henry Miller

**Body:** soft (skin, muscles, fascia, tendons, eyes, nerves, brain, and other organs), hard (bones and teeth), and liquid (blood, lymph, cerebrospinal, tears, respiratory, digestive, and reproductive fluids).

Feed your body with high-quality food free of toxic and degrading ingredients, but consisting of a variety of plant substances, preferably some from your own garden and/or regional organic farmers; with water; with exercise that strengthens and maintains muscle and bone structures, balances the hormones, and improves the cardiovascular system while relieving stress; with healing touch, and by keeping your mind and spirit healthful.

Maintain a regular sleeping pattern.

By doing these things you will have a more prominent base of the telomerase enzyme in the blood, which helps to maintain longer telomeres on your chromosomes, keeping your cells young.

"Man's main task in life is to give birth to himself."
– Erich Fromm

**Mind:** mental, emotional, intellect, talents, craft, skills, yearning, and passions.

Feed your mind with positive thoughts and by managing your emotions; developing your talents, working with your higher passions in ways that uplift and edify; and keeping your body and spirit healthful through high-quality nutrition, exercise, information and study, relationships, intentions, communication, and actions.

"What is a soul? It's like electricity – we don't really know what it is, but it's a force that can light a room."
– Ray Charles

**Energy:** electrical charge being created within, entering, emanating from, and passing through you.

Feed your energy by generating positive and proactive intentional thoughts, and by creating a healthful environment that nurtures and protects wildlife and Nature.

Stimulate your intellect with learning and reading, and by practicing your talents, skills, and abilities.

Stay physically active through daily exercise.

Consume raw, organic plant substances, which are rich in antioxidants, anti-inflammatories, vitamins, minerals, enzymes, amino acids, quality essential fatty acids, and the energy of light nutrients called biophotons.

"Once you have flown, you will walk the earth with your eyes turned skyward; for there you have been, there you long to return."
– Leonardo Da Vinci

**Spirit:** vibrational essence of being, instinct, intuition, infinite intelligence, ether of the infinite, and love.

Feed your spirit by practicing kindness and love, and by keeping a healthful body and mind through a healthy diet, through daily exercise, through intellectual stimulation, through uplifting relationships, through using your talents, and through living intentionally using your higher qualities.

Associate with people who, and read literature, listen to music, and participate in activities that strengthens your resolve to live true to your talents and intellect by using the power of Nature fueling you.

You matter and you are a worthy matter of spirit.

**Community:** all that is in and surrounds you.

Feed it by nurturing good things to happen; by working toward living a sustainable lifestyle; by following a natural, plant-based diet; by, where possible, growing some of your own food; by composting your kitchen scraps into soil; by supporting local organic farmers; by being involved with restoring forests, rivers, lands, and natural habitat; by planting native plants; by protecting wildlands and wildlife; and by working with your talent and craft to bring about an enlightened culture participating in solutions.

**"Love abhors waste, especially waste of human potential."**
– Leo Buscaglia

Wherever you are there is an opportunity for participating in the change you want to see.

Do not concern yourself with gaining the honor and respect of other people. Work from within to be honorable and respectable. True respect and honor originate from the ether of what you are.

Exist within a life that is your solution, your motivation, your better qualities, and higher potential.

# Dream Intention

"As an irrigator guides water to his fields, as an archer aims an arrow, as a carpenter carves wood, the wise shape their lives."
– Buddha

Be inspired to live your intellect and to express your talents, manifesting your desired life, refusing to be conquered by the bombardment of what might otherwise beat you down.

"There are some people who live in a dream world, and there are some who face reality; and then there are those who turn one into the other."
– Douglas Everett

The subconscious mind tends to connect more with words written in longhand and I color, rather than typed, or in black and white.

Using color pens or pencils, write some notes in relation to the following points. Define how they apply to, can take place in, or become present in your life in ways that work with and for you.

1. Connect with your yearning, intellect, and talents, and craft your skills. Your essence is there.

2. Live with purpose.

"Warriors are not what you think of as warriors. The warrior is not someone who fights, because no one has the right to take another life. The warrior, for us, is one who sacrifices himself for the

good of others. His task is to take care of the elderly, the defenseless, those who cannot provide for themselves, and above all, the children – the future of humanity."
– Sitting Bull

3. Make a strategic short list of goals.
Read and adjust it every morning to align your intention.

4. Write an intentional statement every morning declaring what you will focus on and accomplish that day.

5. Organize your space. Dispose of, give away, or sell clutter.

6. Break a sweat every day through exercise, preferably in the morning.
Yoga and calisthenics are free, and can be practiced in a small space. Even prisoners stay fit by doing yoga and calisthenics.

7. Read or re-read at least one book every month that will help fuel personal growth.
Take notes that might end up being your personal book of motivation, inspiration, and reminders of what is important to you. It might also be something worthy to leave behind when you are gone.

8. Spend little, accumulate less, shop less, and save more.

9. State no untrue, slanderous, exaggerated, backbiting, undermining, or unfounded comments that would contribute to pain, fear, dishonor, or troubles in the lives of others, or of yourself.

10. Work hard and take care of yourself. Be inspired and inspiring, uplifted and uplifting, loving, and honorable.

11. Do not buy into other people's self-created drama, or fall into their trap of complications that will rob you of your time, energy, resources, or goodness.

12. Live your truth.
Reread the notebook you are keeping for yourself in tune with point number 7 on this list.

13. Do not participate in the myth and false concept of competition.
There is no competition. You only compete with yourself, to better yourself. Attain the sense of being your own solution.

14. Do not participate in self-hate, self-sabotage, and other self-deceiving thoughts and damaging behaviors.

15. Do not dwell in victimhood or blame.
Don't get stuck in the past.
Focus on the present.
Choose, factor, plan, and work toward your better future.

16. Forgive, let go, and move on with your life – away from your past, and into your future.
No matter what happened, it is past.

17. Stay focused. Stop allowing yourself to be distracted.
Finish projects and experience satisfaction.

"We suffer more often in imagination than in reality. Some things torment us more than they ought. Some torment us before they ought. And some torment us when they ought not to torment us at all. We are in the habit of exaggerating, or imagining, or anticipating sorrow."
– Seneca

How much procrastinating are you going to engage in?
What is it going to take to trigger you to get busy working to accomplish your goals, and stop only holding them within?
Could the issues facing you be more obvious?
When are you going to start to do what you need to do to put your life in a new place?
How long are you going to delay experiencing joy?
Let the activities of improving your life be your new toy.

18. Eat a variety of locally grown organic fruits and vegetables.
Especially be sure to include a variety of green vegetables.
Check out ForksOverKnives.com.

19. Grow some of your own food.
Search for groups involved in motivating and teaching people about growing organic food gardens, food forests, and supporting regional organic produce farms.

20. Refrain from purchasing or consuming junk food, fast food, fried food, foods containing corn syrup, rice syrup, agave, other processed sugars, and processed salt, MSG, or synthetic chemicals, including dyes, flavors, scents, and preservatives.

21. Educate yourself about vegan nutrition. ForksOverKnives is one way. Another is NutritionFacts.org. I also wrote *Plant-based Regenerative Nutrition*. See the documentary "The Game Changers."

22. Plant native trees and a variety of native flowering plants someplace in the surrounding region every year. And/or donate to organizations involved in planting trees, protecting forests, and restoring wildlife habitat. (Research: Forest restoration.)

Humans have decimated forests on every continent, and on island nations. Earth needs billions of more trees on every continent. It needs headwaters forests and river landscapes to be restored and protected. It needs terrain safe for wildlife to flourish.

23. This is important: Work to protect wildlife and to restore its habitat. Support environmental and wildlife protection organizations. Consider the Natural Resources Defense Council, Earth Island Institute, Earth First, Sea Shepherd, Defenders of Wildlife, and the Green World Campaign.

Read *Earth Island Journal*.

24. Live a more environmentally sustainable life.

Learn about permaculture. Research it.

See the documentaries "Seed: The Untold Story," "CowSpiracy," and "Seaspiracy."

"There is one, and only one solution, and we have almost no time to try it. We must turn all our resources to repairing the natural world, and train all our young people to help. They want to. We need to give them this last chance to create forests, soils, clean waters, clean energies, secure communities, stable regions, and to know how to do it from hands-on experience."

– Bill Millison

25. The most important part of the planet is all of it, including where you are living.

What will you do to improve the health of Earth, including in the region where you live? You must do something to help.

Please, get involved in your local environmental groups.

26. Visualize your life the way you want it to be. Then live toward that image.

27. Ask yourself: What would love do if love were the only power fueling your life?

"Be yourself. Everyone else is already taken."
– Oscar Wilde

"I have a personal philosophy in life: kindness begets kindness."
– Drew Johnson

"I don't care what color you are, what sexual orientation you are, what nationality, what religion you are – if you operate out of a place of love, that's a family."
– Sandra Bullock

"Be kind, for everyone you meet is fighting a hard battle."
– Philo Judaeus

"If you want others to be happy, practice compassion. If you want to be happy, practice compassion."
– Dalai Lama

28. Give your self permission to do what you need to do to improve not only your life, but life in general.

"Don't be afraid to ask for what you want – the worst thing that can happen is you won't get it, but if you don't ask, you likely won't get it anyway."
– Cherie Soria

Break free of the normalcy bias, in which you disbelieve the warning signs that Nature is on a path to disaster, and in which you continue on as if it does not impact you. Your denial does not stop the degradation.

We are all here, together on a planet. It is time to be part of the solution. The downfall of Nature does impact you. Stop overlooking the messages and thinking you can go right on living as you have, as if everything will be okay.

You know it is time to make healthy, reasonable, beneficial changes.

"Let it never be said that I was silent when they needed me."
– William Wilberforce

I hope this book helps you to formulate a safe plan for your better life, to plan on living in ways more attuned to true health for you and for those around you, and to be courageous enough to carry through with the plan.

"Courage is like a muscle. We strengthen it by use."
– Ruth Gordon

# Participate in the Solutions

Plant trees.
Plant fruiting bushes to feed wildlife.
Plant native wildflowers to feed wildlife.
Plant an organic food garden to feed yourself.
Follow a plant-based diet.
Support local organic produce farmers.
Protect the rivers, lakes, and oceans.
Protect non-human animals.
Get off petroleum plastic.
Restore wildlife habitat.
Replant the forests.
Replant paradise.

ALDF.org
BiologicalDiversity.org
ClimateNetwork.org
Defenders.org
EarthFirstJournal.news
EarthIsland.org
EarthJustice.org
EdenProjects.org
EndFossil.com
FarmSanctuary.org
FarmUSA.org
FoodAndWaterWatch.org
FoodNotBombs.net
GreenPeace.org
MercyForAnimals.org
PlasticOceans.org
RAN.org
RandchoCompasion.org
SaveTheRedwoods.org
SeaShepherd.com
TheHumaneLeague.org
UPC-Online.org
WeForest.org

# Glossary of Names

## A: Glossary of names

## B: Glossary of names

## C: Glossary of names

## H: Glossary of names

## I: Glossary of names

## J: Glossary of names

## K: Glossary of names

## L: Glossary of names

## M: Glossary of names

## N: Glossary of names

## O: Glossary of names

## P: Glossary of names

## Q: Glossary of names

## R: Glossary of names

E

## Y: Glossary of names

## Z: Glossary of names

# INDEX and TOPICAL GUIDE

## B: Index and Topical Guide

# C: Index and Topical Guide

## D: Index and Topical Guide

237, 259, 314, 414, 421, 428; **Dissect the elements**, 22; **Distance**, admire it from, 30; day, 45; the wind, in the, 137; someone in the, 248; what appear attractive from, 290; yourself, 355; **Distant**, epochs, citizens of, opening pages; held hostage from people from past, 154; stranger, 214; from how church leaders live, 270; communities, 365; seas of thought, end pages; **Distortion**, church, 142; abilities, 221; 229, image of Divinity, 269; understanding, 271; 272, 326, of values, 331; frantic, 328; view of life, 420; of advertising, 421; **Distraction**, 52, 68, 93, 204, 216, 326, 352; **Diversity**, 272; **Divine**, expression of love, 136; mission claim, 141; confidence, 160; 167, thought, 183; don't hold yourself as so, 218; light, 231; **Divinity**, 136, 145, 167, 269, 271, 276, 281, 371, 420; **DNA**, patterns, 194; **Doctor**, witch, 414; **Doctrine**, moral, 139; **Documentaries**, 99, 204, 208; **Dog**, author's 248; attuned to owner, 301; barking, 307; **Dogma**, 287, 347; **Dominion**, unrighteous, 306, anthropocentrism, 384; **Donating money**, 275; **Dopamine** neurotransmitter, 9, 31, 404; **Dormant**, you're lying, 58; forces, 83; areas of brain, 183; quality, 324; **Double life**, author childhood, 227; 271, 319; **Doubt**, 33, self, 51; 52, 66 77, 146, 151, 166, 175, 189, 221, 241, your worth, 351; 353, 356, 397; do not, 423; **Doubts**, believing in and as ruling factor, 60; are traitors, 97; **Downfall as springboard**, 259; **Downtrodden**, lift up, 160; 197; **Dragons**, confront, 83; and princesses, 219; **Drama**, spin in, 164; of former disastrous relationships, 338; and emotions, 416; **Dramatic event, talking of**, 299; **Draw**, in the life, 293; on the substances, 346; **Drawing**, ancient, 55; 175, 187, 392, 400; *Dream Another Dream*, book, 228, 352; **Dream**, 24, 26, 46, 71, proceeds goal, 72; 92, 94, lofty dreams, 186; 241, paintings appear as, 380; chemistry, 398-399; is a microscope, 399; interpretation, 400; intention, some people live in, 437; **Dreaming**, 393, 398-401; **Dreams**, 31, 69, 75, 79, direction of, 83; 95, go in direction of, 187; lie within, 293; and visions, 306; harmonize, 322; give all you got to, 332; go in direction of, 335; and beliefs, fundamental, 342; 354, 395, and body chemistry, 398; might heal you, and digest our day, 399; write down, 400; art, and religious writings, 400; alive, keep your, 417; need completion, 432; **Drudgery and shame**, 233; **Drug**, use, 96; abuse, 414, 402, and stores, 414; interactions, and store clerks uneducated, 415; **Drugged and violated**, author, 253-254; **Drugs**, damaging effects, 41; mind-altering, 375; escapism of, 412-413, farmed animals treated with, 384;

endogenous, 413; prescription, 415; 420; **Drunk**, driving, author's father, 226; 298; **Dull**, 25, the senses, 157, 385; 167; life, 330; you, 410; us, drugs, 414; **Dulling**, 361-362; **Dullness**, perpetual, 341; **Dumbing down of humanity**, 22; **DVDs and children education**, 328; **Dwelling**, in pit, 218; on past, 232; in negative, 233; in past, 258; in shame, 360; in lack of faith, 430; **Dyes**, food, 361, 413, 439; **Dynamics**, group, 367; **Dysfunctional**, environment, 157; relationships, 171; 179, 226, 235, 272, 305, 314-315, 317, 320, 384, 428; **Dysmorphia**, 228

## E: Index and Topical Guide

**Eager feelings**, 414; **Earth First**, 275, what will you do to improve, 440; **Earth Island Institute**, 275, 440; *Earth Island Journal*, 440; **Earth**, and sun revolution, and as center of universe, 48-49; damage to, 56; protect, 112; and Sun energy, 134-135; relationship with, 381; solution for, 422; *Earthlings*, documentary, 208; **Eastern spiritual practice**, 179; **Eating**, emotional, 229, 232; animals, 265, 268; **Eccentric**, 127, 302, 375, 380; **Echo of repulsion**, 199; **Economics**, 42; 130, inequality, 234; **Ecstasy**, 288; **Ecstatic**, 324; **ED (erectile dysfunction)**, 329; **Edify**, 67-68, 434-435; **Editorial bricolage**, 1; **Education**, 17, 62, stigmatization, 98; 126, 130, services, funding, 156; 206, level, 301; 345, heighten, 347; 375, is not the piling on, 428; **Educational**, neglect, 126; videos and infants, 328; **Effervescence** 139; **Eggs**, 339, 384-385, 388, 405; **Ego**, Mormon, 142; 315; **Egotistical**, 286; **Elected officials**, 52; **Electric**, fields, 167, 369; frequency, 170; energy, 168; signals in brain, 237-238; fields of body, 240; charges in body, 334; responses, 379; **Electrically-charged neurochemical biome**, 172; **Electricity and soul**, 435; **Electromagnetic fields**, 129, 238, 264, 267; **Electronic**, media, 2, 365; games, 326; **Electrons**, 133, 312, and photons, 431; **Elegance**, in practices, 68; of your intellect, 158; 256, your, 354; of your spirt, noble, 432; **Elegant power of your spirit**, 194; **Elementary**, truth, 62; forms, 269; particles, 315; **Elicit dramatic response**, 299; **Eliminate**, unnecessary, 293; the problematic, 347; low-quality, 391; **Elite**, universities, 126; and paupers, 162; **Eloquence of your love**, 158; **Emancipate yourself**, opening pages; 130; **Embarrassment**, 244, 262; **Embedded in being problem**, 384; **Emitting energy**, people, 295; **Emotion**, molecules of, 135, 171-172, 183, 199, 206, 238, 241, 295, 322, 334, 369, 379, 384, 389-390; 239;

## F: Index and Topical Guide

173, 200, 209, 213, 231, is teacher, 232; to connect thought and action, 243; experienced, 284; 315, greatest, 335; greatest, 337; 338, 353, 375, organ, 413; **Fair**, time is, 75; -weather friends, 105; life is not, 160; manner, 258; think it's not, 259; **Fairy tales**, 302; **Faith**, 138, 146, 164, 369, in power of mind, 417; only by having, 424; 425, lack of, 430; **Fake persona**, 154, 244, 297; **Fallacies**, 54, 178; **False**, beliefs, 48-50, information, 54; 105; narratives, 160; concepts, 224, hope, 236; 419, 438; concept of competition, 438; **Falsehood**, 54-55, 243; **Fame**, 105, doesn't equal happiness or health, 108; seeking, 112; **Family**, history of ruin, 200; heritage, 201; assignment, role-playing, 229; dying, 246-251; history, 301; conditioning, 315; pressure, 316; farmers, 362; 441; **Famine**, 79; **Fantasies**, 400; **Fantasizing**, 72, 75, 92; **Fantasy**, and belief, 145; nourish a, 173; release, 322; 329, dream, 399; of doing it, 425; **Farmers**, 73; markets, 386; markets, 414; organic, 434-435; **Farming**, animal factory, 384; **Fascia**, 434; **Fashioned information**, 57; **Fast food**, wrappers, 386; 439; **Fasting**, 181-182, 381; **Fat**, 385-386, 388, increased, 402; **Fate**, 190, 274; **Father**, Mark Twain's, 218; author's, 225-227, 247; 357; **Fathom your possibilities**, 131; **Fatigue**, brain, 387; **Fats**, 384, 387, break down, 405; **Fatty liver**, 386; **Fault**, not yours, 230; 301, 351, 421; **Fear**, 34, 50-52, 67, 74, 79, 96-99, free from, 189; of God, 269; acknowledging, 299; 315 -based stagnation, 353; 367, 414, prevents, 432; 438; **Feed grain industry**, 157; **Feedback loops**, 241; **Feeding**, the negative, 216; loneliness, 220; your life, 333; **Feel**, the waves, 234; -good hormones, 240; how they made you, 308; lousy, 354; **Feeling**, alone, 249; like garbage, 254; drained, 335; within themselves, 423; **Feelings**, worthwhile, 233; waste themselves, 355; of the heart, 410; **Feet**, intentions into, 416; **Fellowship**, in religion, 142; programs, 279; **Feral wild land gardening**, 362; **Fermented culture**, 420; **Fertility**, 386; **Fetal**, exposure, and programming, 41; **Fibers connect us**, 370; **Fiction characters**, 304, and emotional connection, 330; **Fifth element**, 431; **Fight-or-flight hormones**, 237; **Fighting**, change, 336; a hard battle, 441; **Fights**, 282; warrior, 437; **Film**, productions, 3; 174, and TV industry, 254; community, 377-378; 379, 400; **Filter**, your, 40; of the mind landscape, 40-46, 229; **Filtering money**, Mormon church, 141; **Final**, destination, 78; no feeling is, 334; **Financial**, stress, 8, 301; insecurity, 121; unrealistic, 254; profitable to sell crap, 329; 353; issues, 311; agreements, TV and film, 326; status, 422; **Find**,

someone to help you, 160; the seed, 346; **Fingerprint**, unique as, 424; **Fingers**, 192; pointing, 209, 300; **Fish**, 168; **Flavorings**, 42, artificial, 361, 413, 439; **Flawed and broken**, 149; **Flawless**, specimen, 16, 337; **Flaws**, so-called, 215; 300, 316; **Flow**, of your mantra, 151; of muck, 353; change, 366; of nutrients, 405; your intentions, 416; **Flower**, 275; bring forth, 346; **Flowering**, of the mind, 432; plants, plant, 440; **Flowing**, in and out, 364; energy through us, 380; **Fluent**, in higher consciousness, 357; in language of your heart, 432; **Focus**, 43, 94, the mind, 181, 432; 164, on present, 162; on future, 218; living with, 291; 293, 339, on wants, 345; 355-356, 367, 419, on things outside themselves, 423; 439; **Focused in the past**, 99; **Follow**, new path, 351; your heart, 390; **Food Not Lawns**, 439; **Food**, gardening, 16, 22, 109, 181, 242, 249, 254, 274, 276, 362, 405, 434, 439; issues, 232; issues, 319; sharing, 323; commercials, 329; shopping, 386; chemicals, 386-388, 407; 408-410, 428, forests, 439; **Footsteps of the wise**, 203; **Force**, transformational, 152; positive change, 338; yourself to prosper, 429; **Forests**, 275, 279, restoring, 371; food, 439; protect, 440; restoration, 435; **Forever chemicals**, 386; **Forget your age**, 334; **Forgiveness**, and church, 143; 166; 218, 229, 252-262, 285, 317, 368, 439; *Forks Over Knives*, documentary, 208, 439-440; **Formal education**, 125; **Former self**, 353; **Formulate**, conditions, 45; reality, 53; a plan, 72; your existence, 165-166; your days, 188; your life, 194, 345, 417; **Fortune**, reversal of, 38; sides with, 69; **Fortunetellers**, 150; **Fossil fuels**, 157, 274, 276; **Fountain of youth**, 118; **FPAS (polyfluorinated alkyl substances)**, 386; **Fractal geometry**, 268; **Fractured**, lives, 200; life, 252; relationships, 347; 360; **Fraternal brotherhood**, Mormon church, 142; **Free**, our minds, 130; yourself, 147; radicals, 240; yourself, 412; **Freedom**, of the mind, 4, 69; to choose, 73; 91, 281; **Frenzied lives of politicians**, 200; **Frequency**, tune your, 166; wavelength, 168; adjustment, 173; vibrational, attuned to, 322; 364, lower your, 410; healthful, 415; of Nature, tune into, 417; 409; **Fresh-foods diet**, 19; **Freudian psychology**, 285; **Fried**, food, 329, 338, 361, 387, 394, 407, 409, 413; **Friends**, dying, 246-251; , 321; appreciate, 430; **Frightened**, 182, 222; **Frivolity**, 325; **Frontal lobes**, 385; **Frugality**, 27; **Fruits and vegetables and advertising**, 329; **Frying**, 384; **Fulfillment**, 164, 347; **Full moon**, fasting, 182; **Functioning**, normal state, 154; mind, 422; **Fundamental**, truths, 49; delusion, 132; law of life, 196; beliefs and dreams, 342;

## G: Index and Topical Guide

## H: Index and Topical Guide

## I: Index and Topical Guide

## J: Index and Topical Guide

## K: Index and Topical Guide

## L: Index and Topical Guide

## M: Index and Topical Guide

# N: Index and Topical Guide

# O: Index and Topical Guide

## P: Index and Topical Guide

of self, 150; 164, 172; **Prosperity**, 90, 147, gospel, 264; 285, 337, force yourself to, 429; **Prostitute**, 96, 272; **Protein**, 19; of body, 133; toxic, 385; **Protons**, space between, 133; **Psyche**, clenched, 315; 362; **Psychedelic**, orange gas, 47, plant medicines, 183-184; **Psychedelics**, 183-184; **Psychic wound**, 231; **Psychoactive drugs**, self-produced, 412; **Psychoanalysis**, 377; **Psychoimmunology**, 238-239; **Psychological**, therapy 155; difficulties, 184; benefits, 203; wound, 209, 234, 306; pain, 216, trauma, 231; 285; ailments, 255, 282, 385, 399, 402; disorders, 388; health, 388, 413; **Psychologist**, 9, 98, 229, 235, 254, 317, 333; **Psychology**, 42, 61, 230, 333, core, 377; **Psychotherapy**, 33; **Psylocybin**, 183-184; **PTSD**, 184, 210, 237-238, 242; **Puella Aeterna issues**, 9; **Puer Aetemrnus issues**, 9; **Puerto Rico**, 55; **Pulitzer Prize**, 379; **Punishment**, and elected officials, 52; and government, 155-156; rewards and, 263; projecting, 279; TV and 326; **Puppet strings**, 244; **Puppy love**, 286; **Purge**, emotional, 232; **Purpose**, without a, 72; and intention, 190, 396; define, 221; of life, 288, 429; weakness of, 291; 347, and meaning, 372; stay focused on, 416; live with, 437; **Pursuit**, conscious, 332; of truth, 411; **Pushover**, 92; **Puzzle of your life**, 194; **Pyramids**, 346

## Q: Index and Topical Guide

**Qualities**, reveal best, 369; **Quantum**, physics, 264, 364; phenomenon dimension, 431; **Questioning assumptions**, 374; **Questions to ask self**, 352; **Quit**, temptation to, 343; **Quran**, 164

## R: Index and Topical Guide

**Race**, 21, 279; running, 355; **Racial**, issues, 311; segregation, 365; **Racism**, 113, Mormon, 141; 224, 273; **Racist**, religions, 139; Brigham Young, 142; 263; **Radcliff College**, 115; **Radical**, transformation, 7, 335; changes through diet, 409; **Rapid eye movement**, 393; **Rapists**, 272; **Rationalization**, denial, 216; 293; 305; **Rats of the Cinematheque**, 378; **Reach**, outward, 315; your goals, 356; out, 422; **Reacting**, 25, and character, 211; harshly, 304; **Reactionary behavior**, 244; **Reading**, and children, 120; books, 206-207, 225, escape, 222; retention, author's, 336; what are you, 352; 391, 438; **Reality**, opening pages, 47, 54, 85, 89, 216, 315, 347, dream, 399; of action, dreams pass into,

401; of creating, 425; **Realization**, 37, spiritual, 274; 318; **Realm of possibility**, 423; **Reason**, for living, 338; 341, we're here, 357; **Rebellion**, 121; **Rebirth**, 157, 283; **Receptors**, cell, 238-239, endorphin, 239; 283, 413; **Recipe for personal disaster**, 375; **Reciprocal arrangement**, 222; **Reconfigure**, logic, 42; 124, relationship with life, 174; 217, body shape, 408; **Recreational drugs**, 22, 42, 414; **Rectal cancer**, 386; **Red blood cells**, 406; **Redeemed**, 62, social conditions, 373; **Rediscover**, the person, 319; strengths, 258; **Reducing yourself**, 211; **Reflection**, 205; of ourselves, 297; **Reformulate**, you, 184; 218; body chemistry, 241; 336; **Refrigeration**, 385; **Refusal**, to open mind, 424; to be conquered, 437; **Refuse**, to be victim, 220; to get caught, 233; to help, 314; to detach from strengths, 430; **Regenerating power**, 164; **Regeneration**, movement, spiritual, 179; 337; **Regret**, 37, 64, 68, 79, 84, 96, 124, 154, 210-211, 233, 237, 258-259, 262, 334, 340, 351, 414, 428, choose with no, 430; **Rehabilitation**, 146, 333; **Rehearsal**, thought is, 185; **Reimagine life**, 2, 5, 215; **Reinterpret past**, 233; **Rejecting the unspiritual**, 417; **Rejection**, 98, 230, 397; **Relationship of self**, 242; **Relatives**, unfortunate, 213; 323; **Relaxation tapes**, 193; **Religion**, originators of, 21; 48-49, 56, stigmatization, 98; scrupulosity, 139, 147; texts, 139; concept, 143-144, 147, 263, 266-268, 270, people, 278; 400; 139-144, 157, 178, 224, 263, 266-267, 269, 280, writings and dreams, 400; being wealthy is their, 420; **Relinquish power**, 82; **Relishing**, in unfortunate, 100; in strength, 286; **Relying**, on others, 157; on other forms of life, 312; **REM**, 393; **Remedy**, for love, 284; 324; **Reminding people of wrongs**, 259; **Remote**, attitudes, 272; control, 330; **Renew awareness**, 217; **Renovate yourself**, 158; **Reparation**, cellular, 399; **Repetition**, 17, of affirmations, 175; 191, of patterns, 194; **Replace thoughts**, 335; **Replicant**, 294; **Replicate**, commercial imagery, 16, 33, 64, 144, 204, 304-305, 327, 375, 420-421; corporate imagery, 304; emotions in dreams, 399; **Replicating past results**, 6; **Replication of cells**, 240; **Reporting child abuse**, 230; **Repressed**, 114, 154, 271, 272; **Reproductive fluids**, 434; **Reptiles of the mind**, 256; **Repulsion**,

## S: Index and Topical Guide

treated like, 214; 271; **Sincerity**, 243, 370; **Sing**, 289, 354, 396; **Single mother**, 225; **Singleness of purpose**, 38; **Sink you**, game that can, 112; **Skewing your life**, 259; **Skills**, atrophy of, 289; **Skin**, issues, 362, 384, 403, 434; **Skyward**, eyes turned, 435; **Slander**, 66, 99-102, 129, 200, 243-244, 258, 296, 367-368, 397, avoid, 430; 438; **Slathered with failure**, 90; **Slave**, ancestors, 201; of your past, 232; owners, 272; **Slavery**, 25, mental, 130; **Slaves**, of the ordinary, 376; to corporate system, 421; **Sleep**, deprivation, 2, too much, 64; 121, 123; pattern, 20, 42, 322, 387, 412, 434; 177, 284, deep, 180; 325, regimen, 388; and testing patterns, 393; aids medications, 394; 391-397, and brain health, 398; 404, 415; **Slothfulness**, 64, 97, 130, 186, 220, 317, 337, 339, 347, 353, 384, 389; **Slow down**, do not 355; **Slowest form of poison**, 384; **Slumber**, 79, 343; **Slumbering powers**, 80; **Smallest act of caring**, 285; **Smell**, 40-42, 194, 210, 295, 384, 389; **Smile**, power of, 285; 422; **Smoothies**, green, 181; **Sneak through**, 375; **Snobby**, 217; **So goes the world**, 432; **Soaking seeds**, nuts, and beans, 338, 414; **Sobriety**, 311, 413; *Social Intelligence: The New Science of Human Relationships*, book, 32; **Social**, media, 2, pressure, 374; 216-217, 224, support, and stimulation, 276, 390; scene, 292; 325-331, 400; club, 157; interaction, 198, 389, 398; being, 295; creatures, 311; exchange, 318; difficulties confront us, 366; entrepreneur, 377; **Socially acceptable**, 356; **Societal pressure**, 316, 352; **Societies**, ancient, 179; **Society**, participation in, 98; 112, 188, transform, 277; perceived, 357; 352, 365, temperament of, 366; nurture, 368; 370, 377, trajectory and design of, and artists, 378, 380; 384, 388, destiny of, 418; hierarchical, and could not remain stable, 419; commercial, 420; **Society's ills**, 400; **Soda**, 388; **Soil**, organisms, 134; 275, of contemplation, 360; **Solar**, electron neutrinos, 133; wind, 134; **Soldier's brains**, 237-238; **Sole purpose**, 25; **Solids**, in the universe, none, 133; 364; **Solitude**, garden of, 64; and idleness, 180; 182, 321, 335; **Solution**, 293, love is, and be part of, 372; 384, become part of, 416; be your, 417; 422; your own, 438; one, 440; **Solutions**, being part of, 13; 60, 280, 314, factor, 360; 367, 373, 393; participate in, 435; **Song**, 280; **Songs**, make you feel, 377; 379; **Sonnets**, your days are, 308; **Sorrow**, 45, keenest, 217; 228, 321, 395; anticipating, 439; **Soul**, on fire, 11; owned by events, 65; disconnected from, 79; 167-168, is dyed, 188; scraped, 218; 239, essential nutrient for, 257; 268, and body, 275; pure, 280; 281-282, needs love, 284; 312, and spirit, 320;

marriage of, 321; alive, 345; global, 364; artist and, 374; do things from, 382; music touches, 396; occurrences of, 399; is writing in dreams, 400; sees through eyes, 403; value, 404; seat of, 409; 435; **Soul's**, house, 403; resources, 426; **Souls**, and music, 193; blossom, and ultimate truth, 324; **Sound**, patterns, 41, 192; replication, 198; **Sounds**, 42; **Spark of life**, 310; **Spatial-temporal reasoning**, 192; **Speaking and nerve wiring**, 391; **Species**, strongest, 336; **Spectacle**, charming, 306; **Spectacular happiness**, 177; **Spectator**, 330, 355, 381; **Spectrum**, of intensity, 8; on the autism, and of behaviors, 129; of trauma, 234; **Speculation**, 428; **Speech**, 122; **Spending**, government, 157; time together, 197; sprees, 330; **Sphere of activity**, 411; **Spiders**, 165; **Spin with drama**, 164; **Spiraling**, opening pages; **Spirit**, behind actions, 52; healing, 124; 167, language of, 181, 379; manifested through parents, 212; we are, 231; work of, 242; energy, 264, 268; and soul, 320; injured your, 333; 338, of your intuition, 357; gathering of, 364; health, 403, 434-435; interact with, 410; of dignity, 416; harmony with your, 427; your, 431; feed your, 435; manifest your, 437; **Spirits**, great, 353; **Spiritual**, nature, 36; process, 52; life, 64; aspect to science, 136; genetics, 136, 201, 243; blackmail, 141; brutality, 141, 264, 270; blessings, Mormon, 142; person, 144; deadness, 167; teachers, 178; practice, 179; regeneration movement, 179; debt, 217; health, 257, 368; beliefs, 263, 264, 270; experience, 265; leader, and inspiration, 273; realization, 274; dwelling in disrepair, 276; force, 280; pain, 285; quality, 324; lobotomy, 331; journey, 373; side and dreaming, 399; essence, 426; awareness, 431; **Spirituality**, 25, and science, 143; , 281; **Spiritually**, troubled, 222; manipulated, 224; advance, 357; disintegrating, 419; impotent, 420; **Spirulina**, 388; **Spitefulness**, 220, 244; **Spleen**, 240; **Splendor of life**, 412; **Spoiled children**, respond like, 299; **Sport**, train for, 162; 175; **Sporting teams**, 367; **Sports**, events, 73; 76,187, 292; **Spreading**, hurt, 219; light, 321; good energy, 397; **Springboard**, use downfall as, 259; **Sprouted**, 19; **Sprouts**, 338, 388, 415; **Squander energy**, 425; **Squash individuality**, 278; **Stage**, world is, 356; universe is your, 427; **Staggering around**, 100; **Stagnant**, 38, energy, 337; 427; **Stagnating**, in religion, 140; 257; **Stagnation**, 154, of fantasizing, 187; 236, 351, fear-based, 353; 388. **Stain your hair**, 375; **Stairs**, step up the, 72, take the steps, 190; 289; fell down the, author's mother, 227; **Standard**, citizenry, 127; lowered, 217;

## T: Index and Topical Guide

# U: Index and Topical Guide

## V: Index and Topical Guide

## W: Index and Topical Guide

## X: Index and Topical Guide

## Y: Index and Topical Guide

## Z: Index and Topical Guide

# About the Author

"I've lost track of the number of people who want to be writers but never actually write anything. Talking about writing, dreaming about writing, can be very fun, but it won't get a book written. You've got to write."
– Laurell K. Hamilton

Daniel John Carey is the author of *Dream Another Dream: Reclaiming and Reimagining Your Life*. This book is an extension of what is explored in that book. He wrote them with the hopes others would not make the mistakes he had made, and live wiser lives, and ones especially closer to Nature.

He's been an author shepherd, helping writers get their manuscripts ready for publication. He has been a ghost co-author on many non-fiction books by a variety of authors.

He is the author of *Plant-Based Regenerative Nutrition: How to Prevent and Reverse Common Chronic and Degenerative Illnesses*.

Carey also is the founder of Screenwriting Tribe script incubation workshop, and the author of *Screenwriting Tribe: Workshop Handbook for Writing and Polishing Film and TV Spec Scripts*. He polishes screenplays for producers, and helps writers to polish their own scripts.

He's worked on hundreds of TV shows and movies as an extra, standin, photo double, hand double, rehearsal actor, and actor.

He is a writer, artist, vegan, food gardener, biker, and runner, and an advocate for wildlife and the environment.

"For business reasons, I must preserve the outward sign of sanity."
– Mark Twain

To contact the author in care of the publisher:
Daniel John Carey
POB 1272
Santa Monica, CA 90406-1272, USA

"In silence between writer and reader, a memory of words and hands takes form.

We learn substance and worth through others' eyes.

Cloth, flesh, ink, skin, paper, dust.

These are but material forms in which ideas dwell.

In the roar of a crowded shelf of books, desert sun and arctic night, distant seas of thought awaken, mingle, and are still.

Minds meet where the reading hand grasps the void and inks its passage in empty margins.

Lost, forgotten, thumbed, split.

We bear scars of patient decades and centuries' dreams.

Whose hands will next hold me, I do not know.

The book too, reads readers in real time."

– Henry Wessells, *The Private Life of Books*

# Make a Difference

"The real meaning of enlightenment is to gaze with undimmed eyes on all darkness."
– Nikos Kazantzakis

"A billion people sitting watching their TV in the room that they call living. But as for me, I see living as loving. And since there is no loving room, I sit on the grass under a tree dreaming of the way things used to be, pre-industrial revolution."
– Woody Harrelson

"The most important lessons in life can never be expressed in black and white, but must be experienced. Experience is the greatest teacher."
– Benny Lewis

"Your profession is not what brings home your paycheck. Your profession is what you were put on earth to do."
– Publius Vergillus "Virgil" Maro

"People are unreasonable, illogical, and self-centered. Love them anyway. If you do good, people may accuse you of selfish motives. Do good anyway. If you are successful, you may win false friends and true enemies. Succeed anyway. The good you do today may be forgotten tomorrow. Do good anyway. Honesty and transparency make you vulnerable. Be honest and transparent anyway. What you spend years building may be destroyed overnight. Build anyway. People who really want help may attack you if you help them. Help

them anyway. Give the world the best you have and you may get hurt. Give the world your best anyway."
— Mother Teresa

"The aim of life is to live, and to live means to be aware, joyously, drunkenly, serenely, divinely aware."
— Henry Miller

"Believe with all your heart that how you live your life makes a difference."
— Colin Beavan

"Walk tall like the trees, live your life as strong as the mountains, be as soft as the spring breezes, keep the warmth of the sun in your heart and the Great Spirit will always be with you."
— Navajo wisdom

"There comes a time when humanity is called to shift to a new level of consciousness, to reach a higher moral ground. A time when we have to shed our fear and give hope to each other. That time is now."
— Wangari Maathai

Thank you for reading my book. Have you found it helpful?

- Let others know about it.
- Post about it on social media.
- Snap a photo of the cover and text it to a friend.
- **Write a customer review on the book's Amazon.com page.**
- Gift a copy to a friend, relative, neighbor, or associate.
- Give a copy to a graduate.
- Drop a copy at a homeless shelter.
- Leave a copy on someone's doorstep.
- Request it at your local library so they add it to their collection.

"We're all simply walking each other home."
— Ram Dass

"No more words. Hear only the voice within."
— Jalal ad-Din Rumi

Made in the USA
Middletown, DE
01 April 2023

27386229R00275